CREATION, LIFE, and PURPOSE

MIKE A. BILLS

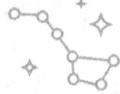

To request permissions,
contact the publisher at mike@GSCYou.com.

ISBN: 979-8-218-59354-4 (Paperback)
First paperback edition January 2025.

Edited by Rebecca Allen | Fort Worth, Texas

Cover Design and Interior Formatting by
KUHN Design Group | kuhndesigngroup.com

Printed in the United States by GSCYou

GSCYou
5332 Sioux Creek Lane
Fort Worth, Texas 76244
GSCYou.com

To my parents, Leroy Michael and Betty Pearl (Beemer) Bills,
who made me go to church,
and to all those who helped shape my faith and curiosity.

THE WINDS OF FATE

Ella Wheeler Wilcox

One ship sails East,
And another West,
By the self-same winds that blow.
'Tis the set of the sails
And not the gales,
That tells the way we go.
Like the winds of the sea
Are the ways of fate,
As we voyage along through life.
'Tis the set of the soul
That decides its goal,
And not the calm or the strife.

Contents

A Letter to My Children

Dear Travis, Joshua, Casey, and Aldyn:

The James Webb Telescope, sitting a million miles out in space, has captured some of the most captivating and awe-inspiring images in recent years—showing us a universe filled with trillions of stars and galaxies. These images stretch our understanding of time and space, hinting at a universe that has evolved over billions of years. This complexity isn't difficult to fathom on its own; however, it becomes challenging when set against the backdrop of the biblical account of creation. How does such an immense and ancient universe fit into the idea of a six-day creation as described in Genesis? On the one hand, the images NASA has shared are profoundly intriguing, offering a glimpse into the vastness of the cosmos. On the other hand, they are unsettling because they seem out of sync with the biblical narrative that I was taught to believe in. It didn't make sense to me.

Adding to this complexity are archaeological discoveries indicating that Homo sapiens—modern humans—have been around for over 200,000 years. This timeline, coupled with the theory of natural selection and evolution proposed by atheists and scientists, suggests a process spanning millions of years.

The more I learned, the more confusing it became. How do these scientific discoveries align with the biblical narrative? Where do Adam and Eve fit in this vast timeline? It felt like trying to piece together a shattered stained-glass window, where each fragment had to find its place in a cohesive picture—but how?

Then there's the question of miracles today. I have to admit, this is something I've struggled with as I've grown older. Miracles, a direct intervention of God like those told in the Bible, seemed clearer when I was younger, or maybe it was just easier to believe in them without question. Today, when I hear people refer to events as miracles—like narrowly escaping a car accident—it often feels more like luck than divine intervention. If it were truly a miracle, then why do so many others not survive such accidents, or emerge from them with life-altering injuries? The concept of miracles today seems inconsistent, especially when looking at the broader reality of our world where suffering and tragedy are all too common.

Anne Frank's story has been one of those troubling examples for me. I listened to her audiobook almost on a whim, not expecting it to affect me as deeply as it did. Her life was filled with hardship, yet she never seemed to give up on God, even in the darkest of times. How do we reconcile the idea of a loving and miraculous God with the harsh reality of history, where so many innocent lives like hers were lost? Where was the miracle in her story, or in the countless other stories of suffering throughout history? These are the questions that keep coming up, and the answers are not easily found.

I began this journey of writing not because I had all the answers, but because I was searching for them. I worried about all of you growing older in a world where faith is constantly challenged by new information and where the teachings of the Bible can seem outdated or irrelevant. You were raised in the church, but I've seen how the world you're growing up in has made it harder for those teachings to take hold. I wanted to understand how all these pieces—the universe, evolution, the Bible, miracles—fit together, and whether they could provide a coherent and believable picture of the world and God.

Starting this journey was like looking at that shattered piece of stained glass, with each piece scattered in a thousand directions, every one of them looking the same. The task of figuring out which piece to pick up first was daunting. I have always believed in the Bible—I was raised that way. Growing up in a humble Christian home, my life was simple, and while the world had its own set of problems and struggles, it was a golden time in my life. I've also always believed in what I can see and what makes sense. So, when science started showing us things that seemed to conflict with the Bible, I knew that every one of those million pieces of glass had to fit together somehow. If they didn't, then either the Bible or science couldn't be true, and that was a troubling thought.

It finally made the most sense to start at the beginning, to go back to my earliest memories and retrace my steps, revisiting a fork in the road here and a twist in the road there. By picking up one piece at a time, I hoped to piece it all together. What I began to discover was that one by one, the pieces started to fit. A fragment of science fit here, and a piece of the Bible's story fit there. Together, they began to form a mosaic of time—more intricate and beautiful than I could have ever imagined without having both. So, I want to invite you to follow along so I can show you what this mosaic has come to reveal. This journey has been one of discovery, faith, and a deeper understanding of how these pieces are creating a picture of something far grander than I ever expected. But before I finish this letter and reveal the full mosaic, I want to share with you how it came together one piece at a time—each a vital part of this story, contributing to a deeper understanding of the world and the faith we hold dear.

CHAPTER 1

My Genesis

The Rouge Complex, conceived in the early twentieth century, was the brainchild of the visionary Henry Ford.[1] Ford's grand plan aimed to create a fully integrated industrial operation capable of transforming raw materials into finished products all within the same facility. This ambitious vision included a vast railway system designed to transport materials and products efficiently throughout the sprawling complex in Dearborn, Michigan. With over ninety miles of internal railway tracks, the Rouge Complex became a bustling hub for railcar manufacturing. This large-scale industrial activity positioned Dearborn as a key manufacturing location, generating countless job opportunities, particularly in the building and maintenance of railcars within the complex.

The Rouge Complex still stands today, a testament to Ford's enduring legacy.[2] The company has renamed it the Ford Rouge Center, modernized it, and it is still successful as a central location for automotive production. This includes the manufacturing of the well-known Ford F-150 and the advanced electric F-150 Lightning.

My story is intricately tied to the early beginnings of the Rouge Complex.

I came into the world in Dearborn, Michigan, on February 20, 1961, a day marked by freezing temperatures and swirling snow. My brother Tim had been born eleven months earlier in Lawton, Oklahoma. My father moved to Dearborn with my mother and brother to work as a welder on the railcars. His mother lived there with his stepdad, and it seemed a perfect place to raise his family.

I can't say I remember those early days of my life, because they were brief. In the 1960s, labor disputes were common in the automotive industry, and the Rouge Complex was no exception.[3] Not long after my father went to work, a disagreement broke out between employee groups about overtime pay during breaks and lunch periods and the resolution resulted in mass terminations to reorganize. So, just as soon as it began, it ended.

Someone once told me that a bottle of whiskey always has a prize in it. Sometimes the drinker will find a little pixie dust to sprinkle around to give everyone a brief sense of joy and happiness. Other times, the prize is a pair of boxing gloves that quickly leads to aggression and conflict. That was the case with my dad's stepfather, who was an alcoholic, so the perfect place to raise a family evaporated quickly.

My mother had grown up in Comanche County, Oklahoma, and her family had deep roots there, with relatives having lived in surrounding small communities for over one hundred years. So, we made an about-face back to Oklahoma, and before I turned two, we were living in the city of Lawton, where my true journey would begin.

Family Life and Times

As a young boy growing up in Lawton, life was pleasantly simple, and the world around me seemed easy to understand. This is the place of my earliest remembrance of existence.

It was the mid-1960s, and we lived at 1911 Andrews Street in a quiet neighborhood that fostered a comforting sense of community. Our home was simple, like most in our area—a modest two-bedroom, one-bath house with a big backyard shaded by towering elm trees and enclosed by a four-foot-high chain-link fence that gave a sense of openness. We tore more than one pair of jeans climbing over it, often catching on the bare wire spikes at the top, which were quite different from the woven spikes on chain-link fences today. My childhood friend, Steve Reichert, who remains a friend to this day, lived on Taylor Street, the next street over, and my maternal grandmother lived just two blocks around the corner. She worked as a beautician and had her salon attached to her home, so I could visit her almost every day.

In this neighborhood, it was not uncommon for my mother to ask me to go to a neighbor's house to borrow a cup of sugar. Most likely, she was short of the two cups of sugar needed to add to a packet of Kool-Aid, which was a daily staple. She would also send my brother and me five blocks away through the neighborhood to Taft Grocery, a small cinderblock building across from Taft Elementary, where we would attend grade school. Our errand usually involved buying a quarter-pound of bologna and occasionally some cheese, bread, or mayonnaise. The store owner would go to the meat counter in the back, pull out a large red plastic-wrapped roll, slice off the meat, and wrap it in white wax paper before handing it over the counter without exchanging money. He would mark the cost down in a ledger, and my dad would pay the bill from time to time.

In the midst of all this, my sister Cricket was born in 1964 (Yes, her real name is Cricket). If I'm being honest, I can't remember much about her while we were growing up. If I had to tell one story, I'm not sure what I would say. I suppose I was too immersed in being a boy and playing with G.I. Joes.

In those days, modern air conditioning was a luxury we did not have. Most homes, including ours, relied on an evaporative water cooler. Ours was positioned in the kitchen window, where it would hum steadily throughout the sweltering summer months, doing its best to cool the house as temperatures climbed to ninety-five degrees or more. The cooler worked by drawing hot air through water-soaked pads, adding a touch of humidity and a faint, damp scent to the air. It provided some relief, but not the sealed-off

comfort of today's air conditioning; the boundary between indoors and outdoors blurred as we kept windows and doors open to let the air circulate.
Yet, despite the heat, the outdoors still held the promise of endless fun with
friends and adventures.

Trips to Taft Grocery weren't chores but adventures and rarely a quick
knight's errand. We would leave our house and make our way to the drainage
ditch, which ran alongside the house next door. At the end of their backyard,
the trail ended in a thicket of trees where we would stop off and hide for a
while and piddle with whatever we could find to do. Then, we would climb
a steep grassy hill to the field where the water tower stood for the surrounding neighborhood. The water tower, as we called it, wasn't a tower at all but a
large round tank on the ground. On the shady side, it would sweat in the hot
summer, and we would push our faces against it to cool off. Tapping it with
a rock never got old, as the deep ocean-like pings it made were mesmerizing.

From there, the next street was a race for survival after carefully timing a
sprint past a neighbor's yard with a big black German shepherd that would
charge the fence like a rabid lion on the African plains. After surviving that,
we would turn the corner for the last two blocks. On the first of the two
blocks was a rare house with a sprinkler system and brass in-ground sprinklers.
Most days, you could lie on the ground and suck on the sprinkler head for a
cool drink of water flavored with a bit of dirt. Past the next stop sign was the
schoolyard with monkey bars, a high metal slide, and a merry-go-round. By
today's standards, all of them were good places to get hurt, but we were all
too willing to tackle the toughness of life in the morning before it got so hot
that we couldn't touch any of it. They made all the playground equipment
out of metal, and by afternoon, you could cook an egg on any of it.

Before leaving the playground, we glanced around the surrounding fence
for pop bottles we could exchange for a nickel. Then across the street to Taft
Grocery, and before going in, we always checked the change cup in the pay-
phone, hoping to find a nickel, a dime, or amazingly, a quarter. Any of those
amounts would allow us to buy a little penny candy or gum.

Winter brought a different ambiance, as we relied on a single in-floor furnace that demanded careful ignition with a long wire and a wooden match. Its feeble warmth barely reached beyond its immediate vicinity in the hallway, but it was a welcome respite from the biting cold outside. On cold nights, when it was freezing in the bedroom, my brother and I would sneak into the narrow hallway and lay in a small space between the furnace and the wall, wrapped in our blankets to stay warm. We quickly learned to avoid rolling over, as the square metal grate was scorching enough to leave an indelible mark.

Summertime always meant vacation. We traveled as far west as Colorado and east to Florida in our cab-over camper that stayed parked in front of the house when not in use. We would camp wherever we found ourselves at the end of the day, most always at Kampgrounds of America (KOA). In the late 1960s and 1970s, KOA campgrounds were emerging as popular destinations for family camping. They were well-known for their clean, safe, and family-friendly facilities designed to meet the needs of travelers, offering amenities such as electrical hookups, hot showers, laundry facilities, and convenience stores.

One unforgettable trip to Colorado put us in a precarious situation with the worst case of poison ivy my brother, dad, and I ever contracted. We were traveling on a high mountain road that wound along the edge of a canyon overlooking a river. As we peered down, my dad noticed the water was teeming with fish resting in a clear, shallow area. Trout—the ultimate catch in that region. Our plans changed quickly as we made an early detour to get him a fishing license and some bait. We found a campsite right along the river, and after setting up, we headed upstream to try our luck. The water wasn't deep, so we crossed to a small island that resembled an Amazon jungle, with dense trees and tall grass, flanked by the river on both sides. The vegetation was so thick that we could only fish from the island's point.

Not long after we got there and cast our lines in, a siren began to wail that, no doubt, you could hear for miles. Since we weren't from the area, we had no idea what it was meant to convey. Unfortunately, my dad ignored it. Not long after, we noticed the river level began to rise. It wasn't alarming at first, but within a few minutes, the river was not only too deep for us to get to the shoreline, but it was also moving way too fast.

What we didn't realize is that the siren was a warning to let anyone know that the floodgates to the dam upstream were being opened, which would violently flood the river and last long into the night. We were trapped before we knew it. Since we were on an island, there was no way to escape it. Our only option was to carve our way back into the jungle to a higher point and try to wait it out. It turns out it was overgrown with poison ivy, and we rolled around in that till evening.

Fortunately, someone had spotted us from the shoreline and notified the local authorities, and they came to get us in a motorboat. But the damage was already done. We didn't catch any fish that day, but we did catch the worst case of poison ivy we could have ever imagined and spent the next several days itching fiercely and covered with calamine lotion.

Life for us during those years was consistent. School, church, cartoons on Saturday mornings followed by bike riding, playing army with the neighborhood kids if we could find a stick of wood or something to use as a gun. Sometimes we would get up a baseball game at the water tower field, but only if someone came up with a baseball and bat. If you didn't have a glove, you could share one with someone who did.

All in all, we were good kids and stayed out of trouble, except for taking bites out of the neighbor's garden tomatoes, according to my mother. To this day, I can't imagine that happening because I hated tomatoes. Nonetheless, we still got a spanking with the ever-present rubber barber's strap that hung on the wall as a reminder.

Faith and Religion

We attended church at a local congregation, the Northwest Church of Christ, and it was an integral part of our lives. It was not only a place to worship but also the central hub for our close family friendships. Every Sunday morning, Sunday evening, and Wednesday night, we were there, only missing for very good reasons, such as being on our deathbeds with uncontrollable fevers. I mention that facetiously, but we rarely missed church when the doors were open. I didn't mind attending as often as we did, except for Sunday evenings. It was the only time I could watch *The Wonderful World of Disney* (1954-1991) or Mutual of Omaha's *Wild Kingdom* (1963-1988), which was probably my favorite entertainment on television. *Wild Kingdom* explored wildlife conservation from the African savannas to American national parks.

The Church of Christ taught us several core beliefs during my childhood that distinctly shaped our faith and daily lives.[4] The focus was on biblical literacy, weekly communion, and the importance of baptism for salvation.

Another distinctive feature of our worship was the absence of instrumental music. The Church of Christ practiced a cappella singing, which set us apart from many other religious organizations. This tradition was based on the belief that early Christian worship, as described in the New Testament, did not include instruments, and thus our worship should follow that pattern.

Prayer was at the core of our beliefs, understanding that asking God to help in our daily lives would bring about miracles of divine intervention. This belief instilled in us a sense of dependence on and trust in God's active involvement in the world. Also important was the belief that creation miraculously happened in six days, and on the seventh day, God rested. This literal interpretation of the Bible underscored a worldview that saw the hand of the divine in every aspect of the natural world.

The Church of Christ held a firm conviction that it was the only true church and the sole path to heaven. This belief was rooted in a strict adherence to the teachings of the Bible, with the view that other denominations were in error. As a child, I accepted these teachings without question. I trusted my parents wholeheartedly and saw our family as a quintessential example of a faithful and righteous life.

I would never, still to this day, change my early religious life. The Church of Christ taught me the Bible extensively, but it also taught me to be judgmental. Maybe it was just my unique personality, but the mixture of this with a grand childhood and happiness, where no misfortune fell upon our family, made it all sensible to me. My father was self-employed and earned a meager living, and my mother stayed at home, but we felt as though we had everything we needed and were rich in that sense. Our lives were marked by a sense of contentment and security, grounded in faith, family, and community.

The World We Lived In

There was a lot going on in the world, including social, political, and cultural changes, but we were shielded from it for the most part. Some notable events included the civil rights movement; the assassination of Martin Luther King Jr.; the women's liberation movement, which sparked the fight for gender equality; and the rise of hippie culture, characterized by antiestablishment sentiments, experimentation with drugs, and the promotion of peace and love. There was the Summer of Love, followed by the Woodstock Music Festival. I'll admit I loved the couple of pairs of bell-bottom pants I had, along with my white leather platform shoes. The assassination of Senator Robert F. Kennedy followed that of his brother, President John F. Kennedy, although I was too young to remember it.

The most notable for us was the Vietnam War and the anti-war protests. From 1964-1969, there was a major US military escalation following the Gulf of Tonkin incident, leading to significant troop deployments. Fort Sill, a major artillery base, was just on the outskirts of Lawton, and there was hardly a time when military cannon shooting practice didn't rattle windows in every home in Lawton.

The Apollo 11 lunar module, named *Eagle*, landed on the moon on Sunday, July 20, 1969, at 3:17 p.m.[5] I was just eight years old, and Tim was nine. Just a few hours later, Neil Armstrong and Buzz Aldrin would walk on the lunar surface, marking one of the most monumental achievements of the decade. The moonwalk was scheduled to happen around 10 p.m., which was way past my brother's and my bedtime. Despite it still being light in the summer, we had to be in bed by 8 p.m. However, our parents allowed us to stay up late that night to watch. We got into our pajamas, and we were so excited to stay up late that we were almost sent to bed before it happened. We managed to calm down, and when the time came, we sat in front of our small black-and-white TV. At 9:57 p.m., we watched Neil Armstrong finally accomplish what had seemed impossible just a few years earlier. Who can ever forget his iconic words that crackled over 238,855 miles of space: "That's one small step for man, one giant leap for mankind."

The Happiest Time of the Year

Christmas was absolutely the best time of the year for us, and it all started with the Sears Christmas Wish Book, an annual catalog filled with dreams and delights.[6] This hefty catalog, often around 400 to 600 pages, was published each year, showcasing everything from toys to exotic gifts. Imagine flipping through pages of mink robes, diamond pendants, handmade Christmas trees, suits of armor, log cabin playhouses, and even one-horse open sleighs! We wore that catalog out, our imaginations running wild. And, of course, there were pages showing women in their underwear, which, for little boys, was endlessly fascinating.

Being members of the Church of Christ, Christmas for us was primarily about Santa Claus and family. The church, known for its strict and sometimes legalistic adherence to the Bible, largely ignored the holiday in its religious cycle. Even if Christmas fell on a Sunday, church services continued as normal, and nativity scenes were considered almost sacrilegious. Despite this, Christmas remained a magical time for us kids.

It was also the only time of year when we would get together with family friends from church and go out to a restaurant for dinner. We never went out to eat, so this was a special occasion. The place we always went to was Underwoods Cafeteria, a rustic spot with the best BBQ brisket I've ever eaten. You would never have guessed we didn't have much money in those days.

Christmas Eve was always a big event. The whole day was filled with the bustle of cleaning, Mom cooking, and the excitement of wondering what gifts awaited us that night. We usually received about ten nice gifts from our parents, relatives, and friends. The twinkling foil Christmas tree and the sound of tearing wrapping paper added to the anticipation of Santa Claus arriving in the morning. Christmas programs playing in the background added a special magic to the day, especially those timeless classics broadcast year after year.

This era, particularly the 1960s and 1970s, was filled with memorable holiday specials that became part of our annual traditions, forming a nostalgic backdrop to the holiday season. It was the golden age of Christmas television, where each program had a charm and warmth that still resonates today. Some of the most iconic specials during this time were:

- *Rudolph the Red-Nosed Reindeer* (1964)
- *A Charlie Brown Christmas* (1965)
- *How the Grinch Stole Christmas!* (1966)
- *The Little Drummer Boy* (1968)
- *Frosty the Snowman* (1969)
- *Santa Claus Is Comin' to Town* (1970)
- *A Christmas Carol* (1971)

These specials brought together friends and family, bonding us as we gathered around the TV. They taught timeless lessons of kindness, generosity, and love—ideas that filled our hearts, much like the spirit of Christmas itself. These classic programs didn't just tell stories; they became the stories of our childhoods, etched into our holiday memories forever.

This time in history was particularly special, not just because of these programs, but because they emerged during a simpler time when Christmas was a magical experience for children. These shows brought animation, music, and the joy of the season into our homes, forever tying our Christmas memories to these cultural touchstones.

Then came Christmas morning, when Santa Claus came to town. At the crack of dawn, we would wake up to find an unbelievable assortment of gifts, like bicycles or BB guns—everything we had been dreaming of from the Sears catalog—magically arranged in our spots around the silver tree. Our modest home was filled with warmth, laughter, and the unmistakable scent of cinnamon apple cider made with Red Hots. These moments, rich in sensory detail, made Christmas the happiest time of the year.

One of my most vivid memories is our Christmas stockings, which we still have today. They were like a whole Christmas in a stocking. One year, I remember finding 100 one-dollar bills in mine—what an incredible surprise! Our stockings were handmade by my mother from an old white textured bedspread, scraps of material, buttons, and sequins. Mine had the face of Santa Claus outlined in gold sequins, with brass buttons for eyes and a large red button for his mouth. His hat was made from a piece of red corduroy with a gold button at the top, and a blue Star of David embroidered on the toe, with a black button in the center. My name, *Mike*, was embroidered in red yarn along the bottom.

Tim's stocking featured a red candy cane made from the same corduroy, outlined with gold sequins, and two green embroidered bells at the top. There was also a Star of David in black, with a black button in the center, and a green Christmas tree on the toe decorated with four green pearl buttons. His name, *Timothy*, was embroidered in red along the bottom.

Cricket's stocking had an angel with a blue gown outlined in silver sequins and yellow wings, along with blue and yellow embroidered stars, brass and burnt yellow buttons, and her name, *Cricket*, embroidered at the bottom.

On Christmas morning, our stockings always contained an apple, an orange, old-fashioned ribbon candy, nuts, small gifts, and a new Christmas ornament. These simple treats were extra special to us because we didn't often have things like fresh fruit or candy throughout the year. This part of Christmas has never faded from my memory. It inspired the three-foot-long, ten-inch-wide stockings your mother and I made for you kids growing up—no doubt you remember them as being just as special as ours: a whole Christmas in a stocking. It was a wonderful idea, but I must admit, those stockings became expensive to fill as the years went by!

Thanksgiving—When Family Came Together and Fell Apart

While Christmas was always just our immediate family—Mom, Dad, me, and my siblings—Thanksgiving brought together our extended family on my mother's side. My father was the only child of my grandmother, Grandma Goode. When she was young, she had married a much older man from Michigan who already had fourteen children. Not long after, my father was born into a family whose roots traced back to the first immigrant Bills family that came to America in 1899. The original log cabin burned in 2012 in a freak fire, but the land is still owned by the Bills family today, and they host large family reunions every year.

When my father was seven, my grandmother left her husband, believing he had only married her to care for his children after their mother died. She left the family, and my father became a distant memory. However, they never forgot him, and when my dad was seventy-five, his four oldest half-sisters found him in Faxon, Oklahoma, and it was a joyful reunion that he cherished until his passing in 2018.

Our early Thanksgivings were spent at either my Granny's house or at Mamo's (her mother and my great-grandmother) on the south side of Lawton. Mamo was a lively character—tough, joyful, and a sports enthusiast. She would sit in her rocking chair with a sports event blaring on the TV and another game on the radio, yelling at both while smoking her way through four packs of cigarettes a day and drinking coffee. Before Thanksgiving dinner, her house needed thorough cleaning a week before to clear out the thick cigarette smoke that had soaked into everything.

Granny's cranberry salad was the most memorable dish every Thanksgiving, and I often helped her make it the day before. I remember grinding whole cranberries, pecans, and quartered oranges (peel and all) in her hand-crank food grinder, and then watching her mix it all into a sweet gelatin. That salad, with its cold, dense, sweet-and-sour crunch, was the perfect complement to the turkey. Everyone brought their signature dishes—green bean casserole with fried onions, creamy broccoli and cheese rice casserole, and Mamo's famous scalloped corn casserole. My Aunt Dixie (actually, my mother's aunt) always made a seven-layer salad, and my mother's pumpkin pie was second to none.

As the years passed, Thanksgiving moved to Aunt Dixie's home in Mustang, Oklahoma, about one hundred miles north of Lawton. The colder weather often meant rain or snow, and her house, nestled in the country and surrounded by towering pecan trees, became the new gathering spot. There, we started the tradition of playing bingo after dinner and before the Dallas Cowboys game. Aunt Beverly (my mother's sister) would collect small closeout items throughout the year for prizes, and we'd keep playing until everyone had a chance to win something.

Rea Jade Bennett

The most captivating Thanksgiving was the year Rea Jade had a surprise to show everyone. Rea was Dixie's granddaughter, who was five years old and born with spina bifida. The type, *myelomeningocele,* had required immediate surgery and led to her being crippled and unable to walk.

After everyone had finished dinner, we gathered in the front room for Rea to show everyone her surprise. Her mother laid her on the floor on her belly, and she was smiling from ear to ear. The room was completely silent as everyone watched intently. Everyone knew of her struggle, and in my mind, I thought, *Finally, she is going to stand and take a few steps.*

Rea glanced at her mother, Debbie, who nodded to her that it was time. You wouldn't have thought the room could get any quieter, but it did. Rea's smile disappeared, replaced by pure determination. She slowly pushed herself up, supporting herself with her arms. She was looking toward the floor, and little drops of sweat began to form on her forehead. Her body was shaking, and then, with all her might, she struggled with every ounce of energy and pushed herself backward while dragging her knees forward, inch by inch, until she was finally on her hands and knees.

She was completely exhausted, but she had just climbed the highest mountain on the planet right in front of our eyes. A little five-year-old girl, with a horrible crippling disease and paralyzed since birth, had done it. She had touched the top of the mountain. She looked up, her hair wet from perspiration, and as everyone broke out in applause, her smile showed a sense of unbelievable accomplishment that, in that moment, surpassed everything else in the world.

This time in my life was a harsh reminder of how hard life could be. It influences me to this day and is why through the years, when someone is complaining about mowing the lawn or walking somewhere they were too lazy to walk to, I would say, "Rea would give anything to walk behind a mower or walk from here to there."

That Thanksgiving would be the closest Rea ever came to walking. As she grew older and the reality of her condition set in, she relied on a wheelchair for the rest of her life. I will always remember that her smile never faded, nor did the love and support of her family. Rea passed away when she was twenty-seven.

Christopher Jaye Bills

In 1971, my little brother Christopher was born. Thanksgiving was always a happy occasion. Life was busy throughout the year, and this was a time we all gathered, creating a sense of unity and stability in our family. However, Thanksgiving 1990 was overshadowed by Christopher's death in a car accident while driving home one night to my parents'.

Chris was special in our family. When he was born, he brought a fresh energy and new dynamic that reignited excitement and joy at home, keeping our family young at heart. Tim, Cricket, and I all formed unique and special bonds with him, as we took on quasi-parental roles—changing diapers, giving him a bottle, and sharing life lessons we had learned. This fostered a deep sense of responsibility and affection. He was especially attached to me when he was a toddler. He had asthma as a child and sometimes had to sleep in a playpen with a water vaporizer blowing into it, covered by a makeshift tent. For some reason, he wouldn't cry and would go to sleep if I slept in the playpen with him. I did it many times, as he dealt with frequent bouts of illness.

Thanksgiving was different the first time Chris wasn't there. There was a huge void that everyone felt but didn't quite know how to address. The atmosphere carried an unmistakable sense of loss, as if a shadow had settled over our usual festivities. People didn't know what to say, really. The silence felt heavier than usual, filled with the weight of words left unsaid. My parents, I knew, would welcome any mention of Christopher; they needed to talk about him, to keep his memory alive, but the discomfort and uncertainty kept most of us silent.

Christopher would never be at another Thanksgiving gathering, and that realization hung in the air. It was a somber reminder of our fragile existence. The clatter of dishes and the hum of conversation continued, but beneath it all, there was a shared grief, an ache that connected us with our collective loss. That Thanksgiving, we celebrated as best as we could, but Christopher's absence was a presence, a silent echo in the room, reminding us of the love and life that had been abruptly taken away. Chris had died when he was just eighteen.

As I look back on those early years, filled with both joy and loss, I see now that they were slowly building up the questions I would face later in life—questions about faith, the world, and how it all fits together.

Cherishing Each Moment

Both Rea and Christopher's brief lives were a somber reminder of our fragile existence. When Chris died, it was the first time we experienced such a substantial loss. The bond between parents and children, or between brothers and sisters, is incredibly strong, built on deep emotional connections, shared experiences, and unconditional love. The past had its grip on Chris, while the future pulled us forward, slowly tearing us apart from him. It was catastrophic, leaving an emptiness that only time could attempt to fill. The loss was not just an absence but a life-altering disruption to our family's sense of unity and purpose, forever altering the landscape of our lives.

Through these experiences, I learned that goodness doesn't shield us from life's storms. While I had once believed that living a righteous life would somehow protect us from tragedy, I came to understand that we all live in a world that can be harsh and unpredictable. Life's adversity does not discriminate between the righteous and the wicked. Dying is part of living, and we live with that reality always. Life is short—shorter for some than others—but ultimately, life is just a moment in time.

This underscores the value of the two voices that can guide you through life—the voice of Nature and the wisdom of the Bible. Together, they are invaluable for living your life to the fullest in the time you have on this planet we call Earth.

When I was in grade school, I came to have a little blue robin's egg. How I came about it, I don't recall, but I like to think I didn't steal it from its mother's nest. But as little boys often do, I probably did. Regardless, I took it into the house, found an empty shoebox and a heating pad, and attempted to hatch it. It only takes about two weeks for a robin's egg to hatch, so in less time, it did. Amazing—I had a tiny bird.

My dad helped me figure out how to feed it. He mixed cornmeal with water, and with the tip of a popsicle stick, I would feed it. Since I was in school, my dad helped take care of the bird, and in less than two weeks, it was a fledgling covered in fluffy, downy feathers with a mix of muted brown and rusty hues. It was curious and always alert to me, hopping around energetically, testing its wings and wanting to explore its surroundings. So my dad decided it was time to keep it outside.

We had an old rabbit pen that was perfect for it, except that you had to tilt it up off the ground to put the bird under it. It was a wood-framed box lined with chicken wire and about four feet square. It was fairly heavy, but my dad would tilt it up, and I would put the bird under it, then my dad would lower it back down.

Being outside in this new pen was much better because the bird could get a real taste of nature, learn to use its wings, and maybe find a bug to eat on its own. We would take it out, and I would put it on the four-foot-high chain-link fence in the backyard, then run to the center of the yard about twenty-five feet away, and it would try to fly to me. It couldn't fly upward yet, but it could fly on a descent almost to where I was standing. It wouldn't be long before its journey from an egg to an independent robin would be complete.

A day or two after being in its new environment, I rushed home from school before my dad was home from work and wanted to help it practice flying. I flew into the house and out into the backyard, and he was hopping around, ready to get out. Getting him out was not hard. The pen was heavy, but as soon as I lifted it, he jumped out from under it, ready to go. Like always, I put him on the fence, and he would fly to me, and we would do it again. In the next coming days, his feathers would become sleek and developed, and he would be on his way.

After we finished, it was time to put him up. My dad still hadn't got home, but I felt like I could do it myself. I held my bird in one hand and knelt down and leaned against the pen with my shoulder, grabbing under the edge of it with my free hand and pushed it up just enough that I could pitch the bird under it. I did that and then dropped the pen, but the instant the bird touched the ground he hopped to get out, like he always did, and to my horror, the edge of the pen crushed him squarely in his back.

I have tears in my eyes sharing the end of this story, over fifty years later, remembering how I watched him die in front of me. It was horrible—within just a few seconds, I saw the life fade out of him. I don't think I ever cried so much as a child.

The voice of Nature was stern, teaching me a myriad of lessons in one moment. And they were hard lessons at the expense of a little bird. It taught me the importance of leaving nature to tend to its own, not to take on tasks

I can't do alone, and to be ever mindful of the care required when someone's life or happiness is on the line. It taught me heartbreak, responsibility, and the weight of unintended consequences.

Also, this experience, though painful, was a powerful teacher in understanding the fragility of life. Life is not a race from moment to moment, but an opportunity that is precious and irreplaceable. We should do our best to give our full attention to the little bits of time we have in order to recognize the delicate balance of life. By doing so, we remind ourselves to live fully, love deeply, and appreciate the small yet significant moments that make up our existence, for they could be the last.

The Bible has always offered timeless wisdom for navigating the time we have in life. One verse that captures the essence of cherishing the moments we have is Job 14:1-2: "Mortals, born of woman, are of few days and full of trouble. They spring up like flowers and wither away; like fleeting shadows, they do not endure." This verse touches on the significance of the fleeting nature of our existence and the importance of making the most of our short time on earth.

By embracing the wisdom of the Bible, we learn to value each day as a gift and to approach life with a heart full of gratitude and mindfulness. It teaches us to seek balance, to love one another deeply, and to live with intention and purpose. In this way, we can truly appreciate the moments that matter and make sure that we fill our lives with meaning and joy.

From City Lights to Country Nights

Our lives underwent a dramatic transformation in 1974 when we moved about twelve miles (as the crow flies) south of Lawton, leaving behind the familiar hustle and bustle of the city for the tranquil, open expanses of the country. This move was more than just a change of address; it was a distinct shift that brought new opportunities, challenges, and a deeper connection to the natural world around us.

The catalyst for this move was Camp Lu-Jo KISMIF (*Keep It Spiritual Make It Fun*), a church camp my brother and I attended each summer with great anticipation as soon as the school year ended. The camp occupied fifty acres and contained three old army barracks: one for the boys, one for the girls, and one serving as a mess hall. It was only used one month a year during the summer, and the rest of the time, it remained unattended. Being in the middle of nowhere and left unoccupied for so long, it was frequently vandalized. Hunters in the area would shoot out windows and engage in other mischievous acts. To combat this, the local churches that built and supported the camp decided to find a family to move a mobile home onto the property to look after it and, at the very least, keep it from being vandalized. We were that fortunate family.

The country was a new world for us and marked the start of the next chapter in our lives. We were older now, and I became more aware of the stars without city lights to hide them. The Milky Way stretched out across the sky and looked like a river of light flowing through a pitch-black sky. Thousands more stars in a deeper darkness made the universe look bigger, and you couldn't help but notice the vastness of God's creation. This is what David must have experienced in Psalm 8:3-4, describing what I was seeing: "When I consider your heavens, the work of your fingers, the moon and the stars, which you have set in place, what is mankind that you are mindful of them, human beings that you care for them?"

When we were living in the city, we could often make out the brighter parts of constellations, such as the Big Dipper, which is a prominent part of the Great Bear (Ursa Major) constellation. However, the detail of the Great Bear constellation, including its fainter stars, was not noticeable. Now they stood out in vivid detail and formed a bright canopy of light that shined over us, no differently than they have done for everyone who has ever lived. I had studied stories of the Bible all my life, but now they seemed to come to life. I could easily see the evidence of what Moses wrote of in Job 9:9: "He is the Maker of the Bear and Orion, the Pleiades and the constellations of the south," and by the unknown writer in Job 38:31, where God asks, "Can you bind the chains of the Pleiades? Can you loosen Orion's belt?" No matter the time or place in which you lived in the world's history, it somehow became apparent that we all looked up into the same sky, saw the same sun, moon, and stars, and in some small way, we have been connected.

Not only was the night sky clearer and more revealing, but the night air was like crystal. Sounds echoed in the night. From the open fields and deep woods that lined Pecan Creek, the sounds of nature's nocturnal creatures came alive. Crickets and frogs created a symphony of rhythmic chirps and croaks, blending seamlessly into a harmonious tapestry of nighttime life. The occasional hoot of a lone owl added a haunting melody to the rustling leaves that whispered secrets as gentle breezes swept through the dark woods and grasses of the open fields, while the distant howl of a coyote brought a touch of wild mystery. These sounds, which replaced the noise of city life, became a vivid reminder of the rich, living world around us, a world that thrived and sang its own songs under the cover of darkness.

There were mysterious sounds to learn of in the part of the country we were in. As we settled into our new home, every so often, we would hear a clattering and knocking that came from a far distance just south of us. It would occur at no particular time—sometimes at night and sometimes during the day. Sometimes it was fast, and sometimes it was slower. Figuring it out wasn't easy because as soon as it started, it ended, and we didn't have time to drive and investigate.

One day our curiosity got the best of us, so we got in the pickup with my dad and drove in the general direction, not knowing what we were looking for. We lived in the middle of the section (one-mile stretch of road along a field), so we drove a half mile south and turned to the west for a mile on the dirt road that cut through grassy pastures and wheat fields. We turned back south at the T-intersection and after about a mile came up on an old metal bridge set high over West Cache Creek.

West Cache Creek is a tributary of the Red River, flowing through the fertile plains of Comanche County. The creek has been significant for centuries. In the seventeenth century, Spanish explorers, including Father Juan de

Salas, ventured into the Wichita Mountains (which were visible to us on the horizon) near the creek in search of gold and to spread Christianity among the indigenous tribes. These early expeditions laid the groundwork for future exploration and settlement.

We proceeded across the bridge, and just like that, we found the source of the noise. The sound was coming from this rusty old Pratt or Warren truss-designed steel bridge with wooden planks; it was unmistakable. The cupped planks would rock and knock on the steel framing when a car or truck rolled across them, and the noise could be heard for miles. The bridge was named Cutty Bridge and was most likely built before the 1930s; many of them crossed the creeks that snaked around all over the surrounding counties.

The history of Native Americans in Comanche County, Oklahoma, is rich and complex, especially during the early 1900s. The area was originally part of the Kiowa-Comanche-Apache (KCA) Reservation. Non-Indian settlers gained access to the land that later became Comanche County through a land lottery held on August 6, 1901. This event, while opening up land for settlers, caused deep tension and grief for the Native tribes, as it marked the loss of their ancestral lands and further displacement. Little did we know that the sounds of this distant past still echoed across the fields and plains at night.

One evening, after the sun had dipped below the horizon, we heard a sound that no doubt terrified early settlers when wagon trains in the East began heading West in the early 1830s. It was the rhythmic beat of drums, accompanied by faint, melodic chanting, as though spirits of the Native Americans who once roamed this land were reaching out across time. It wouldn't have surprised me if an arrow flew out of the dark night and into the front door. However, these Native Americans didn't shoot arrows at early settlers; they went to school with us instead. The sound was that of the Indian family that lived a mile and a half down the road, and the drums were actually a recording they would play loudly to practice the chanting they would do for local powwows, which were common in the area.

A Fresh Start

As the days went by, we quickly became accustomed to the sounds of the country. It was a great awakening to the natural order of things, something we could never have learned in the city. In a sense, we had taken a step back in time to a simpler and quieter life. It was an education in the ways of creation that aligned perfectly with the teachings of the Bible. Nature became a living testament to the words we had read and studied so many times in our church, reinforcing our faith and understanding of the world.

With school starting in about a week, I was a little apprehensive about adjusting to a new group of people. It's not something I have ever liked to do, and yet I couldn't help but feel less stressful. During the 1970s, Tim and I had attended Tomlinson Junior High School in Lawton. It was a time when the school experienced significant racial tensions as part of broader societal shifts in the United States. The integration of schools following desegregation mandates led to clashes between white and black students, reflecting the ongoing struggles for civil rights and equality during that era. The Lawton public school system was actively working to comply with federal desegregation laws, which included busing students from predominantly black neighborhoods to schools in other areas of the city, and it wasn't the best of times.

We enrolled in school in the small town of Faxon, Oklahoma, five miles away from our new home and would ride the bus to school. I was in the seventh grade, my brother Tim was in the eighth grade, and Cricket was in the fourth grade.

The original Faxon School House, built in 1910, was a red brick building that housed grades 1-8. It burned down on March 14, 1911, and a new school was constructed shortly after, complete with modern features, including a basement for protection against storms, all too common in Oklahoma.

The building we attended, similar to the original, was a two-story, red-brick, four-room schoolhouse with just four teachers, one of whom also served as the principal, baseball coach, and basketball coach. The school bus driver also served as the janitor and maintenance person, and lastly, and most importantly, there was the cafeteria cook. First and second grades were in one room, third and fourth grades in another, fifth and sixth in another, and seventh and eighth grades in the last room, which had a connecting door to the principal's office so that our teacher could step out to be the principal when needed. It was not uncommon for him to step out to quickly debate the fate of a student who was causing trouble of some sort. The principal was the judge, jury, and executioner, and his judgment was immediately carried out decisively with a wooden paddle, which, when used, was loud enough for everyone in the school to be reminded that order was the rule of law in those days.

There were four of us in the seventh grade on one side of the room, and Tim and the rest of the eighth grade sat on the other side. That was a nice surprise because Tim was in the same room with me. The teacher would teach one side at a time while the others worked on an assignment, whether it be Math, English, Reading, Writing, or Social Studies.

Tim graduated at the end of the year and the next year moved to Chattanooga High School and Elementary, another five miles away. The school bus would stop at Faxon, where I would jump off with the other kids attending there, and then head on to Chattanooga. In 1975, I graduated from the eighth grade with Mont, Kelly, and Michelle. The four of us joined the ninth grade in Chattanooga with fewer than ten other students, most of whom had attended since the first grade.

Chattanooga High School (Chatty), like Faxon, had a history deeply rooted in the community's development. The high school is relatively small, with a student body that has varied over the years but has typically remained under one hundred students. Chattanooga was a slightly bigger school, serving grades 1-12. To give an example of how much bigger it was, there were two cooks in the cafeteria instead of just one at Faxon.

The school district emphasized a well-rounded education, and they were accomplished. From Tim's graduating class, Mike Phillips (Colonel Michael D. Phillips) went on to serve as the Department Head of Mathematical Sciences at the United States Military Academy at West Point from June 2006 to June 2016. From my class, Pamela Bohl became an accomplished accountant and moved to Russia to join a firm there. She now lives in Paris, France. The school had a strong focus on athletics (baseball and basketball) and extracurricular activities such as the Future Farmers of America (FFA), which is significant given the agricultural heritage of the area. Most students participated in FFA and entered at least one animal to show in county fairs. Some kids showed steers, but mostly lambs and pigs were the animals of choice.

Tim and I showed pigs each spring and fall (with Mike Phillips). We also raised pigs and at one time had as many as three sows, which would have a litter of pigs twice a year. Sometimes the litters were small with five to seven piglets, and other times there could be over a dozen. To say the least, things could get really busy at times. Once the piglets got older, we would select the best ones to show in upcoming fairs and sell the rest. Taking care of the pigs was part of our daily chores when we got home from school, and my father fed them most mornings after we got on the school bus. We won several champion awards through the years, always with a crossbreed hog of Chester White descent.

Baseball and basketball seasons, harvest, and seasonal stock shows defined our years in high school, which went by without major event. I played both sports, although I wasn't particularly good at either. However, Tim excelled at baseball and was exceptional on the field. He had a strong left arm and pitched through the years and his natural curve ball was hard to hit. Tim graduated in 1978, and I graduated in 1979 with only thirteen in our graduating class.

From City Kids to Country Boys

At the time of our new adventure from the city to the country, Tim and I were unaware that our move to Faxon and the Chattanooga area would reconnect us with our family history. Our great-grandfather on my mother's side, Jesse Beemer, was a notable figure in the Chattanooga, Oklahoma, area in the early 1900s. He was born on March 24, 1887, and became a prominent cowboy who owned a ranch outside of Chattanooga. He farmed and raised horses, mules, and shorthorn cattle. He had legendary experiences in his life, including going hunting with President Theodore Roosevelt. Jesse Beemer passed away on April 2, 1952, and is buried in the Chattanooga Cemetery alongside his wife, who we called Granny B, and my grandfather, Jay Beemer.

Beemer's life intersected with some of the most significant personalities of his time, including Will Rogers. Will Rogers, born in 1879 in the Cherokee Nation in Oklahoma, was a vaudeville performer, actor, and humorist who became one of the most famous personalities in America during the early twentieth century. His charm and wit made him a beloved figure, and he often drew on his cowboy heritage in his performances.

We also discovered that our grandmother (Granny) and her sisters had all graduated from Chattanooga High School in the 1930s, and the school had included their pictures among the senior class pictures displayed in the hallway.

Church in Rural America

Not long after we moved out into the country, the drive back into town only continued to link us back to a life we were quickly leaving behind. The church my parents found to attend was in Chattanooga, which not only was closer but gave us a place to worship with the people we now shared our lives with.

The church, like the school in Faxon, was small. Still today, it sits on the corner of a grassy lot just across the street from Chattanooga High School. On the same block, on the opposite corner, is the Presbyterian church built with light-colored brick in simple ecclesiastical architecture. Its prominent steeple, topped with a pointed finial over the entrance, and landscaping of narrow cedar trees is both inviting and emblematic of traditional church designs, providing a quaint yet dignified presence in the community's heart.

Across the street from the Presbyterian church is First Baptist Church, constructed of light red bricks, setting itself apart with a sense of stability in a traditional, beautiful style. From above, it is built in the shape of a cross, with a fellowship hall behind it. The solid double-entry doors, stained dark brown with a circular wooden framed window above, and a wide set of stairs lead up to a small portico supported by beige columns, adding a simple elegant touch to the town's main street.

The Chattanooga Church of Christ, which we attended, is by far the simplest of the three churches. Two large elm trees stand in front of the white plastered block walls of the rectangular building, modest and charming, reflecting the simplicity and humility often associated with small rural communities. Just inside are two restrooms on either side of the small foyer, which is separated from the auditorium by another set of aged wooden glass doors. Stepping through, you'll find two small classrooms in the back and then the auditorium, which seats about one hundred people. In the front, there is a small, elevated platform with a pulpit, with a communion table set below it. Centered behind the pulpit is the baptistery, with two additional classrooms on either side. The old wooden pews creaked and squeaked in this building with the scent of the outdoors, all washed in light that shone through frosted windowpanes lining each side of the building. The simplicity and warmth of the Chattanooga Church of Christ embodied the heartfelt devotion and close-knit community spirit that defined our town.

Each of these churches reflected the overtones of faith in God that permeated this small country town with a population of about 400, not including the surrounding families living in the area. These churches, set in the middle of town and close to each other, conveyed the message of freedom of religion, encouraging individuals to worship God in their own way. The Church of Christ and the Presbyterian church actually shared the parking lot between them, and the community people simply united in God. This proximity and shared space underscored a sense of unity and mutual respect among different denominations, reinforcing the town's collective faith and communal spirit.

Wheat Harvest

Probably our greatest adventure was the summer after tenth grade. I had just turned sixteen, and Tim was seventeen when we went on the seasonal wheat harvest with a local farmer, Mark Scherler. Mark was a well-known German farmer just outside of Faxon. Harvest lasted for two months, consuming most of our summer. We first cut all the wheat that Mark had planted in Comanche County, which took about a month, then we loaded the Gleaner combines onto forty-foot A-frame trailers and pulled them with a twenty-four-foot-long wheat truck on a thousand-mile journey. There were five of us, including Mark and a couple of other adult hired hands.

Our route took us through Kansas, where we cut wheat for local farmers on our way to Colorado. This first leg of the journey was an adventure in itself, as we moved from one farm to another, experiencing both the hospitality and challenges of different communities. Our final destination was Cheyenne Wells, Colorado, where Mark's son farmed several sections of land. Not only did I cut wheat for that season, but I also stayed behind to plow the land and prepare it for the next crop. The land was vast, with sprawling fields, so much so that it took a full hour just to plow around the field one time.

The harvest experience was a rite of passage, providing us with a sense of responsibility and the satisfaction of hard work. Each day began before dawn and ended well after sunset, filled with the rhythmic hum of combines and the dust of the wheat fields. We faced mechanical breakdowns, unpredictable weather, and the relentless pace of the harvest season. Despite the challenges, the camaraderie among the crew and the joy of completing a field made it all worthwhile.

This adventure not only strengthened the bond between Tim and me but also Steve, my lifelong friend from Taylor Street, who hired on with Mark as well. For all of us, it instilled a strong work ethic and a deeper appreciation for the agricultural community. Those two months of harvest were a formative period in our lives, filled with hard work, new experiences, and lasting memories.

We often thought of this adventure as reminiscent of the movie *The Cowboys*, released in theaters in 1972. It was the journey of boys thrust into the adult world of a cattle drive, facing dangers and learning essential life skills.

Similarly, our harvest adventure required us to step up and take on responsibilities beyond our years, fostering growth and maturity. Just as the boys in the movie formed a tight-knit group under the guidance of John Wayne's character, we too developed a strong sense of camaraderie and learned valuable lessons that would stay with us for a lifetime.

I still often think about Mark Scherler. Mark was one of the biggest and strongest men I have ever met. He was like Paul Bunyan, a giant of a man, and I never saw him in anything but a pair of overalls and a button-down, short-sleeved plaid shirt. He walked with the sway of John Wayne, usually with one pant leg caught on the top of his cowboy boot, always wearing a ball cap and maintaining a focused demeanor. On rare occasions, we could coax a crooked smile across his face. Farming is a tough business, and there was work to do from sunup to sundown.

Mark's hands were more like enormous bear paws, with a bit of a shake, and it was always alarming when you were holding something with him on the other end of a sledgehammer. But somehow, he never missed. It was always best to just look down and be really still. What you didn't want to do was make him mad because that never went well. He was quiet most of the time, but when he spoke, it was usually with a stern, no-nonsense tone that let you know he meant business.

Without a doubt, the last thing you ever wanted to see while cutting wheat with your combine was Mark heading your way in his white dual pickup with side toolboxes. If he was taking the long way around to avoid running over uncut wheat, it meant you were doing something wrong—but it was manageable. However, if he was barreling straight through uncut wheat directly toward you, it was best to stop, put the combine in neutral, and brace yourself for his fury. He would jump out of his pickup and climb onto the side ladder of your combine, and it felt like he might tip it over. The door of the cab would swing open, flooding the cabin with the roar of the engine, wheat chaff, and hot summer dust, followed by his booming voice, trained directly on you—a sound and experience you would never forget.

The thing was, Mark was always right. He had been a farmer all his life, and he knew how things should be done—not because he simply wanted it done his way, but because it was the best way to do it and, most importantly, the safest way to do it. Farming is dangerous, and he accepted full responsibility for our safety. His stern demeanor and seemingly harsh methods were not just about efficiency, but about ensuring that everyone made it home safely.

Mark's wisdom and experience were invaluable lessons that went beyond the fields. He taught us the importance of hard work, discipline, and doing things the right way, even when it was the harder path to take. His influence instilled in us a deep respect for the land and the work it took to cultivate it. As I reflect on those days, I realize that Mark Scherler was more than just a boss—he was a mentor and a guardian, whose tough love and unwavering standards left a lasting impact on all who had the privilege of working under him.

Sanctuary in the Wichita Mountains

Throughout my life, whether in the city or country, the Wichita Mountains have always been a place of escape and renewal. Their steady presence on the horizon, with their soft bluish-gray tones and rugged boulders, has been a constant reminder of the natural beauty that surrounds me. From the clear mornings to the golden hues of sunset atop Mount Scott, these mountains have remained a source of peace and inspiration, grounding me in the wonders of the world around us.

The Wichita Mountains Wildlife Refuge, established in 1901, is one of the oldest managed wildlife facilities in the United States.[7] It holds a significant place in conservation history as the oldest managed wildlife facility within the US Fish and Wildlife Service system. It spans over 59,000 acres and serves as a sanctuary for wild roaming buffalo, elusive elk, deer, and over 50 mammal species, 240 bird species, and a variety of reptiles, amphibians, and plants— all of which you would encounter frequently.

The refuge holds a distinct character, where an Old West toughness meets the rich scents of the western prairies. The fresh, slightly sweet fragrance of

Eastern Red Cedar often fills the air, mingling with the earthy aroma of oak trees and the blanket of musty leaves beneath them, especially after a rain. The scent of sun-dried fields and flowing streams adds to this natural tapestry, creating an atmosphere that both invigorates and soothes the senses— embodying the true spirit of the western plains wilderness.

Every Season—A Reason to Go

The Wichita Mountains had unique allures as they transitioned throughout the year. In spring, the landscape burst into life with vibrant wildflowers, green grassy plains, and newborn calves of the buffalo and long-horned cattle that roamed wild. Rains filled the streams that cut through the red granite mountains, replenishing our favorite swimming spot, the locally famous forty-foot hole, which, much of the time, was the only reason the Wichitas even existed for us.

The hike to this spot was always an adventure in and of itself. It was about a mile through rugged mountain trails, ending with a climb down into a deep canyon. Along the way, we passed a massive cobblestone dam that formed a lake at the start of our journey. After the rainstorms, it was picturesque, watching the water tumble down over the meticulously placed stones. The sound could be deafening as the water crashed over thousands of cobblestones into the granite riverbed below, each stone a testament to the "cannon ball architecture" style adopted by the Civilian Conservation Corps in the 1930s. This structure was not just a marvel of natural beauty but also a symbol of human resilience and craftsmanship from a difficult time in American history.

What makes this place memorable to me isn't just its uniqueness; it's the life lesson I learned about rushing through life and missing out on fleeting moments.

One day, I was with my brother Tim and friends Mike Phillips and Mark Washburn from high school. We had timed our outing perfectly, catching the aftermath of a big storm that poured water into the forty-foot hole, making the experience even more exhilarating. I couldn't wait to get there, so after we passed the dam, I rushed ahead, eager to be the first to reach the spot. Somehow, being first always felt like a small victory.

When I arrived, I wasn't disappointed—the water was wild, churning, and powerful. It promised an exciting day of jumping from the high boulders. As I got ready, taking off my shoes and shirt, I realized that the others hadn't caught up yet. Ten minutes passed, then twenty, and they still weren't there. Concerned, I put my shoes and shirt back on and started back to find them.

What I discovered hit me like a ton of bricks: I had missed one of the greatest adventures of our time. After I rushed ahead, they had floated down the river from the dam, riding the roaring rapids straight to the forty-foot hole. I met them as they arrived—but I had missed the entire experience.

That day has stuck with me my entire life. I learned an important lesson: life isn't always about rushing to the destination. It's about savoring the journey, especially when shared with those around you. The best experiences in life can come when you least expect it, if you take the time to enjoy the path you're on.

Summer's heat transformed the refuge into a rugged, resilient terrain that we challenged on frequent occasions. Long hikes without bottled water (bottled water started becoming more accessible to the average consumer in the 1980s) and our refusal or inability to carry a canteen often left us parched—actually, beyond parched. I vividly remember the feeling of desperation, thinking we would die of thirst before reaching a campsite where an old rusty water pump awaited us. Finally, we would get a cold drink of water—rainwater filtered through the rocky strata, giving it the uniquely clean taste of the Wichitas, which sadly is no longer available today.

Fall painted the trees in rich hues of red, orange, and yellow, creating a breathtaking mosaic that was a feast for the eyes during our hikes. It was a time of cooler weather, making hiking and camping more comfortable. Campfires at night brought welcome warmth and the nostalgic smell of the outdoors. We filled those evenings with laughter and a deep appreciation for the time we spent together, creating memories that have lasted a lifetime.

Winter, with its occasional blankets of snow and ice, turned the mountains into a serene, almost mystical wonderland. Sometimes the ice would be so heavy that the woods echoed with the cracking and breaking of tree branches that crashed to the ground. It was a cycling of life. One of the most memorable times I spent with my best friend, Steve, was a weekend when we were both teens and too young to drive. My mother dropped us off on Friday with plans to pick us up on Sunday. When we arrived, it was cold but dry. As the sunset began to cast its shadows across the refuge and our campsite began to dim under a dark gray and cloudy sky, it slowly began to snow in the quiet stillness of the mountains. We were the only campers at sunset, and it was so quiet you could hear the snowflakes falling through the dried leaves on the trees like rain.

When we woke up the next morning, we discovered ourselves covered in six inches of snow from our small two-man pup tent. The pristine, white landscape was breathtaking, and the sense of solitude and connection with nature was humbling. The snow muffled all sounds, creating an atmosphere of peaceful isolation. It was a magical experience, one that forged a deep bond between us and left an indelible mark on our memories.

These times in life made the refuge not just a haven for wildlife, but also a haven for us. Each hike along its trails, each moment spent climbing the mountains, brought a deep sense of peace and connection to something greater than ourselves. The Wichita Mountains were a sanctuary where the hustle and bustle of everyday life faded away, leaving only the pure beauty of nature. Here, amidst the ancient rocks and whispering trees, was a place where you could experience simplicity. It was an escape from the trials of city life, homework, and mowing lawns—it was a reminder of the timeless rhythms of the earth, greater than anything we could learn from the classroom or daily chores.

The Seasons Bring Rains—The Rains Bring Change

The Wichita mountain range felt like a looking glass back in time, offering us the freedom to explore and learn about the delicate balance of complex ecosystems that support life on earth. It was a living testament to the self-sustaining intricacy of God's creation. Every visit uncovered new discoveries, deepening our appreciation for the interconnectedness of the natural world. As far back as I could imagine, listening to the voice of nature in the soft wind and the peaceful songs of meadowlarks and canyon wrens, I would stand still, taking in the scene. I tried to see creation as it might have been at the beginning of time—how the sun rose and set over this land for thousands of years, while nothing disturbed the natural cycles of plant life, buffalo roaming the plains, or the migration patterns of North Canadian Geese flying south ahead of the harsh northern winters.

These mountains became home to early indigenous peoples, including the Wichita and Comanche tribes, who relied on the land for hunting and gathering. Traces of early explorers also linger in the region. Notably, Francisco Vázquez de Coronado, the Spanish explorer, led an expedition in 1541 through parts of the southwestern United States, including the area around the Wichita Mountains. One enduring relic of that era is a cave known as Spanish Cave, a place where we, much like the young men and boys of the past, once stood. Inside, marks left by past visitors—whether stains, paint, or carvings—serve as a reminder of those who came before. People still leave their marks today, connecting us to the past in a timeless tradition.

Figures from the Old West, such as Jesse James, are said to have passed through these mountains. According to local lore, James, while carrying gold, was forced to take shelter during a severe winter storm near Buzzard's Roost, just east of the Wichita Mountains. A carving he made in the soft stone to mark the location of hidden treasure can still be seen today, fueling the imaginations of treasure hunters. The search for gold also drew hopeful miners to the region, though the riches they sought remained elusive. Scattered empty mines across the refuge stand as silent reminders of those futile quests for fortune, testifying to the dreams of prosperity that never materialized.

In a way, the Wichita Mountains offer a glimpse into the evolution of mankind in this part of the world—a history that began in simplicity yet was often marked by struggle. One tragic chapter in this history is the Cutthroat Gap Massacre, which occurred in 1833, a year remembered by the Kiowa as "The Year the Stars Fell," due to the famous Leonid meteor shower.[8] During this event, the Osage tribe ambushed a Kiowa camp at a location now known as Cutthroat Gap, on the northern border of the Wichita Mountains.

At the time, most of the Kiowa warriors had left to hunt buffalo, unaware that a band of Osage, who had been hunting in Kiowa territory, had been observing them. On the day of the massacre, a young Kiowa boy, tending to his family's horse, saw an Osage warrior hiding behind some rocks. Though he rushed back to warn the camp, it was too late. The Osage attacked swiftly, killing approximately 150 Kiowa women, children, and elders. Two young siblings, a boy named Thunder and a girl named White Weasel, were taken captive.

When the Kiowa warriors returned, they found the horrific aftermath: the bodies of their loved ones decapitated, and their heads placed in cooking pots. This brutal massacre left a deep scar on the Kiowa tribe. In 1834, White Weasel was returned to the Kiowa as a peace offering, but her brother, Thunder, had tragically died in captivity.

The Evolution of Civilization in the Wichita Mountains

As early settlers began to arrive in the region, the clash between those who lived according to the natural laws of the land and those who came with a more refined cultural understanding, shaped by teachings like those found in the Bible, became evident. This cultural tension, much like the challenges Adam and Eve faced as they sought to bring order and understanding to a wild and untamed world, revealed the difficulties in bridging two very different ways of life. The wilderness, with its own set of rules, was often at odds with the structured, moral guidance passed down through generations. It became clear that to settle and civilize the area, something more than just pioneering spirit was required—it demanded a force capable of maintaining peace and order. Thus, the United States saw the necessity of establishing Fort Sill, a military post designed to help tame the land and manage relations with the Native peoples.

The establishment of Fort Sill in 1869 marked a significant chapter in the transformation of this region. While it represented progress for settlers, it also signaled the difficult task of integrating the Native American tribes, who had lived in balance with the land for centuries. This process of "taming" the land, much like the biblical task of taming the wilderness, mirrored what Adam and Eve faced—bringing structure to a world shaped by the laws of nature. The Native American tribes, like the Comanche and Kiowa, were not primitive but represented an earlier stage in the evolution of human society, deeply connected to the natural world.

One figure who stands out during this time is Quanah Parker, the last chief of the Comanche. Quanah's story is an extraordinary blend of both worlds— born to Cynthia Ann Parker, a white woman captured by the Comanche, and a Comanche chief, Quanah grew up within the tribe but later navigated the challenging transition into Western society. His leadership helped his people through a difficult period of transition, as they were forced to abandon their traditional ways and assimilate into the culture being imposed upon them.

Quanah's connection to the land and his ability to guide his people into a new chapter mirrors the difficult but necessary transitions that often occur in history. His leadership was grounded in the strength and resilience of his people, even as they adapted to life on the reservation.

Quanah's granddaughter, Anona Alice "Nona" Birdsong, was the daughter of Laura Neda Parker Birdsong, Quanah Parker's daughter.[9] She was born in 1884, not long after the days of the Indian Wars, and lived much of her life in the Wichita Mountains area. The Star House, Quanah Parker's famous home with red stars painted on the roof of the two-story white-frame house, served as a center for Comanche culture, keeping the traditions and history of the tribe alive.

As time went on, this part of regional history became intertwined with my own family's story. My mother's uncle, whom we called Uncle Pete, married

Nona. I remember her well from Thanksgiving dinners at my great-grand-mother Mamo's home. By then, she was much older—a quiet presence at our gatherings, but with a toughness that left a lasting impression on me.

In Mamo's garage, I remember seeing the rusty metal brands used by Quanah Parker. He raised cattle on the lands of the Wichita Mountains in his later life, which was certainly a change of pace, I'm sure. Those brands were a quiet reminder of a past not so far removed—a past where the land, the people, and the way of life were much different than the world I knew growing up. Civilization refines wilder ways of life and propels humanity forward, but it's important to remember the cost of that progress and the people who had to adapt to survive.

This reflection gave me a foundation for understanding the challenges faced at the very beginning of humanity. Adam and Eve entered a world that had existed for hundreds of thousands of years, filled with mankind much like the early indigenous people here. The transformation of a people, whether it's the story of Adam and Eve in the Bible or the Comanche under Quanah Parker, is never easy. The challenges faced by those who live in a world governed by the laws of nature, without the guidance of a moral or cultural framework, are formidable. But just as God sought to bring Adam and Eve into a fuller understanding of their purpose, so too does the progress of civilization aim to bring people into a more structured, purposeful existence.

Beyond Nature: The Search for Divine Moral Guidance

Stories like the Cutthroat Gap Massacre highlight the harsh realities of living in a world where humanity has consistently failed to create sustainable moral laws. Societies often devolve into selfish oppression and conflict. Moral laws based solely on humanity's evolutionary development seem to ground themselves in a cynical alternative to the Golden Rule: those who hold the power make the rules. This principle harnesses itself to a narrow, self-serving intent instead of something universal and encompassing. The further one is driven from their moral roots, the more brutal the decline becomes.

From the very beginning of our lives, I believe we possess a sense of moral law and a basic understanding of right and wrong. This instinct is universal and unchanged in children throughout history. It is not a product of maturity but a fundamental building block of our creation. Life challenges this sense more than it develops it. If anything, selfish desires often corrupt it.

Richard Dawkins, a prominent evolutionary biologist and atheist, is well known for his critical perspectives on the origin of moral laws. In *The God Delusion*, Dawkins asserts that moral laws are byproducts of evolutionary survival mechanisms. His perspective, shaped by his background in evolutionary biology, emphasizes that moral laws evolved through gradual changes and may not be inherent or constant from birth but rather shaped by societal and environmental influences.

This reminds me of one of my favorite funny stories about two little boys testing out cussing for the first time. Kids don't inherently cuss—they pick it up by listening to others. One day, two brothers were raking in the front yard. The older brother, Mark, says, "Hey, at breakfast tomorrow, let's try saying a cussword." The younger brother, Tommy, nods with excitement. "Yeah! You go first." So, the next morning, their mom asks, "What do you boys want for breakfast?" Mark smiles and replies, "Oh hell, Mom! Give me some of those Cheerios!" Their mom grabs him by the ear, drags him up the stairs, and yells, "You can go to school without breakfast, young man!" Then she comes back downstairs, looks at Tommy, and gruffly asks, "Now, what do you want for breakfast?" Tommy says, "Well, I don't want any of those DAMN Cheerios!"

This story captures the idea that our sense of right and wrong is present from birth, but external factors and life experiences can corrupt it. When children first encounter morally offensive language, there's a moment of internal conflict—a discomfort—indicating an inherent moral awareness. It's only after influence from the external world that this moral compass gets tested or corrupted.

The Wichita Mountains were not only a place of endless adventure for us but also a place where the search for a higher power began. Just as civilization has done for thousands of years, we found that the mountains, with all their wonders, pointed toward a higher intelligence of design. This reflection aligns with Psalm 19:1-2: "The heavens declare the glory of God, and the sky above proclaims his handiwork. Day to day pours out speech, and night to night reveals knowledge." Nature, in all its majesty, invites contemplation on the existence of a Creator, encouraging a journey of discovery and understanding.

CHAPTER 2

In Search of Our Origins

Throughout history, ancient civilizations sought to understand their origins and the universe through creation stories. These beliefs shaped entire cultures, many of which lasted for centuries until scientific understanding replaced them. Yet, even as myths and legends, these stories still reflect humanity's deep longing to make sense of the cosmos. Just as the mountains spoke to us of a grand design when we were growing up, early peoples looked to the heavens and the earth, crafting narratives that would define their cultures and beliefs.

The Sumerian, Egyptian, and Babylonian creation stories are among the oldest known accounts, preserved on clay tablets, papyrus, and stone.[10] These myths provide valuable insight into the evolution of human thought about the world and humanity's place within it. They highlight the diverse ways cultures have attempted to explain the universe's origins and their role within it.

Many of these ancient myths continue to resonate today, preserved through cultural traditions, religious practices, and modern storytelling. Disney's *Moana*, for example, draws from Polynesian mythology, introducing ancient stories to contemporary audiences, while Marvel's portrayal of Norse gods like

Thor keeps Norse mythology alive in popular culture.[11] These modern adaptations ensure that ancient myths remain relevant, allowing them to endure in the history of humankind.

A recurring theme across many of these myths is the concept of a great flood.[12] This narrative appears in the stories of Sumer, Greece, and others, often bearing striking similarities to the biblical flood. While not scientific evidence, the widespread presence of these flood myths across different civilizations suggests a shared recognition of a significant event in human history.

Although modern science has debunked the literal interpretations of these ancient myths, it's important to acknowledge that science, while excellent at explaining the "how" of the universe, is limited when addressing deeper questions of purpose and existence. These matters—where ancient myths, the true religion of the Bible, and a relationship with God offer insight—lie in the realms of philosophy and faith. This ongoing quest for not only *how*, but also *why*, leads naturally to the exploration of the four major belief systems that dominate the world today.

The Evolution of Belief Systems

As humanity's understanding of the universe evolved, so too did its spiritual beliefs. While early mythologies provided imaginative explanations for creation and the forces of nature, they eventually gave way to more structured religious systems. These major belief systems not only address creation but also offer deeper theological frameworks to answer life's most profound questions. Today, four major belief systems—Hinduism, Islam, Buddhism, and Judeo-Christian traditions—continue to guide the spiritual and philosophical lives of billions. Each presents unique perspectives on the nature of existence, the origin of the universe, and humanity's place within it.

Hinduism

Belief: Hinduism has multiple creation stories, but one of the prominent accounts is from the Rigveda and the Puranas. In this tradition, the universe goes through endless cycles of creation, preservation, and destruction, governed by the Trimurti: Brahma the creator, Vishnu the preserver, and Shiva the destroyer. The story often starts with the primordial waters, from which a lotus emerges with Brahma, who then creates the world.

Flood Account: The Hindu Puranas include a flood story where the god Vishnu, in the form of a fish (Matsya), warns the ancient king Manu about an impending deluge.[13] Manu builds a boat and saves himself, the seven great sages, and seeds of all plants, ensuring the continuation of life.

Modern Presence: Hinduism remains one of the world's largest religions, with over 1.2 billion followers primarily in India and Nepal. Its stories and teachings are integral to cultural practices, festivals, and daily life.

Islam

Belief: In Islam, the creation story is found in the Quran and closely resembles the story of creation found in the book of Genesis from the Bible.[14] Allah (God) is described as the singular creator of the universe. Allah created the heavens and the earth in six days, though the specific details of each day are not as elaborately described as in Genesis. Allah created the earth and spread out mountains and rivers, and then created all living beings, including humans, with Adam being the first human created from clay. The Quran emphasizes the power, wisdom, and mercy of Allah in the creation of the universe.

Flood Account: The Quran also includes a flood story similar to that of Noah in the Bible. Prophet Nuh (Noah) is commanded by Allah to build an ark to save himself, his family, and pairs of animals from a great flood meant to cleanse the earth of corrupt humanity.

Modern Presence: Islam has over 1.9 billion followers worldwide. The creation story is a fundamental part of Islamic teachings and is recited and reflected upon in religious practices.

Buddhism

Belief: Buddhism does not have a single, unified creation story in the way that some other religions do. This is largely because Buddhism is more focused on the path to enlightenment and the nature of suffering than on cosmological origins. However, various Buddhist cosmological texts provide different perspectives on the creation and structure of the universe. In Buddhist cosmology, the universe is seen as cyclical and eternal, going through endless cycles of creation and destruction, aligning with the concept of *samsara*, the cycle of birth, death, and rebirth.[15] The universe undergoes periods called *kalpas*, which are incredibly long epochs of time during which the universe is created, exists, decays, and is eventually destroyed, only to be created again. Stories and teachings from different Buddhist traditions, such as the Pali Canon and the Avatamsaka Sutra, describe the world system being created through natural processes without a creator deity, emphasizing the cyclical nature and the interconnectedness of all things.

Modern Presence: Buddhism has approximately 500 million followers worldwide. Its teachings on creation and the nature of existence continue to influence spiritual practices and philosophies.

Judeo-Christian

Belief: The most popular creation story in history, particularly in the Western world, is the Judeo-Christian creation story as found in the book of Genesis in the Bible. While the biblical creation story is not the oldest in terms of written records, its theological significance and the belief in its primacy remain central to many religious traditions. The biblical creation story is traditionally dated to around 1000-500 BC based on linguistic, archaeological, and historical evidence. The existence of older written myths does not necessarily negate the validity of the Genesis account from a faith perspective. Instead, it highlights the rich tapestry of human attempts to understand our origins, whether through divine revelation, oral tradition, or mythological storytelling.

Flood Account: The Genesis account of Noah's ark describes God commanding Noah to build an ark to save himself, his family, and pairs of every animal species from a great flood meant to cleanse the earth of human wickedness.

Modern Presence: Christianity has about 2.4 billion followers, and Judaism has around 14 million followers globally. The Genesis creation story is foundational to the beliefs and practices of these religions.

In the Judeo-Christian tradition, the book of Genesis in the Old Testament details the creation story. According to this account, God created the universe in six days and rested on the seventh.

Day 1: *God created light, separating it from darkness.*
Day 2: *He created the sky.*
Day 3: *He gathered the waters to create dry land and made vegetation.*
Day 4: *He created the sun, moon, and stars.*
Day 5: *He created the creatures of the sea and birds of the air.*
Day 6: *He created land animals and humans in His own image.*
Day 7: *He rested, sanctifying it as a day of rest.*

Note of Interest: The Seven-Day Week God created the world in six days and rested on the seventh day, which is known as the Sabbath (Genesis 1-2:3). This seven-day cycle became deeply embedded in Jewish religious practice and Christianity later adopted it. The biblical creation story's seven-day structure played a significant role in shaping the concept of a weekly cycle in Western culture.

The Bible's account of creation stands alone from all other myths and traditions because of its monotheistic framework, where a single, omnipotent God creates the universe by divine command, as opposed to the polytheistic and often mythological narratives found in other traditions. This account emphasizes an orderly, intentional creation process, culminating in creating humans in God's image, which establishes a unique relationship between the Creator and humanity.

The biblical narrative integrates with a historical and prophetic context, culminating in a plan of redemption. It highlights a continuous divine intervention in human history, which is distinct from the cyclical and mythological elements prevalent in Hindu, Islamic, and Buddhist creation stories. This combination of theological depth, historical continuity, and moral purpose underscores the Bible's unique position among the world's creation accounts.

The Tension Between Science and Faith: A Closer Look

As we transition from ancient myths and legends to the modern day, it's important to acknowledge the extraordinary advances science has made in understanding our universe. The scientific method has helped unravel the mysteries of physics, biology, cosmology, and more. Yet, there remains a growing tension between science and faith, particularly when it comes to the origins of the universe and life itself.

It's no secret that many within the scientific community view religious belief systems with skepticism, even contempt. From creation myths to deeply held theological beliefs, there has been an ongoing effort to push religious explanations aside as mere fables. And in many cases, there is some merit to that view—stories of gods emerging from primordial chaos, shaping the earth from bones and blood, and wielding magical powers may seem far-fetched in light of what we now know about the cosmos.

Science tells us that the universe began in a moment of rapid cosmic expansion, a singular event that sparked the formation of everything we know today.[16] Whether you call it the Big Bang or the "moment of rapid cosmic expansion," the essence remains the same—an instantaneous, universe-defining event. It's a narrative that both science and religious belief share in their fundamental understanding: the universe came from nothing, and its origins align in striking ways with the ancient account in Genesis.

However, the Bible's creation account, specifically the one found in Genesis, stands apart in a way that demands deeper reflection. While early civilizations were making guesses about how the world came to be, the account recorded by Moses thousands of years ago—an account originating in an ancient, pre-scientific world—manages to reflect a sequence of events that strikingly aligns with what modern science has only recently confirmed.[17]

Consider this: Moses's creation story describes an ordered process that begins with the creation of light, followed by the separation of the heavens and the earth, the appearance of dry land, the creation of vegetation, the emergence of celestial bodies, the formation of sea and land creatures, and finally, the arrival of humankind. This sequence, written long before the dawn of telescopes or microscopes, mirrors the same general stages of cosmic development that science now teaches—starting with an instantaneous beginning and moving through an ordered progression of the universe's formation. The Bible described these events with a remarkable degree of accuracy, given the limitations of human understanding at the time.

What the scientific community fails to explain—and often refuses to even consider—is *how* this ancient manuscript could have been so accurate. How could Moses, writing thousands of years ago, have possibly known the correct sequence of the universe's formation?[18] The criticism levied against all religious beliefs, including Christianity, is that they involve a creator, a deity, something that cannot be measured or tested in a laboratory. Science, they argue, deals in facts, not in faith. But herein lies the irony: *science itself admits that the universe had a beginning.* It agrees that all matter and energy exploded into existence at a singular moment in time—out of nothing, ex nihilo.

This is where the waters become murky for science. While the Big Bang theory provides a framework for what happened at the beginning, it offers no satisfactory explanation for why it happened or how it was triggered. Despite the incredible precision needed for the universe to exist in the first place—an explosion so perfectly fine-tuned that any deviation in force would have caused it to either collapse back into itself or expand too rapidly for stars, planets, or galaxies to form—there is still no answer for the cause of it all. Science agrees that the universe had a definite starting point, but it falls short of explaining how something came from nothing. This very mystery, which science acknowledges but cannot solve, is explained clearly and decisively in the biblical account: "In the beginning, God created the heavens and the earth."

For centuries, religion has been the object of ridicule from the scientific community because it dares to claim a Creator—*a personal God*—was responsible for the existence of the universe. Yet, when asked to explain the cause behind the Big Bang, or what existed before the universe, science draws a blank. Theories are thrown around—perhaps it was a multiverse, perhaps it was quantum fluctuations, or perhaps it was something beyond our understanding. These theories, however, are no more provable than the divine narrative that Moses presented. The difference is that science remains stuck with no conclusive answer, while the Bible provides one.

What we face today is not simply a disagreement over facts. It is a refusal from much of the scientific establishment to acknowledge that their very understanding of the universe aligns with the ancient biblical story. The sequence of events that science teaches—from the Big Bang to the formation of stars and planets, from the emergence of life in the seas to the creation of humankind—is almost perfectly mirrored in Genesis. The only difference is that the Bible assigns this process to the hand of a Creator, while science claims it was all random and purposeless.

As we prepare to delve deeper into the details of creation and science, it is critical to remember this: both the Bible and science agree that the universe had a beginning. Both agree that this beginning happened in an instant. Both agree on the order in which the universe unfolded. The only disagreement lies in the cause. Science is left searching for answers, while the Bible offers a clear explanation—one that was recorded millennia ago and remains unchanged to this day.

This book is not an attack on science. Science is an incredible tool, and its discoveries have enriched our understanding of the world in unimaginable ways. But science has its limits, particularly when it comes to explaining the origins of the universe. It can tell us what happened, but it cannot tell us why or how.

As we move forward, this book will explore the alignment of the biblical creation story with the scientific record. It will unravel how these two seemingly opposing forces—faith and science—are not in conflict but in harmony when understood through the right lens. And while science has reached the limits of what it can explain about the origin of the universe, the Bible steps in to reveal the deeper truth behind that moment of creation.

The Logical Arguments for Christianity

I like to think that my reasoning for being a Christian and firmly believing in the Bible's story of God, His creation, purposeful design, and redemption would have led me to this conclusion no matter where I was born, simply because it is logical. Living in the United States offers a unique opportunity to be exposed to the Bible, with Christianity being the dominant faith, represented by over 350,000 individual churches nationwide. As I mentioned in the first chapter, the small town of Chattanooga, where I attended school, had three churches so close that you could throw a rock and hit any of them from the schoolyard.

Additionally, I had the unique experience of working most of my life in the funeral industry, which gave me a broader perspective on the world's leading religions. Working as a funeral director allows you to witness firsthand how different faiths respond to life and death. In Fort Worth, Texas, where I spent much of my career, the religious landscape is incredibly diverse, reflecting a wide array of faiths and denominations. If there is ever a moment when a person's beliefs are laid bare, it is at the time of death, when the community comes together to reflect and reaffirm their faith. Sadness mingles with what we remember, and the beauty of life crystalizes into cherished memories.

In these moments, I've observed the rich tapestry of religious traditions and the deeply ingrained rituals that different faiths employ to honor the dead and comfort the living. From the solemn chants of Buddhist monks to the reverent formality of the Catholic Church, and the vast variety within Christian rites, each tradition offers a glimpse into its core beliefs and values.

These ceremonies are not merely rituals but meaningful expressions of a community's understanding of life, death, and what lies beyond.

I've probably attended over 4,000 funeral services, and I can tell you the number one destination people hope for—*Heaven*. Even if the family didn't regularly attend church or have a minister to preside, at this pivotal moment in life, Heaven is what they long to hear about. People often speak of their loved ones being "in a better place" or "reunited with those they've lost." It seems that no matter one's background, an eternal home with God is an innate human desire.

It reminds me of the story of two brothers, known as the town's most notorious scoundrels. When one of the brothers passed away, the other went to the local minister to plan the funeral. He told the minister, "You can say whatever you want during the service, but at some point, you must refer to my brother as an angel." The minister, knowing full well the reputation of the deceased, was in a tough spot. On the day of the funeral, the minister spoke honestly about the brother's life, acknowledging his faults and failings. Then, with a pause, he added, "But compared to his brother sitting here today, he was an absolute angel."

It's a humorous story, but it highlights a broader truth: no matter how someone has lived their life, the hope for something better, something eternal, shines through at the end. It's as if the desire for Heaven is embedded in the human spirit, regardless of religious affiliation or personal history.

So, why is it that across so many cultures and religious practices, there is this common thread—a belief in something beyond this life, an eternal home? It's this deep-seated desire for Heaven that points to something more than just an evolutionary quirk or cultural tradition. It points to the possibility that we were, in fact, created with eternity in mind. This longing seems like a clue left by our Creator, leading us toward the truth. Even the Egyptians, despite being misguided in their worship of multiple gods, went to incredible lengths to prepare for the afterlife.

This is where I believe Christianity stands apart. While many belief systems point toward an afterlife or paradise, Christianity offers something unique—a logical sequence of events, supported by modern discoveries, that corresponds with both our spiritual longings and the natural world as we know it. The Bible's account of creation, though written thousands of years ago, aligns with modern scientific discoveries in a way no other religious text does. Christianity doesn't just offer hope for an eternal home; it provides a rational, coherent explanation for creation, life, and purpose—along with the path to redemption.

Christianity's Historical Grounding: Jesus was a *Real* Person

The historical evidence for Jesus's existence is robust and supported by multiple sources, both Christian and non-Christian.[19] These sources collectively confirm that Jesus was a real person who lived in the first century, was crucified under Pontius Pilate, and had a significant impact on the people and societies of his time. This historical grounding is believable, providing a factual basis for the faith that has influenced billions of people throughout history.

New Testament Writings

- **The Gospels:** The books of Matthew, Mark, Luke, and John provide detailed accounts of Jesus's life, teachings, death, and resurrection. The authors of these texts wrote within a few decades of Jesus's death and either knew Jesus personally or were closely connected to his disciples.

- **The Letters of Paul:** Some of Paul's letters were written as early as twenty-thirty years after Jesus's death and provide early testimony to Jesus's existence and the early Christian belief in his resurrection. The historical existence of Paul the Apostle is well-supported by multiple sources. His own letters, some of the earliest Christian documents written between AD 50 and 60, provide firsthand accounts of his missionary work and theological teachings.

Early Christian writings, such as those by Clement of Rome and Ignatius of Antioch, further validate Paul's influence and martyrdom.

Clement of Rome

- Clement of Rome is considered one of the earliest Church Fathers. His writings, specifically First Epistle of Clement (circa AD 96), are some of the earliest known Christian texts outside of the New Testament. In this epistle, Clement addresses the church in Corinth, discussing issues of order and unity. While Clement doesn't explicitly describe Paul's martyrdom, he does mention Paul as an example of faithful endurance. This letter is significant in early Christian history because it confirms the wide influence of both Paul and Peter in the Christian communities and their strong presence in Rome.

- Clement's writings validate Paul's missionary activities and his leadership in the early church, highlighting Paul's contribution to spreading Christianity throughout the Roman Empire.

Ignatius of Antioch

- Ignatius of Antioch, another important Church Father, was a bishop of Antioch and an early Christian martyr. He wrote a series of letters (circa AD 110) to Christian communities on his way to martyrdom in Rome. In these letters, Ignatius refers to Paul's influence, indicating that Paul's teachings and missionary work had a lasting impact on the Christian communities Ignatius was connected to.

- Ignatius's writings also demonstrate the deep respect early Christians had for Paul's theological teachings and his role in spreading the gospel, confirming Paul's legacy in the early church.

Archaeological and Roman Records

While there are no direct Roman records specifically documenting Paul's life, his travels fit well within the known historical context of the Roman Empire. Archaeological discoveries, such as inscriptions and references to the cities and regions Paul visited (like Corinth, Philippi, and Ephesus), align with Paul's missionary journeys as described in his letters and the Acts of the Apostles. These findings support the historical reality of Paul's missionary work and the spread of Christianity during this period.

Roman and Jewish Historians

- **Tacitus:** A Roman historian, Tacitus, wrote about Jesus in his *Annals* around AD 116.[20] He mentions Christus (Latin for Christ) and his execution by Pontius Pilate during the reign of Tiberius. This account provides an early non-Christian reference to Jesus's existence and crucifixion.

- **Suetonius:** Another Roman historian, Suetonius, mentions Chrestus in his work *The Twelve Caesars*, written around AD 121. Historians believe that this reference relates to Jesus and the disturbances caused by his followers in Rome.

- **Josephus:** A Jewish historian, Josephus, provides two references to Jesus in his *Antiquities of the Jews*, written around AD 93-94. The most significant passage, known as the Testimonium Flavianum, describes Jesus as a wise man, a doer of wonderful works, and mentions his crucifixion under Pontius Pilate. While there is debate over the authenticity of parts of this passage, most scholars agree it provides valuable historical testimony to Jesus's existence.

Other Ancient Sources

- **Pliny the Younger:** In a letter to Emperor Trajan around AD 112, Pliny the Younger, a Roman governor, describes the worship of

Christ by early Christians, further attesting to the historical presence and influence of Jesus.

- **Lucian of Samosata:** A second-century Greek satirist, Lucian refers to Jesus in his work *The Death of Peregrine*, mocking Christians for worshiping a man who was crucified in Palestine.

Archaeological Evidence

While direct archaeological evidence of Jesus's existence is sparse, archaeological findings have corroborated many aspects of the historical and cultural context described in the Gospels, such as the discovery of the Pool of Bethesda and the ossuary of Caiaphas, the high priest involved in Jesus's trial. (An ossuary is a small stone chest for bones.)

In 2012 Southwestern Baptist Theological Seminary in Fort Worth hosted the Dead Sea Scrolls and the Bible exhibit, which I attended. The elaborate display included the *Genesis 37-38* fragment, which is owned by the Kando family of Bethlehem and is considered to be the largest Dead Sea Scroll segment held by a private collector. Five other major fragments were also on display, including *Genesis 33*, *1 Kings 13:22*, *Isaiah 28:23-29*, *Amos 7:17- 8:1*, and *Joel 3:9-10*. The chance to view portions of the Dead Sea Scrolls usually requires an overseas trip to a Near East nation, such as Israel or Jordan, so it was a lone chance to step back in time and see a piece of Christian history in this small collection of Roman artifacts.

One of the items I found most interesting was an ossuary found in 1941 in a tomb in the Kidron Valley, Jerusalem, that bears the inscription *"Alexander, son of Simon."* It is thought to be connected to Simon of Cyrene, the man who carried the cross for Jesus. Simon of Cyrene is mentioned in the Gospels (Matthew 27:32, Mark 15:21, Luke 23:26) as the man compelled by the Romans to carry Jesus's cross on the way to the crucifixion.

The inscription on the ossuary has led some scholars to speculate that it could indeed belong to the family of Simon of Cyrene. The full inscription reads, "Alexander (son of) Simon." Given the relatively rare combination of names and the context provided by the Gospels, this has been considered significant evidence by some researchers linking it to the historical figure mentioned in the New Testament.

In ancient Jewish customs, ossuaries were used during the Second Temple period around the first century BC to the first century AD, particularly in Jerusalem and the surrounding region.

While this connection is intriguing, it remains a subject of scholarly debate, as definitive proof linking the ossuary to Simon of Cyrene and his son Alexander is still lacking. However, such findings do provide a fascinating glimpse into the historical context of the New Testament narratives.

One of the most well-known ossuaries is the James Ossuary, which was discovered in the early 2000s and bears an Aramaic inscription that translates to *"James, son of Joseph, brother of Jesus."*[21] The authenticity of this ossuary has been subject to much debate, but it highlights the importance of ossuaries in understanding early Jewish burial practices and potential connections to historical figures from the Bible.

It's things like this that make the Bible, the life of Christ, and Christianity personal beyond all other religious beliefs in the world. It's not a fairytale of mystic wonders that can't be touched in at least some small way. There's a tangible historical connection to the figures, places, and events described within its pages, which distinguishes it from many other belief systems. These are not just allegories of gods interacting in unreachable realms or disconnected myths from a distant past—they are accounts rooted in the reality of human history.

Consider other creation stories, such as those from Egyptian or Norse mythology: grand tales of deities emerging from chaos or gods forming the earth from their remains. These narratives, while fascinating, often focus on mythological explanations that lack the same historical or archaeological grounding that the Christian story provides. Christianity, by contrast, offers a direct link to real historical figures like Jesus, Paul, and Peter, supported by archaeological findings, writings from ancient historians, and the consistent preservation of biblical texts over the centuries. The Bible exists within real places, real time, and real people, giving it a unique authenticity.

Moreover, when we examine belief systems like Buddhism, Hinduism, and Islam, the contrast becomes even clearer. Buddhism, for instance, often points to a cyclical, abstract spiritual existence where ultimate reality is a state of Nirvana—a concept that seems distant and intangible. There's no personal relationship with a creator, and the goal is not eternal life in a physical sense, but rather an escape from suffering and rebirth. In Islam, while there is a promise of paradise, the focus on physical rewards like rivers of wine and companions in the afterlife doesn't offer the same personal connection to God that Christianity emphasizes. Hinduism, with its pantheon of deities and belief in cycles of reincarnation, often presents a mystic, abstract understanding of life and death, where the ultimate goal is merging with a universal spirit, which can feel detached from personal experience.

By contrast, Christianity offers not just a coherent and historically verified story, but a personal relationship with the Creator, a direct path to eternal life, and a narrative grounded in historical reality. This is why I find Christianity convincing: it provides not only hope for the afterlife but also a grounded and intimate understanding of God's purpose for humanity.

It's this historical and personal connection that sets the Bible apart. When you read the Gospels, you are engaging with testimonies passed down through generations—stories believed and cherished by countless individuals for millennia. Unlike myths that seek to explain the unknown through imaginative tales, Christianity offers a logical framework grounded in historical events and real people who walked the earth.

When we examine the evidence, the desire for Heaven doesn't stem from a myth but from a deeper understanding that we are more than beings destined to perish. We are part of a story that has been unfolding since the beginning of time, a story written by the Creator Himself. This is what makes Christianity not only believable, but also deeply personal.

Consistency and Historical Continuity in the Christian Tradition

- Christianity's creation narrative, as detailed in the Bible, provides a coherent and consistent account of the origin of the universe, life, and humanity. Unlike the cyclical or mythological elements seen in other traditions, the biblical story offers a linear and purposeful progression from creation to redemption.

- The historical continuity of the Christian tradition is evident in the preservation and transmission of biblical texts over millennia. This unbroken chain of faith and documentation provides a solid foundation for understanding human history and divine interaction.

Moral Purpose and Divine Plan

- The Christian narrative emphasizes a moral purpose for creation. Humans are created in the image of God, endowed with intrinsic value and a unique role in the divine plan. This stands in contrast to other traditions where humans may be seen as incidental or part of an endless cycle.

- Christianity offers a clear and compelling plan of redemption. The story of Jesus Christ's life, death, and resurrection provides a path to salvation and eternal life, addressing the human condition and the problem of sin in a way that is both personal and universal.

Unique Relationship Between Creator and Humanity

- The relationship between God and humanity in Christianity is deeply personal and loving. God is not distant or impersonal but intimately involved in the lives of His creation. This is exemplified in the incarnation of Jesus Christ, God becoming man, to bridge the gap between the divine and the human.

- Divine intervention in human history is a hallmark of the Christian faith. From the creation of the world to the covenants with the patriarchs and the life and resurrection of Jesus, God's actions are consistently aimed at guiding, redeeming, and sustaining humanity.

Distinctive Differences Between Christianity and Judaism

- **Messiah and Prophecies:** Christians believe that Jesus Christ is the Messiah, fulfilling the prophecies of the Old Testament. In contrast, Judaism does not recognize Jesus as the Messiah, expecting a future human leader to fulfill these prophecies.

- **Interpretation of Scripture:** Christianity views the New Testament as the fulfillment of the Old Testament prophecies, emphasizing the life and teachings of Jesus Christ. Judaism relies solely on the Hebrew Bible (Tanakh) and does not accept the New Testament as canonical.

- **Salvation:** Christianity teaches that salvation is achieved through faith in Jesus Christ as the Savior, emphasizing grace and faith over works. Judaism emphasizes righteous living, repentance, and adherence to the commandments as the path to maintaining the covenant with God.

In my experience, the teachings of the Bible and the experiences of life have led me to embrace Christianity as the logical and profound truth. The Christian faith provides a consistent and historically grounded narrative, a moral purpose, and a deeply personal relationship with the Creator. These elements offer convincing answers to the existential questions of origin, purpose, and destiny, reaffirming my belief in Christianity as the path to redemption and eternal life.

Yet, this journey toward understanding God and His creation does not stop with just history or theology. The Bible reveals God's specific plan for humanity, but we also see His design, His creativity, and His power through

Nature. These two distinct yet harmonious voices—the voice of Nature and the voice of Scripture—work in tandem to reveal the fullness of God's presence and purpose.

Nature, as God's general revelation, speaks to all people, displaying the wonder of creation, the fine-tuning of the universe, and the intricacies of life. Through the natural world, we glimpse the vastness and intentionality of God's design. At the same time, the Bible serves as His specific revelation, detailing the moral and spiritual truths that shape our relationship with Him and one another.

As we move forward, let's explore how these two voices—Nature and the Bible—work together to paint a fuller picture of God's intentions for creation. In the next chapter, we will examine how scientific discoveries align with biblical teachings and what both Nature and Scripture reveal about the Creator. This dual testimony underscores the depth of God's character, His creativity, and His ultimate plan for redemption.

CHAPTER 3

Which Way Do I Go?

I
n the nonsensical story of Alice in Wonderland, at the beginning of her journey, after she fell into the rabbit hole, Alice is driven more by curiosity than by a specific goal of finding her way. Her initial concern is not about reaching a particular destination, but about exploring the strange and wondrous world she finds herself in. However, as time goes on, Alice encounters increasingly bizarre and nonsensical situations, and her desire for direction and understanding grows. This is evident when she comes to a crossroads in the woods, with signs pointing in every direction and pathways doing the same. In her conversation with the Cheshire Cat, this confusion is highlighted:

> **Alice:** *"Would you tell me, please, which way I ought to go from here?"*
> **Cheshire Cat:** *"That depends a good deal on where you want to get to."*
> **Alice:** *"I don't much care where—so long as it gets me somewhere."*
> **Cheshire Cat:** *"Then it doesn't matter which way you go."*

The Cheshire Cat's response to Alice is indeed insightful. It highlights a critical truth about life and decision-making: if you have no clear goal or destination in mind, then it really doesn't matter which way you go—any way you go will get you somewhere. This interaction underscores the importance of having direction and purpose in one's journey. Not knowing where you want to end up means the choices you make lack significance; any choice will lead you somewhere, but not necessarily to where you need or want to be. This existential quest for meaning and direction is something everyone faces.

Amazingly, God knew our purpose before the beginning of time and the direction we should go to accomplish it:

> *Even before he made the world, God loved us and chose us in Christ to be holy and without fault in his eyes. God decided in advance to adopt us into his own family by bringing us to himself through Jesus Christ. This is what he wanted to do, and it gave him great pleasure.* (Ephesians 1:4-5, NLT)

This passage highlights that God's plan for redemption through Jesus Christ was established before the foundation of the world. It was a beginning specifically designed with the end in mind and makes that known in two guides—Nature: God's General Revelation and the Bible: God's Special (Divine) Revelation.

These two voices of God offer the necessary framework to navigate the complexities of life with purpose and clarity, contrasting sharply with the arbitrary and often conflicting guidance found in other belief systems. By attuning ourselves to these voices, we can walk a meaningful path that leads not just anywhere, but toward a life aligned with God's intentions. This harmonious dual revelation offers a coherent direction, guiding us away from the aimless wandering exemplified by Alice's initial lack of purpose in Wonderland.

Discovering God in Nature

The ever-present voice of God is whispered by the universe itself. Nature is a general revelation that reveals God's attributes and creative power through its complexity, order, and beauty.[22] This concept is often linked to passages such as Psalm 19:1-4, which states:

> *The heavens declare the glory of God, and the sky above proclaims his handiwork. Day to day pours out speech, and night to night reveals knowledge. There is no speech, nor are there words, whose voice is not heard. Their voice goes out through all the earth, and their words to the end of the world. In them he has set a tent for the sun.*

Nature speaks a universal language, filling the world around us with beauty and wonder. From the vastness of the oceans, teeming with life and stretching beyond the horizon, to the rhythmic waves that shape coastlines, the sea holds a mesmerizing power. Standing by the shore, we feel the deep pull of the tides and the endless motion of the water, a reflection of the eternal nature of God's presence. Beneath the surface, the mysteries of marine life unfold—creatures of all shapes and sizes, vibrant coral reefs, and hidden depths that remind us how much of God's creation remains unseen and unexplored.

Even in the heart of bustling cities like New York, places such as Central Park provide a sanctuary where nature speaks clearly. Walking through the park, the air is alive with the sounds of birds, the rustling of trees, and the hum of life that never seems to be quiet. Water fountains scattered throughout the world bring the soothing sound of flowing water to urban landscapes, allowing people to feel connected to nature, even in the midst of concrete. The sound of water resonates deep within us, offering a calming rhythm that reminds us of the rivers and streams that carve paths through the land.

Whether it's the grandeur of a mountain range, the stillness of a forest, or the gentle cascade of a fountain, nature surrounds us with reminders of God's handiwork. It speaks not just through what we see but through what we feel—the sensation of wind on our skin, the scent of flowers in bloom, and the sound of water flowing nearby. These experiences of nature stir something deep within, awakening a sense of wonder and drawing us into a closer connection with the Creator.

These wonders in nature represent some of the most extraordinary natural phenomena on Earth, inspiring awe and respect for the natural world and highlighting the diversity and grandeur of our planet's natural heritage. They not only showcase the beauty and complexity of God's creation but also serve as reminders of His power and majesty, evoking an emotional connection to the divine for all who witness them.

These observations around the world have led countless individuals throughout history to recognize the hand of a higher power at work. Without formal knowledge of God, these unique geographical wonders give rise to diverse tapestries of ancient civilizations' beliefs, myths, and legends. Philosophers like Plato and Aristotle pondered the order and purpose evident in nature, leading them to theorize the existence of a Prime Mover or a divine architect.[23] In more recent times, scientists like Isaac Newton and Albert Einstein expressed awe at the natural laws governing the universe, viewing them as evidence of an underlying intelligence.

But beyond the beauty of our surroundings on Earth, there is another realm of creation that equally captures our awe and curiosity—the heavens above.

The Celestial Connection

The heavens are unique. This sense of wonder and recognition is universal, cutting across cultures, religions, and epochs, uniting humanity in the acknowledgment of something greater than ourselves. Regardless of where one is born or lives on this planet we call Earth, everyone has witnessed the very same sun, moon, and stars in their vastness and constellations. This shared experience is a powerful reminder of our collective existence and the universal wonders that we all observe.

Since the beginning of time, the rotation of the earth daily creates a slowly changing display of an astonishing celestial sphere, highlighting the unchanging and majestic order of the heavens. The constellations move across the night sky in an ordered sequence, like floats in a parade celebrating genius design. The Pleiades (the Seven Sisters), Orion (the Hunter), and the Bear (Ursa Major, the Great Bear) were specifically mentioned over 4,000 years ago by Moses who wrote about them in Job 38:31-33 (NIV): "Can you bind the chains of the Pleiades? Can you loosen Orion's belt? Can you bring forth the constellations in their seasons or lead out the Bear with its cubs? Do you know the laws of the heavens? Can you set up God's dominion over the earth?"

Various cultures have recognized constellations throughout history, using their predictable appearances as markers of seasonal changes and navigation aids. As a kid playing outside at night with friends, I can't count how many times we would gaze up at the night sky, searching for the Big Dipper and Little Dipper. These asterisms—prominent patterns of stars—are found within the constellations of Ursa Major (the Great Bear) and Ursa Minor (the Little Bear). The Big Dipper, in particular, has served as a guiding light for travelers and sailors for centuries, its comforting, constant presence in the night sky offering direction and stability.

The shared experience of observing the heavens connects all of humanity. From the sun and moon to the stars and constellations, these celestial bodies have inspired wonder, guided exploration, and marked the passage of time across cultures and epochs. They serve as a reminder of our shared existence and the grandeur of the natural world, inviting us to look up and reflect on the majesty of creation and the Creator who set these wonders in motion.

The Moon's Universal Appeal

And what human being who has ever lived hasn't looked up to explore the moon? The moon, with its phases, has been a source of wonder and a timekeeper for millennia. Its cycles influence tides, and its beauty is a common sight in the night sky. The same moon that guided ancient navigators and inspired poets is the one we see today. The moon's gravitational interaction with Earth stabilizes our planet's axial tilt, which is crucial for maintaining a relatively stable climate and seasonal variation over long periods.[24]

This stabilization is important for the development and sustainability of life on Earth.

Additionally, the occurrence of solar and lunar eclipses, where the apparent sizes of the moon and the sun align perfectly, allows for total solar eclipses—a phenomenon unique to Earth among the planets in our solar system.

These things amaze me and no doubt have amazed all of humanity. They are a reflection of God's majesty and care, deeply embedded in the fabric of nature, rather than the result of an inexplicable explosion—a "Big Bang" that suggests something came from nothing without reason or purpose. Through these observations, nature itself becomes a testament to God's creative power and intentional design, offering a clear and coherent understanding of His existence and attributes. This harmonious revelation through nature complements the detailed guidance provided by the Bible, collectively pointing us toward a meaningful and purposeful life aligned with God's intentions.

The Voice of Nature's Instructions in Life

Nature is a silent teacher, offering profound lessons about life to those willing to observe and listen. In its rhythms and patterns, we see reflections of our own experiences—of growth, struggle, renewal, and interconnectedness. The cycles of nature, from the changing seasons to the slow growth of a tree, mirror the processes of life itself, providing a framework for understanding our own journeys.

One of the most striking lessons nature teaches is the value of patience. The growth of a tree, from a small seed to a towering giant, does not happen overnight. It takes years of slow, steady progress, weathering storms, enduring droughts, and basking in the sun. Similarly, life's greatest achievements and personal growth require time, perseverance, and faith in the process. Nature reminds us that the most lasting and meaningful things are those that grow slowly, over time.

Resilience is another key lesson. After wildfires ravage a forest, new growth begins to emerge from the ashes. Flowers bloom again, trees take root, and life regenerates. This resilience mirrors our own ability to recover from life's setbacks. No matter how devastating the circumstances are, there is always the potential for renewal. Nature teaches us to trust in the possibility of restoration and to have faith that after the storms, there can be new beginnings.

The interconnectedness of all living things also offers a significant lesson. In an ecosystem, every element, from the tiniest insect to the tallest tree, plays a role in maintaining balance. Each life form is dependent on others, and the actions of one ripple through the entire system. In this, we see a reflection of our own lives. No one exists in isolation. Our choices, relationships, and contributions are all part of a greater whole. Nature reveals the importance of community and the delicate balance that sustains life, teaching us that our lives are interwoven with the lives of others.

Nature also teaches us the importance of stillness and reflection. Amidst the busyness of modern life, moments of quiet can seem rare, yet in nature, stillness is abundant. A walk through the woods or a moment spent by a quiet stream invites us to slow down, breathe, and reconnect with something larger than ourselves. In these quiet moments, we find clarity, peace, and the opportunity to reflect on life's deeper meaning.

Lastly, humility is perhaps one of nature's greatest lessons. Standing on the shore of an ocean, gazing up at a star-filled sky, or walking through a towering forest, we are reminded of how small we are in the vastness of the universe. And yet, within this immensity, each of us has a role, a purpose. Nature humbles us, but it also inspires awe, reminding us that we are part of something far greater than ourselves.

One personal experience I recall reminds me of nature's ability to teach us about resilience and the unforgiving side of life. Several friends and I planned a deep-sea fishing trip out of Port Aransas, Texas, a three-day venture sixty miles out on the ocean. We left Fort Worth early that morning, expecting plenty of time to make it to the docks for our 4 p.m. departure. However, car trouble struck along the way—fortunately, we found a local shop to replace a failed coil, but we lost valuable time. With about two hundred miles to go, we called the dock to let them know we might be twenty or thirty minutes late. I still remember speaking to one of the crew members, and his response was, "Good luck, and I hope you make it by 4, because that's when we're leaving."

That felt harsh at the time, but as I've reflected on it over the years, I've come to understand his perspective. Life on the ocean, governed by nature, can be unforgiving, and so was he. There's no negotiating with the tides or delaying a storm—you must be ready when the moment comes. Fortunately, we managed to pick up speed and arrived with a few minutes to spare, but the lesson stayed with me. Just as the ocean teaches those who live and work on it to respect its rhythms and harsh realities, life also teaches us that some opportunities come only once, and we must be prepared to meet them.

In all these ways, nature is a constant guide, showing us the truths that are often hidden in the noise and rush of daily life. By observing nature's cycles, we learn about our own lives—how to grow with patience, how to recover with resilience, how to live in balance with others, and how to find peace in stillness. Ultimately, nature reminds us that life, like creation itself, is both fragile and enduring, interconnected and purposeful, always pointing back to the Creator who designed it all.

The Voice of God in Scripture

The Bible is the foundational text for Christianity. It is not only a religious text but also a historical and literary treasure. Its manuscripts, discovered across various regions—ranging from the deserts of the Middle East to the libraries of Europe—have been preserved through meticulous efforts by ancient scribes. From the Dead Sea Scrolls found in the caves of Qumran, to early New Testament manuscripts discovered in Egypt and other parts of the Mediterranean, these ancient texts carry God's timeless wisdom and guidance. Over the centuries, they have inspired billions of people, shaping cultures, guiding moral principles, and offering insight into the divine plan for humanity.

The Bible is divided into two primary parts: the Old Testament and the New Testament. No other religion in world history has a text with the same level of extensive documentation, scholarly preservation, and widespread historical verification as the Bible.

The Old Testament

This historical text, also known as the Hebrew Bible, consists of writings composed over many centuries, spanning from approximately 1200 to 165 BC. It includes the Torah (the first five books, also known as the Pentateuch), historical books, wisdom literature, and the writings of the prophets. Significant discoveries of Old Testament manuscripts include the Dead Sea Scrolls, found in 1947 in the Qumran Caves near the Dead Sea, which date back from the third century BC to the first century AD, and the Masoretic Text, compiled by Jewish scribes between the seventh and tenth centuries AD. The Septuagint, a Greek translation of the Hebrew Bible completed in the third and second centuries BC, was widely used by Hellenistic Jews and early Christians.

The New Testament

The writers composed this section of the Bible in the first century AD. It includes the Gospels, the Acts of the Apostles, the Epistles, and the Book of Revelation. The earliest New Testament manuscripts are papyrus fragments dating from the second to third centuries AD, such as the Rylands Library Papyrus P52, which contains a fragment of the Gospel of John. Important complete manuscripts include the fourth-century Codex Vaticanus and Codex Sinaiticus, both written in Greek and housed in the Vatican Library and the British Library, respectively. Scribes transmitted the New Testament through handwritten copies, with thousands of Greek manuscripts and early translations into other languages discovered, enabling scholars to reconstruct the original text with high confidence.

The Bible's Diverse Authorship

The Bible was written by over forty different authors from various walks of life, including kings, prophets, fishermen, and scholars. Their diverse backgrounds and experiences provide a multifaceted view of religious and historical events, making the Bible a unique and comprehensive text. The meticulous efforts of these individuals in writing, preserving, and transmitting these texts have ensured their accuracy and consistency throughout history, contributing to the Bible's status as one of the most reliable historical texts.

Old Testament Authors

Moses (Prophet, Leader—c. 1400-1200 BC): Traditionally credited with writing the first five books of the Bible (Genesis, Exodus, Leviticus, Numbers, Deuteronomy), also known as the Pentateuch. Some traditions also attribute the book of Job to Moses, highlighting its potential connection to the wisdom literature of the early biblical period.

Joshua (Military Leader—c. 1350-1200 BC): The book of Joshua.

Samuel (Prophet—c. 1100-1000 BC): Parts of 1 Samuel and potentially other historical books.

Nathan (Prophet—c. 1000 BC): Contributed to historical books like Samuel, Kings, and Chronicles.

Gad (Prophet—c. 1000 BC): Contributed to historical books like Samuel, Kings, and Chronicles.

David (King—c. 1000-970 BC): Many of the Psalms.

Solomon (King—c. 970-931 BC): Proverbs, Ecclesiastes, Song of Solomon.

Isaiah (Prophet—c. 740-700 BC): The book of Isaiah.

Jeremiah (Prophet—c. 627-580 BC): Jeremiah and Lamentations.

Ezekiel (Prophet—c. 593-571 BC): The book of Ezekiel.

Daniel (Prophet, Advisor—c. 605-530 BC): The book of Daniel.

Hosea (Prophet—c. 755-710 BC): The book of Hosea.

Joel (Prophet—c. 835-800 BC): The book of Joel.

Amos (Shepherd, Prophet—c. 760-750 BC): The book of Amos.

Obadiah (Prophet—c. 586 BC): The book of Obadiah.

Jonah (Prophet—c. 785-760 BC): The book of Jonah.

Micah (Prophet—c. 740-700 BC): The book of Micah.

Nahum (Prophet—c. 650 BC): The book of Nahum.

Habakkuk (Prophet—c. 610-605 BC): The book of Habakkuk.

Zephaniah (Prophet—c. 640-630 BC): The book of Zephaniah.

Haggai (Prophet—c. 520 BC): The book of Haggai.

Zechariah (Prophet—c. 520-518 BC): The book of Zechariah.

Malachi (Prophet—c. 430 BC): The book of Malachi.

Ezra (Priest, Scribe—c. 450 BC): The book of Ezra and possibly Nehemiah.

Nehemiah (Cupbearer, Governor—c. 445-420 BC): The book of Nehemiah.

Mordecai (Advisor—c. 400 BC): Traditionally attributed with writing the book of Esther.

New Testament Authors

Matthew (Tax Collector, Apostle—1st century AD): The Gospel of Matthew.

Mark (John Mark, Companion of Peter—1st century AD): The Gospel of Mark.

Luke (Physician, Historian—1st century AD): The Gospel of Luke and Acts of the Apostles.

John (Fisherman, Apostle—1st century AD): The Gospel of John, 1 John, 2 John, 3 John, and Revelation.

Paul (Pharisee, Apostle—c. 5-67 AD): Romans, 1 Corinthians, 2

Corinthians, Galatians, Ephesians, Philippians, Colossians, 1 Thessalonians, 2 Thessalonians, 1 Timothy, 2 Timothy, Titus, Philemon, and possibly Hebrews.

James (Brother of Jesus, Leader in Jerusalem Church—1st century AD): The book of James.

Peter (Fisherman, Apostle—1st century AD): 1 Peter and 2 Peter.

Jude (Brother of Jesus—1st century AD): The book of Jude.

These authors wrote over a period of approximately 1,500 years, from around 1400 BC to AD 100. Despite the diverse authorship and the span of centuries that would not have allowed the authors to confer with each other, the Bible maintains a compelling consistency and unity, which Christians attribute to the divine inspiration guiding its composition.

How We Got the Bible

The Bible's history focuses on significant milestones in making the Scriptures accessible to the masses, notably through the Septuagint and the Latin Vulgate. The translations of the Bible into Greek and Latin were pivotal in the history of Christianity. The Septuagint made the Hebrew Scriptures accessible to the Hellenistic world, while the Vulgate provided a standardized and enduring Latin text for the Western Christian tradition. Both translations reflect ongoing efforts to make the sacred texts available to a wider audience, ensuring their preservation and continued influence.

The process of compiling and translating the Bible into its current form involved significant historical developments. The Council of Carthage in AD 397 confirmed the canon of the New Testament, solidifying the collection of texts deemed authoritative by the early church.[25] St. Jerome's Vulgate, commissioned by Pope Damasus I in the late fourth century, used Hebrew texts for the Old Testament and Greek manuscripts for the New Testament, creating a translation that became the Western Church's standard for centuries.

The invention of the printing press by Johannes Gutenberg in the fifteenth century revolutionized Bible availability, with the Gutenberg Bible, printed in 1455, making the Scriptures more accessible. The King James Version, completed in 1611, became one of the most influential English translations, known for its accuracy and literary style, impacting English-speaking Christianity and literature.

The Septuagint

The Septuagint is the earliest Greek translation of the Hebrew Bible.[26] It was created during the Hellenistic period (323 BC to AD 31). This era began with the death of Alexander the Great in 323 BC and ended with the Roman conquest of Egypt and the defeat of Mark Antony and Cleopatra at the Battle of Actium in 31 BC.

Cleopatra was a member of the Ptolemaic dynasty and was the last active ruler of the Ptolemaic Kingdom of Egypt. The Ptolemaic rulers, particularly Ptolemy II Philadelphus, were known for their patronage of scholarship, and the renowned Library of Alexandria served as a hub for this translation effort. Ptolemy II Philadelphus, who ruled from 285 to 247 BC, sought to enrich the Library of Alexandria with translations of major works, including the Hebrew Scriptures.

While the exact details of the translation process are not fully known, historians accept that Jewish scholars in Alexandria took on the task of translating the Hebrew Scriptures into Greek. The term "Septuagint" refers to the tradition that seventy (or seventy-two) scholars were involved in this work. This translation was vital for Greek-speaking Jews and later for early Christians who used it extensively.

New Testament Quotes from the Septuagint
Matthew 1:23:

Septuagint: Isaiah 7:14: "Therefore the Lord himself will give you a sign: The virgin will conceive and give birth to a son, and will call him Immanuel."

Matthew: "Behold, the virgin shall conceive and bear a son, and they shall call his name Immanuel" (which means, God with us).

Acts 7:14:

Septuagint: Genesis 46:27: "With the two sons who had been born to Joseph in Egypt, the members of Jacob's family, which went to Egypt, were seventy-five in all."

Acts: "Then Joseph sent and called his father Jacob and all his relatives to him, seventy-five persons in all."

Hebrews 1:6:

Septuagint: Deuteronomy 32:43: "Rejoice, you heavens, with him, and let all the angels of God worship him."

Hebrew: "And again, when he brings the firstborn into the world, he says, 'Let all God's angels worship him.'"

These examples illustrate how the New Testament writers utilized the Septuagint, demonstrating its influence on early Christian thought and Scripture.

The Latin Vulgate

In the late fourth century, St. Jerome, a scholarly monk, undertook the monumental task of translating the Bible into Latin. This translation, known as the Vulgate, was commissioned by Pope Damasus I to create a standardized and accessible version of the Scriptures for the Western Christian world. Jerome's work on the Vulgate spanned over twenty-three years, during which he translated most of the Old Testament directly from Hebrew and revised the existing Latin translations of the New Testament based on the best Greek manuscripts.

Jerome's translation was revolutionary because he chose to translate the Old Testament from Hebrew rather than the Greek Septuagint, which was the standard practice at the time. This decision was met with resistance, but Jerome persisted, emphasizing the importance of accuracy and fidelity to the original texts. His fluency in Latin, Greek, and Hebrew allowed him to produce a translation that was both scholarly and accessible.

The Vulgate became the standard Bible for the Western Christian world for over a millennium. It was used by scholars, clergy, and laypeople alike and played a crucial role in shaping Western Christianity's theology and liturgy. The Council of Trent (1545-1563) later affirmed the Vulgate as the official Latin Bible of the Catholic Church. Jerome's meticulous work ensured that the Scriptures were preserved and transmitted accurately to future generations.

Historical Accuracy

What makes the Bible unique among religious texts is not only its unparalleled spiritual teachings but also its historical and prophetic accuracy. Archaeological discoveries and historical research have corroborated many events, places, and people mentioned in the Bible, lending credibility to its accounts. For example:

1. **The Siege of Lachish:** Archaeological excavations at the ancient city of Lachish have uncovered evidence of the Assyrian siege described in 2 Kings 18:13-17. The discovery of the Lachish Reliefs, which depict the siege in detail, corroborates the biblical account.

2. **The Hittites:** The Bible mentions the Hittite civilization numerous times, although it was long thought to be a mythical people by historians. However, the discovery of Hittite cities and records in the nineteenth and twentieth centuries confirmed their existence and importance in ancient history, as described in Genesis 15:20 and other passages.

3. **The Pool of Bethesda:** John 5:1-15 describes the healing of a paralyzed man at the Pool of Bethesda.[27] Excavations in Jerusalem

have identified the location and structure of this pool, matching the description provided in the Gospel of John.

4. **The Dead Sea Scrolls:** Discovered between 1946 and 1956, the Dead Sea Scrolls include some of the oldest known manuscripts of the Hebrew Bible.[28] These texts have provided invaluable insight into the accuracy and preservation of the biblical texts over millennia.

The discovery of the Dead Sea Scrolls demonstrated the impressive accuracy with which the biblical texts were preserved over millennia. These scrolls, along with other ancient manuscripts, show a high degree of consistency with later copies of the Bible.

Biblical scholarship, involving experts in various fields such as history, linguistics, and archaeology, continues to affirm the Bible's historical reliability. While debates and discussions persist, the general consensus is that the Bible provides a valuable and accurate record of historical events, cultural practices, and religious beliefs of the ancient world.

Christians believe that the Bible is inspired by God, meaning that the human authors wrote under the guidance of the Holy Spirit. This divine inspiration ensures that the Scriptures convey God's truth accurately and authoritatively. As stated in 2 Timothy 3:16-17, "All Scripture is breathed out by God and profitable for teaching, for reproof, for correction, and for training in righteousness, that the man of God may be complete, equipped for every good work."

Of Special Interest: The Calendar System

The calendar system that marks time as of now, for example, the year 2024, is based on the traditionally calculated year of the birth of Jesus Christ of the Bible. This dating system, known as Anno Domini (AD) for years after the birth of Christ and Before Christ (BC) for years before, has become the most widely used calendar system worldwide.

Global Standard. The Gregorian calendar, which uses the BC/AD system, has been adopted globally for civil and administrative purposes.[29] Pope Gregory XIII introduced this calendar in 1582 to correct inaccuracies in the Julian calendar. Over time, it became the international standard, largely due to the influence of European colonization and global trade.

Secular Terms. To provide a more inclusive and secular approach, the terms Common Era (CE) and Before Common Era (BCE) are used interchangeably with AD and BC, respectively. These terms maintain the same starting point, which is traditionally recognized as the year of Jesus Christ's birth.

CHAPTER 4

Genesis of Creation

When exploring the origins of the universe, the path inevitably leads to the intricate interdependence of time, space, and matter—three fundamental elements that science recognizes as the very fabric of creation. Albert Einstein introduced the theory of relativity, which includes the concept of the space-time continuum.[30] This theory combines space and time into a single, interconnected entity, with matter interacting within this fabric. It is a cornerstone of modern physics and underscores the intrinsic interconnectedness of time, space, and matter.

The notion that time, space, and matter could create themselves is a logical impossibility, as it would require them to exist before they existed. Matter requires space to exist, as it occupies a physical location, and without space, matter would have no place to be. Likewise, matter defines space itself, shaping it and causing it to curve—this curvature is what we perceive as gravity. Without matter, space would lack these defining characteristics. Similarly, time is essential for the existence of both matter and space, as it provides the framework within which events unfold and change occurs. Without time, there would be no *when* for matter to exist or for space to be defined.

The Bible, in its very first verse, encapsulates a truth so profound that it defies the limitations of the era in which it was written. Genesis 1:1 states, "In the beginning, God created the heavens and the earth." These words, simple yet remarkable, affirm the simultaneous creation of time, space, and matter—concepts that modern science has only begun to unravel. "In the beginning" signifies the creation of time itself; "the heavens" represents the vast expanse of space; and "the earth" refers to the formation of matter. The precision with which this ancient text captures the fundamental elements of the universe is nothing short of extraordinary, revealing a depth of understanding that the writers could not have known on their own. The necessity of a cause for this creation leads us to the undeniable conclusion: that cause is God.

I would not interrupt this exploration of deep science now were it not for the incredible theme that echoes throughout the entire Bible, beginning from the very first verse. The writers of the Bible, who lived in times when humanity was just beginning to grasp the rudimentary principles of science and the mysteries of the universe, inexplicably articulated a truth that aligns with what we now understand. They possessed a knowledge that transcended their time, a knowledge that can only be attributed to divine inspiration.

This essential interdependence of time, space, and matter is precisely why they must have come into existence simultaneously—a concept that modern science supports through the Big Bang theory.[31] This theory proposes that time, space, and matter, along with energy, all emerged at the same moment in a catastrophic, universe-defining event. By the 1970s and 1980s, the scientific community widely accepted the Big Bang theory, and by the 1990s, it had emerged as the dominant cosmological model for explaining the origin and evolution of the universe.

I can't remember exactly when I first heard of the Big Bang theory, but I recall the mixed emotions it stirred within me. Proponents of the theory of evolution seemed to claim victory with the Big Bang, while the church vehemently opposed it. People often depicted the theory as a disbelief in God or any causal effect by a higher power. Yet, on another level, it made perfect sense God would create the universe in this way. Why wouldn't He? The elegance and simplicity of such an event seemed to align with a Creator, who is both powerful and ingenious. However, it was the church's staunch rejection of the theory that led me to block it out as implausible, even though, deep down, it felt entirely reasonable that God could have started creation through such a magnificent event.

Why the Big Bang (Rapid Expansion) Makes Sense

How does one create a universe? It makes sense to start off with a gigantic explosion. I mean, that's how I would do it!

The Big Bang theory begins with an unimaginable burst of energy that marked the origin of everything we know. This explosion wasn't an explosion in space but rather an explosion of space itself, expanding outward from an initial singularity—a point of infinite density and temperature. From this singularity, all the matter, energy, space, and time of our universe emerged.

One of the first and most crucial elements to form after the Big Bang was hydrogen, the simplest and most abundant element in the universe.[32] Hydrogen atoms began to form as the universe cooled just minutes after the Big Bang. These atoms, composed of just one proton and one electron, were the building blocks for everything that would come later.

As the universe continued to expand and cool, gravity began to pull these hydrogen atoms together, causing them to coalesce into dense clouds. Over time, the pressure and temperature within these clouds increased until the hydrogen atoms began to fuse together, forming helium through a process called nuclear fusion. This fusion process released enormous amounts of energy, leading to the birth of the first stars.

Remember the periodic table in science class, the elements from hydrogen (number 1) to uranium (number 92) and beyond? Element number 1, hydrogen, is the basic building block of the universe. To get element number 2, helium, you fuse two hydrogen atoms together (1+1=2). To create lithium (number 3), you combine one helium atom with one hydrogen atom

(2+1=3). Then, to get to element number 4, beryllium, you fuse two helium atoms (2+2=4), and so on, continuing this process until you have all the elements known to man. These elements, formed through nuclear fusion within stars, make up the very fabric of our world and everything in it.

These stars, acting as cosmic forges, continued to fuse hydrogen into helium, and then into even heavier elements like carbon, oxygen, and iron.[33] The temperature at which a star burns varies greatly depending on the type of star and its stage in the stellar lifecycle.

- **Main Sequence Stars:** Red Dwarfs, the smallest and coolest stars, have surface temperatures of around 2,500 to 4,000 K, while sun-like stars, such as our own, have surface temperatures around 5,500 K and core temperatures reaching 15 million K. Blue Giants, among the hottest stars, can have surface temperatures ranging from 20,000 to 50,000 K, with core temperatures in the tens of millions K.

- **Giant and Supergiant Stars:** Red Giants have cooler surface temperatures, typically ranging from 3,000 to 5,000 K, but their cores can reach temperatures of up to 100 million K. Blue Supergiants can have surface temperatures exceeding 20,000 to 50,000 K, with even hotter cores.

- **White Dwarfs:** These remnants of stars that were not massive enough to end in a supernova can have surface temperatures exceeding 100,000 K when they first form, though they gradually cool over time.

- **Neutron Stars:** Formed from supernova explosions, neutron stars are incredibly hot, with surface temperatures around 1 million K shortly after formation, and core temperatures that are even more extreme.

In their cores, the intense heat and pressure allowed for the creation of the elements necessary for planets, life, and everything we see around us today. The heaviest element their intense heat can create is iron (number 26). The death of massive stars in supernova explosions generates even greater temperatures. During a supernova, temperatures can briefly reach billions of Kelvin in the core.[34] This extreme heat allows for the fusion of elements heavier than iron, which are then scattered throughout the universe, seeding space with the building blocks for new stars and planetary systems.

As the universe expanded further, more stars formed, bringing light to the cosmos and leading to the formation of galaxies. Over billions of years, these galaxies collided, merged, and evolved, creating the complex structures we observe in the universe today.

Among the myriad stars and planets that formed, one particular planet—Earth—emerged in a small galaxy we call the Milky Way. Earth was forged from the remnants of ancient stars, with its core elements born in the hearts of stars that lived and died long before our solar system came into being. The same processes that formed the stars also laid the foundation for the planets, moons, and other celestial bodies, including our own world.

The Big Bang, far from being a chaotic and random event, set into motion a series of natural processes that, over time, led to the formation of everything in the universe. This grand design, with its precise and intricate mechanisms, reflects the brilliance and foresight of a Creator who would set such a magnificent process in motion. It's a process that not only makes sense scientifically but also aligns beautifully with the idea of a purposeful creation that is simply genius.

What Science Offers

People often view science and religion as opposing forces, but in reality, they can complement each other in meaningful ways. Science doesn't deal with matters of theology, the relationship we have with God, or the redemption the Bible teaches. Likewise, the Bible is not a science book that explains the intricacies of nature's laws. However, science serves as a powerful magnifying glass, allowing us to explore and understand the details of God's amazing creation. Science gives us insight into the *how* of the universe, while the Bible addresses the *why*.

Take the human body, for example. We can live our entire lives without fully understanding the complex biological processes that sustain us. Many people enjoy perfect health without ever concerning themselves with the science behind it. But when something goes wrong—when we don't feel well or when our bodies fail to function as they should—medical science steps in to provide explanations. It tells us why our bodies work the way they do, how they maintain balance, and what happens when that balance is disrupted.

Driving a car is another example. A person needs to know little more than how to turn a key (or push a button), put it in gear, push the accelerator, and go—never thinking for a minute about the incredible understanding and harnessing of nature's laws that science figured out to make that possible. Behind the simple act of driving lies a complex interplay of physics, chemistry, and engineering, all working together seamlessly to move us from place to place.

And then there's the incredible accomplishment of flight. Science has enabled us to take thousands of tons of metal and human beings, defy gravity, and soar through the air at hundreds of miles per hour. The principles of aerodynamics, once a mystery, have been mastered to the point that we can travel across continents and oceans in a matter of hours—something that would have taken days, weeks, or even months in less advanced societies. The ability to harness the wind and propel massive aircraft around the globe is a testament to human ingenuity and the power of scientific understanding.

These examples show how science reveals the intricate mechanisms of the world around us. It doesn't diminish the wonder of creation; rather, it enhances our appreciation for the intelligence and design behind it all. Science gives us the *how*, allowing us to marvel at the complexity, while faith provides us with the *why*, giving our journey meaning and purpose.

In the same way, science helps us explore the universe, offering insights into how it operates and how it came to be. It allows us to understand the mechanisms behind the stars, the planets, and life itself. But it doesn't address the deeper, more philosophical questions of purpose and meaning. That's where the Bible comes in, providing us with the reason behind creation, the purpose of life, and the nature of our relationship with the Creator.

By embracing both science and faith, we can gain a fuller understanding of the world around us. Science enhances our appreciation for the complexity and beauty of creation, giving us a glimpse into the incredible wisdom and power of God. It shows us the intricate processes that sustain life and the universe, processes that were set into motion by a Creator with infinite foresight and intelligence. Rather than being at odds, science and faith can work together to bring us closer to the truth—revealing both the details of how the universe operates and the deeper meaning behind it all.

The Timing of God

So the story of creation begins. What we now know, based on scientific evidence, is that the universe most likely began 13.8 billion years ago with a Big Bang—a term that doesn't even begin to describe the almost incomprehensible explosion of time, space, and matter into existence. We know this in large part due to the observations made by the Hubble Space Telescope, which was designed by a team of engineers at NASA and launched into space on April 24, 1990.[35] The telescope has provided us with unprecedented images and data that have allowed scientists to better understand the origins and expansion of the universe.

When we see light from stars, we are essentially looking back in time. The light we observe today from distant stars and galaxies has traveled across the vastness of space for millions or even billions of years before reaching us. This is because light travels at a finite speed—approximately 299,792 kilometers per second (about *186,282 miles per second*). The distance that light travels in one year is called a light-year, and when we observe celestial objects, we are seeing them as they were when their light first began its journey to us.

The Hubble Space Telescope can detect light from some of the most distant objects in the universe, capturing images of stars and galaxies as they were billions of years ago. For example, when Hubble observes a galaxy that is thirteen billion light-years away, the light it captures left that galaxy thirteen billion years ago, long before Earth even existed. To calculate these immense distances, astronomers use a method called redshift. As light travels through the expanding universe, it stretches and shifts toward the red end of the spectrum. By measuring how much the light from a galaxy has shifted, scientists can determine how far away it is and, consequently, how long its light has been traveling to reach us. This ability to peer into the distant past has provided critical insights into the formation and evolution of galaxies, stars, and the universe itself.

But time isn't just something that scientists measure across billions of years—it's something we all experience in our everyday lives, sometimes in ways that are surprisingly similar. When you kids were little, I remember how naive you were about time and how long it would take for me to get things done. Whether we were taking a short drive or heading out on a longer adventure, like our camping trips to Bear Lake in the Colorado mountains, the whole journey was filled with questions: "Are we there yet? Are we there yet? When are we going to get there?" You were so eager to reach our destination that you couldn't quite grasp the concept of time passing during the trip. This is why we often traveled through the night, hoping you would sleep and lose track of time, so the journey would feel quicker and less tedious.

But back to this story. The Bible simply states, "In the beginning, God created the heavens and the earth." The only reference to time in this statement is "the beginning." There's no mention of how long this event took. At the time Genesis was written, it's unlikely that people could even comprehend a million years, much less nine billion years. The time and numbers in Genesis reflect the understanding of the ancient world, where people dealt with time in terms of days, weeks, months, years, and generations. The idea of vast epochs spanning millions or billions of years was beyond their comprehension. Instead, they closely tied their time-related concepts to their agricultural, social, and religious practices, emphasizing the rhythms of life, seasons, and generational continuity.

So the creation story is like a *Reader's Digest* version of what happened. Think of it as if we left for Colorado and you fell asleep—at the time of creation, everyone was more than asleep; no one even existed. You wake up at the campground and think it was instantaneous. But it wasn't; it took nine hours. The text suffices to say that God created time, space, and matter while you were asleep. Now the perspective of the story shifts to Earth. Billions of years have passed and creation continues (and you are still asleep).

Verse 2: "And the earth was without form, and void; and darkness was upon the face of the deep. And the Spirit of God moved upon the face of the waters." This is the beginning of the six days of creation and would take another 4.6 billion years.

God's timing is not like our timing on earth. In 2 Peter 3:8, the Bible states, "But do not overlook this one fact, beloved, that with the Lord one day is as a thousand years, and a thousand years as one day." It emphasizes that God is not bound by time as we are; He exists outside of time and views it differently. What may seem like a long time to us is just a moment to Him, and vice versa.

Time in the Bible is not always a straight line. Throughout Scripture, there are instances where time references can seem confusing or difficult to interpret. For example, in the New Testament, Jesus says, "Truly, I say to you, this generation will not pass away until all these things take place" (Matthew 24:34). This statement has puzzled many because it seems to suggest that those hearing Him speak would witness His return within their lifetime. Similarly, the Apostle Paul wrote to the Thessalonians with a sense of urgency, suggesting that some believers might be alive to see Christ's return:

> For this we declare to you by a word from the Lord, that we who are alive, who are left until the coming of the Lord, will not precede those who have fallen asleep. For the Lord himself will descend from heaven with a cry of command, with the voice of an archangel, and with the sound of the trumpet of God. And the dead in Christ will rise first.

Then we who are alive, who are left, will be caught up together with
them in the clouds to meet the Lord in the air, and so we will always
be with the Lord. (1 Thessalonians 4:15-17)

Yet nearly two thousand years have passed, and these events have not occurred as expected, leading to various interpretations about the timing of the Second Coming. Clearly, the seemingly simple is endlessly complex.

Additionally, when Jesus was on the cross, He told the criminal beside Him, "Truly, I say to you, today you will be with me in paradise" (Luke 23:43). This statement has raised questions about what *today* meant and how it relates to the afterlife, especially given differing views on time in eternity versus time on earth. Another example is the phrase "three days and three nights" that Jesus used to describe His time in the tomb, which has led to debates because it doesn't align perfectly with our modern understanding of time. By the traditional timeline, Jesus was crucified on Friday and resurrected on Sunday, which doesn't seem to cover a full three days and three nights (it was three days and two nights). However, in Jewish tradition, any part of a day could be counted as a whole day, which helps explain this apparent discrepancy.[36]

My intent here is not to try and decipher what any of these references were trying to convey about time, but simply to say that sometimes I think it's not really about the timing. It's about the message.

To put this in perspective with something more familiar, think about how often we say, "Give me a minute," knowing full well we need more than a minute to do what someone is asking. We're not asking for a literal sixty seconds; rather, we're conveying that given the context of time in that moment, it will only take a short while to address the task. It's a way of expressing urgency without being tied down to exact timeframes, much like how some of the biblical references to time should be understood. The focus is not on the precise duration but on the intent and the message behind it.

I believe, as science will verify, the days of creation are one of these misunderstood periods of time. After each day of creation, it is said, "And the evening and the morning were the first day." So on and so forth for each day or "yom" of creation. *Yom* is from the original text written in Hebrew.

It's important to note that the Hebrew language, in which the Old Testament was originally written, had about 3,000 root words. In contrast, the English language, which was later used to translate these texts, has over 600,000 words. This vast difference in vocabulary can lead to challenges in translation, as the original Hebrew words often had to serve multiple purposes and could carry more than one meaning depending on the context.

One of the key examples is the word "yom." While it is commonly translated as "day," in Hebrew, "yom" can also refer to any undefined period of time, not just a twenty-four-hour day.[37] It could signify a day, a season, an age, or even an era. This flexibility in meaning allows for a broader interpretation of the "days" of creation, which could correspond to much longer periods of time as understood by modern science. Therefore, when we read the creation story, it's crucial to consider that the word "yom" may not strictly mean a literal day as we understand it, but rather, it could represent a significant period in the process of creation.

The Devil Is in the Details

When I attended Central State University in Edmond, Oklahoma, in 1983 (now the University of Central Oklahoma), I took an accounting course as part of my minor. Toward the end of the semester, we were given a test that heavily contributed to our final grade in the class. Twenty percent of the test was based on one problem—balancing a company bank account. If you failed that portion of the test, the best possible score would be 80, so there was a fine line between passing and failing. But at that point in the class, if you couldn't balance the books, then it raised the question—what's the point? The problem included a starting balance for the account, a number of checks that the company had written, and also the deposits that were made to the account. This had to be reconciled to the bank statement balance. I started with that problem first, and when I finished, I was $0.36 off. So, I did it again.

Still—$0.36 off. Panic started to creep into my mind, but I set it aside and worked on the rest of the test. I finished with about ten minutes to spare and tried reconciling the account again, with the same result. I could not get it to balance. What was I missing?

Then, one check caught my attention. The amount was $12.73. If it had been meant to be $12.37, the difference would be exactly $0.36. I thought, "No way the professor transposed the numbers." But with just a couple of minutes left, I decided to mark out the 73 cents and change it to 37 cents. The account balanced, and I turned in my test, walking out of the classroom thinking, "What a disaster."

A few days later, the professor returned the graded tests. Before handing them back, he had something to say. To my surprise, he admitted that he had inadvertently transposed the check amount from $12.37 to $12.73. Finding the error and correcting it was the right thing to do to reconcile the account. Out of about forty students in the class, only four, including myself, caught the error and made the change. All of the students in the class were given the same beginning and ending amounts, yet they didn't catch the subtle detail in the middle, which was a transposition, and therefore couldn't reconcile the account to the bank statement. They had all the right numbers—they had the 3 and they had the 7—but misinterpreted the data because they didn't recognize the transposition. What came next infuriated everyone else, but such is life. Since four people interpreted the numbers correctly, the professor counted it in the overall score and those who couldn't balance the account failed that portion of the test. Many ultimately failed the test as a result. Ouch.

I realize this isn't a perfect analogy because some may argue that the Bible itself does not contain errors. I agree that the original message is true, but what was originally written in Hebrew and later translated into English could lead to misunderstandings due to differences in language. Just as the students who missed the transposed number on the test were working with the correct information but still arrived at the wrong conclusion, misinterpretation can occur in the translation of ancient texts. When I took that test,

I knew that the beginning and ending amounts were correct and that they couldn't be changed logically. I had to carefully analyze the details to understand what the professor intended because the discrepancy was somewhere in the middle. Similarly, with the Bible's account of creation, we know the overall message and what was created each day. We also know, based on scientific understanding, how long these processes took. But when the original Hebrew text, with its limited vocabulary, was translated into English with its vast vocabulary, there was potential for misinterpretation. It's in this middle ground—between translation and interpretation—where subtle discrepancies can arise, leading to potential misunderstandings of the original message.

A Short Life and a Long Life—Both a Moment in Time

In the thousands of words of comfort I have listened to spiritual leaders speak at funerals throughout my thirty-five years in the funeral industry, few have stayed with me more than this one statement: "There is no difference between a short life and a long one; both are a moment in time." Although it may not offer the intended comfort when you're burying a ten-year-old who tragically drowned in a family pool, as any parent or sibling suffering the loss of a child or little brother or sister will tell you, it holds a deep and undeniable truth. The fleeting nature of life, whether short or long, is something that becomes profoundly evident when one spends years witnessing both the joy and sorrow of a life's final farewell.

Take Anne Frank, for example. She was just a young girl when she died in the brutal cold of a concentration camp in Auschwitz, Germany—her life cut short by the horrors of war and persecution. Her brief time on Earth, however, has left an indelible mark on history, her words resonating across generations as a testament to the resilience of the human spirit.

Contrast this with the life of Thomas Jefferson, who passed quietly in his bed at Monticello after a long and meaningful life that helped shape a nation. His was a life of great length and significance, yet in the grand scheme of time, it too was but a moment—a blink in the vast continuum of history.

And then there was my Granny, who meant the world to me. She died at seventy in her sleep quietly and unexpectedly on a night when it snowed, covering the city of Lawton in winter's wonder. Her passing was peaceful, her life full of love shared with those around her. The snow came as a surprise and fell softly that night, as she too quietly slipped away in the silence of snowflakes.

Whether it's a life cut tragically short or one that spans many decades, the truth remains: there is no difference between a short life and a long one— as time moves forward into history, memories slowly blend into moments. Thomas Jefferson hinted at this when he wrote to his friend John Adams upon the death of his wife, Abigail:

> *The public papers, my dear friend, announce the fatal event of which your letter of Oct. 20 had given me a proximate warning. Tried myself in the school of affliction, by the loss of every form of connection which can rive the human heart, I know well, and feel what you have lost, what you have suffered, are suffering, and have yet to endure. The same trials have taught me that, for ills so immeasurable, time and silence are the only medicine. I will not therefore, by useless condolences, open afresh the sluices of your grief, nor, although mingling sincerely my tears with yours, will I say a word more where words are vain; but that it is of some comfort to us both that the term is not very distant at which we are to deposit in the same cerement, our sorrows and suffering bodies, and to ascend in essence to an ecstatic meeting with the friends we have loved and lost and whom we shall still love and never lose again.*

Whether you consider the days of creation to be 24 hours or 240,000 years, it doesn't really matter. In the grand scheme of time, both are just a moment. The genuine wonder lies in the act of creation itself—the complexity, beauty, and order that emerged from nothing. Whether short or long, the time frame is insignificant compared to the magnificence of what was created.

The universe, Earth, and life itself are far more significant than the duration it took for them to come into being. It's not the time that matters, but that these miraculous processes occurred at all. Creation is a testament to a power and intelligence far beyond our understanding, and that is where the focus should be—not on how long it took, but on the fact that it happened.

When I consider the "yoms" of creation, the Hebrew word used to separate each period of time, it is entirely logical to interpret it as conveying any length of time. Each "yom" marks the beginning and end of a specific phase—not necessarily a twenty-four-hour day, but a defined period. This word provides a clear separation of time for each step in the creation process. Whether you view it as a short period or a long one, both are merely moments in the vast timeline of the universe. In the days when Genesis was written, and when readers could not comprehend the concept of millions of years, understanding "yom" as a literal day made perfect sense. And today, now that we can grasp the idea of millions or even billions of years, understanding it as a million years still makes perfect sense—well, it can.

God's Timing: The Flexibility of Creation Days

What I shared previously in *"The Timing of God"* is a viewpoint based on the predominant interpretation of the Bible regarding the text, "And the evening and the morning were the first day." This phrase comes from the King James Version (KJV) of the Bible, one of the most popular and widely recognized translations in the English-speaking world. First published in 1611, the KJV has profoundly influenced English literature, language, and culture. Known for its majestic and poetic language, it has served as the standard Bible for many English-speaking Christians for centuries.

I am familiar with this version, as it was the most popular Bible translation during the 1960s and 1970s when I grew up and spent every Wednesday evening and Sunday morning studying it. Although the King James Version has remained unchanged since its original publication, Benjamin Blarney made minor updates in 1769, known as the Oxford Standard Edition. These updates focused on standardizing spelling, punctuation, and some word choices to reflect changes in the English language since the seventeenth century. The 1769 edition is the version most people refer to as the King James Version today.

The second most popular version of the Bible today is the New International Version (NIV). First published in 1978, the NIV has since become one of the most widely used modern translations. It is known for its balance between readability and accuracy, making it accessible to a broad audience while staying true to the original texts. The NIV is favored by many Protestant denominations and is often used in churches, Bible study groups, and personal reading.

The NIV uses the wording for the text at the conclusion of each day of creation as, "And there was evening, and there was morning—the first day." This wording is very similar to the King James Version, with the main difference being the punctuation and the inclusion of an em dash before "the first day," which helps to emphasize the transition. The NIV maintains the same essential meaning as the KJV but uses more contemporary language and punctuation conventions.

Given the influence of the King James Version over the centuries, whether reading the KJV or the NIV, the lines of text are almost unanimously understood to mean that the events of each day of creation happened within a single twenty-four-hour period.

However, as I look deeper into the story of creation and the text that describes it, I think we have to keep in mind that the Bible, while infallible in its spiritual truths, is not a science book. As our understanding of the universe expands, our interpretations of these texts must evolve to keep the Bible's message relevant and comprehensible in the modern age. This does not mean altering the message to be more tolerant; rather, it means ensuring that our interpretations align with the knowledge we now have, making the Bible's teachings even more thoughtful and meaningful.

History has shown us the dangers of rigidly adhering to traditional interpretations without considering new information. Take, for example, the case of Galileo Galilei. Galileo's groundbreaking assertion that Earth orbits the

Sun was met with fierce opposition by the Catholic Church, which held to the geocentric view that Earth was the center of the universe.[38] The church leaders of the time interpreted the Bible in a way that supported this outdated view, and as a result, Galileo was condemned, forced to recant his findings, and spent the rest of his life under house arrest.

Galileo was right. His scientific understanding did not contradict the Bible itself, but rather the prevailing interpretation of it. The Bible's spiritual truths remained intact, but the leaders of the time failed to see beyond their limited understanding of the physical world. Today, we recognize Galileo's contributions as foundational to our understanding of the cosmos, and we see that his discoveries did not diminish the Bible's message but enriched our appreciation of the Creator's work.

Now, in our time, science has provided us with an even greater understanding of how the world came into existence. We find ourselves at a similar crossroads, where new discoveries challenge long-held interpretations. Science today is rattling the longstanding interpretations of the Bible, particularly in the ongoing controversy between young earth creationists, who believe the world was created in six literal twenty-four-hour days, and old earth creationists, who see the "days" as long periods of time. Meanwhile, atheists often use these debates as proof that many Christians don't have any viable answers, casting doubt on the compatibility of faith and reason. It is here that I choose to take the road less traveled—not to challenge the authority of Scripture, but to explore how our growing knowledge of the universe can deepen our understanding of God's magnificent creation.

As with my college accounting test, where I knew the beginning and the end and had to deduce the correct interpretation of the middle, I see the creation narrative in the same way. When the beginning of creation and its culmination don't add up as they should, it only makes sense that the interface—the middle—is where we must make interpretations against both sides of the argument between theology and science. If the truths of the Bible and the revelations of science don't align, the issue isn't with the truths present but with the information or interpretations we're working with to reconcile the two. The Bible and the universe—which science examines to uncover its intricacies—*must* interface perfectly. The challenge is not to change what the Bible says but to recognize that translations, interpretations, or even scientific assumptions may need reevaluation. When approached this way, reconciling theology and science becomes not only possible but essential, ensuring both reveal the full depth of truth.

From the story of *"My Genesis,"* you already know that Christmas is a favorite time of year for me. Consider a familiar Christmas song like "The Twelve Days of Christmas." Each verse introduces something new, yet it always returns to the refrain: *"And a partridge in a pear tree."* This refrain acts as more than a repeated line—it provides a rhythmic anchor, giving each verse context and continuity while creating a cadence that ties the entire song together.

This structure mirrors the cadence of the creation narrative in Genesis. Just as a song uses a refrain to emphasize rhythm and meaning, Moses employs the phrase "And there was evening, and there was morning" to punctuate the six days of creation. This rhythmic separation helps us grasp the deliberate and majestic process through which the universe was brought into existence—not in six twenty-four-hour days, but in six distinct periods spanning 4.5 billion years. Let me say that again: 4.5 billion years.

Now, I will admit, that thought almost didn't translate from my mind to my fingers to type it. The staggering difference completely contradicts what I've been taught my entire life. But the evidence from the knowledge we've gained in the last few decades is eye-opening. The advancements in our understanding of geology, astrophysics, and biology clearly reveal a universe that has been carefully and methodically crafted over billions of years. The fossil record, the movement of tectonic plates, the formation of stars and planets, and the evolution of life all speak to a process that required time—billions of years, not days.

What we know isn't to diminish the power or authority of God; rather, it's enhancing our understanding of the Creator of the universe. The Bible was written for people who lived in a time when the concept of billions of years was unimaginable. The writers used language and metaphors that suited their understanding, just as we use scientific language that suits ours. By recognizing this, we can appreciate the depth and richness of the biblical narrative in a new way, seeing it not as a static account that becomes no longer relevant, but as a living, breathing text that speaks to us in the context of our expanding knowledge.

This realization inspires me to go back to what was originally written in Hebrew and look at it again to see if we've misunderstood something. To seek out a truer meaning that aligns with both our faith and our growing understanding of the universe.

Below is the original text written by Moses through divine intervention by God and the possible meaning of each word. Keep in mind that the Hebrew language only consisted of about three thousand words to describe everything in the world at the time Genesis was written. The world then was less complex than it is today, but it was still a challenge to describe it in clear detail with so few words. Single words often represented entire phrases, and words were chosen to encompass a wide range of meanings and variations depending on the context. The Hebrew text and various meanings of each word for the creation account's refrain is:

Vayehi-erev vayehi-voker, yom echad

1. **Vayehi**—"And there was," "and it came to be"
2. **Erev**—"Evening," "dusk," "twilight"
3. **Voker**—"Morning," "dawn"
4. **Yom**—"Day," "time," "age," "era," "period"
5. **Echad**—"One," "first," "single"

Direct translation:

"And there was *Vayehi* evening *erev*, and there was *Vayehi* morning *voker*, day *Yom* one *echad*"

Equivalent direct translations:

"And there was evening, and there was morning, *day* one."

"And there was evening, and there was morning, *time* one."

"And there was evening, and there was morning, *age* one."

"And there was evening, and there was morning, *era* one."

"And there was evening, and there was morning, *period* one."

So, the question is, which one makes the most logical sense given all we know now?

The traditional interpretation of this text has often been that the phrase "evening and morning" defines *yom* as a twenty-four-hour day. Given the knowledge available throughout much of history, that interpretation has made sense. However, as our understanding of the universe has evolved, this interpretation seems less adequate. This highlights the inherent complexity of translating and interpreting ancient texts.

It's crucial to recognize that there is no absolute authority in translating Hebrew texts; every translation is, to some extent, an interpretation shaped by the perspectives and knowledge of those who produce it. This is evident in the numerous versions of the Bible available today, each reflecting different interpretative choices. Ultimately, any translation is an informed opinion, validated by those who find it credible.

Translating Hebrew text is particularly complicated because ancient Hebrew, like many ancient languages, did not use punctuation marks such as commas, periods, or quotation marks. Instead, meaning was conveyed through word order, context, and sometimes through the use of conjunctions or particles. The lack of punctuation in the Hebrew text leaves room for interpretation. The reader must infer the relationships between phrases based on context and the overall narrative structure. There are traditional methods of dividing the text that indicate shifts in thought, such as paragraph divisions (parashot) and verse divisions. However, these are not as clear-cut as modern sentence and paragraph breaks. The lack of consistent division means that much of the interpretation relies on context and traditional readings.

This is what Hebrew text looks like:

בְּרֵאשִׁית בָּרָא אֱלֹהִים אֵת הַשָּׁמַיִם וְאֵת הָאָרֶץ וְהָאָרֶץ הָיְתָה תֹהוּ וָבֹהוּ וְחֹשֶׁךְ
עַל פְּנֵי תְהוֹם וְרוּחַ אֱלֹהִים מְרַחֶפֶת עַל פְּנֵי הַמָּיִם וַיֹּאמֶר אֱלֹהִים יְהִי אוֹר
וַיְהִי אוֹר וַיַּרְא אֱלֹהִים אֶת הָאוֹר כִּי טוֹב וַיַּבְדֵּל אֱלֹהִים בֵּין הָאוֹר וּבֵין הַחֹשֶׁךְ
וַיִּקְרָא אֱלֹהִים לָאוֹר יוֹם וְלַחֹשֶׁךְ קָרָא לָיְלָה וַיְהִי עֶרֶב וַיְהִי בֹקֶר יוֹם אֶחָד

Hebrew text in manuscripts of the Hebrew Bible (Tanakh) is not written in a line-by-line format. Instead, it is written in continuous prose, with the words arranged according to the grammar and syntax of the Hebrew language, rather than English. Additionally, Hebrew is written from right to left, whereas English is written from left to right.

The order provided below is an attempt to break down the text for clarity and to show how the words translate directly. However, in the actual Hebrew text, the words would not be aligned in this way, nor would they be on separate lines. Instead, the text would be continuous, with each verse following the previous one.

Line 1: בְּרֵאשִׁית | בָּרָא | אֱלֹהִים | אֵת | הַשָּׁמַיִם | וְאֵת | הָאָרֶץ

B'reishit | bara | Elohim | et | ha-shamayim | v'et | ha-aretz

In the beginning | created | God | (no direct English translation) | the heavens | and | the earth

Line 2: וְהָאָרֶץ | הָיְתָה | תֹהוּ | וָבֹהוּ | וְחֹשֶׁךְ | עַל | פְּנֵי | תְהוֹם

V'ha-aretz | hay'tah | tohu | vavohu | v'choshech | al | p'nei | t'hom

And the earth | was | formless | and void | and darkness | upon | the face of | the deep

Line 3: וְרוּחַ | אֱלֹהִים | מְרַחֶפֶת | עַל | פְּנֵי | הַמָּיִם

V'ruach | Elohim | m'rachefet | al | p'nei | ha-mayim

And the spirit | of God | hovered | over | the face of | the waters

Line 4: וַיֹּאמֶר | אֱלֹהִים | יְהִי | אוֹר | וַיְהִי | אוֹר

Vayomer | Elohim | y'hi | or | vay'hi | or

And said | God | let there be | light | and there was | light

Line 5: וַיַּרְא | אֱלֹהִים | אֶת | הָאוֹר | כִּי | טוֹב | וַיַּבְדֵּל | אֱלֹהִים | בֵּין | הָאוֹר | וּבֵין | הַחֹשֶׁךְ

Vayar | Elohim | et | ha-or | ki | tov | vayavdel | Elohim | bein | ha-or | uvein | ha-choose

And saw | God | the | light | that | [it was] good | and separated | God | between | the light | and | the darkness

Line 6: וַיִּקְרָא | אֱלֹהִים | לָאוֹר | יוֹם | וְלַחֹשֶׁךְ | קָרָא | לָיְלָה

Vayikra | Elohim | la-or | yom | v'lachoshech | kara | laila

And called | God | the light | Day | and the darkness | [He] called | Night

Line 7: וַיְהִי | עֶרֶב | וַיְהִי | בֹּקֶר | יוֹם | אֶחָד

Vayehi | erev | vayehi | boker | yom | echad

And there was | evening | and there was | morning | day | one

This visual representation illustrates the challenges of interpreting ancient texts and the potential for different readings based on the structure of the language itself. The Hebrew text is broken out into seven lines, but the majority of Bible translations combine these lines for better flow and readability. They also add filler words for the same reason. For example, Line 7 in the KJV includes a slight variation:

Hebrew direct translation: "And there was evening and there was morning day one."

King James translation: "And the evening and the morning were the first day."

The difference between the Hebrew text and the KJV translation may seem subtle, but it carries an acute implication. The direct Hebrew translation reads, "And there **was** evening and there **was** morning." This phrasing shows that evening and morning "occurred"—they were distinct events in the sequence of creation.

In contrast, the KJV translates this as, "And the evening and the morning *were* the first day." By changing "was" to "were," the translation subtly shifts the meaning, presenting evening and morning as a collective unit that defines the day. This seemingly small alteration leads readers to view the day as a single twenty-four-hour period, rather than as a sequence of events marking the passage of time. The Hebrew text suggest two separate time periods, a complete rotation of the earth and a period of time it defined as being "one."

This shift in language influences how one interprets the nature of the "days" in the creation account, moving from the idea of distinct events occurring to a more unified concept of a twenty-four-hour day. Understanding this difference is crucial when considering the broader implications of how we interpret the creation narrative in light of both theological tradition and scientific discovery.

In the Hebrew Bible, when the length of time that "yom" (day) is meant to represent is specified with a number, a numerical value is usually given explicitly. This is typically done with a cardinal number (e.g., "echad" for "one," "sheni" for "second," etc.) or an ordinal number. The descriptive language, such as "and there was evening and there was morning," is not used to specify the length of time; instead, it serves more as a literary or structural device within the text, indicating the passage of a day as Earth completed a 360-degree rotation. It is entirely logical to separate these phrases into distinct events, as they describe different aspects of the creation process rather than defining the term "yom." "Yom One" refers to the entire creative process, and it could be arranged as follows:

Line 7: | וַיְהִי | בֹּקֶר | יוֹם | אֶחָד |

Vayehi | erev | vayehi | boker

And there was | evening | and there was | morning

Line 8: וַיְהִי | עֶרֶב

yom | echad

period | one

Here's what the first period of creation would look like:

- Create Heaven and Earth

- Create Light

- Separate Light from Darkness

- Name Light "Day" and Darkness "Night"

- Let Earth make a full rotation (refrain)

Yom (Period) One

This interpretation suggests that after each distinct period of creation—whether it was the separation of light from darkness that took one billion years, the formation of the sky that took 500 million years, or the emergence of land that took another billion years—a twenty-four-hour day marked the end of that period before the next one began.

I understand the phrase "And there was evening and there was morning" to serve as a conclusion—a refrain marking the completion of the entire creative process for that period. *Yom* then names the period in sequence, leaving it up to the reader to determine how long it took to accomplish the creative elements in that period, if they choose to do so. The length of time doesn't matter—it's a flexible interpretation. The phrase suggests that after completing the events of creation, God took a step back, reviewed what He had accomplished, deemed it good, and allowed a day to pass, marking the end of that creative phase. Each phase of creation is put in order with the passing of time—Yom 1 | Yom 2 | Yom 3 | Yom 4 | Yom 5 | Yom 6 | Yom 7.

Day (Period) 7: Reinforcing the Interpretation

The common refrain that ends every day of creation was "And there was evening and there was morning." However, it wasn't used on the seventh day of rest. Why not? The seventh day is an integral part of the creation story and part of the process, the model of which is referred to in the Bible and is responsible for our current seven-day workweek. Six days of work and one day of rest.

As I reflect on the creation narrative, I find the omission of the familiar refrain to be particularly revealing. This absence, I believe, is not a mere stylistic choice but a deliberate indication that the refrain has nothing to do with defining the length of time "yom" is meant to convey.

Throughout the first six days of creation, the refrain consistently marks the completion of each creative period, suggesting a rhythm and structure to God's work. If this refrain during the six days was intended to define *yom* as a literal twenty-four-hour period, it would be logical for the seventh day to follow the same pattern. However, the absence of this refrain on the seventh day disrupts that expectation, leading me to conclude that "And there was evening, and there was morning" is a separate event from "yom" in the creation narrative. The period of *yom* is defined by creation events *plus* the one twenty-four-hour period.

While some might argue that the seventh day of God's rest is ongoing to explain its omission, this interpretation overlooks the practical and symbolic meaning behind the original structure of the workweek—both for humanity and for God. The seven-day workweek, which is rooted in the creation story, establishes a clear rhythm: six days of work followed by one day of rest. This pattern is not designed to suggest an indefinite rest period, but rather a finite and purposeful pause before returning to activity.

If we follow this logic, God's rest on the seventh day wasn't meant to stretch indefinitely. It was a temporary period of refreshment and reflection on all of His work completed, just as our weekly Sabbath is a time to rest and recharge. After this day of rest, the expectation is to return to work, and this is exactly what we see happen in the biblical narrative. God doesn't remain in an ongoing state of rest. The seventh day ended God's process of creation; that was His work He rested from, and then He resumes His role as the active manager of the universe.

It is worth noting that some young earth creationists argue that the days of creation must be twenty-four-hour periods because God instituted the Sabbath, based on Exodus 20:11: "For in six days the Lord made the heavens and the earth, the sea, and all that is in them, but he rested on the seventh day. Therefore the Lord blessed the Sabbath day and made it holy." However, time is experienced differently for God, as 2 Peter 3:8 reminds us: "With the Lord a day is like a thousand years, and a thousand years are like a day." This distinction reinforces the idea that God's "days" of creation may not be bound by our human understanding of twenty-four-hour periods.

Thus, the seventh day of rest appears to have followed the same practical work-rest rhythm that we experience: work six days, take one day off, and then return to the responsibilities at hand. If we adhere to this understanding, it becomes clear that God's rest was a finite, specific event—just one short period of time—after which He resumed His active management of the world.

Suggesting that God is still "resting" undermines the clear biblical examples of His active involvement in human history following creation.[39] The flood, the call of Abraham, and God's interactions with His people are all examples of a return to divine activity, just as we return to our work after our own Sabbath rest.

Mastery Takes Time

In considering the days of creation, I find it impossible to overlook a fundamental truth that we all experience in our daily lives: mastery takes time. Whether it's a piece of art, a meticulously crafted meal, or a relationship built over years, it reflects the depth of care, the quality of the result, and the emotional impact it leaves. This principle, so deeply ingrained in human experience, offers indirect yet powerful support for the idea that *yom* in the creation narrative represents long periods of time rather than literal twenty-four-hour days.[40]

Time is more valuable than money, more precious than any material gift. It is the most personal thing we can offer to someone, a reflection of our deepest emotions and our commitment to their hopes and well-being. Consider the difference between throwing money at a problem and investing time to truly understand and resolve it. A wealthy parent may buy their child everything they desire, but if they don't invest time in building a relationship, the child may grow up feeling emotionally neglected. Similarly, a spouse who is showered with expensive gifts but is denied quality time may feel disconnected and unloved.

This idea resonates with the way we understand God's creation. If God had simply thrown a universe together in 144 hours because He could, what message would that convey about His care and love for His creation?[41] It would be like a parent giving a gift without thought or personal involvement. But that's not what the Bible tells us. Instead, it says that after each day, God looked at what He had done and saw that it was good. This isn't the behavior of someone rushing through a task; it's the careful reflection of a Creator who is deeply invested in every detail of His work.

When I think about the time I've spent preparing gifts for my children or my late wife, Laura, I see a reflection of this divine care. It was never just about the gift itself. It was about the thought, the attention to detail, the time spent making sure that everything was perfect. Whether it was a basket full of summer shorts, shoes, candies, gardening tools, balloons on the floor, or flowers carefully arranged, the time I invested was a way of showing how much I cared. I wanted those moments to be special, to convey my love in a way that words alone couldn't.

This personal understanding of time and care sheds light on why the idea of a hastily created universe feels so at odds with God's nature. Why would God simulate age on the wonders of creation? Why would He make things look older than they really are, as some interpretations suggest? To me, this idea overlooks the incredible time and care God invested in crafting such an indescribable place for humanity. It's as if we're missing the point of the story, overlooking the love that God poured into every detail of creation.

For me, when I spend so much time and effort on something, only for it to be dismissed or unrecognized, it's deeply disheartening. I want the recipient to understand how much I care, to see the value of the time I invested in them. I believe God feels the same way. He spent billions of years dotting trillions of i's and crossing trillions of t's in the creation of the universe. For us to overlook that, to see His work as something hastily thrown together, is to miss the profound message of His love and dedication.

The creation story, when viewed through the lens of time, becomes a testament to God's mastery, His infinite care, and His desire for us to recognize and appreciate the incredible world He has made for us. It's not just about the end result; it's about the journey, the process, the time spent creating something truly magnificent.

Creation Timeline

Day 1: Light and Darkness

- **Approximate Beginning:** 4.6 billion years ago

- Events: The formation of the sun and Earth from a collapsing molecular cloud, Earth's molten state transitioning to a solid crust, and the initial separation of light from darkness as Earth's atmosphere begins to clear and stabilize.

Day 2: Separation of Waters

- **Approximate Beginning:** 4 billion years ago

- **Events:** The formation of Earth's early atmosphere and the development of oceans. This period could also mark the beginning of water cycling and the stabilization of the planet's surface.

Day 3: Land, Seas, and Vegetation

- **Approximate Beginning:** 3.5 billion years ago

- **Events:** The formation of continents and the appearance of the first simple life-forms, including cyanobacteria, which contributed to oxygenating the atmosphere. The first plants likely began to emerge in the latter part of this period.

Day 4: Sun, Moon, and Stars

- **Approximate Beginning:** 1 billion years ago

- **Events:** The atmosphere becomes clearer, allowing the sun, moon, and stars to be visible from Earth's surface. This period also includes the development of more complex life-forms, such as algae and the first multicellular organisms.

Day 5: Sea Creatures and Birds

- **Approximate Beginning:** 600 million years ago

- **Events:** The Cambrian Explosion occurs, leading to the rapid diversification of life in the oceans. Fish and other sea creatures dominate, followed by the emergence of the first birds and flying insects.

Day 6: Land Animals and Humans

- **Approximate Beginning:** 300 million years ago

- **Events:** The rise of land animals, including reptiles, mammals, and eventually primates. The latter part of this period sees the emergence of hominins, Neanderthals, and early Homo sapiens, culminating in the special creation of Adam and Eve (modern humans) around 11,500 to 10,000 BC.

While I have provided specific beginnings for each of the days (periods) of creation, it is important to understand that these times are not precise. They offer a general framework to understand the broad phases of Earth's development, rather than fixed durations. Each day reflects not only a distinct creative act but also the interconnectedness of God's work. For instance, life introduced in Day 5, such as delicate bird species and marine creatures, continued to flourish and progress well into Day 6, adapting to the changing ecosystems as land animals and humans began to dominate. This seamless flow from one phase of creation to the next reflects the complexity and intentionality of God's design, sustaining the diverse forms of life we experience today.

By presenting creation as a continuous and overlapping process, this approach harmonizes the biblical account with the vast timeline revealed through scientific discovery, highlighting the unity of faith and reason in understanding the majesty of God's work. As the Bible describes, God commanded the earth to "bring forth living creatures according to their kinds," and she did so over time, fulfilling His word through the intricate processes He set into motion before deeming the period of creation good and moving on to the next phase. This unfolding of creation reflects both the divine authority of God's command and the patient, intentional nature of His design, sustaining the diverse forms of life we experience today.

The Days of Creation
Day 1: Light and Darkness

Genesis 1:1-5

In the beginning, God created the heavens and the earth. The earth was without form and void, and darkness was over the face of the deep. And the Spirit of God was hovering over the face of the waters. And God said, "Let there be light," and there was light. And God saw that the light was good. And God separated the light from the darkness. God called the light Day, and the darkness he called Night. And there was evening and there was morning, the first day.

Hebrew Text with Direct Translation

IN THE BEGINNING CREATED GOD THE HEAVENS AND THE EARTH AND THE EARTH WAS WITHOUT FORM AND VOID AND DARKNESS WAS OVER THE FACE OF THE DEEP AND THE SPIRIT OF GOD WAS HOVERING OVER THE FACE OF THE WATERS AND SAID GOD LET THERE BE LIGHT AND THERE WAS LIGHT AND SAW GOD THE LIGHT THAT IT WAS GOOD AND SEPARATED GOD BETWEEN THE LIGHT AND BETWEEN THE DARKNESS AND CALLED GOD THE LIGHT DAY AND THE DARKNESS CALLED NIGHT AND THERE WAS EVENING AND THERE WAS MORNING DAY ONE

The book of Job, attributed to Moses, offers a poetic description of the universe at this early stage of creation. In Job 9:5-9, we find a description that resonates with our modern understanding of the cosmos:

> *He who removes mountains, and they know it not, when he overturns them in his anger, who shakes the earth out of its place, and its pillars tremble; who commands the sun, and it does not rise; who seals up the stars; who alone stretched out the heavens and treadeth on the waves of the sea; who made the Bear and Orion, the Pleiades and the chambers of the south.*

This passage reflects a remarkable awareness of the universe's vastness and the forces at play, knowledge that the writers of the time could not have known in detail, yet it aligns poetically with modern scientific concepts.

The Biblical and Scientific Perspective. Nine billion years had passed since God initiated the creation of the universe. During this time, the cosmos expanded—just as it continues to do today. Galaxies drifted apart as the very fabric of space stretched outward, a process still observable, with galaxies billions of light-years away moving at incredible speeds.

Amid this vast, dynamic universe, Earth began to take shape around 4.6 billion years ago, forming from the collision and accumulation of countless planetesimals in the young solar system. Initially a molten sphere, Earth gradually cooled over millions of years, forming a thin crust and becoming a water-covered planet. But it was not yet the vibrant blue world we know today. Enveloped in darkness, its deep waters lay silent, waiting. This was the stage upon which God's Spirit hovered, poised to bring order and purpose to the formless Earth.

Around 4.5 billion years ago, Earth was shrouded in darkness. The sun and stars were obscured from view by a dense, thick atmosphere dominated by gases and water vapor. The biblical depiction of God "hovering over the waters" aligns with this scientific understanding of a planet waiting to emerge into light.

During this time, a cataclysmic event—the Giant Impact Hypothesis— forever altered Earth's trajectory. A Mars-sized body, known as Theia, collided with the young Earth. The impact ejected significant debris into space, which eventually coalesced to form the moon. This collision profoundly reshaped Earth's geological and environmental conditions, melting the planet's surface into a "magma ocean" and contributing to the differentiation of Earth's layers— core, mantle, and crust. Heat from the collision vaporized much of Earth's water and volatile substances, forming a temporary "rock vapor" atmosphere.

As Earth cooled, water vapor condensed to reform oceans, initially shallower than today's seas. Additional water was delivered over millennia through impacts from water-rich comets and asteroids. Over time, the atmosphere thinned, allowing sunlight to pierce through and illuminate the planet's surface. The sun and moon became pivotal transformations, separating the light from the darkness as described in Genesis 1:3-4, and preparing Earth for the emergence of life.

The collision with Theia also established Earth's rotational speed and axial tilt, crucial factors for maintaining seasons and a stable climate. These precise conditions finely tuned Earth to support life.

While the exact sequence of these events remains partially shrouded in mystery, their outcomes were transformative. Earth became uniquely suited for life, a testament to both its complexity and the divine orchestration behind its formation. The incredible precision of these developments laid the foundation for the diversity and intricacy of life to come.

Alternative Narrative for Day 1: A Logical Explanation (Personal View). From a logical perspective, the Genesis account's description of "Let there be light" aligns remarkably with a transformative event in the history of the universe: the ignition of the sun.

Scientific understanding suggests that both the sun and Earth began forming approximately 4.6 billion years ago, originating from the same collapsing cloud of gas and dust. The sun formed first due to its larger mass, followed by the planets, including Earth, which coalesced from the remaining material in the protoplanetary disk within one to three million years. During this early period, the cosmos in this region remained dark. The sun existed as a protostar—dim, unstable, and not yet fully ignited—leaving the Earth "formless and void" in the vast expanse.

As the sun accumulated mass, its core temperature rose steadily. However, nuclear fusion could not begin until the core reached approximately 15 million K. Once fusion ignited, the sun transformed into a stable, luminous star capable of providing consistent and life-sustaining light to the solar system. This monumental event, estimated to have occurred 30 to 50 million years after the sun's initial formation, marked the first time light could consistently bathe the solar system, including Earth.

Earth's formation overlapped this timeline, occurring within 10 to 60 million years. This synchronization fits seamlessly with the Genesis description. As God spoke, "Let there be light," this could signify the transformative moment when the sun ignited, dispelling the darkness that enveloped Earth and illuminating it for the first time. This was not merely light but the beginning of order and stability, symbolic of God's intervention to bring order out of chaos.

What makes this explanation so powerful is its harmony with both science and Scripture. It acknowledges the sun's existence before this moment, as science has revealed, while emphasizing the significance of Job 9:7—God's divine timing and orchestration of light: "who commands the sun, and it does not rise; who seals up the stars." These words beautifully reflect Earth's initial state, shrouded in darkness, until the sun's light, at God's command, pierced through the thick and gaseous atmosphere.

Yet, it was in God's timing that the light was revealed, and with the moon, separated day from night, preparing Earth for the life that would follow. This intricate process also foreshadowed the establishment of plant life on Day 3, further highlighting the masterful order in which God shaped the universe and our world.

This perspective underscores the precision and intentionality of creation. It shows that the Bible offers unique insights into our origins, presenting truths that harmonize with scientific discovery. It lends credence to the Bible's divine inspiration, allowing writers thousands of years ago to record knowledge they could not have known without God's guidance.

While this explanation is one of many, it provides a logical and awe-inspiring interpretation of "Let there be light." Whether understood as literal light breaking through the atmosphere or the ignition of the sun, this phrase encapsulates the divine orchestration that transformed the universe into the masterpiece we see today.

Day 2: The Separation of Waters

Genesis 1:6-8

And God said, "Let there be an expanse in the midst of the waters, and let it separate the waters from the waters." And God made the expanse and separated the waters that were under the expanse from the waters that were above the expanse. And it was so. And God called the expanse Heaven. And there was evening and there was morning, the second day.

Hebrew Text with Direct Translation

AND SAID GOD LET THERE BE AN EXPANSE IN THE MIDST OF THE WATERS AND LET IT SEPARATE THE WATERS FROM THE WATERS AND MADE GOD THE EXPANSE AND SEPARATED BETWEEN THE WATERS WHICH WERE UNDER THE EXPANSE AND BETWEEN THE WATERS WHICH WERE ABOVE THE EXPANSE AND IT WAS SO AND CALLED GOD THE EXPANSE HEAVEN AND THERE WAS EVENING AND THERE WAS MORNING DAY TWO

The Biblical and Scientific Perspective. Over millions, perhaps hundreds of millions, of years, Earth began to stabilize following the catastrophic collision with Theia. This event had left the planet in a molten, hellish state, vaporizing its water and reshaping its surface. Over time, water vapor condensed from the thick atmosphere, falling as rain to replenish the oceans. Impacts from comets and asteroids delivered additional water, and eventually, Earth was once again blanketed by a global ocean.

This second phase of creation marked a pivotal step in shaping Earth's atmosphere and environment. It established the "expanse," or "heaven," dividing the waters above from the waters below, setting the stage for the planet's next transformative era.

As the planet continued to cool, volcanic activity released vast amounts of gases, including water vapor, carbon dioxide, and nitrogen, creating a thick and dense atmosphere. This early atmosphere trapped heat and maintained surface temperatures suitable for liquid water, despite the sun emitting only about seventy percent of its current energy output.

The biblical phrase "separation of waters from the waters" can be understood as the division of Earth's global water in the oceans from the water-dense atmosphere above. As volcanic outgassing and the loss of lighter elements to space began thinning the atmosphere, a clearer expanse, or sky, emerged. This process laid the groundwork for more complex atmospheric systems, including weather patterns and the eventual oxygenation of the atmosphere—essential for supporting advanced life-forms.

This separation of waters also initiated Earth's hydrological cycle. Water vapor condensed into clouds, marking the division between the waters below—the oceans—and the waters above—the dense, vapor-laden atmosphere. The newly formed atmosphere regulated surface temperatures through a greenhouse effect, stabilizing conditions and enabling the persistence of liquid water. These early systems foreshadowed the intricate processes of weather and climate that continue to sustain life on Earth.

The expanse created during this phase not only became the medium for Earth's water cycle but also served as a protective barrier. It shielded the planet from harmful solar radiation and helped regulate temperature, ensuring a stable environment. Over time, this atmosphere would transform further, eventually allowing light to penetrate and the celestial bodies to become visible on Day 4.

This phase reflects the extraordinary balance required to sustain life. The hydrological cycle, established billions of years ago, continues to operate as it did in the beginning—through rain, rivers, and the replenishment of water supplies. The separation of waters described in Genesis resonates with this enduring system, underscoring the precision and continuity of Earth's design.

Day 3: Land, Sea, and Vegetation

Genesis 1:9-13

And God said, "Let the earth sprout vegetation, plants yielding seed, and fruit trees bearing fruit in which is their seed, each according to its kind, on the earth." And it was so. The earth brought forth vegetation, plants yielding seed

according to their own kinds, and trees bearing fruit in which is their seed,
each according to its kind. And God saw that it was good. And there was eve-
ning and there was morning, the third day.

Hebrew Text with Direct Translation

AND SAID GOD LET BE GATHERED THE WATERS UNDER THE
HEAVEN TO ONE PLACE AND LET APPEAR THE DRY GROUND
AND IT WAS SO AND CALLED GOD THE DRY GROUND LAND
AND THE GATHERING OF THE WATERS CALLED SEAS AND
SAW GOD THAT IT WAS GOOD AND SAID GOD LET PRO-
DUCE THE EARTH VEGETATION SEED-BEARING PLANTS
AND TREES BEARING FRUIT WITH SEED IN IT ACCORDING
TO THEIR KINDS AND IT WAS SO AND PRODUCED THE
EARTH VEGETATION SEED-BEARING PLANTS ACCORDING
TO THEIR KINDS AND TREES BEARING FRUIT WITH SEED
IN IT ACCORDING TO THEIR KINDS AND SAW GOD THAT
IT WAS GOOD AND THERE WAS EVENING AND THERE WAS
MORNING DAY THREE

The Biblical and Scientific Perspective. On the third day of creation, God
commanded the waters to gather, allowing dry land to appear and vegetation
to flourish. This transformative event mirrors Earth's tectonic activity, where
shifting plates gave rise to continents and ocean basins, separating land from
the global oceans. In this newly defined environment, God called forth vegetation, introducing the foundation for sustaining life through photosynthesis.

After Earth's surface cooled and stabilized around 4 billion years ago, tectonic activity began shaping the planet. Movements of the lithosphere caused
landmasses to rise and form continents while ocean basins deepened, defining the boundaries between land and sea. Volcanic eruptions further contributed to the formation of solid ground, while minerals from these geological
processes enriched the soil, creating conditions conducive to plant growth.

Life first emerged in the oceans around 3.5 billion years ago with simple organisms like cyanobacteria. These photosynthetic microorganisms were instrumental in transforming Earth's atmosphere, producing oxygen and triggering the Great Oxidation Event approximately 2.4 billion years ago. This increase in atmospheric oxygen allowed for the eventual development of more complex life forms.

As Earth's atmosphere continued to stabilize, early ecosystems of algae and microbes thrived in aquatic environments, paving the way for plant life on land. Multicellular algae appeared around 1 billion years ago, followed by the first nonvascular land plants, such as mosses and liverworts, approximately 470 million years ago. These pioneering plants slowly adapted to life outside water, eventually giving rise to vascular plants like ferns and the evolution of seed-bearing species.

The fossil record offers a glimpse into this progression, with stromatolites—layered structures created by cyanobacteria—serving as some of the earliest evidence of life. Similarly, early terrestrial plants began to shape Earth's surface, stabilizing the soil and altering the atmosphere by absorbing carbon dioxide and releasing oxygen.

This monumental chapter in creation illustrates the transformative interplay between geological and biological processes, marking the emergence of a world capable of sustaining vibrant and diverse forms of life.

Day 4: Sun, Moon, and Stars

Genesis 1:14-19

And God said, "Let there be lights in the expanse of the heavens to separate the day from the night. And let them be for signs and for seasons, and for days and years, and let them be lights in the expanse of the heavens to give light upon the earth." And it was so. And God made the two great lights—the greater light to rule the day and the lesser light to rule the night—and the stars. And God set them in the expanse of the heavens to give light on the earth, to rule

over the day and over the night, and to separate the light from the darkness.
And God saw that it was good. And there was evening and there was morn-
ing, the fourth day.

Hebrew Text with Direct Translation

AND SAID GOD LET THERE BE LIGHTS IN THE VAULT OF
THE SKY TO SEPARATE THE DAY FROM THE NIGHT AND
LET THEM SERVE AS SIGNS TO MARK SACRED TIMES AND
DAYS AND YEARS AND LET THEM BE LIGHTS IN THE VAULT
OF THE SKY TO GIVE LIGHT ON THE EARTH AND IT WAS
SO GOD MADE TWO GREAT LIGHTS THE GREATER LIGHT
TO GOVERN THE DAY AND THE LESSER LIGHT TO GOVERN
THE NIGHT HE ALSO MADE THE STARS GOD SET THEM IN
THE VAULT OF THE SKY TO GIVE LIGHT ON THE EARTH
TO GOVERN THE DAY AND THE NIGHT AND TO SEPARATE
LIGHT FROM DARKNESS AND SAW GOD THAT IT WAS GOOD
AND THERE WAS EVENING AND THERE WAS MORNING
DAY FOUR

The Biblical and Scientific Perspective. On the fourth day of creation, the
focus shifts from shaping Earth's physical environment to the purposeful
placement of celestial bodies to govern the cycles of time and light. This day
establishes the framework for life's rhythms on Earth, marking the moment
when the sun, moon, and stars became visible from the planet's surface. Their
visibility signified their roles as "lights in the expanse of the sky" to separate
day from night and to mark seasons, days, and years, further enhancing the
order and intentionality of creation.

When we closely examine the original Hebrew language used in the text,
we can understand the account of the fourth day in Genesis in relation to the
events on Day 1. The Hebrew verb used in this verse, *asa*, is often translated
as "made" in English. However, Hebrew verbs do not have tenses directly

corresponding to those in English. Instead, the tense or aspect of a Hebrew verb is determined by context and the surrounding narrative.

In this case, the verb *asa* does not necessarily imply the creation of the sun, moon, and stars at this moment. Rather, it can suggest an action completed earlier that is now being emphasized or brought into focus. The verse states that God "made" the two great lights—the sun and the moon—to govern the day and the night and to separate light from darkness. This separation of light from darkness had already occurred on the first day, as described in Genesis 1:4: "And God saw the light, that it was good: and God divided the light from the darkness."

This repetition indicates that the celestial bodies were created as part of the initial creation of the universe. What the fourth day highlights is not their material creation but their visibility and specific function. The sun, moon, and stars had always been present but were not yet visible due to the thick, hazy atmosphere that enveloped the early Earth.

As the atmosphere cleared—an event that aligns with the Great Oxidation Event—the sun, moon, and stars became visible in the sky, fulfilling their role in governing the day and night and marking the passage of time. The phrase "to set them in the vault of the sky" reflects this shift in visibility, emphasizing their role as markers for time, seasons, and natural cycles essential for life on Earth.

This interpretation harmonizes both the biblical text and scientific understanding of Earth's early history, where the clearing of the atmosphere allowed celestial bodies to be seen from Earth's surface. By understanding the context of the Hebrew verb *asa*, we recognize that Day 4 is not about the initial creation of the sun, moon, and stars but about their visibility and the establishment of their roles in the natural order.

God's act of making the sun, moon, and stars visible symbolizes the establishment of order and regularity in the cosmos. This act provided a predictable environment essential for sustaining life. The cycles governed by these celestial bodies—day and night, seasons, and years—are crucial for natural behaviors like feeding, breeding, and migration. Their visibility on the fourth day represents a pivotal moment in creation, preparing Earth for the emergence of complex life forms.

Day 5: Marine Life and Birds

Genesis 1:20-23

And God said, "Let the waters swarm with swarms of living creatures, and let birds fly above the earth across the expanse of the heavens." So God created the great sea creatures and every living creature that moves, with which the waters swarm, according to their kinds, and every winged bird according to its kind. And God saw that it was good. And God blessed them, saying, "Be fruitful and multiply and fill the waters in the seas, and let birds multiply on the earth." And there was evening and there was morning, the fifth day.

Hebrew Text with Direct Translation

AND SAID GOD LET SWARM THE WATERS WITH SWARMS OF LIVING CREATURES AND LET FLY THE BIRDS ABOVE THE EARTH ACROSS THE EXPANSE OF THE HEAVENS SO CREATED GOD THE GREAT SEA CREATURES AND EVERY LIVING CREATURE THAT MOVES WHICH THE WATERS SWARMED ACCORDING TO THEIR KINDS AND EVERY WINGED BIRD ACCORDING TO ITS KIND AND SAW GOD THAT IT WAS GOOD AND BLESSED THEM GOD SAYING BE FRUITFUL AND MULTIPLY AND FILL THE WATERS IN THE SEAS AND LET THE BIRDS MULTIPLY ON THE EARTH AND THERE WAS EVENING AND THERE WAS MORNING DAY FIVE

The Biblical and Scientific Perspective. Creation is nearing its culmination—ninety percent complete. Four billion years of careful crafting have shaped Earth into a thriving and dynamic world, with just under 500 million years remaining to perfect its conditions. Humanity is on the horizon, but before its arrival, a critical phase unfolds. On this day, God fills the seas and skies with a rich diversity of life, marking a pivotal moment in the preparation of Earth as the ideal environment for mankind.

The seas began teeming with an astonishing variety of marine life, from the smallest fish to the most magnificent sea creatures. The fossil record supports this flourishing of life, particularly during the Cambrian Explosion approximately 541 million years ago. This period saw the rapid emergence of countless marine organisms, including mollusks, arthropods, and the early ancestors of fish—many of which laid the groundwork for the vibrant ecosystems that still exist today.

As life thrived in the oceans, the skies came alive with the creation of birds. The biblical account of birds taking flight harmonizes with scientific findings that birds evolved from theropod dinosaurs. Archaeopteryx, the earliest known bird, appeared around 150 million years ago during the late Jurassic period, displaying both reptilian and avian features. Whether by divine intervention or through God's purposeful use of evolutionary processes, these early birds diversified over millions of years into the countless species that fill our skies today.

The ecosystems of the seas and skies became interconnected, flourishing in complexity and beauty. Yet, these developments were not merely evolutionary milestones—they were integral steps in God's divine plan. Each intricate design within the waters and skies served as a foundation for what was to come.

All of creation up to this point had been building toward the arrival of a new kind of being—a human being. However one chooses to understand how all that we know came into existence, the focus is not on the process but on the purpose—the reason life exists at all. This purpose would soon be revealed in the crowning moment of creation.

Day 6: Land Animals and Mankind

Genesis 1:24-31

And God said, "Let the earth bring forth living creatures according to their kinds—livestock and creeping things and beasts of the earth according to their kinds." And it was so. And God made the beasts of the earth according to their kinds and the livestock according to their kinds, and everything that creeps on the ground according to its kind. And God saw that it was good.

Then God said, "Let us make man in our image, after our likeness. And let them have dominion over the fish of the sea and over the birds of the heavens and over the livestock and over all the earth and over every creeping thing that creeps on the earth." So God created man in his own image, in the image of God he created him; male and female he created them. And God blessed them. And God said to them, "Be fruitful and multiply and fill the earth and subdue it and have dominion over the fish of the sea and over the birds of the heavens and over every living thing that moves on the earth." And God said, "Behold, I have given you every plant yielding seed that is on the face of all the earth, and every tree with seed in its fruit. You shall have them for food. And to every beast of the earth and to every bird of the heavens and to everything that creeps on the earth, everything that has the breath of life, I have given every green plant for food." And it was so. And God saw everything that he had made, and behold, it was very good. And there was evening and there was morning, the sixth day.

Hebrew Text with Direct Translation

AND SAID GOD LET THE EARTH BRING FORTH LIVING CREATURES ACCORDING TO THEIR KINDS LIVESTOCK AND CREEPING THINGS AND BEASTS OF THE EARTH ACCORDING TO THEIR KINDS AND IT WAS SO AND MADE GOD THE BEASTS OF THE EARTH ACCORDING TO THEIR KINDS AND THE LIVESTOCK ACCORDING TO THEIR KINDS AND EVERYTHING THAT CREEPS ON THE GROUND ACCORDING TO ITS KIND AND SAW GOD THAT IT WAS GOOD AND SAID GOD LET US MAKE MAN IN OUR IMAGE ACCORDING TO OUR LIKENESS AND LET THEM HAVE DOMINION OVER THE FISH OF THE SEA AND OVER THE BIRDS OF THE

HEAVENS AND OVER THE LIVESTOCK AND OVER ALL THE
EARTH AND OVER EVERY CREEPING THING THAT CREEPS
ON THE EARTH AND CREATED GOD MAN IN HIS IMAGE IN
THE IMAGE OF GOD HE CREATED HIM MALE AND FEMALE
HE CREATED THEM AND BLESSED THEM GOD AND SAID
TO THEM GOD BE FRUITFUL AND MULTIPLY AND FILL THE
EARTH AND SUBDUE IT AND HAVE DOMINION OVER THE
FISH OF THE SEA AND OVER THE BIRDS OF THE HEAVENS
AND OVER EVERY LIVING THING THAT MOVES ON THE
EARTH AND SAID GOD BEHOLD I HAVE GIVEN TO YOU
EVERY PLANT YIELDING SEED THAT IS ON THE FACE OF ALL
THE EARTH AND EVERY TREE THAT HAS FRUIT WITH SEED
IN IT YOU SHALL HAVE THEM FOR FOOD AND TO EVERY
BEAST OF THE EARTH AND TO EVERY BIRD OF THE HEAV-
ENS AND TO EVERYTHING THAT CREEPS ON THE EARTH
THAT HAS THE BREATH OF LIFE I HAVE GIVEN EVERY GREEN
PLANT FOR FOOD AND IT WAS SO AND SAW GOD EVERY-
THING THAT HE HAD MADE AND BEHOLD IT WAS VERY
GOOD AND THERE WAS EVENING AND THERE WAS MORN-
ING DAY THE SIXTH

The Biblical and Scientific Perspective. Day 6 marks the most dynamic and transformative period of creation, as God began to fill the land with diverse life-forms. It is worth noting a significant shift in the naming of this period compared to the five prior periods—Yom one, Yom two, Yom three, Yom four, and Yom five. The original Hebrew text uniquely refers to this as "Yom the Sixth," using a definite article. This shift is deliberate and significant, setting this period apart from the previous phases.

The use of the definite article here is reminiscent of old-world titles like "Robert the Bruce" or "Catherine the Great," where the naming confers a sense of importance and distinction. Similarly, "Yom the Sixth" elevates this period to a position of prominence, emphasizing the climactic nature of this phase of creation, where God's ultimate purpose comes into view. This was not merely another period of creation; it was the moment when humanity was brought into existence—God's image-bearers, set apart from all other living creatures. This significance will be explored in greater detail in chapter 5, which focuses on this extraordinary pinnacle of creation.

Marine animals and birds had been flourishing for hundreds of millions of years, but now it was time for the land to come into its own. Diverse land animals emerged, each playing a critical role in the intricate balance of Earth's ecosystems. Yet, all of this was but a prelude to God's ultimate act of creation: the formation of human beings. Humanity was not just another addition to creation but the crowning achievement, imbued with God's image and given dominion over the Earth.

The naming of "Yom the Sixth" reflects the culmination of God's creative work and the special significance of this period. It serves as a deliberate literary marker, highlighting the fulfillment of God's purpose in creation. Just as the titles of old-world figures distinguish their prominence, so too does this naming set "Yom the Sixth" apart, inviting us to recognize its critical place in the Genesis narrative. This detail underscores that Genesis is not merely a sequence of events but a story rich with theological and symbolic meaning—one that invites us to see the interconnectedness of creation, life, and humanity's unique purpose within it.

The Age of Dinosaurs: Earth's Giants Take the Stage

Growing up in the 1960s and 1970s, dinosaurs were an undeniable part of our cultural landscape, yet they were often a source of quiet confusion—not just for those of us raised in the church, but for society at large. How could this be? For those with religious teachings, the Bible made no mention of dinosaurs, and the world was often taught to be only six thousand years old. For others, dinosaurs raised different kinds of questions about history and science, sparking a sense of wonder and uncertainty. Yet, somehow, these prehistoric giants captured the public's imagination, their story told in ways that often blurred the line between fact and fantasy.

Shows like *The Flintstones* (which aired from 1960 to 1966) and *Land of the Lost* (which aired from 1974 to 1976) brought dinosaurs into living rooms across America, framing them in playful, lighthearted narratives. This seemed to reflect how society at large—regardless of religious belief—often handles unsettling or difficult truths: by making light of them. Dinosaurs, mysterious and larger than life, seemed to leave everyone grappling with questions about the past and where they fit into the broader story of the Earth. Despite the inaccuracies, these portrayals captured the imagination of children and adults alike, making dinosaurs a familiar and fascinating part of cultural consciousness.

I can still remember visiting the Museum of the Great Plains. Though the details are a little fuzzy after more than fifty years, one display stands out clearly in my mind. It was housed under a plexiglass box in the center of a spacious room—either given special significance or oddly tucked away in an empty room at the back of the museum. The display seemed out of place, standing in stark contrast to the rest of the exhibits. The box, about five feet by five feet and maybe eighteen inches high, showcased a dramatic scene with characters six to eight inches tall. Underneath the glass, cave dwellers in animal-skin skirts and moccasins, armed with spears, were locked in a life-and-death battle with a mammoth. They had already thrown a couple of spears into the massive beast and were surrounding it, poised for the kill.

The display always intrigued me. I'll admit, at the very least, it was just a cool scene—kudos to whoever created it. I wanted one of my own.

Yet, there was also a sense of shock. The display further solidified these prehistoric creatures in the public consciousness, even as they contradicted the belief system I was taught in church. Dinosaurs were a cultural phenomenon that was hard to ignore, yet equally hard to accept. The church often dealt with this by simply not addressing it, leaving us to grapple with the contradictions on our own. Dinosaurs either didn't exist, or they were some kind of puzzle God created and buried in the ground to give adults something to find and try to piece together for fun. Whatever they were, if it wasn't on *Captain Kangaroo* (which aired from 1955 to 1984), then it couldn't have happened—or so we thought.

Science has confirmed that dinosaurs did indeed exist, roaming the Earth for millions of years. Dinosaurs lived during the Mesozoic era, which is divided into three major periods: the Triassic, Jurassic, and Cretaceous. They first appeared around 230 million years ago during the Triassic period and became the dominant land animals through the Jurassic and into the Cretaceous.

This era saw an incredible diversity of dinosaur species, ranging from the towering Brachiosaurus of the Jurassic to the fearsome Tyrannosaurus rex of the late Cretaceous. Dinosaurs flourished in a world vastly different from our own, adapting to a wide range of environments. But their reign ended in a mass extinction event, likely caused by a combination of an asteroid impact, volcanic activity, and climate shifts, wiping out the dinosaurs and paving the way for mammals to rise.

Dinosaurs, while not directly tied to humanity's creation in the biblical sense, contributed significantly to shaping Earth's environment and ecosystems in ways that ultimately impacted the future of life—including the emergence of humans. As dominant species for over 160 million years, dinosaurs played a crucial role in maintaining ecological balance, regulating predator-prey dynamics, and influencing vegetation and climate. Their presence shaped the land and its resources, laying the groundwork for what would come after them.

Perhaps most importantly, the extinction event that wiped out dinosaurs 66 million years ago became a turning point in Earth's biological history. This mass extinction cleared the way for mammals to diversify and thrive, eventually leading to the emergence of human-like species. Without the disappearance of dinosaurs, it is unlikely that mammals—and, ultimately, humans—would have become the dominant life-forms on Earth.

Dinosaurs, through their long reign and eventual extinction, helped prepare the Earth for the emergence of humankind. Their existence reminds us of the intricate processes that have shaped life on this planet and the extraordinary interconnectedness of creation. Though they may not be part of humanity's direct lineage, their story is a testament to the complexity and intentionality of God's design. Dinosaurs were not a random anomaly or a footnote in history; they were part of a grand narrative, one that ultimately points to the Creator who orchestrates all things with purpose and precision.

As their chapter came to a close, the stage was set for a new era: the rise of mammals and the emergence of human-like species. This progression marks the beginning of God's most extraordinary creation: Human Beings.

Evolution and the Confusion Surrounding Humanity's Origins

Few topics have sparked as much debate and confusion as the idea of human evolution. For much of my life, I believed it was a concept bordering on blasphemy or, at best, an enigma too complex to reconcile with the Bible. However, as scientific discoveries expand our understanding of life's complexity, it becomes increasingly clear that evolution and faith are not inherently contradictory but can be viewed as complementary facets of a greater truth.

For centuries, the religious community has wrestled with the concept of human evolution, often perceiving it as a challenge to the biblical narrative of humanity's unique creation on the sixth day. This belief in humanity's special status has been central to Christian theology. Yet, with the discovery of ancient fossils and the rise of evolutionary theory—most notably through Charles Darwin's *On the Origin of Species*—many felt the biblical narrative was being directly challenged. This tension between science and faith grew into an uneasy conflict that persists to this day.

Reconciling Science and Faith

The church's initial reaction to Darwin's theory was largely one of rejection. The suggestion that humans could have developed from earlier life-forms seemed to contradict the Genesis account and was seen as undermining the foundation of Christian doctrine. Over time, this rejection deepened the divide between science and religion, leaving many believers in a state of cognitive dissonance, struggling to reconcile the fossil record with Scripture.

The discovery of hominins, Neanderthals, and other early human species only added to the challenge, presenting evidence that seemed at odds with a literal interpretation of Genesis. For many, this created a stark choice: reject scientific evidence in favor of a strict biblical interpretation or embrace science and risk questioning the Bible's reliability. This perceived dichotomy has left many feeling they must choose between faith and reason—a deeply unsettling prospect for those who view the Bible as the inerrant word of God.

John Adams once said, "Truth is a stubborn thing." While truth does not diminish with time, it can feel elusive—hidden beneath layers of complexity and seemingly contradictory perspectives. Yet, truth constantly tugs at one's mind and curiosity, as if encouraging the seeker to discover it. Some theologians suggest that Genesis was never intended as a scientific account but as a theological narrative emphasizing God's relationship with humanity. While this perspective has merit, remaining silent on the questions raised by scientific discoveries does little in the discovery of the truth and risks making the Bible seem irrelevant in the modern search for knowledge.

A Divine Process: Evolution as God's Tool

I find it reasonable to view evolution as a process God used to shape life on Earth. This perspective enriches, rather than diminishes, the biblical narrative. Genesis may not disclose the exact mechanisms God employed before creating Adam and Eve, but reliable scientific evidence deepens my awe of His creative genius. The story of evolution is not one of randomness or chance but one marked by divine intentionality. God's fingerprints are visible throughout the process, shaping, refining, and preparing the way for beings uniquely capable of reflecting His nature.

Insights from Hominins and the Role of DNA

Discoveries of hominins, such as Neanderthals and Homo erectus, have provided valuable insights into early human development. These extinct relatives, while not explicitly mentioned in Scripture, reveal glimpses of how God may have shaped humanity through progressive refinement.

Homo neanderthalensis exhibited complex social structures, tool-making, and burial rituals, reshaping assumptions about early humans. Fossils like Australopithecus afarensis ("Lucy") highlighted traits like bipedalism, paving the way for adaptability long before larger brain capacity developed.

Advances in genetics further illuminate humanity's intricate origins. Modern humans share DNA with Neanderthals and Denisovans, revealing interbreeding that passed on critical adaptations like improved immune responses and the ability to thrive in diverse climates. Mitochondrial Eve, traced through mitochondrial DNA, underscores humanity's interconnectedness across geographic and racial divides, highlighting the divine orchestration behind our shared existence.

Homo sapiens: The Culmination of Creation

Homo sapiens, emerging around 300,000 years ago, became the sole surviving species of the genus Homo by approximately 11,500–10,000 BC. Distinguished by advanced cognitive abilities, cultural development, and capacity for language, Homo sapiens laid the foundation for ancient civilizations. Their interactions with Neanderthals and Denisovans further shaped early Homo sapiens, setting the stage for the emergence of humanity's unique spiritual and moral capacities.

The Missing Link in Evolution: The Origin of Moral Conscience

The origin of consciousness and moral reasoning—the innate sense of right and wrong—represents a philosophical mystery in evolutionary theory. While evolution explains survival behaviors, it struggles to account for humanity's leap to abstract thinking, spiritual longing, and artistic expression.

Philosopher David Chalmers describes consciousness as "The Hard Problem," questioning how physical processes in the brain produce subjective experiences. Similarly, morality—acts of justice and self-sacrifice—cannot be fully explained by mechanisms like kin selection or reciprocal altruism, as these behaviors often contradict survival instincts.

This gap underscores the limitations of materialistic explanations and points to divine intervention. The origin of moral conscience is best understood as a reflection of God's nature, instilled in humanity through the soul.

A Divine Perspective: Humanity's Spiritual Nature

The evolutionary process, guided by God, reveals a Creator who works through time and nature to achieve His purpose. From the formation of DNA to the intricate interconnections between ancient hominins and modern humans, every step reflects divine artistry and expertise. This journey, culminating in the creation of Adam, showcases the brilliance of God's plan and His desire to create beings capable of reflecting His own nature.

Rather than diminishing faith, these discoveries invite us to marvel at the Creator's ingenuity, deepening our understanding of His methods and purpose. The story of human origins is not merely a scientific narrative but a testament to God's intentionality, preparing humanity for its role as bearers of His image.

A Shift in Creation—Adam, Plants, Land Animals, Birds, and Then Eve?

The order of creation in Genesis 1 and Genesis 2 has been a point of contention among critics and scholars for a long time. Many critics argue that the different orders of creation in these two chapters suggest inconsistencies or contradictions in the biblical narrative, which some view as evidence of multiple sources or errors in the Bible.

Genesis 1:

The creation follows a structured six-day sequence:

1. *Light and darkness*
2. *Separation of waters (sky and sea)*
3. *Land and vegetation*
4. *Sun, moon, and stars*
5. *Birds and sea creatures*
6. *Land animals, then humans (male and female)*

Genesis 2:

The order is different:

1. *God forms man (Adam) from the dust of the ground first.*
2. *Plants a garden (Eden) and brings forth vegetation.*
3. *Forms land animals then birds.*
4. *Creates woman (Eve) from Adam's rib.*

There are several explanations that scholars and apologists offer in response to these criticisms of Genesis 1 vs. Genesis 2:

- **Different Focuses and Contexts:** *Chronological Account vs. Adam's Relationships*

- **Complementary, Not Contradictory:** *Strict Chronology vs. Not Focusing on Order*

- **Theological Intent vs. Literal Sequence:** *Order of events vs. Theological Themes*

- **Different Literary Sources:** *Priestly Order vs. Anthropocentric Narrative*

- **Interpretation of Hebrew Terms:** *Creation Order vs. Presented-to-Adam Order*

Despite the range of explanations offered by scholars and apologists, none has emerged as a universally accepted interpretation that fully resolves the apparent discrepancies between the Genesis 1 and Genesis 2 narratives. Each theory provides valuable insight, but the truth seems to have remained elusive and nags for a better explanation as ongoing debates continue. This highlights the complexity of the creation accounts and the depth of their theological and literary significance.

The Explanation of Genesis 1 and Genesis 2 Narratives: Two Creations

As the creation story unfolds in Genesis, a significant shift occurs in the second chapter—a move from the grand cosmic scale of the universe to the intimate and detailed formation of the garden within the land called Eden.

Genesis 2:8 explicitly states: "Now the Lord God had planted a garden in the east, in Eden; and there he put the man he had formed." While Genesis 1 paints the creation of the heavens and the earth on a vast canvas, Genesis 2 zooms in on a specific corner of creation, a garden meticulously created for humanity in the land of Eden. The narrative in Genesis 1 ends with the creation of Adam and Eve. Genesis 2 picks up where Genesis 1 leaves off and moves forward in reverse order—a reflection of the first creation.

This perspective—the idea that Genesis 1 describes the creation of all things over 4.6 billion years while Genesis 2 focuses on the localized and purposeful preparation of Eden around 11,500 to 10,000 BC—offers the most reasonable explanation. It upholds the literal accuracy of events described in the Hebrew writings while affirming the detailed plan God laid out for the unique and central role of mankind in His creation.

In Genesis 2, the point of view shifts—from the universe to the earth, and finally to the land of Eden. It is here that God brings all of creation together in the cradle of civilization. This region now takes precedence, becoming the focal point of God's undivided attention. The order is far from redundant— it is entirely new. It is not about the vastness of creation but about the precise formation of man's home, with every detail carefully orchestrated.

This shift in creation can be seen in a few key verses. In Genesis 1, God speaks creation into order, yet the earth brings forth life. Notice the sentiment in these verses when the Earth was the point of view:

- **Genesis 1:11:** "And God said, '**Let the earth** sprout vegetation, plants yielding seed, and fruit trees bearing fruit in which is their seed, each according to its kind, on the earth.' And it was so."

- **Genesis 1:24-25:** "And God said, '**Let the earth** bring forth living creatures according to their kinds: livestock and creeping things and beasts of the earth according to their kinds.' And it was so. And God made the beasts of the earth according to their kinds and the livestock according to their kinds, and everything that creeps on the ground according to its kind. And God saw that it was good."

- **Genesis 1:20:** "And God said, '**Let the waters** swarm with swarms of living creatures, and **let birds fly** above the earth across the expanse of the heavens.'"

In Genesis 2, the focus shifts from the entire world to the specific region of Eden. This second creation isn't a retelling; it highlights the intimate care God took in preparing a special place for humanity from the ground of this specific region of land. Notice how the sentiment changes when the **land** or **ground** is the point of view:

- **Genesis 2:7:** "Then the Lord God **formed** the man of dust **from the ground** and breathed into his nostrils the breath of life, and the man became a living creature."

- **Genesis 2:9:** "And **out of the ground** the Lord God **made** to spring up every tree that is pleasant to the sight and good for food. The tree of life was in the midst of the garden, and the tree of the knowledge of good and evil."

- **Genesis 2:19:** "Now **out of the ground** the Lord God had **formed** every beast of the field and every bird of the heavens and brought them to the man to see what he would call them. And whatever the man called every living creature, that was its name."

This new, second creation sequence—**man, plants, land animals, birds,** and then **woman**—is not about Adam's relationships, it's not a lack of focus on order, or about theological themes or how creation was presented to Adam— this creation narrative is about establishing a land called Eden within the whole of earth, where a sacred place, the Garden of Eden, would be established. It is a place where God would walk and talk with mankind and begin the moral order of the universe.

This shift in focus has been overlooked for centuries. God was not finished in Genesis 1; His ultimate plan extended far beyond. This understanding becomes even clearer when we examine the linguistic nuances in the original Hebrew text, which reveal key distinctions often overlooked in traditional translations.

Misunderstanding in the Translation

A closer look at Genesis 2:4-7 reveals that early translations accurately reflect the shift in narrative in verses 5 through 7, using localized terms such as "land" and "ground." However, the shift is misinterpreted in verse 4, particularly in its conclusion: "in the day that the Lord God made the earth and the heavens." To match the succeeding narrative, the verse should be understood as follows, reflecting the shift from the global to the local perspective:

Genesis 2:4-7:

[4] These are the generations of the heavens and the earth (global) when they were created, in the day that the Lord God made the **land** and the **sky** (local).

[5] When no bush of the field was yet in the **land** and no small plant of the field had yet sprung up—for the Lord God had not caused it to rain on the **land**, and there was no man to work **the ground**,

[6] and a mist was going up from the **land** and was watering the whole face of **the ground**

[7] then the Lord God formed the man of **dust from the ground** and breathed into his nostrils the breath of life, and the man became a living creature.

This subtle adjustment aligns the verse with the localized focus of Genesis 2, marking the transition from a universal perspective to the specific and sacred narrative of Eden. It reorients the reader's perspective, narrowing from the vast heavens and earth to the land of Eden, where God's most intimate creative work takes place.

This shift is not merely linguistic; it highlights the unique purpose of humanity in creation. Genesis 2 emphasizes the preparation of Eden—a sacred, purposeful environment where God would dwell with humanity, setting the stage for the moral and spiritual order of the universe.

By refining the translation, we uncover the deliberate intent behind this second account. It clarifies that Genesis 2 is not a repetition of Genesis 1 but a focused continuation, demonstrating God's meticulous care in preparing Eden as the cradle of civilization and His relationship with mankind.

This linguistic refinement not only clarifies the narrative but also underscores God's deliberate design, transitioning from the vastness of creation to the intimate preparation of Eden, where His relationship with humanity would begin.

The Linguistic Argument for "Land" and "Sky"

As we delve deeper into the text of Genesis 2:4, it's essential to explore the linguistic tones of the original Hebrew. The Hebrew words *eretz* and *shamayim* are commonly translated as "earth" and "heavens," but their meanings are flexible and context-dependent. To fully understand the significance of the second creation account, we must re-examine these words and their application to the localized setting of the Garden of Eden. This brings us to the linguistic argument for interpreting *eretz* as "land" and *shamayim* as "sky" in Genesis 2:4.

Romanized Hebrew (Genesis 2:4):

"Elleh toledot hashamayim veha'aretz behibaram beyom asot Adonai Elohim **eretz v'shamayim**"

Common Translation (English):

These are the generations of the heavens and the earth when they were created, in the day that the Lord God made the earth and the heavens.

Translating *Eretz* and *Shamayim*

ERETZ:

- The word *eretz* can mean "**earth**" in the general sense, referring to the whole planet. However, it can also mean "**land**"—a specific region of the earth, such as the land of Canaan (Genesis 12:1). In Genesis 2, it is reasonable, if not prudent, to interpret *eretz* as "**land**," particularly referring to the Garden of Eden or the region where humanity is placed. God is no longer creating the entire earth but focusing on the land where Adam and Eve will dwell—the Garden of Eden. The word *eretz* here clearly refers to this specific area, making "land" a more accurate translation than the broader "earth."

SHAMAYIM:

- The word *shamayim* typically means "**heavens**" or "**sky.**" In Genesis 1, it refers to the vast heavens, encompassing space, stars, and the cosmos. In Genesis 2, however, where the focus is on a specific habitat for humanity, *shamayim* can be interpreted as "sky," referring to the immediate atmosphere above the land of Eden, where birds are formed. Genesis 2 refers to the sky above the land, the realm where birds were formed, rather than the broader heavens described in Genesis 1.

The Clear Translation Using "Land" and "Sky"

GENESIS 2:4:

"These are the generations of the heavens and the earth when they were created, in the day when the Lord God made the land and the sky."

This refined translation not only clarifies the text but also underscores the shift in focus from the global creation of Genesis 1 to the localized and intentional creation of Eden in Genesis 2.

The Argument for Precision in the Wording

By interpreting "land" and "sky," we uncover the precise nature of the Genesis 2 account. This narrative is a detailed description of how God prepared a perfect and sacred environment for humanity to begin. Both accounts of Genesis 1 and Genesis 2 are crafted with divine precision, yet they serve distinct purposes.

This interpretation also clarifies the structure of Genesis 2:4, which, in traditional translations, seems redundant: "These are the generations of the heavens and the earth when they were created, in the day that the Lord God made the earth and the heavens."

Such phrasing appears repetitive without new information. To understand this better, consider the term "generations" (Hebrew: *toledot*), which consistently introduces what comes next or what is produced, as in Genesis 5: "These are the generations of Adam." This phrase implies a lineage or development—what follows from Adam—naming his descendants Seth, Enosh, Kenan, and so on. Applying the same logic to Genesis 2:4, we would expect the "generations of the heavens and the earth" to reveal what came next, not simply echoing their creation. Thus, a more precise rendering is for the verse to say, "from the heavens and the earth, came the land and the sky of Eden," resolving the redundancy. This pattern aligns seamlessly with the use of *toledot* found elsewhere in Scripture.

Eden: The Pinnacle of Creation

God's creation of Eden represents a pinnacle of divine design, a sacred space deliberately prepared for humanity to thrive in harmony with His presence. Throughout Scripture, we see a consistent pattern: God establishes holy places, set apart from the untamed world, where His divine presence dwells, His purposes are fulfilled, and humanity finds redemption. From the Garden of Eden to the tabernacle in the wilderness to the temple in Jerusalem, these sacred spaces reflect God's intentionality and care, where nothing is left to chance—much like the intricate details of the temples He later designed, where every element worked in harmony.

Eden was not merely a physical location but a sanctuary where humanity would begin its sacred journey. Unlike the untamed world outside, shaped over millennia by natural processes, Eden was a tamer, controlled environment—a place of divine perfection, uniquely suited for Adam and Eve. Around 11,500 to 10,000 BC, God created Adam and Eve in this refined setting, distinct from the hunter-gatherer existence that characterized life beyond Eden. Their role as farmers and shepherds signaled a new chapter in creation: one of harmony, purpose, and a closer relationship with God.

This distinction is evident in the creation of the plants, animals, and birds of Eden. These were not duplicates of the creatures created in Genesis 1, which had multiplied and filled the earth. Instead, they were a refined creation, uniquely suited to coexist in harmony with Adam and Eve. Much like the deliberate design of the temple, where every detail served a purpose, the creatures of Eden were perfectly crafted to contribute to the peaceful environment God intended. These animals were companions and helpers, existing in harmony with humanity rather than as threats or prey. This may explain why Eve was not alarmed when approached by the serpent—a creature that, under Satan's influence, would ultimately corrupt humanity.

The distinction between these two creations is reflected in the language of Scripture. Genesis 1 describes the creation of the "beasts of the earth" (*chayat ha'aretz*), wild animals inhabiting the untamed world. In Genesis 2, however, the focus shifts to the "beasts of the field" (*kol chayat hasadeh*), animals formed specifically for the localized region of Eden. This shift underscores the unique purpose and harmony of Eden's ecosystem, where survival instincts like "kill or be killed" were absent. Instead, these creatures embodied a finely tuned balance, supporting humanity's sacred role in the garden.

Eden's design reflects God's intimate care and intentionality. It was a place where humanity could encounter God, carry out their role in His design, and find redemption. Within this sanctuary, Adam and Eve were uniquely crafted as bearers of God's image, endowed with living souls and destined for eternity. Their innocence and divine likeness set them apart, enabling them to reflect God's character and will. From this sacred space, their influence could extend to the broader pre-Adamic populations (early Homo sapiens) through inter-mixing over time, aligning with God's ultimate design: a world fully reflecting His glory and purpose.

The animals and plants of Eden further emphasize its sacred nature. These were not merely creations of necessity but of beauty, harmony, and purpose, reflecting the full potential of life as God envisioned it. Eden was a glimpse of divine perfection, a sanctuary that stood apart from the evolutionary processes that shaped the rest of the world. Here, humanity would begin its sacred journey, cultivating the garden, living in harmony with its creatures, and fulfilling the divine purpose for which they were created.

Eden was not just a place of peace but a deliberate preparation for humanity's unique role in creation. It was a sacred sanctuary where God placed Adam—a being uniquely crafted to reflect His image and equipped to fulfill humanity's sacred work. From this sanctuary, the story of God's relationship with mankind would ripple outward, carrying the harmony and purpose of Eden to the world beyond.

The Purposeful Creation of Adam

Genesis 2:7

Then the Lord God formed the man of dust from the ground and breathed into his nostrils the breath of life, and the man became a living creature.

Hebrew Text with Direct Translation

AND FORMED THE LORD GOD THE MAN DUST FROM THE GROUND AND BREATHED INTO HIS NOSTRILS THE BREATH OF LIFE AND BECAME THE MAN A LIVING SOUL

The Biblical and Scientific Perspective. The creation of Adam, occurring approximately between 11,500 and 10,000 BC, was a pivotal moment in humanity's history. While evolutionary processes had shaped life on Earth for millions of years, Adam's creation marked a deliberate act of divine intervention—a culmination of God's purpose and the natural progression He orchestrated. Unlike the earlier days of creation, where God called the Earth to bring forth life, this moment in Eden was deeply personal. God Himself formed Adam from the dust of the ground and breathed life into him, completing a design that had been meticulously prepared over time.

The phrase "formed from the dust of the ground" highlights humanity's deep connection to the Earth. Throughout Scripture, the land is depicted as both a physical source of life and a spiritual foundation for humanity's relationship with God. From the Garden of Eden, where God provided everything necessary for life, to the Promised Land of Canaan, the Bible repeatedly emphasizes the land's central role in sustaining and fulfilling God's covenant with His people. This sacred act of creation took place in Eden, the sanctuary God had meticulously prepared for humanity's beginning, where the unspoiled ground reflected the purity of God's divine plan.

Genesis 2:5-6 describes the untouched purity of Eden's soil—an environment where no life had yet emerged because there had been no rain and no one to work the ground. It was from this sacred, unspoiled ground that God formed Adam. When He breathed life into Adam, He transformed a physical body into a living soul, creating a temple where the divine and the material coexisted in perfect harmony. This act of breathing life was far more than animation—it was the culmination of divine intent, a moment where Adam became the bearer of God's image, endowed with a soul capable of moral reasoning, free will, and spiritual awareness.

Central to Adam's creation was the role of DNA, the intricate blueprint for life. Over millions of years, genetic material had evolved, growing increasingly complex under God's guidance. In Adam, this refinement reached its pinnacle—not merely for physical survival but for spiritual and moral capacity, reflecting God's image. His genetic makeup was the culmination of both natural refinement and divine craftsmanship, perfectly suited to house the breath of God.

Adam's DNA also contained the blueprint for humanity's growth and balance. The XY chromosomes in his genetic code introduced a system for determining biological sex, ensuring a balanced male-to-female ratio essential for human flourishing. This intricate mechanism demonstrates the harmonious design intended for humanity's relationships and reproduction, aligning with God's command to "be fruitful and multiply."

Through Adam's DNA, God established the framework for humanity's physical and spiritual existence. It encoded not only the traits necessary for survival but also the moral and spiritual capacities that define what it means to be made in God's image. From Eden, Adam's creation would ripple outward, setting the stage for humanity to flourish and reflect God's glory across all creation. Adam was not simply the first human—he was the embodiment of God's craftsmanship, a living testament to His glory.

The Preparation of Eden and Adam's Task

Genesis 2:8-20

And the Lord God planted a garden in Eden, in the east, and there he put the man whom he had formed. And out of the ground the Lord God made to spring up every tree that is pleasant to the sight and good for food. The tree of life was in the midst of the garden, and the tree of the knowledge of good and evil.

A river flowed out of Eden to water the garden, and there it divided and became four rivers. The name of the first is the Pishon. It is the one that flowed around the whole land of Havilah, where there is gold. And the gold of that land is good; bdellium and onyx stone are there. The name of the second river is the Gihon. It is the one that flowed around the whole land of Cush. And the name of the third river is the Tigris, which flows east of Assyria. And the fourth river is the Euphrates.

The Lord God took the man and put him in the garden of Eden to work it and keep it. And the Lord God commanded the man, saying, "You may surely eat of every tree of the garden, but of the tree of the knowledge of good and evil you shall not eat, for in the day that you eat of it you shall surely die."

Then the Lord God said, "It is not good that the man should be alone; I will make him a helper fit for him." Now out of the ground the Lord God had formed every beast of the field and every bird of the heavens and brought them to the man to see what he would call them. And whatever the man called every living creature, that was its name. The man gave names to all livestock and to the birds of the heavens and to every beast of the field. But for Adam there was not found a helper fit for him.

Hebrew Text with Direct Translation

AND PLANTED THE LORD GOD A GARDEN IN EDEN IN THE EAST AND THERE HE PUT THE MAN WHOM HE HAD FORMED AND OUT OF THE GROUND MADE THE LORD GOD TO GROW EVERY TREE PLEASANT TO THE SIGHT AND GOOD FOR FOOD AND THE TREE OF LIFE IN THE MIDST OF THE GARDEN AND THE TREE OF KNOWLEDGE OF GOOD AND EVIL AND A RIVER WENT OUT OF EDEN TO WATER THE GARDEN AND FROM THERE IT PARTED AND BE-CAME FOUR RIVERS THE NAME OF THE FIRST IS PISH-ON IT ENCIRCLES THE WHOLE LAND OF HAVILAH WHERE THERE IS GOLD THE GOLD OF THAT LAND IS GOOD THERE IS BDELLIUM AND THE ONYX STONE THE SE-COND RIVER IS GIHON IT ENCIRCLES THE WHOLE LAND OF CUSH THE THIRD RIVER IS TIGRIS WHICH FLOWS EAST OF ASSYRIA AND THE FOURTH IS EUPHRATES AND TOOK THE LORD GOD THE MAN AND PUT HIM IN THE GARDEN OF EDEN TO TEND IT AND KEEP IT AND COMMANDED THE LORD GOD THE MAN SAYING FROM EVERY TREE OF THE

GARDEN YOU MAY EAT BUT FROM THE TREE OF KNOWL-
EDGE OF GOOD AND EVIL YOU SHALL NOT EAT FOR IN
THE DAY YOU EAT FROM IT YOU SHALL SURELY DIE AND
SAID THE LORD GOD IT IS NOT GOOD THAT THE MAN
SHOULD BE ALONE I WILL MAKE FOR HIM A HELPER SUIT-
ABLE FOR HIM. NOW OUT OF THE GROUND THE LORD
GOD FORMED EVERY BEAST OF THE FIELD AND EVERY
BIRD OF THE HEAVENS AND BROUGHT THEM TO ADAM
TO SEE WHAT HE WOULD CALL THEM AND WHATEVER
ADAM CALLED EVERY LIVING CREATURE THAT WAS ITS
NAME AND GAVE ADAM NAMES TO ALL THE LIVESTOCK
AND TO THE BIRDS OF THE HEAVENS AND TO EVERY
BEAST OF THE FIELD BUT FOR ADAM THERE WAS NOT
FOUND A HELPER SUITABLE FOR HIM

The Biblical and Scientific Perspective. At first glance, the mention in Genesis of "It encircles the whole land of Havilah where there is gold. The gold of that land is good; there is bdellium and the onyx stone" may seem out of place. After all, Adam and Eve, living in their early simplicity, had no need for gold, bdellium, or onyx, given the lack of technology to utilize such materials. However, modern archaeology and geology reveal that the regions often associated with Eden, such as the Fertile Crescent, are rich in minerals, precious stones, and fertile land—aligning with the biblical description. This detail is far from incidental. It reflects a deeper significance: the divine quality of the land and its sacred purpose in God's creation.

Throughout Scripture, God demonstrates exacting standards for constructing sacred spaces meant to house His presence. Whether it was the tabernacle, the temple, or the Holy of Holies, these spaces were meticulously crafted with the finest materials—gold, precious stones, and purest fabrics—symbolizing their holiness and divine purpose. God's instructions for the tabernacle were explicit: "Exactly as I show you concerning the pattern of the tabernacle, and of all its furniture, so you shall make it" (Exodus 25:9). This precision underscores the sanctity of sacred spaces and reflects God's intentionality in dwelling among His people.

The sacred nature of Adam's creation parallels this meticulous care. Just as the tabernacle and temple were designed as dwelling places for God's presence, Adam's body was created as a sacred vessel, a living temple for God's Spirit. As Paul later writes in 1 Corinthians 6:19-20: "Do you not know that your body is a temple of the Holy Spirit within you, whom you have from God? You are not your own, for you were bought with a price. So glorify God in your body."

Like the temple, built with the finest materials, Adam was formed from the purest elements of the Earth—an intentional design that speaks to the sacredness of human life.

The temple built by Solomon continued this tradition of excellence. Constructed with cedar wood, gold, and precious stones, its inner sanctuary—the Holy of Holies—was overlaid with gold and housed the Ark of the Covenant. This sacred space, so holy that only the high priest could enter after rigorous purification, was a testament to the extraordinary care devoted to creating places for God's presence. The same divine care was evident in Eden, where the land's richness reflected its sacred purpose.

This narrative is not about providing resources for Adam and Eve to use but about the divine quality of the land itself. Adam and Eve were more than just living beings—they were living temples, holy and set apart, formed with the utmost care to embody God's Spirit and purpose.

In every instance—whether preparing sacred spaces like the tabernacle and temple or creating Adam's body—God used the finest materials and gave meticulous attention to every detail. The land of Eden, abundant with gold, bdellium, and onyx, was not incidental but intentional, reflecting the sanctity of God's design. It was the perfect environment for humanity's creation, just as Adam's body was the perfect vessel for the soul—a sacred dwelling place for the Spirit of God.

The Timing of Adam's Tasks

The Bible emphasizes Adam's responsibilities before the arrival of Eve. He was tasked with naming the animals—a process that likely required time, observation, and thoughtful consideration. This was not merely about assigning labels but about understanding and appreciating the unique qualities of each creature, reflecting his role as a steward of God's creation.

The timeline for this period remains unspecified, but it is difficult to imagine it all happening in a single day. Naming every animal, caring for the garden, and learning to tend the plants were significant undertakings that could have spanned weeks, months, or even years. This extended period serves as a reminder of the divine pace of creation—a rhythm that allows for growth, preparation, and reflection through spans of time.

Despite the richness of Eden and the fulfillment of his work, Adam still experienced a sense of incompleteness. God, in His wisdom, recognized this need for companionship, declaring, "It is not good that the man should be alone" (Genesis 2:18). When God presented Eve, Adam's reaction—*"At last!"*—reveals his deep anticipation and the unfolding of God's perfect timing.

Eve: Wonderfully Made with Beauty and Purpose

Genesis 2:21-22

So the Lord God caused a deep sleep to fall upon the man, and while he slept took one of his ribs and closed up its place with flesh. And the rib that the Lord God had taken from the man he made into a woman and brought her to the man.

Hebrew Text with Direct Translation

AND CAUSED TO FALL THE LORD GOD A DEEP SLEEP ON THE MAN AND HE TOOK ONE OF HIS RIBS AND CLOSED UP THE PLACE WITH FLESH AND FROM THE RIB THE LORD GOD BUILT INTO A WOMAN AND BROUGHT HER TO THE MAN

The Biblical and Scientific Perspective. While the creation of Adam marked the formation of humanity in God's image, the creation of Eve, the first woman (*also created in the image of God*), was a masterpiece of divine ingenuity. The female body, with its unique abilities and complexities, was designed with precision and purpose. Eve's creation introduced the balance to the human experience that would be essential for the survival and flourishing of humanity.

The Ingenuity of the Female Body. The female body, with its incredible capacity to bear and nurture life, is a marvel comparable to the greatest designs of the universe. Eve was not just a counterpart to Adam, but the vessel through which all future generations—*created in God's image*—would come. Her body was designed to carry and protect *new* life, a responsibility of unimaginable importance. The delicate balance of strength and tenderness that defines the female form was embodied in Eve.

Her mind, too, was crafted with extraordinary sophistication. The reasoning capability of a woman operates in ways that are often different from a man's—rooted in a stubborn resilience that allows her to face unreasonable odds with unwavering determination. This protective instinct, especially when it comes to her children, drives her to fight for them in ways that defy logic, a fierce power instilled by God from the very beginning.

The intricacy of a woman's thought is unquestionably incredible. One can compare it to the depths of the ocean, equal to a man's intellect but often immeasurably mysterious and nuanced. Her mind operates on multiple levels, considering not only the immediate but the long-term, the practical and the emotional, the needs of others before her own. Unlike men, who are typically able to focus on a single train of thought effectively, Eve was designed with an extraordinary ability to process information across numerous channels of thought at the same time. This multitasking capacity allows her to juggle the many responsibilities of life—family, work, and emotional needs—all at once, often without missing a beat.

An example of this occurred when my daughter Aldyn was about four.

We were sitting in church, and she was nestled between her mother Laura and me. Like many children, she appeared to be lost in her own world, coloring on a page, seemingly oblivious to what was happening around her. Yet, to my surprise, she suddenly burst out laughing and looked up at me with a grin, saying, "That was funny!" I was amazed because, while she had been focused on her drawing, she had also been attentively listening to the minister's sermon. This moment reminded me of how females, even from a young age, often exhibit an innate ability to tune into the subtleties of the world around them, seamlessly balancing multiple streams of information with amazing precision.

Just as Eve was designed to be uniquely different from Adam, women's ability to multitask and process information on multiple levels is a trait that often goes unacknowledged. It reflects a broader reality about gender diversity, particularly when it comes to parenting and perhaps why children are unequivocally drawn to their mothers.

Like the ocean, the helpmate for mankind, Eve was created with a calm that can be as tranquil as the sunset's serenity as it drops below the horizon, yet her strength can be as fierce as a hurricane, transforming everything in its path. This duality—the calm and the storm—makes the female mind a force to be reckoned with, one that complements and challenges the male mind in equal measure.

The Bible itself speaks to the balance of strength, wisdom, and nurturing spirit in women. Proverbs 31:25-26 captures this beautifully: "Strength and dignity are her clothing, and she laughs at the time to come. She opens her mouth with wisdom, and the teaching of kindness is on her tongue." This passage reflects the multifaceted ability of a woman to embody strength and courage while offering meaningful wisdom and compassion.

Proverbs 14:1 also highlights the transformative power of a woman: "The wisest of women builds her house, but folly with her own hands tears it down." This verse acknowledges her constructive ability to nurture and protect, balanced by an intensity capable of altering circumstances entirely.

Ecclesiastes 3:1-8 provides a broader lens to understand this duality. Solomon reflects, "For everything there is a season, and a time for every matter under heaven … a time to love, and a time to hate; a time for war, and a time for peace." A woman's temperament can transition seamlessly in sync with these times, embodying the calm of peace when needed and the fierceness of protection in moments of conflict.

One of the most striking examples of this balance is found in the story of two mothers who came before Solomon for judgment, as recorded in 1 Kings 3:16-28. Two women living in the same house gave birth days apart. Tragically, one mother's child died during the night, and in her grief, she took the living child of the other mother and claimed it as her own. The dispute was brought before Solomon. To discern the true mother, Solomon proposed dividing the living child in two and giving half to each woman.

The true mother's reaction encapsulates the depth and adaptability of a woman's nature. Overwhelmed with a mother's protective instinct, she immediately abandoned her claim, crying out, "Oh, my lord, give her the living child, and by no means put him to death!" (1 Kings 3:26). Her selflessness in the face of loss—prioritizing the child's life over her own grief—revealed her as the true mother. Solomon, understanding this protective instinct and the heart-wrenching sacrifice a mother is willing to make, declared her the rightful parent.

This story illustrates the extraordinary depths of a woman's heart, capable of fierce determination and selfless love. It is this duality—the ability to transition seamlessly from the calm of nurture to the strength of protection—that makes the female nature uniquely powerful. Eve, as the first woman, embodied this balance, reflecting a divine design that brought harmony and depth to the human experience. Her creation was not merely as a helper but as a complement to Adam, enriching the sacred design of humanity with her strength, resilience, and complexity.

To my children: The description of the female nature and nurturing spirit undoubtedly brings to mind your mother, Laura. She was, for the thirty-two incredible years we were married, a living embodiment of these qualities. I often described her as the ocean—deep, mysterious, and as beautiful as a sunset, drawing everyone near to who she was. She carried a loving bohemian spirit, a blend of creativity, freedom, and authenticity that made her both grounded in her belief and uniquely herself.

Her bohemian soul gave her a natural openness to life's beauty and a deep connection to the world around her, paired with the strength and resilience to face challenges with calmness at times and other times with strength of mind. She embraced life with a free-spirited energy that never compromised her faith but instead expressed it in intensely personal ways. She was deeply loving, adventurous in thought and action, and always willing to break from convention when her heart and convictions led her to do so.

She was a force to be reckoned with at times, fierce in her love for her family and unyielding in her devotion to her children. She brought an unmatched vibrancy to our lives, and the bond you shared with her is a testament to the nurturing, protective, and selfless mother she was. I know you carry her love and spirit with you every day, and I see so much of her in each of you.

Eve: The Mother of All Living

Genesis 3:20

The man called his wife's name Eve, because she was the mother of all living.

This verse has sparked considerable debate, with many interpreting it to mean that Eve was the biological mother of all humans. However, both scientific discoveries and the linguistic nuances of the biblical text suggest a richer, more comprehensive understanding of Eve's role.

The Scientific Challenge: Mitochondrial Eve

Modern genetic studies have identified a figure called Mitochondrial Eve, a common matrilineal ancestor who lived roughly 150,000–200,000 years ago. While all humans share her mitochondrial DNA, Mitochondrial Eve was not the only woman alive in her time. She represents a lineage that persisted, while others died out. This does not align with the biblical Eve's timeline, nor does it reduce her theological significance.

The Bible's description of Eve goes beyond her biological creation, inviting us to consider her spiritual significance. She was not merely the first woman, but the first female bearer of the image of God—a unique endowment that distinguishes humanity from animals and earlier hominins.

Chai vs. Nephesh Chayah: Mother of Living Souls

The Hebrew word *chai* (חַי) in Genesis 3:20 translates simply to "living." In contrast, the term *nephesh chayah* (נֶפֶשׁ חַיָּה)—used in Genesis 1 and 2—describes all living beings, including animals, as recipients of the breath of life. If Eve were the mother of all living in the broad sense, it would imply she was the mother of animals as well—a notion that is neither biblically supported nor logical.

Eve's title as the "mother of all living" must therefore refer to something deeper: her role as the mother of all *living souls*—those created in God's image. This image, characterized by moral awareness, spiritual capacity, and an eternal soul, distinguishes humanity from all other creatures. Eve's significance lies not in biological ancestry but in her spiritual role as the starting point of humanity's divine lineage.

Eve's Spiritual Role in Humanity's Lineage

Eve's role as the mother of all living souls is evident in the biblical narrative. When she gives birth to Cain, she proclaims, "I have gotten a man with the help of the Lord" (Genesis 4:1). This statement reflects her deep recognition of God's active involvement in the creation of life. She understood that her role in bearing children was part of a divine partnership—where God not only brought forth physical life but also endowed each person with a soul, reflecting His image.

Further affirmation of Eve's spiritual significance comes with the birth of

Seth: "When Adam had lived 130 years, he fathered a son in his own likeness, after his image, and named him Seth" (Genesis 5:3). This mirrors the language of Genesis 1:27, where humanity is described as being created in God's image. Seth, born in Adam's image, represents the continuation of this divine image through Eve's descendants. This lineage ultimately leads to Christ, who would become the true "life-giver," offering eternal life to all who bear God's image.

Eve as the Portal of Souls

Eve's creation marked the beginning of a new phase in God's plan. Through her, humanity was not only given physical life but also spiritual life. She became the portal through which all future souls, created in God's image, would enter the world. This spiritual inheritance transcended biology and DNA, spreading through her descendants to all humanity.

While pre-Adamic humans may have existed, Eve's creation signified the moment when humanity was imbued with the image of God. This image, passed on through her lineage, was spiritual rather than genetic. Even Cain, who likely took a pre-Adamic wife, carried this divine image, which spread through intermixing and eventually encompassed all humanity.

Eve's Legacy and Christ

Eve's role as the mother of all living souls finds its ultimate fulfillment in Christ. Born of a descendant of Eve, Christ became the true "life-giver," offering redemption and eternal life. His sacrifice restored what was lost through Adam and Eve's disobedience, reaffirming the divine image in humanity.

Through Eve, God established a spiritual lineage that would carry His image into the world. Her title as the "mother of all living" is not about biology but about her role in the propagation of humanity's divine identity. It was through her that God's image entered the world, setting the stage for His redemptive plan.

Eve's significance lies not in her biological motherhood but in her spiritual legacy. She was the first woman created in God's image, the starting point of humanity's divine lineage. Through her, the soul—the essence of what it means to be made in God's image—was passed on to all humanity. Her role as the "mother of all living" is ultimately about the propagation of God's spiritual image, a legacy fulfilled in Christ.

This understanding not only resolves the scientific and theological tensions surrounding Eve but also elevates her role in God's grand narrative. She was not just the first woman but the mother of all who bear the divine image, a role that underscores her pivotal place in creation and redemption history.

The Sacredness of Life in the Womb

The Bible consistently affirms the sanctity of human life, presenting it as a divine creation imbued with purpose and value. It is the divine way in which God designed the soul of mankind to enter the world. One of the most powerful expressions of this truth is found in Psalm 139, which speaks to God's intimate involvement in the formation of life:

> *For you formed my inward parts; you knitted me together in my mother's womb. I praise you, for I am fearfully and wonderfully made. Wonderful are your works; my soul knows it very well. My frame was not hidden from you, when I was being made in secret, intricately woven in the depths of the earth. Your eyes saw my unformed substance; in your book were written, every one of them, the days that were formed for me, when as yet there was none of them.* (Psalm 139:13-16)

From the moment of conception, life is portrayed as sacred, a reflection of divine craftsmanship. It is not merely biological but spiritual, a gift imbued with God's image and purpose. This intertwining of the physical and spiritual underpins humanity's unique value and role in creation.

The sanctity of life extends even to the unborn, as illustrated in Exodus 21, where harm to a pregnant woman or her child carries severe consequences:

> *When men strive together and hit a pregnant woman, so that her children come out, but there is no harm, the one who hit her shall surely*

be fined, as the woman's husband shall impose on him, and he shall pay as the judges determine. But if there is harm, then you shall pay life for life, eye for eye, tooth for tooth, hand for hand, foot for foot, burn for burn, wound for wound, stripe for stripe. (Exodus 21:22-25)

This passage emphasizes the immense value God places on human life, both of the mother and the unborn child, from its earliest stages. The directive imposes severe consequences if harm comes to either, emphasizing that both lives are sacred and deserving of protection. Through this law, God commands justice and accountability, safeguarding the vulnerable and highlighting the divine sanctity of life.

The Father-Daughter Relationship: At the Core of Humanity

One of the most primal and foundational bonds in humanity is the relationship between fathers and daughters. This bond is deeply embedded in the fabric of creation, reflecting themes of trust, love, and protection.

A stark portrayal of the fragility of this bond is seen in the HBO series *Game of Thrones*, in which Stannis Baratheon sacrifices his daughter Shireen. This act of betrayal shocked viewers, not merely for its brutality but because it defied the sacred role of a father—to protect, nurture, and care for his daughter. This portrayal resonated because it violated a universal moral understanding that a father's love for his child should be unconditional and unwavering.

Daughters represent the next generation of souls God brings into the world. This divine design underscores the significance of women in creation, not merely as bearers of life but as integral to God's plan for humanity. Their ability to nurture and sustain life is a tremendous gift—one that God holds in the highest regard. This responsibility is best fulfilled when daughters, who may one day become mothers, are nurtured to be emotionally, spiritually, and physically healthy.

A father's role in his daughter's life is unparalleled. This unique relationship, rooted in selfless love and free from ulterior motives, provides a secure foundation for her emotional and spiritual development. A father's care influences how a daughter perceives her worth, her sense of safety, and even her understanding of God as a loving and protective Father.

No other man can replicate this security. A father's role is to create an environment where his daughter knows she is valued and protected, free from fear or ulterior motives. When this trust is upheld, it reflects God's own fatherly love, becoming a cornerstone of resilience and self-assurance in a daughter's life. However, when this trust is broken—when a daughter, through neglect, seeks a father's love elsewhere—it can lead to lasting emotional and spiritual wounds, highlighting the gravity of this sacred responsibility.

In this way, the father-daughter relationship mirrors the ultimate relationship between humanity and God. Just as a father's love shapes his daughter's understanding of her worth, God's love defines our identity as His children, guiding us to trust in His provision and care. This divine pattern emphasizes the irreplaceable role of fathers in reflecting God's character and nurturing the spiritual and emotional health of their daughters.

Honoring God's Design in Parenthood

When fathers and mothers honor their divine roles, they reflect God's love and wisdom in the lives of their children. By nurturing them with care and guidance, they prepare the next generation to embrace their sacred role in creation—both as fathers and mothers of life and as reflections of God's image.

This calling is not merely about the continuation of physical life but about the propagation of God's spiritual purpose for humanity. In this way, the family becomes a sacred cycle of love, trust, and faith, mirroring God's relationship with His creation.

Scripture frequently portrays God as a Father who nurtures, protects, and guides His children. This divine example sets the standard for earthly fathers and mothers, calling them to embody trust, unconditional love, and unwavering care in their relationships with their children. By design, they provide a unique and sacred bond—a love that fosters trust and security without expectation or condition and establishes a foundation of confidence, self-worth, and spiritual identity.

In this way, parents not only contribute to the sacred cycle of life, but also to the unfolding of God's grand design—a creation imbued with His image, love, and purpose, and carried forward through each new generation.

Day 7: God Rested

Genesis 2:1-3

Thus the heavens and the earth were finished, and all the host of them. And on the seventh day God finished his work that he had done, and he rested on the seventh day from all his work that he had done. So God blessed the seventh day and made it holy, because on it God rested from all his work that he had done in creation.

Hebrew Text with Direct Translation

AND WERE FINISHED THE HEAVENS AND THE EARTH AND ALL THEIR HOST AND FINISHED GOD ON THE DAY THE SEVENTH HIS WORK WHICH HE HAD DONE AND RESTED ON THE DAY THE SEVENTH FROM ALL HIS WORK WHICH HE HAD DONE AND BLESSED GOD THE DAY THE SEVENTH AND MADE IT HOLY BECAUSE IN IT HE RESTED FROM ALL HIS WORK WHICH GOD CREATED TO DO

Completion of the Creation Process. The most extraordinary aspect of God's creation is creation itself—a world of beauty, complexity, and balance that reflects the magnitude of the Creator's work. On the seventh day, or as the original Hebrew phrases it, "in the day, the seventh," the prominence of this period stands apart from the others, marked by a unique naming that reflects its unparalleled significance in the creation narrative. On the seventh day, God rested, marking the completion and perfection of His creation. This rest was not out of necessity but as a declaration that His work was finished—a moment to reflect on the harmony and stability of the world He had made.

In nature, rest is essential for sustainability. Ecosystems thrive on cycles of activity and renewal, mirroring the wisdom of rest in creation. God's rest on the seventh day established the principle of the Sabbath: a time to pause, reflect, and rejuvenate. This rhythm of work and rest is woven into the fabric of creation, teaching humanity the importance of balance, appreciation, and restoration.

The seven-day week, rooted in the biblical account of creation, became a defining rhythm for humanity. God's six days of creation followed by a day of rest inspired the Sabbath, central to Jewish law and life. The Hebrew text's unique naming of "the day, the seventh" emphasizes its sanctity and purpose, setting it apart as a period of completion and reflection rather than creation. This practice profoundly influenced cultures over time, eventually shaping global society. By AD 321, the Roman Emperor Constantine adopted the seven-day week, marking Sunday as a day of rest in honor of Christ's resurrection—a tradition that persists today.

The enduring rhythm of the seven-day week reflects the balance between work and rest, productivity and renewal. It serves as a reminder of the Creator's wisdom in designing a world where rest is not idleness but a vital component of life's flourishing.

CHAPTER 5

A Tumultuous Beginning

As a child, hearing the story of Noah's Flood is like stepping into a fantastical adventure. It's a colorful, almost whimsical tale, in which a white-bearded old man embarks on a grand journey. The images of giraffes with their heads poking out of a gigantic wooden ark, surrounded by hippopotamuses, deer, bears, monkeys, and penguins waddling alongside elephants, are enchanting. The idea of every creature from every corner of the globe—polar bears and kangaroos, tigers and pelicans—boarding a single ark, united for a voyage, seems like a magical vision of perfect harmony.

Yet, as we grow older, the story transforms into a paradox. On one hand, it's part of the Bible, a sacred text for millions, and therefore, believers often feel a sense of obligation to accept it. But the logistical challenges of such a tale become difficult to ignore and the sheer scale of it strains credulity.

Did penguins and sloths, animals from vastly different climates, actually traverse thousands of miles to get to the ark? What about the vast variety of species? How could every single animal type find its way to this boat? And once they arrived, how did Noah manage to accommodate thousands of animals, along with the specific foods they required, for a full year? The idea that these creatures, each needing different habitats, were housed together in one ark seems incredible. Could a koala bear truly survive on a ship in the same space as a predator like a tiger?

This story that was once wonderfully fantastical in childhood comes to a crossroads in the mind of an adult, where the path of reality begins to look strikingly similar to that of myth. What's the difference between this story and the one Walt Disney Animation Studios tells about Moana, the strong-willed daughter of a chief in a coastal village of ancient Polynesia, who is chosen by the ocean itself to set sail and find Maui, a legendary demigod, in hopes of returning the mystical green emerald heart to Te Fiti and saving her people? Both are tales of epic journeys, filled with challenges and magical elements. I'll admit that retrieving Maui's magical fishhook from the realm of monsters, guarded by the giant coconut crab Tamatoa, was a clear giveaway that Moana's story is a myth designed to teach lessons about bravery, perseverance, and self-discovery—but hopefully, you get my point.

If Noah's story doesn't align with what we understand about the natural world, it risks being relegated to the same category—a well-intentioned but ultimately mythical narrative, rather than a historical event. The challenge, then, is to reconcile the story with reality in a way that preserves its theological significance without dismissing the critical faculties we've developed as we've matured. If we can't make sense of the flood narrative, it could become just another legend, losing its power to inspire faith and understanding. It's crucial to explore interpretations that allow the story to remain both meaningful and plausible, ensuring it retains its place as a cornerstone of biblical teaching rather than being dismissed as a mere fairy tale.

For someone who has grown up in the church their entire life, it can be easy to place difficult stories like Noah's Flood on the "faith" shelf, tucked away in the closet of unquestioned beliefs. This is especially true if you're part of a close-knit community of believers in a small town like Faxon, Oklahoma, where I grew up. Such an environment can provide a buffer against the harsh scrutiny one might face in a more critical world. It was easier to maintain these beliefs when our understanding of the universe was limited, but times have changed. As we learn more about the natural world, it becomes increasingly challenging to keep those stories on the shelf without confronting the reality that they may not align with what we now know to be true.

It's even more disheartening when this single story becomes one of the most criticized by unbelievers, challenging the validity of the entire Bible. For those who don't have a strong foundation in faith or who are just beginning to explore their beliefs, this can become a significant stumbling block. Skeptics often use the story of Noah's Flood to discredit the Bible as a whole, and for someone who hasn't had the opportunity to reconcile these challenges with a deeper understanding, it can create doubt and confusion. This can be particularly troubling for young adults, students, or anyone newly grappling with questions of faith and science, who may find it difficult to reconcile this ancient narrative with the realities of the world they see around them.

President Dwight D. Eisenhower once commented in a 1956 speech that farming often seems simpler than it is. He remarked, "Farming looks mighty easy when your plow is a pencil, and you're a thousand miles from the cornfield." Over the years, I've adapted that thought to say: "It's easy to be a farmer when your field is a sheet of paper, and your plow is a pencil, and you're a thousand miles away from the cornfield."

This speaks directly to the disconnect people can have when they are far removed from a situation. When you aren't standing in someone else's shoes, it's easy to simplify or misunderstand their challenges. For someone questioning their faith or approaching Christianity from the outside, even simple Bible stories can become significant barriers to belief. When these questions go unanswered, it creates a gap between faith and reason that can be difficult to bridge.

Even if the flood narrative isn't a point of contention for you, understanding its cultural and historical context allows all believers to engage more meaningfully with the Bible. It opens the door to reconciling scientific evidence with biblical accounts. This approach doesn't diminish the spiritual or moral lessons of the story; rather, it enhances our ability to discuss it in a modern context. Making an effort to understand this event equips Christians to respond thoughtfully and rationally to challenges, while also offering a path for those seeking truth beyond simple answers.

So, how do we reconcile the logistics, the scientific evidence, and the spiritual significance of such an event? Did the flood truly cover the entire world, submerging every mountain? And if so, how did life survive in such conditions? As adults, serious questions start to emerge:

Where did it happen?

When did it happen?

And most importantly, **why**?

By exploring these questions, we can begin to unravel the complexities of the Noah story, finding answers that bridge the gap between ancient text and modern understanding. In doing so, we not only strengthen our own faith but also offer a more compelling narrative to those who might be struggling with these very questions.

Where Did the Flood Happen? Global vs. Local

Before diving into this narrative about the location of the flood, I want to take a moment to reflect on a key argument made earlier in *"A Shift in Creation—Adam, Plants, Land Animals, Birds, and Then Eve?"* In that section, we explored how the narrative of Genesis shifts focus from the entire cosmos in Genesis 1 to the localized region of Eden in Genesis 2. The terms "land" and "sky" in Genesis 2 logically refer specifically to the environment where Adam and Eve lived—the Garden, within the land of Eden—marking a clear distinction from the broader creation account. God's attention shifted from the global to the local—a specific place where He carefully orchestrated every detail to create a perfect environment for His launch of humanity, made in His image.

To begin answering the questions of *where*, *when*, and *why*, it's important to recognize that the lack of detailed knowledge about this period in history has led to ongoing debates for as long as anyone can remember. In just five chapters, the Bible covers a huge swatch of human history—from the creation of the world to the corruption that ultimately led to the flood.

Genesis Chapter 1: The Creation of the World *(Big Bang to Adam and Eve)*

Genesis Chapter 2: The Seventh Day of Rest *(Adam, Eden, Land Animals, Birds, and Eve)*

Genesis Chapter 3: The Fall *(Adam and Eve Cast from the Garden of Eden)*

Genesis Chapter 4: Cain and Abel *(Cain Kills Abel)*

Genesis Chapter 5: Adam's Descendants to Noah

This vast period of time, spanning hundreds if not thousands of years, is condensed into less than three pages in most Bible translations. Yet, in this short narrative, we learn insightful truths about God—His creative power, His desire for relationship with humanity, His justice in response to sin, and His ongoing involvement in the world He created.

The rapid pace of these chapters is not a reflection of the events being insignificant, but rather of the Bible's focus on conveying key theological principles over exhaustive historical detail. Within these chapters, we see God as a Creator, a Judge, a Sustainer, and a Redeemer. These foundational truths about God's nature are crucial as we move into the story of the flood. The God who created the world with such precision and intention is the same God who responds to its corruption in the narrative of Noah.

The story of the flood, as told in Genesis 6-9, must be understood in continuity with what we've learned in the first five chapters. The debate that has been at the center of the flood narrative for decades is more than just about semantics—it profoundly affects how we understand God's actions and how the Bible intersects with our modern understanding of nature. If the story of the flood is viewed as a global event, it stands in stark contrast to the character of God as revealed in the first five chapters of Genesis.

A global flood suggests a God who disregards the natural order He established, choosing to wipe out all life on Earth in an act of sweeping judgment—a punishment of the many for the actions of a few. This interpretation can seem at odds with the depiction of a just and righteous God who is deeply invested in humanity and the creation He declared "good." It raises questions about God's consistency and the proportionality of His judgment, particularly when the corruption described in Genesis appears to have been localized within a specific human population.

Viewing the flood as a regional event reaffirms God's nature as just, purposeful, and sovereign within the framework of the natural laws He created. This perspective demonstrates God's ability to target His judgment precisely, addressing the wickedness of a specific region while preserving the broader creation. It portrays a God who acts with precision and care, balancing justice with mercy, and working within the natural order rather than overriding it.

By understanding the flood as a regional event, we uphold a consistent image of God—powerful yet restrained, upholding the natural laws He established while responding to human sinfulness with measured judgment. This view harmonizes the theological truths of the Bible with scientific understanding, offering a narrative that is both spiritually meaningful and intellectually reasonable.

Sometimes, we tend to perceive God as a more imposing figure than He may have intended for us to understand. This often stems from our limited grasp of how things truly work—much like when we were children, captivated by the idea of the entire planet being engulfed in water. We expect God to manifest in dramatic, extraordinary ways, perhaps misunderstanding that true greatness is often demonstrated through restraint and harmony with the universal laws He designed to keep everything in balance.

To further illustrate this concept, imagine two little boys getting into a squabble. One says to the other, "My dad can beat up your dad!" Of course, neither boy fully understands the reality of what they're saying—they're just trying to win the argument without risking what we used to call a "five-knuckle Nellie" to the face. Lacking the skills to resolve the conflict themselves, they call in reinforcements, using their dads as pawns to escalate the disagreement. Meanwhile, the dads would likely respond, "Whoa, what are you talking about? Speak for yourself and leave me out of it."

In much the same way, when we approach the story of the flood, we must be careful not to project our own limited understanding or exaggerations onto the text. Instead, we should seek to uncover what the text is truly communicating about God's actions and intentions. This requires asking the right questions—questions that guide us toward a deeper understanding of the narrative's meaning and relevance.

What was God's temperament when He decided to flood the earth? In Genesis 6, God's response to the corruption and wickedness of humanity is described not with wrath but with sorrow. The Bible tells us, "The Lord regretted that he had made man on the earth, and it grieved him to his heart" (Genesis 6:6). This powerful statement reveals a God who is heartbroken, not angry. His decision to send the flood arises from deep grief over what humanity had become. He saw the violence and corruption filling the earth and acted out of sorrow, not rage. If anything, God's temperament at this moment shows His overwhelming sadness, rather than the image of a vengeful deity many have come to imagine. His justice is intertwined with grief, not uncontrolled fury. This succinct understanding of God's emotions at the time of the flood helps us grasp His true nature as a just, yet sorrowful, Creator.

Where, When, and Most Importantly, Why?

By exploring these questions, we deepen our understanding of the flood story, appreciating its theological depth while engaging with it through a lens that values both faith and reason.

A key concept emphasized in this book is that while God is undeniably powerful, He consistently chooses to operate within the laws of physics He established when creating the universe. This principle is illustrated when Jesus was tempted by Satan in the wilderness. When Satan challenged Him to jump from the pinnacle of the temple, citing that angels would protect Him, Jesus responded, "Do not put the Lord your God to the test" (Matthew 4:7). This speaks volumes about God's nature—even Jesus acknowledged that God doesn't perform miracles merely for display or in ways that break the order He created. Instead, His power works within the system He designed, emphasizing a respect for the very laws He set in motion.

In this light, we can see other miraculous acts similarly. For instance, when Jesus fed the five thousand, He didn't create food from nothing but started with five loaves and two fish. Why did He begin with this young man's offering instead of producing food from thin air? What did these items provide Jesus with? They gave Him the "recipe"—the DNA structure that contained the design to replicate the fish and bread. In doing so, Jesus honored the natural order, using the building blocks of creation as a foundation. Perhaps this shows us that even in miracles, Jesus worked within creation's established patterns, utilizing the "blueprint" of life encoded in DNA and respecting the system's laws.

This approach aligns with a God who interacts with creation in a way that preserves and even elevates the natural world He so carefully crafted. Rather than bypassing the physical structures He designed, Jesus's miracles demonstrate a harmony with creation, suggesting that divine power often operates through, rather than outside, the order of nature.

The flood of Genesis, traditionally understood as a global event that wiped out all life, may also fit this pattern. The story—whether in the original event, the words chosen to write it, or the words used to translate it—may reveal more about our evolving understanding of the universe than about what actually happened. For centuries, society unquestioningly accepted this version of an incredible event, but does it hold up with today's understanding of the natural world? In reexamining the flood through the lens of God's established natural order, we might find a view of this event that is not only faithful to the text but also harmonious with the physical laws of the universe.

Nature and the Bible: Understanding the Universe

Just as Einstein's theory of relativity revealed that space and time are intricately woven together, so too are the Bible and nature interconnected. Each offers a pathway to better understanding the other. What we learn through nature can deepen our understanding of the Bible, helping us to grasp its true meaning. As we explore the universe, ancient biblical descriptions gain new depth, often aligning with scientific truths in ways that transcend time.

For example, the discovery of the universe's expansion resonates with ancient words from the Bible. In Jeremiah 10:12, we read praise for God who "stretched out the heavens." At the time, this might have seemed purely poetic, yet modern science reveals that the universe began with a rapid expansion of matter and is still expanding today, as observed by Edwin Hubble. This connection brings new depth to Jeremiah's words, illustrating how biblical descriptions can harmonize with our expanding understanding of the cosmos.

A Local Flood within the Laws of Nature

Reflecting on the story of the flood in light of what we know today, it seems unlikely that a global flood occurred as traditionally believed for centuries. Again, this isn't to suggest that God couldn't do anything He desires—He certainly could. But the question arises: would He violate the natural laws He established by covering the entire surface of the earth with water?

The account of the flood describes a natural process, divinely guided. The Bible tells us that it rained for forty days and forty nights (Genesis 7:12), causing the waters to rise and flood the earth. Afterward, the waters prevailed on the earth for 150 days (Genesis 7:24), then gradually receded. This process follows a natural progression—rain causing flooding, waters prevailing, and receding slowly. This reinforces the idea that God's power operates within the framework He designed, respecting the natural order rather than bypassing it.

If the flood were global, it would be anything but a natural event. The Bible says the waters rose above the mountain tops, covering them by 15 cubits (Genesis 7:19-20)—around 22.5 feet above the highest peaks. Covering the entire earth with water to such a height presents significant challenges to the laws of nature.

Challenges of a Global Flood

If we consider the possibility of a global flood covering the highest mountains—such as Mount Everest, which stands over 29,000 feet (5.5 miles above sea level)—the volume of water required would vastly exceed the total amount of water available on Earth. Scientifically, this scenario becomes implausible without the miraculous creation of an immense quantity of additional water. Such an event would contradict the narrative in Genesis, which describes the flood as a natural occurrence within the established order of creation.

The Earth's water cycle is a closed system, meaning the water present in the oceans, lakes, rivers, glaciers, polar ice caps, groundwater, and atmospheric water vapor is already contained within its natural reservoirs. Approximately 97.5% of Earth's water is in the oceans, with about 2.5% in freshwater reservoirs. The water vapor in the atmosphere, while vast, would only be sufficient to cover the Earth by about one inch if condensed—nowhere near enough to submerge even the lowest hills, let alone mountain peaks in the region of Eden like Mount Ararat (16,854 feet) or Everest. To raise sea levels to cover these mountain peaks, an additional influx of water far beyond what exists in Earth's current system would be necessary. Even if we melted every glacier and ice cap and condensed all atmospheric moisture, it still wouldn't suffice.

The Bible references the "fountains of the great deep" breaking open (Genesis 7:11), which some interpret as a source of subterranean water. However, even the largest underground aquifers wouldn't hold nearly enough water to significantly raise global sea levels. Adding thirty percent more water from subterranean sources, for example, would only raise sea levels by around 3,600 feet—nowhere near enough to cover the Earth's highest mountains.

This leaves two possibilities: either the floodwaters would need to come from outside Earth's system, or the atmosphere would need to be fundamentally altered to accommodate these flood conditions, necessitating the creation of water *ex nihilo* (from nothing)—both of which would violate known laws of physics and the Law of Conservation of Mass, which states that matter cannot be created or destroyed.

Impractical Amount of Precipitation

Exceeding 29,000 feet with rainfall would require 725.55 feet of water to fall every day for forty days. Even during catastrophic weather events like hurricanes, the amount of rainfall is nowhere near the levels needed for this scenario.

Let's take a moment to think about the scale we're discussing when interpreting the flood story with this much rainfall. The most rainfall ever recorded in twenty-four hours is six feet. Now imagine the amount needed to reach 725.55 feet a day—it would be devastating! This imagery highlights the real challenges in interpreting such a flood as global. The laws of nature, as we know them, make this scenario implausible.

Consider the rainfall itself. At that intensity, the size of raindrops and the sheer volume of water would have catastrophic consequences. The falling water, particularly at the necessary speed and volume, would not simply flood the Earth; it would batter the surface relentlessly, beating everything to death. The impact would be akin to a continuous, violent deluge, more like high-pressure water cannons exceeding even hard rains that we might envision.

Temperature, Freezing, and Breathable Air

At high altitudes—such as the peak of Mount Everest, which stands at 29,022 feet—the temperatures are extremely cold, often well below freezing. Rain falling at such heights would instantly freeze, turning into snow or ice rather than remaining liquid. This would make it incredibly difficult for a global flood to maintain liquid water at such elevations, as vast ice caps would form instead of the continuous covering of water described in the flood narrative.

Even more challenging are the atmospheric conditions at the elevation where the ark would have been floating. At high altitudes, oxygen levels drop significantly as the air becomes thinner, making survival for humans and most animals impossible without supplemental oxygen. For Noah, his family, and all the animals, surviving such altitudes for an extended period would be unfeasible. The breathable air would be too thin to sustain life, and the freezing temperatures would make survival without significant intervention equally unlikely.

In these extreme conditions, the animals on the ark—particularly those adapted to specific environments—would face insurmountable challenges. The freezing temperatures and lack of breathable air would create a scenario in which survival would be virtually impossible, especially considering that they would have had to endure these conditions for months.

Ecological Balance

The sudden introduction and subsequent removal of such vast amounts of water would have catastrophic effects on Earth's ecosystems. Forests, grasslands, deserts, and other habitats rely on specific conditions to sustain life, and flooding of this magnitude would obliterate these delicate environments.

Even if some species were able to survive temporarily on the ark, severe soil erosion, altered climates, and the disruption of food chains would jeopardize the long-term survival of many ecosystems. Ecosystems are intricate, interdependent networks, and a flood of global proportions would permanently destabilize these relationships.

A global flood wouldn't merely kill all living beings; it would devastate life for centuries, if not longer. The immense volume of water would submerge entire landscapes under miles of water, drowning all forms of life and eroding land masses beyond recovery. The weight of this water would trigger tectonic shifts, volcanic eruptions, and earthquakes, destabilizing the Earth's crust. These violent events would compound the destruction with long-lasting consequences that could make recovery impossible for millennia.

A Perplexing New Beginning

As Noah and his family stepped off the ark, the scene described in Genesis 8-9 portrays peace and renewal. The floodwaters had receded, the land was dry, and Noah's first act was to build an altar to offer sacrifices in thanksgiving. God blessed Noah's family, commanded them to be fruitful and multiply, and set the rainbow as a sign of His promise never to flood the earth in such a way again. It appears almost idyllic—a fresh start with life ready to resume.

However, a flood of such magnitude—a global catastrophe that submerged the highest mountains, such as Mount Everest or Ararat—raises significant questions. The sheer volume of water required would have annihilated Earth's ecosystems, leaving a barren wasteland rather than a fertile, habitable environment. The planet's climate would have been drastically altered, with volcanic ash and debris filling the atmosphere, blocking sunlight, and causing temperatures to plummet. Recovery would take centuries, if not ages.

Yet, the biblical account describes a world seemingly unaffected by such catastrophic events. Noah steps into a landscape ready to sustain life, with plants growing, birds flying, and his family beginning to rebuild. There are no mentions of ecological collapse or the barren conditions we would expect after a global flood, leaving us to wonder how such harmony could emerge so quickly after such destruction.

This raises a perplexing question: *how does the world Noah steps into bear no signs of the global destruction that a flood covering the highest mountains would inevitably cause?* The narrative as described doesn't align with the level of destruction we've discussed—a world submerged in water for months, landscapes obliterated, ecosystems annihilated, and soil washed away. The quick return to normalcy in Genesis suggests much less severe aftermath, leading one to consider whether the flood was localized rather than global.

Noah's new beginning, as depicted, doesn't reflect the aftermath of an apocalyptic global event. Instead, it points toward a recovery that could only be possible if the flood affected a specific region rather than the entire planet. The peaceful resumption of life, as Noah and his family step off the ark, seems far more plausible in the context of a localized flood—a flood that judged humanity in one area while leaving the broader creation intact.

This is what makes the idea of a global flood that wipes out all life while allowing for a swift recovery scientifically and logically implausible, as the recovery from such catastrophic devastation would take far longer than the biblical timelines suggest.

The Bible is deeply relevant, but when presented in ways that seem to contradict our understanding of the natural world, it risks losing that relevance. Scientists, endowed with the God-given gift of discovery, often struggle to reconcile certain interpretations of Scripture with the physical laws they study daily. Yet these same individuals—whether scientists or those who trust primarily in what they can observe—might engage more deeply with faith if interpretations embraced discovery and understanding rather than requiring leaps of faith alone. By viewing the flood as a local event, we not only harmonize the narrative with the natural laws God established but also uphold the significant theological truths of His judgment and mercy.

What Does the Bible Actually Say About the Flood Zone?

The Bible offers insight into the extent of the flood's coverage, beyond what tradition has often taught. Psalm 104:9, which reflects on day three of creation, says, "You set a boundary that they may not pass, so that they might not again cover the earth." This verse refers to the moment when God gathered the waters under the sky into one place, establishing the seas and setting boundaries for them. It speaks to God creating natural limits that prevent the waters from overwhelming the earth. This suggests that God would operate within the natural laws He established, and once those boundaries were set, they were meant to remain, ensuring the waters could never cover the entire earth again.

An interpretation of Scripture suggesting otherwise—such as Noah's flood covering the entire planet above the highest mountains—seems to present a contradiction, offering yet another opportunity for critics to claim biblical errancy.

The New Testament Perspective on the Extent of the Flood

Although there isn't a specific New Testament verse that explicitly discusses the extent of Noah's flood, we can infer how biblical writers perceived the world through their language and descriptions. Several passages suggest that even in New Testament times, writers expressed their views within the geographical and cultural understanding of their era, which could imply a more localized interpretation of "the world."

For example, in Luke 2:1, Caesar Augustus issues a decree for a census: "In those days a decree went out from Caesar Augustus that all the world should be registered." Here, "all the world" clearly refers to the Roman Empire—the known world of the time—not the entire globe. This demonstrates that in New Testament writings, "world" was often understood in a more limited, localized sense, reflecting the geographic knowledge of the time.

Similarly, in Acts 2:5, the Bible describes people from "every nation under heaven" being in Jerusalem for Pentecost: "Now there were dwelling in Jerusalem Jews, devout men from every nation under heaven." Again, this doesn't literally mean *every nation on the globe* but rather all the nations within the known world, likely referring to the Roman Empire and nearby regions.

These examples highlight that the knowledge available at the time shaped the perspectives of biblical writers. While the original texts of the Bible are divinely inspired, translators and interpreters have had to consider these cultural and linguistic contexts, which can significantly affect the meaning conveyed to modern readers.

The Importance of Translation Differences in the Bible

When reading the Bible, it's important to recognize that translation plays a major role in shaping the text we encounter today. Most modern Bibles are translated from ancient sources, such as Hebrew (for the Old Testament), Greek (for the New Testament), and sometimes Aramaic. These ancient manuscripts—like the Masoretic Text, the Septuagint (a Greek translation of the Hebrew Bible), and the Dead Sea Scrolls—provide the foundation for translations. However, various factors influence how translators render the text into English or other languages, resulting in significant differences between versions. These factors include:

- **Translation Philosophy:** Some Bibles are translated word-for-word (literal translation), such as the King James Version (KJV), while others follow a thought-for-thought approach (dynamic equivalence), like the New International Version (NIV). This affects how certain words or phrases are interpreted.

- **Historical Context:** Translators consider the historical content of words, which can change over time. Terms that made sense in ancient languages may not have direct equivalents in modern languages.

- **Theological Perspective:** Different denominations and theological viewpoints can influence the way certain passages are translated, especially when dealing with key doctrinal issues.

- **Cultural and Linguistic Evolution:** Language evolves over time, so translations made centuries ago (like the KJV) may use words or phrases that no longer carry the same meaning in today's context, requiring updated translations (like the NIV) to resonate with modern readers.

Understanding the Translation of *Ha'aretz* in the Flood Narrative

At the heart of the argument surrounding the extent of the flood zone is the Hebrew term *Ha'aretz,* commonly translated as "earth" in many English Bibles. This translation has led many—if not nearly everyone— to conclude that the flood was global in scope, affecting the entire planet.

However, the term *Ha'aretz* is also frequently used in Hebrew to mean "land," referring to a specific region rather than the entire Earth. In the flood narrative, translating *Ha'aretz* as "land" allows for a localized interpretation of the flood, aligning better with the cultural and geographical understanding of the time and opening the possibility that the flood was more regional than global.

To illustrate this, consider two examples where *Ha'aretz* clearly refers to a specific region:

Genesis 12:1—The Call of Abram

- **Hebrew (Romanized):** "Vayomer Adonai el-Avram: Lech-lecha me'artzecha umimoladtecha umibeit avicha el-**ha'aretz** asher ar'eka."

- **Traditional English Translation:** "Now the Lord said to Abram, 'Go from your country and your kindred and your father's house to **the land** that I will show you.'" (Genesis 12:1)

- **Context:** Here, *Ha'aretz* is translated as "land," clearly referring to a specific region, not the entire earth.

Isaiah 13:9—Judgment on the Land

- **Hebrew (Romanized):** "Hinei yom Adonai ba, achzari v'evrah v'charon af l'sum **ha'aretz** l'shmama v'chataeiha yashmid mimena."

- **Traditional English Translation:** "Behold, the day of the Lord comes, cruel, with wrath and fierce anger, to make **the land** a desolation and to destroy its sinners from it." (Isaiah 13:9)

- **Context:** In this prophecy, *Ha'aretz* refers to a specific land or region that will be laid waste by God's judgment.

In both examples, *Ha'aretz* is understood to mean "land," a specific location or region. This localized meaning contrasts with the traditional translation of

Ha'aretz as "earth" in the flood narrative, which implies a global event. However, this contrast provides a more logical and contextually accurate understanding of the flood as a regional event rather than a global catastrophe.

The Flood Zone in Perspective: A List of Verses in Genesis 6-9

Given the accepted translation of the words *ha'aretz, ba'aretz,* and *va'aretz,* this list of verses in Genesis recounting the flood includes all instances of the root word *'erets.* In every case, replacing "earth" with "land" aligns with Hebrew grammar and does not violate any linguistic rules.

To maintain focus, I've highlighted several key verses where translating *'erets* as "land" provides a more accurate and contextually consistent understanding, suggesting that the text describes a local flood. At the time of the flood, there is no archaeological evidence of large, cultured civilizations existing globally. Early civilizations, such as those in Mesopotamia and Egypt, were beginning to emerge, but these societies were still regional and relatively small. Beyond these areas, most human populations lived in smaller, tribal communities. This understanding aligns with the Bible's narrative, which consistently focuses on the history of mankind within the Middle East as we know it today, without venturing into the broader global context.

Genesis Chapters 6–9: Key Verses
Genesis 6:1

- **Traditional Translation:** "When man began to multiply on the face of the earth …" (ha'arets)

- **Revised Translation:** "When man began to multiply on the face of the land …"

- *Explanation:* "In the Land" is the more accurate translation here, as humanity in the biblical narrative was localized to a specific region during this time, even though archaeological findings indicate broader human populations across the earth.

Genesis 6:6

- **English:** "And the Lord regretted that He had made man **on the earth**, and it grieved Him to His heart." (ba'aretz)

- **Revised Translation:** "And the Lord regretted that He had made man **in the land**, and it grieved Him to His heart."

- *Explanation:* "In the Land" is the more accurate translation here, as humanity was localized to a specific region during this time, even though archaeological findings indicate broader human populations across the earth.

Genesis 6:13

- **English:** "And God said to Noah, 'I have determined to make an end of all flesh, for **the earth** is filled with violence through them. Behold, I will destroy them with **the earth**.'" (both ha'arets)

- **Revised Translation:** "And God said to Noah, 'I have determined to make an end of all flesh, for **the land** is filled with violence through them. Behold, I will destroy them with **the land**.'"

- *Explanation:* "In the Land" is the more accurate translation here, as humanity was localized to a specific region during this time, even though archaeological findings indicate broader human populations across the earth.

Genesis 7:17

- **Traditional Translation:** "The flood continued forty days on **the earth**. The waters increased and bore up the ark, and it rose high above **the earth**." (both ha'arets)

- **Revised Translation:** "The flood continued forty days on **the land**. The waters increased and bore up the ark, and it rose high above **the land**."

- *Explanation:* "The land" makes more sense here, as it is more geographically precise in reference to where the ark *is* and the focus of the narrative is regional.

Genesis 8:13

- **English:** "Noah removed the covering of the ark and looked, and behold, the face of **the earth** was dry." (ha'arets)
- **Revised Translation:** "Noah removed the covering of the ark and looked, and behold, the face of **the land** was dry."
- *Explanation:* "The land" makes more sense here, as Noah would not have been able to see the whole of earth.

Genesis 9:17

- **English:** "'This is the sign of the covenant that I have established between me and all flesh that is on **the earth.**'" (ha'aretz)
- **Revised Translation:** "'This is the sign of the covenant that I have established between me and all flesh that is on **the land.**'"
- *Explanation:* "In the Land" is the more accurate translation here, as humanity was localized to a specific region during this time, even though archaeological findings indicate broader human populations across the earth.

Intensifying the Support for a Localized Flood

In Genesis 6-9, the term "earth" is referenced forty-six times in thirty-five verses. In the appendices of this book, all of these verses are provided in their traditional English translation, alongside the Hebrew (Romanized) and a revised translation where the word "earth" is rendered as "land." Additionally, the full text of these chapters is presented with "earth" consistently translated as "land," offering a clearer perspective on the flood narrative.

In every instance from this comprehensive list, the word "earth" can be convincingly translated as "land" or "region" rather than implying a global scope. This interpretation is strongly supported by the Hebrew term *ha'aretz*, which can refer to a specific land, region, or territory depending on the context, rather than the entire planet. Many of these verses, when considered in their historical and cultural context, are more logically understood as describing a localized event.

It's important to highlight one particularly telling example: **Genesis 7:22.** This verse is unique in that it explicitly uses a Hebrew term that necessitates a more specific translation—"on the dry land"—while many of the other verses leave room for interpretive flexibility based on the writer's intent or context. The deliberate choice of "dry land" here, as opposed to the more subjective translations of "earth," speaks volumes about the intent of the writer and strongly supports a localized interpretation of the flood's conclusive result. This key distinction sets a precedent for understanding the flood as an event affecting a specific region rather than the entire globe.

- **English:** "Everything **on the dry land** in whose nostrils was the breath of life died."

- **Hebrew (Romanized):** "Kol asher nishmat ruach chayyim b'apav mikol asher **bacharavah** metu."

The word *bacharavah*, meaning "on the dry land," is used several times in the Old Testament to describe specific geographic locations or events involving dry land. Some key examples include:

1. **Exodus 14:22:** When the Israelites crossed the Red Sea, the phrase **"on dry land"** *(bacharavah)* is used to describe their crossing while the waters were parted.

2. **Joshua 3:17:** Similarly, when the Israelites crossed the Jordan River, the priests stood **"on dry ground"** *(bacharavah)* in the riverbed, once again referring to a localized event.

3. **Exodus 15:19:** The term is used again in the celebration after the crossing of the Red Sea, emphasizing that the Israelites walked "**on dry land**" *(bacharavah)* while Pharaoh's forces were swallowed by the sea.

In all these instances, *bacharavah* consistently refers to specific, localized areas of dry land. This reinforces the idea that in Genesis 7:22, the phrase could similarly indicate a regional flood rather than a global event. The specific use of "on the dry land" suggests that the flood affected a certain area, rather than the entire globe, supporting the interpretation that the flood was a localized occurrence.

How Many Instances Should Be Translated as "Land"?

Based on virtually all forty-six instances of "earth" in Genesis 6-9, every instance could be more accurately translated as "land" or "region," making the flood account more consistent with a localized event. This interpretation avoids contradictions with natural laws and aligns with what we know about ancient geography and human settlement at that time.

This interpretation aligns seamlessly with both the ancient worldview and our modern understanding of natural processes. It avoids the severe ecological, atmospheric, and geological consequences that a global flood would have triggered—such as the destruction of the earth's vegetation, the core foundation for food sources and oxygen production, which would have made post-flood survival impossible for Noah, his family, and the animals. By interpreting the flood as a regional event, we see how the rest of the world's ecosystems could have continued to function, maintaining the balance necessary for life.

We can understand phrases like "all flesh" and "under heaven" as referring to the people and creatures within the specific region affected by the flood, rather than the entire planet. This interpretation is consistent with other biblical examples of localized divine judgment, such as the destruction of Sodom and Gomorrah or the plagues in Egypt.

Understanding the flood as a regional event provides a thoughtful perspective of God's actions within the natural laws He established, demonstrating that the flood was not a miraculous suspension of these laws, but a divinely guided event within the natural processes already in place. This perspective not only reconciles the biblical account with scientific understanding, but also preserves the theological significance of the flood as a momentous act of judgment.

This perspective of a localized flood not only aligns with the natural laws God established but also helps address some of the logistical challenges traditionally associated with the flood narrative. One of the most debated questions, for example, is how Noah managed to gather and care for all the animals. Could this, too, be better understood through the lens of a regional flood?

The Local Flood and the Animals on the Ark

The story of Noah's ark has long raised questions about logistics. How could so many animals fit on the ark? How did they even get there? And once the floodwaters receded, how did these animals return to their far-flung habitats? The mental image of penguins waddling thousands of miles from Antarctica, kangaroos hopping across oceans from Australia, and polar bears lumbering down from the Arctic stretches the imagination. These questions challenge the feasibility of a global flood and raise another critical issue: What does the Bible mean by "kinds"?

The Hebrew word *min*, often translated as "kind," refers to broad categories of animals rather than the modern scientific concept of species. In ancient Hebrew, vocabulary was based on observable traits, such as appearance or behavior, rather than the detailed biological classifications we use today. For example, in Leviticus 11:7-8, when God forbade the Israelites from eating pigs, the command stated: "And the pig, though it has a divided hoof, does not chew the cud; it is unclean for you. You must not eat their meat or touch their carcasses; they are unclean for you."

This directive didn't distinguish between wild boars, domestic pigs, or any other variation within the "pig kind." It referred to all animals within that category, emphasizing the practical and broad nature of Hebrew terms like *min*. Applying this same logic to Noah's ark, when God instructed Noah to bring "kinds" of animals, it likely meant all species within each kind—just as "pig" in Leviticus covered all suids. This interpretation suggests that Noah was tasked with bringing pairs (or seven pairs for clean animals) of all species within the "kinds" native to the region impacted by the flood.

By using this understanding of *min*, the narrative becomes more feasible. Noah would not have needed to gather animals from distant continents or every corner of the earth. Instead, he focused on preserving the biodiversity of the land of Eden and its surroundings. This aligns seamlessly with the Genesis account and makes logistical sense within the context of a localized flood.

A Localized Flood: The Story of Eden Revisited

The Genesis account offers a significant clue. On Day Six of creation, God created animals and birds specifically for the land of Eden, the region where Adam and Eve were placed to begin humanity's story. These animals were unique to Eden, designed to live in harmony with Adam and Eve in a carefully crafted environment. If the flood was localized to this region, Noah's mission to preserve life becomes far more plausible.

Instead of needing to gather creatures from across the globe, Noah's task was to save the life-forms specific to Eden—those that were integral to the ecosystem and humanity's existence in the region. The ark wasn't a floating global zoo but a carefully purposed vessel, preserving the creatures that were under God's direct care and part of His unfolding story with humanity. This perspective not only aligns with the Genesis account but also makes the logistics of Noah's mission far more realistic.

This interpretation aligns with the biodiversity of the region surrounding the land of Eden today. Animals such as sheep, goats, cattle, various birds, and smaller land-dwelling creatures dominate this ecosystem. Even accounting for all species in the area, the number of animals Noah would need to save might range from five hundred to one thousand species. With two of each unclean animal and seven pairs of each clean animal, this reduces the total number of individual animals aboard the ark to as low as two thousand to five thousand—a far cry from the millions implied by a global interpretation.

A Fresh Start for Humanity

The localized flood narrative also fits seamlessly with the theological message of Genesis. The flood was not about destroying all life on Earth but about resetting the land of Eden, where humanity's moral failures had reached their peak. Just as God had once started with Adam and Eve, He now chose Noah and his family—four tested and faithful couples—to restart creation in the region. This ensured a foundation of resilience and experience, accompanied by the animals and birds of Eden, to begin anew.

Addressing the Numbers

When we consider the ark's size, the logistics become even more plausible. The ark, with its 101,250 square feet of space across three levels, could easily accommodate the animals of Eden. If we assume a high estimate of 5,000 animals (2,500 pairs), each pair would have approximately 40.5 square feet of space. Pens measuring 5 feet by 8 feet—providing 40 square feet each—align perfectly with this need, leaving additional room for pathways, storage, and food supplies. The math supports the narrative, showing how Noah's task was feasible within the ark's dimensions.

Resolving the Challenge of Rapid Diversification

Skeptics argue that if Noah carried only a few thousand pairs of "every kind of bird, of every kind of animal, and of every kind of creature that moves along the ground" (Genesis 6:19-20) from the entire earth, the millions of species we see today would require an implausible rate of diversification—over ten new species per day since the flood.[42] However, if the flood was regional and the animals were specific to Eden, this challenge disappears. Noah's mission was not to preserve the genetic potential for every species on Earth but to save the creatures vital to the land of Eden's ecosystem and humanity's survival. This interpretation aligns the story with observable natural laws and eliminates the need for rapid post-flood speciation, making the narrative both scientifically plausible and consistent with the Genesis account.

By situating the flood within the land of Eden and its surroundings, the story of Noah's ark becomes both theologically rich and logistically feasible. God's purpose was to reset the region where He had been actively working with humanity, preserving its biodiversity and giving humanity a fresh start. Noah's faithfulness ensured the continuity of God's plan, while the animals aboard the ark symbolized the renewal of life in Eden.

This interpretation resolves long-standing questions about the feasibility of the ark and aligns the flood story seamlessly with the broader narrative of Genesis. It shows how God's actions were not only purposeful but also consistent with His established natural laws, making the story of Noah's ark both believable and deeply meaningful.

In the next sections, we will explore the implications of this understanding by addressing when it happened and why it holds such significant meaning in both ancient and modern contexts.

When Did the Flood Happen?

Nowhere in history do we find clear evidence of the flood of Noah. This becomes especially significant when we consider the traditional view of a young Earth, which suggests the world and the creation of Adam and Eve—the first humans—occurred around 4000 BC. If this were the case, the global flood would have been placed around 2400 BC, coinciding with the flourishing of advanced civilizations like the Egyptian Old Kingdom and the Sumerian city-states.

Problems with the 2400 BC Flood Timeline

Continuous Existence of Civilizations

Around 2400 BC, several advanced civilizations were thriving:

- The **Egyptian Old Kingdom** (c. 2700–2200 BC), which built the Great Pyramids.

- The **Sumerians** (c. 3100–2000 BC), in Mesopotamia, with their development of writing and advanced cities.

- The **Indus Valley Civilization** (c. 3300–1300 BC), known for its urban planning.

It can be argued that, in the grand span of time, a one-year event like the flood would be nearly undetectable were it not for the continuous records left by ancient civilizations. These records show no evidence of a global flood disrupting them.[43] If such a catastrophic event had occurred, it would have left clear signs of destruction. Yet, the pyramids, temples, and artifacts of these civilizations show no indication of being submerged by water. If a global flood had occurred, these civilizations would have had to restart from zero, but the continuity in their development suggests otherwise.

Lack of Geological Evidence

A global flood around 2400 BC would have left a universal sediment layer.[44] However, no such evidence exists. While localized floods, like those in Mesopotamia, are well-documented, there is no geological proof of a global event. The absence of a universal sedimentary layer further undermines the concept of a global flood at this time.

Historical Records

Advanced cultures such as the Sumerians, Egyptians, and Chinese, who kept written records during this period, do not mention a worldwide flood. These sophisticated societies would likely have recorded such an event if it had occurred.

- **Sumerian Records:** The Sumerians were among the earliest civilizations to develop writing (cuneiform) and kept detailed records of events, myths, and kingship lists. While they do have flood myths, such as the *Epic of Gilgamesh*, their records do not describe a global flood event around the time often associated with Noah's flood (around 5000–3000 BC). Instead, the Sumerian flood narrative is more regional, reflecting localized flooding along the Euphrates and Tigris Rivers, typical of the Mesopotamian environment.

- **Egyptian Civilization:** Ancient Egypt, which maintained sophisticated records through hieroglyphics during the same time period (and earlier), shows no record of a catastrophic global flood event. Egyptian history, from the Early Dynastic Period (c. 3100 BC) through the Old Kingdom (c. 2686–2181 BC), was relatively continuous. They maintained detailed inscriptions of their kings, wars, and natural events like the annual Nile floods, but there is no mention of a global deluge disrupting their civilization. A global flood would have likely destroyed Egypt's infrastructure, but no such event appears in their records.

- **Chinese Civilization:** Ancient Chinese records from the early dynasties, such as the Xia (traditionally dated to around 2070–1600 BC), contain no mention of a worldwide flood either. Instead, like other ancient cultures, they had regional flood legends, such as the story of Yu the Great, who controlled the flooding of the Yellow River. If a worldwide flood had occurred, it would likely have impacted this region, but their extensive chronicles remain silent on such an event.

Genetic Diversity

In the traditional interpretation of the flood account, a global flood, with only eight survivors, would have caused a significant genetic bottleneck. However, modern genetic evidence shows no drastic reduction in human population around 2400 BC.[45] Instead, the genetic diversity we see today reflects a continuous population expansion rather than a collapse and sudden repopulation.

A More Plausible Timeline: The Flood of Noah Around 6000 BC

In light of archaeological evidence, it seems more plausible to place the flood of Noah around 6000 BC, coinciding with the Black Sea Deluge.[46] This shift brings the flood into alignment with known environmental and cultural developments of the time.

Placing the creation of Adam and Eve between 11,500—10,000 BC suggests that the flood occurred 4,000 to 5,500 years later, around 6000 BC. This timing better aligns with archaeological evidence of regional floods and cultural transitions. While this differs from the traditional biblical timeline of approximately 1,700 years after creation, this extended timeline will prove to be more plausible by the end of this section, aligning with both theological interpretations and the broader biblical narrative.

The Black Sea Deluge, which some scientists date to around 5600 BC, is a prime candidate for a significant regional flood. This event would have caused widespread flooding as melting glaciers from the end of the Ice Age raised water levels, inundating surrounding regions. The rapid influx of water into the Black Sea, which had been a freshwater lake, dramatically expanded its boundaries, drowning large areas of habitable land. I am not suggesting that this event was merely a random act of nature, but rather that these conditions may have been part of how God used natural forces to accomplish His purpose, reflecting His consistent nature of working through creation. This regional catastrophe could have provided the basis for the flood story passed down through generations, including the biblical account of Noah's flood.

Although this flood would have been a local event rather than a global one, its scale and impact on early human societies would have been enough to leave a lasting cultural memory. Such a flood, orchestrated by God, still held the divine purpose of cleansing and renewing humanity. The fact that Noah spent around one hundred years building the ark under God's direction, gathering animals, and preparing for the flood speaks to the significant spiritual and moral weight of this event.

The idea that the floodwaters came from within the natural environment aligns with the law of conservation of mass, suggesting that God used existing waters to accomplish His purpose. The Black Sea Deluge fits this narrative well, as the waters already present in glaciers and seas were redirected to bring about the flood.[47] The region is surrounded by the Black Sea and the Caspian Sea, making it a natural basin for such an event. This divine orchestration did not necessitate a global inundation but rather a significant regional catastrophe with far-reaching implications.

Although there is no historical record of a global flood around 6000 BC, this could be understandable given the lack of advanced written language at the time. However, evidence of regional floods, such as the Black Sea Deluge, aligns with the biblical account of Noah's flood. These events likely shaped the flood stories found in various ancient cultures, demonstrating how a catastrophic event could resonate through generations.

Historical Context and Population Growth

After Noah and his family exited the ark, the renewal of humanity began, specifically among those in the region where God was actively working to shape a people in His image. This aligns with evidence of population growth and cultural development in the ancient world. While the Bible focuses on Noah's family as the agents of repopulation, genetic diversity and archaeological findings suggest that humanity's post-flood expansion was part of a broader and ongoing process shaped over millennia.

Repopulation and Post-Flood Expansion

Following the flood, Noah's descendants—Shem, Ham, and Japheth—spread out across the Earth, fulfilling the renewed directive to "be fruitful and multiply, and fill the earth" (Genesis 9:1). Their migration likely led to interactions and intermingling with pre-existing populations, similar to what occurred during the time of Adam and Eve. This blending of lineages contributed to the expansion of human societies throughout the region and beyond.

The Neolithic Revolution and Early Civilizations

By 6000 BC, permanent agricultural settlements such as Jericho and Çatalhöyük were flourishing, marking a major transition from hunter-gatherer societies to farming communities. These early civilizations enabled population growth, technological advancements, and the rise of complex societies. Jericho, located near the Jordan River, is one of the oldest continuously inhabited cities, while Çatalhöyük, in modern-day Turkey, is recognized as one of the most significant Neolithic settlements in Anatolia.

Both of these locations were likely outside the flood region described in the biblical account, suggesting that long-standing civilizations continued to develop independently of the event. The ark's landing, traditionally associated with the mountains of Ararat, would have been approximately five hundred miles to the east of Çatalhöyük, further emphasizing the localized nature of the flood and its impact.

After the flood, the Bible describes Noah's family as moving westward, eventually reaching the plain of Shinar (Genesis 11:2), where the Tower of Babel was later built. This migration narrative fits with the idea of Noah's descendants settling in regions where civilization was already thriving, such as areas near Çatalhöyük and Jericho. Their movement westward aligns with the broader human story of growth and expansion, contributing to the diversity and development of early societies across the region.

Genetic Studies and Human Diversity

Modern genetic studies indicate that human diversity developed over tens of thousands of years through gradual adaptation and population growth. This means that neither Adam and Eve nor Noah's family needed to account for all the genetic diversity observed today. Instead:

- Adam and Eve's Role (11,500–10,000 BC): They may represent a pivotal point in the human story, coinciding with the early stages of the Neolithic Revolution and the beginnings of agriculture.

- Post-Flood Intermingling (6000 BC onward): After the flood, Noah's descendants likely intermingled with pre-existing populations, incorporating and spreading genetic diversity that had already developed.

Bridging Faith and Science

By placing the flood around 6000 BC, potentially aligning it with events like the Black Sea Deluge, we can harmonize the biblical narrative with historical and scientific evidence. The flood serves as a theological turning point, emphasizing God's judgment and mercy, while human societies continued to grow and diversify through natural processes that God set in motion.

Another Puzzle: The Tower of Babel and Rapid Growth

However, this introduces another puzzle into the timeline. Genesis 10:25 tells us that during the time of Peleg, "the earth was divided," which many understand to refer to the Tower of Babel event. After the flood, the descendants of Japheth go one direction and the descendants of Ham go the other. According to the young earth creationist timeline, based on the genealogies in Genesis 11, the flood occurred in 2348 BC, and the Tower of Babel was built in 2242 BC—106 years later. Peleg was born 101 years after the flood, meaning he would have been around six years old when this event took place, which fits the young earth timeline.

The question arises: How did society multiply so rapidly from just eight people (Noah and his family) to a population large enough to build a civilization capable of constructing the Tower of Babel within 106 years?

Rapid Population Growth and Technology

After the flood, the first few generations would likely have focused on survival—establishing agriculture, hunting, and securing basic resources. With an initial population of only eight people, each generation would need time to mature, reproduce, and establish stable family units. Even assuming six children per family, high infant mortality rates, disease, and other challenges typical of early post-flood conditions would likely slow population growth. At best, the population might have reached a few hundred to one thousand people by the time of Babel, still a small number for constructing a monumental tower and founding cities with distinctive cultures.[48]

Cultural Development

The Tower of Babel represents a moment of high civilization. The development of advanced building techniques and coordination required to construct something as complex as the Tower of Babel would have demanded more than just population numbers. It would require a society with established roles, knowledge sharing, and organization—something difficult to achieve with even one thousand people spread across multiple generations. Not only did this require technological advances but also a shared cultural unity. How could these developments have taken place in only 106 years?

Falling Away from God

Perhaps most puzzling, how could humanity have so quickly fallen away from God after the flood—a divine event meant to cleanse the earth of wickedness? In just over a century, the descendants of Noah were once again in rebellion against God, building a tower that symbolized their desire to reach the heavens and become like God.

I'm sixty-four years old, and in my lifetime, I've only had four children, and they've had less than a dozen. They're still in school and have yet to start families of their own. How, then, could Noah's descendants have multiplied enough in such a short period of time to accomplish what is described in Genesis?

The Intersection of Genesis Genealogies and Historical Development

The explanation may lie in missing generations. It is possible that the genealogical record in Genesis 11 compressed and omitted certain generations between Shem and Abram. The flexibility of the Hebrew language supports this theory. The specific details in the text suggest that the author only mentioned the most significant figures, while omitting others, thus compressing the timeline and creating the appearance of a continuous, shorter lineage. The author presents the narrative as though hundreds of years elapsed, while likely omitting thousands of years of history.

If we accept the possibility of missing generations, we can reconcile the long timeline required for the development of early civilizations, the spread of agriculture, and the rise of complex societies like those in Mesopotamia and Egypt. This will allow for:

- The population to grow significantly.

- The development of technologies like brickmaking.

- The spiritual and cultural shift away from God that led to the rebellion at the Tower of Babel.

I am a firm believer that science can help us understand what really happened. While it may not always be exactly right, it guides us toward the truth—and when it leads you to an alignment, then you more than likely have the truth. Genesis tells the story of Adam and Eve as the beginning of the Neolithic Revolution. God taught them to be gardeners—farmers who would start the civilization of the world by growing grains, domesticating animals, and establishing agricultural societies around 10,000 BC. It's a story that spans thousands of years as society develops into complex civilizations capable of monumental achievements, such as the Tower of Babel.

This theory of compressing generations bridges the biblical narrative with the scientific understanding of human history, explaining how the events described in Genesis 11 could have unfolded over a much longer period than a literal reading of the genealogies might suggest.

Interpreting Biblical Genealogies: Bridging Time and Scripture

In order to align the biblical timeline with the scientific record, we recognize that the genealogies presented in the Bible, especially in Genesis 5 and Genesis 11, are likely compressed—meaning they focus on key figures while omitting many intervening generations. This approach was not uncommon in ancient cultures, where genealogies often highlighted only the most important individuals for a particular narrative, leaving out less significant ancestors.

The Hebrew language itself allows for such flexibility. Key words used in genealogical lists, like *yalad* (begat) and *ben* (son), can denote both direct father-son relationships and broader ancestral connections, meaning that the "son" of someone may actually be a descendant many generations removed.

A Key Clue: Shem, Father of Eber's Children

Genesis 10:21 contains a significant clue that supports this theory: "To Shem also, the father of all the children of Eber, the elder brother of Japheth, children were born." Shem is called the "father" of all the children of Eber, even though Eber does not appear in the genealogy until much later—not to mention that the Bible specifically says they are Eber's sons. This is the Bible's way of telling us that Shem is not necessarily the biological father of Eber's sons, but they are tier ancestors. This broad use of "father," which is common in the Hebrew language, confirms that genealogies can skip generations. Here are similar examples in the Bible:

- The genealogy of Jesus in Matthew 1: The genealogy lists David (1000 BC) as the father of Jesus, even though there are generations between David and Jesus. Matthew's genealogy intentionally skips several names to focus on key figures, demonstrating how the biblical use of "father" and "son" can mean ancestor and descendant.

- Eve is called the "mother of all living" (Genesis 3:20), even though not every individual on Earth was directly born from her. This reflects the representative use of "mother" to signify that Eve is the matriarchal figure for all humanity, just as "father" is used to denote key ancestors in genealogies.

- In Genesis 10:31, after defining the territory in which the sons of Eber and their descendants lived, stretching from Mesha toward Sephar in the hill country of the east, the text states: "These are the sons of Shem, by their clans, their languages, their lands, and their nations."

These examples reflect the flexibility in the biblical usage of familial terms, showing how genealogies often focus on key individuals rather than listing every generation in detail. These telescoping generations, when collapsed, allow the narrative to glide through the centuries, highlighting key figures while skipping less significant generations. This method emphasizes the continuous lineage through important eras, ultimately linking to Jesus.

In biblical genealogies, the word "begat" (as used in older translations like the King James Version) is often translated from the Hebrew word *yalad* (יָלַד), which means "to bear" or "to bring forth." In the context of genealogies, *yalad* is commonly translated as "fathered" or "became the father of." It generally signifies parenthood, though in some cases, it may refer to a more general lineage, such as "ancestor of," rather than implying a direct father-son relationship. The word "son" (*ben*) can mean descendant, grandson, or even a more distant relative, not exclusively a direct son.

One of the most significant examples of this is in the New Testament. In Luke Chapter 3 is the genealogy of Jesus Christ. As the narrative works its way backward in time from Jesus to Adam, it comes to the time of Noah's generations and here is where a missing generation is shown. In Luke 3:36, an extra figure named "Cainan" appears between Arphaxad and Shelah: "the son of Abraham, the son of Tarah, the son of Nahor, the son of Serug, the son of Reu, the son of Peleg, the son of Eber, the son of 'Shelah', the son of 'Cainan', the son of 'Arphaxad', the son of Shem…"

Cainan is missing from the genealogy in Genesis 11. His time is compressed in the Old Testament account and suggests that the biblical genealogies may omit some names, depending on their significance to the story. For whatever reason, it was important to mention it in the book of Luke, but not in Genesis.

Reconciling Time from Seth to Abraham: What Science Has Discovered

The genealogy in Genesis 11:10-26 suggests only 290 years passed between Shem, who had just walked off the ark, and Abram. Taken literally, this short period poses challenges when we consider the scientific evidence of thriving civilizations like Egypt and Mesopotamia, which developed much earlier.

If we accept a strictly literal timeline, consider what would need to be condensed into this brief biblical window of just 290 years:

- **Jericho:** Known as one of the world's oldest settlements, Jericho dates back to 9000 BC, with advanced urban planning, defensive walls, and a population of 2,000–3,000. Its gradual evolution into a thriving community would need to fit within this compressed framework.

- **Çatalhöyük:** By 6000 BC, this settlement in Anatolia showcased complex societal structures, including agriculture, religious practices, and art. Collapsing 4,000 years of cultural development into a few centuries strains the plausibility of such rapid progress.

- **Mesopotamian Cities:** Early cities like Uruk, forming around 4000 BC, laid the groundwork for writing, governance, and organized religion—milestones that require long-term societal development.

- **Ancient Egypt:** Unified under centralized pharaohs by 3100 BC, Egyptian civilization's achievements, such as the pyramids, reflect centuries of gradual progress.

- **The Tower of Babel:** Building such an advanced structure, with fired bricks first used around 3500 BC, would have required a significant population and technological knowledge—unlikely within the restricted timeline.

Beyond these challenges, the demographics of the time further complicate the compressed timeline. Most of the population would have been women and children, with only a fraction of men available for large-scale projects like the Tower of Babel. The practical limitations of such undertakings underscore the need for a broader timeline.

Acknowledging Genealogical Compression

By recognizing that the genealogies in Genesis may compress generations, skipping over less significant figures, we align the biblical account with the historical record. This perspective allows for the thousands of years necessary for the gradual rise of civilizations, the development of technology, and the unfolding of God's plan.

Rather than undermining the biblical narrative, this approach enriches it, providing a framework that respects both the integrity of Scripture and the discoveries of modern science. It acknowledges the vast timeline required for humanity to thrive in places like Jericho, Çatalhöyük, and Mesopotamia, while affirming God's hand in guiding the process.

Unveiling Gaps: How the Hebrew Language Compresses Time in Genesis

In the genealogies of Genesis, we can observe how the Hebrew language toggles between different meanings, depending on the context. When the text specifically mentions multiple children or a "son," it shows they are the biological children or son of the father. However, when the narrative mentions only one child without specifying their gender as a "son," it compresses generations and focuses on a key figure or later descendant, suggesting the skipping of some generations. This compression allows the Bible to highlight key individuals while leaving out less significant generations, which might overwhelm the clarity of the text.

I'll admit this sounds like a riddle my father used to tell when I was a little boy. The riddle goes like this:

> There was a man who had been in prison for 20 years. During those 20 years, he never had a visitor. One day after his 20th year in prison, a man came to see him. The guard was very surprised and curious who the visitor was. So, the guard went to the prisoner and asked him who the visitor was. The prisoner replied: "Brothers and sisters I have none, but this man's father is my father's son." How was the visitor related to the prisoner? *(Answer at the end of this section.)*

Understanding this riddle is much like deciphering the genealogies in the Bible. Unveiling the hidden generations involves subtle omissions, but as we look closer, they become noticeable. To get a clearer picture, let's examine Genesis 10:21-29, where the relationships are established and sons are specifically mentioned, which I've highlighted:

> [21] To Shem also, the father of all the children of Eber, the elder brother of Japheth, children were born.
>
> [22] The **sons of Shem**: Elam, Asshur, Arpachshad, Lud, and Aram.
>
> [23] The **sons of Aram**: Uz, Hul, Gether, and Mash.
>
> [24] Arpachshad fathered Shelah; and Shelah fathered Eber.
>
> [25] To **Eber were born two sons**: the name of the one was Peleg, for in his days the earth was divided, and his brother's name was Joktan.
>
> [26] Joktan fathered Almodad, Sheleph, Hazarmaveth, Jerah,
>
> [27] Hadoram, Uzal, Diklah,
>
> [28] Obal, Abimael, Sheba,
>
> [29] Ophir, Havilah, and Jobab; all these were the **sons of Joktan**.

This chapter is about the nations descended from Noah, establishing the generations of Shem, which are further detailed in Genesis 11. Notice in verse 24 that Arpachshad fathered Shelah, and Shelah fathered Eber. There is no mention of Shelah or Eber being the "**sons**" of Arpachshad or Shelah. This is where the hidden generations begin to emerge. Genesis 10: 21-29 lays out the father-son relationships and family structure, while Chapter 11 focuses on the lineage and timeline.

Here's how the lineage appears in Genesis 11, where we now know that Arpachshad, Peleg, and Abram are biological sons of Shem, Eber, and Terah:

>   **Shem** *(100 years old)* fathered Arpachshad—**his son**
>
>   **Arpachshad** *(35 years old)* fathered Shelah—his descendant
>
>   **Shelah** *(30 years old)* fathered Eber—his descendant
>
>   **Eber** *(34 years old)* fathered Peleg—**his son**
>
>   **Peleg** *(30 years old)* fathered Reu—his descendant
>
>   **Reu** *(32 years old)* fathered Serug—his descendant
>
>   **Serug***(30 years old)* fathered Nahor—his descendant
>
>   **Nahor** *(29 years old)* fathered Terah—his descendant
>
>   **Terah** *(70 years old)* fathered Abram—**his son**
>
>   **Abram** *(Abraham)*

This appears to be a continuous succession of father-son relationships. However, the text does not specifically say that Shelah, Eber, Reu, Serug, Nahor, or Terah were father-son relationships. This could, in fact, mean:

>   **Shem** *(100 years old)* fathered Arpachshad—**his son**
>
>   **Arpachshad** *(35 years old)* fathered a son, who fathered a son, who fathered a son, and so on, until Shelah—Arpachshad's descendant

Shelah *(30 years old)* fathered a son, who fathered a son, who fathered a son, and so on, until Eber—Shelah's descendant

Eber *(34 years old)* fathered Peleg—**his son**

Peleg *(30 years old)* fathered a son, who fathered a son, who fathered a son, and so on, until Reu—Peleg's descendant

Reu *(32 years old)* fathered a son, who fathered a son, who fathered a son, and so on, until Serug—Reu's descendant

Serug *(30 years old)* fathered a son, who fathered a son, who fathered a son, and so on, until Nahor—Serug's descendant

Nahor *(29 years old)* fathered a son, who fathered a son, who fathered a son, and so on, until Terah—Nahor's descendant

Terah *(70 years old)* fathered Abram—**his son**

Abram *(Abraham)*

The genealogies from Seth to Abraham may seem to span only 290 years, but it likely represents a much longer timeline, with hundreds of years between key figures. The focus was on significant individuals, and many generations were omitted. This approach conserved space, which was crucial given the limited resources available for writing. Manuscripts were written on materials like papyrus or parchment, which were not as easily available or abundant as paper is today. The process of writing was labor-intensive, and scribes would prioritize essential information. Since the genealogies have served their purpose effectively for thousands of years without issue, it suggests that these details weren't critical to the broader narrative of God's unfolding plan.

To better understand how this compression works, here's an example of what the timeline looks like when telescoped:

Shem *(100 years old)* fathered Arpachshad—**his son**

Arpachshad *(35 years old)* fathered a son

who *(35 years old)* fathered a son

who *(35 years old)* fathered a son

who *(35 years old)* fathered a son

who *(35 years old)* fathered **Shelah**—**Arpachshad's** descendant

Shelah *(30 years old)* fathered a son

who *(35 years old)* fathered a son

who *(35 years old)* fathered a son

who *(35 years old)* fathered a son

who *(35 years old)* fathered **Eber**—**Shelah's** descendant

The advantage of this style becomes clear when we consider the writer's intent and purpose in the narrative. The lineage is effectively conveyed while conserving time, space, and resources, yet still accounting for what may represent hundreds of years of history. This writing style is genius in that it efficiently condenses the timeline while maintaining the essential links between generations and key figures.

Answer to the Riddle

The visitor is the prisoner's son.

A Broader View of Time Before the Flood

Recognizing how the post-flood genealogy is compressed sheds light and perhaps answers a couple of perplexing questions in the time before the flood and in the pre-flood genealogy. This better explains why Adam's descendants could have become so misguided in the shorter period of time between creation and the flood. Most likely because the time to forget their origins was two or three times longer than we realized. This period of time could have spanned not 1,700 years but 5,000 years. It's a big difference. It also can explain why so many patriarchal figures lived at the same time—they didn't.

Before the flood, the lives of these key individuals seemed to overlap sig-nificantly. Each patriarch, from Adam to Noah, was born roughly one hun-dred years apart, with most living for nearly nine hundred years. At one point before the flood, there may have been nine patriarchs alive at the same time. During this time, there was a period of over six hundred years during which Seth through Jared all lived. After the flood, a similar pattern occurred, with ten key figures living concurrently.

Pre-Flood	*Post*-Flood
Adam	Noah
Seth	Shem
Enosh	Arpachshad
Kenan	Selah
Mahalalel	Eber
Jared	Peleg
Enoch	Reu
Methuselah	Serug
Lamech	Nahor
	Terah

In the broader perspective of the Old Testament, outside the early chapters of Genesis leading up to the Tower of Babel, key figures generally lived in suc-cession rather than concurrently. This vertical stacking of patriarchs—where ten men from Adam to Noah are said to have lived for nearly one thousand years each within a span of about 1,700 years—seems puzzling when com-pared to the rest of biblical history. It's far more plausible that these men rep-resent significant moments in time across a horizontal timeline, with many generations between them. This understanding allows for a more consistent progression of events, where each patriarch's life spans centuries, ensuring the continuity of God's message and guidance through successive generations, rather than overlapping lifetimes.

Pre-Flood Lifetimes in Succession

Seth > Enoch > Kenna > Mahalalel > Jared > Enoch > Methuselah > Lamech > Noah

Post-Flood Lifetimes in Succession

Noah > Shem > Arpachshad > Selah > Eber > Peleg > Reu > Serug > Nahor > Terah > Abram

If we view these key figures not as *concurrently* living giants but as linear figures whose long lifespans symbolize extended patriarchal roles, the narrative aligns more naturally with the leadership pattern seen in Old Testament history. Just as the prophets and kings of Israel provided guidance across different periods, each patriarch's life would overlap with the next, offering continuity of leadership. This interpretation suggests that their extended lives allowed them to guide humanity through distinct eras, much like the successive reigns of Israel's leaders ensured stability and direction throughout the Old Testament.

Compressed Generations Before the Flood

The genealogy in Genesis 5, which records the line from Adam to Noah, follows a consistent reference to the relationships. Like Genesis 11, there are *three* father-son relationships:

Adam *(130 years old)* fathered Seth—**his son**

Seth *(105 years old)* fathered Enosh—his descendant

Enosh *(90 years old)* fathered Kenan—his descendant

Kenan *(70 years old)* fathered Mahalalel—his descendant

Mahalalel *(65 years old)* fathered Jared—his descendant

Jared *(162 years old)* fathered Enoch—his descendant

Enoch *(65 years old)* fathered Methuselah—**his son**

Methuselah *(187 years old)* fathered Lamech—his descendant

Lamech *(182 years old)* fathered Noah—**his son**

Noah

The timeline appears to span 926 years from Seth to Noah, but it likely spanned almost five thousand years from around 11,500 BC to 6000 BC. Expanding this timeline would likely look like this:

Adam *(130 years old)* fathered Seth—**his son**

Seth *(105 years old)* fathered a son

who *(90 years old)* fathered a son

who *(90 years old)* fathered **Enosh**—Seth's descendant

Enosh *(90 years old)* fathered a son

who *(90 years old)* fathered a son

who *(90 years old)* fathered **Kenan**—Enosh's descendant

Kenan *(70 years old)* fathered a son

who *(90 years old)* fathered a son

who *(90 years old)* fathered **Mahalalel**—Kenan's descendant

Mahalalel *(65 years old)* fathered a son

who *(90 years old)* fathered a son

who *(90 years old)* fathered **Jared**—Mahalalel's descendant

Jared *(162 years old)* fathered a son

who *(90 years old)* fathered a son

who *(90 years old)* fathered **Enoch**—Jared's descendant

Enoch *(65 years old)* fathered Methuselah—**his son**

Methuselah *(187 years old)* fathered a son

who *(90 years old)* fathered a son

who *(90 years old)* fathered **Lamech**—**Methuselah's** descendant

Lamech *(182 years old)* fathered Noah—**his son**

Noah

From the creation of Adam to the birth of Noah, this broader view of time can easily span thousands of years. It likely contains hidden generations not mentioned between these patriarchs, expanding the timeline into one more aligned with archaeological records.

This interpretation respects the integrity of the biblical text while recognizing the possible limitations of ancient writers and their concise style—God's brief way of telling a grand story. The entire universe, complex and vast, is summarized in just one sentence: "In the beginning, God created the heavens and the earth." Perhaps the idea was: why write the story down when you can just open your eyes and see it?

This reminds me of my time in the funeral industry and having access to early records, where case files spanning decades were filled with handwritten records and notes. However, during World War II, resources were scarce. Wartime files were sparse, with every inch of paper used—notes even filling the margins. This reflected the need to conserve materials. Women during that time painted lines down their legs to mimic stockings because nylon and silk, used for hosiery, were rationed for the war. It was a creative way to maintain appearances amid shortages.

This resonates with how ancient manuscripts were likely written. Limited resources and the labor-intensive process required brevity, conserving precious space without sacrificing meaning. In the original Hebrew, words lacked spaces, paragraph breaks, or punctuation. Hebrew often omits filler words, focusing only on core meaning. Verbs imply subjects, and words are combined into efficient phrases, giving it a concise, sometimes "choppy" feel. For example, Genesis 1:1-3 was likely written continuously, like this:

בראשיתבראאלהיםאתהשמיסואתהארץוהארץהיתהתהוובהוחשךעלפניתהום

ורח אלהימםרחפתעלפנימהימוייאמראלהימיהיאורויהיאור

By expanding biblical timelines, we're not altering the story but enriching it. As ancient writers conserved resources while preserving truth, we must ensure the biblical narrative remains relevant without being confined by outdated interpretations. Our responsibility is to keep the Bible aligned with modern understanding to avoid confusing future generations. Like those before us, we must preserve the integrity of the Bible, balancing faith with reason.

Understanding the Flood: Two Perspectives

The story of the flood in the Bible is rich with meaning, spanning thousands of years and involving complex dynamics of human behavior, divine intervention, and moral decay. Given the complexity and significance of this well-known biblical event, I've provided two versions of the following chapter to cater to different reading preferences.

For those who prefer a concise overview, there is a condensed version that captures the essence of the narrative and key insights without delving into extensive details. This version is ideal if you're looking for a quick yet comprehensive understanding of why the flood happened, with clear takeaways about its significance.

For those who enjoy a more thorough exploration, the detailed version offers a deeper dive into the timeline, the cultural and moral landscape of the time, and the spiritual significance behind the events. It examines the evolution of mankind, the long lifespans of the patriarchs, and the theological implications of the sons of God and the Nephilim, all while weaving in perspectives from biblical, historical, and scientific contexts.

Both versions aim to provide clarity on the flood's purpose, but the choice of how deep to go is yours. Whether you prefer the concise summary or the comprehensive explanation, I hope this chapter offers valuable insight into one of the Bible's most significant events.

The Condensed Version: Why Did the Flood Happen?

Reflecting on the story of the flood, it's challenging to grasp how humanity could have drifted so far from walking with God in Eden to a point where they no longer remembered Him. The timeline between Adam's creation and the flood spans over five thousand years, which may seem like a long time. However, when we consider the extraordinary lifespans of that era—often close to one thousand years—lived in overlapping but largely consecutive succession, with each generation transitioning from one to the next, it becomes clearer how, over this extended period, the human condition could deteriorate to the point that only one man, Noah, found favor in the eyes of the Lord.

Understanding the Flood

The story begins with **Genesis 6:1-8**, which offers insight into why the flood occurred:

- **Section 1:** Humanity began multiplying, and "the sons of God" took "daughters of men" as their wives, driven by physical attraction.

- **Section 2:** God decides to limit man's lifespan to 120 years, as the Nephilim and mighty men roamed the earth.

- **Section 3:** Humanity's wickedness grieved God, who regretted creating mankind.

- **Section 4:** God resolves to wipe out humanity, sparing only Noah, who had found favor in His eyes.

At first glance, these verses may seem disjointed, shifting from marriages to moral corruption and the introduction of the mysterious Nephilim. However, as we look closer, a clearer picture emerges of why God chose to intervene so drastically.

Three Interpretations

Scholars have long debated the identity of the "sons of God" and the reasons their actions precipitated the flood. The three most popular theories are the Fallen Angels theory, the Sethite theory, and the Divine Kingship theory. Each, however, presents challenges.

- The **Fallen Angels theory** suggests that the "sons of God" were angels who had children with humans, resulting in the Nephilim. However, this theory conflicts with biblical teachings about the nature of angels, particularly the idea that they do not marry or reproduce.

- The **Sethite theory** posits that the "sons of God" were descendants of Seth, who intermarried with the "daughters of man," understood to be Cain's descendants. While this theory fits into the broader biblical lineage, it lacks clear scriptural support to explain why these marriages would lead to such severe judgment.

- The **Divine Kingship theory** suggests that the "sons of God" were rulers or kings claiming divine authority, perhaps through coerced marriages to common women. However, this theory doesn't fully account for the moral decline described in the narrative, nor does it align with the historical context of advancing civilizations during that period.

A Plausible Explanation

The missing element is science. By integrating biblical teachings with our understanding of human history, a more plausible explanation emerges. Early Homo sapiens existed long before Adam and Eve, but through Adam and Eve, God imparted a unique spiritual quality—the soul—connecting humanity to Him. Adam's descendants, the "sons of God," were intended to uphold this divine relationship and maintain moral order as they multiplied to fill the earth.

However, they failed to live righteously as bearers of God's image, choosing wives based on physical beauty and succumbing to sins of the flesh. They disregarded their role as the sons of God and their spiritual focus in filling the earth, which led to widespread moral corruption. The Bible emphasizes human wickedness, not the actions of angels, as the cause of the flood. Genesis 6:5 states, "The Lord saw that the wickedness of **man** was great in the earth." This marks the true cause of the flood: humanity's failure to maintain righteousness.

Noah: Humanity's Hope

In contrast to the widespread corruption, Noah stands as a beacon of hope. He chose to walk with God, demonstrating that it was possible to live righteously, even in a world that had forgotten its divine origins. Noah's faithfulness, including his decision to delay starting a family until the age of five hundred and possibly marrying much later in life, suggests a man who made wise, God-centered choices. He raised his sons in the same way, particularly Shem, whose lineage would eventually lead to Jesus.

God's Judgment: Local or Global?

The phrase "from the face of the land" in Genesis 6:7 likely refers to a specific region, most plausibly the Fertile Crescent, where civilization first flourished and moral collapse occurred. This interpretation aligns with the geographical and historical context of the time, suggesting that God's judgment was localized and just, focusing on the sin in that land rather than a global flood. By this time, humanity had already begun spreading across the world, and the flood was directed at the region where the descendants of Adam had failed to live up to their divine calling.

Conclusion

The flood was not an arbitrary punishment but a reset—a divine response to humanity's moral collapse. Noah's faithfulness showed that living righteously was possible, and through him, God preserved a remnant. By wiping away the corruption caused by spiritual compromise, God began anew with those who still remembered Him. Noah's story serves as a reminder that God's expectations, while high, are achievable through faithfulness and dedication.

The Detailed Version: Why Did the Flood Happen?

Reflecting on the story of the flood, it's challenging to grasp how humanity could have drifted so far from walking with God in Eden to a point where they no longer remembered Him. The timeline between Adam's creation and the flood spans over five thousand years, which may seem like a long time. However, when we consider the extraordinary lifespans of that era—often close to one thousand years—lived in overlapping but largely consecutive succession, with each generation transitioning from one to the next, it becomes clearer how, over this extended period, the human condition could deteriorate to the point where only one man, Noah, found favor in the eyes of the Lord.

Recognizing that numerous generations may have been collapsed in the biblical narrative, with key figures living consecutively across centuries, this long span of time becomes easier to understand. This was the dawn of human intellect, and as history has shown, it took thousands of years for this intellect to fully emerge and shape civilization.

This perspective doesn't aimlessly stretch time but accounts for the full period that actually existed. It helps us understand why, over such a long span, humanity's moral decline became so severe that, in the end, only Noah's faithfulness allowed him to find favor in the eyes of the Lord.

In the world of modern technology, we often use systems to protect and recover valuable data. Take the example of a RAID array in a computer system, where data is distributed across multiple hard drives. This is done so that if one drive fails, the remaining drives can reconstruct the missing data back onto the new replacement drive. The system can reconstruct the information, even when a large section of the information is missing. Now, let's take this concept and apply it to the story of humanity before the flood.

It all began with a piece of fruit, Eve, a serpent, the Tree of Knowledge of Good and Evil, and the exercise of free will—these elements set off a chain of events that would shape the fate of humanity to this day. What gave cause to the flood is written in Genesis 6:1-8, which says:

- **Section 1: 1** "When man began to multiply on the face of the land and daughters were born to them, **2** the sons of God saw that the daughters of man were attractive. And they took as their wives any they chose."

- **Section 2: 3** "Then the Lord said, 'My Spirit shall not abide in man forever, for he is flesh: his days shall be 120 years.' **4** The Nephilim were on the earth in those days, and also afterward, when the sons of God came in to the daughters of man and they bore children to them. These were the mighty men who were of old, the men of renown."

- **Section 3: 5** "The Lord saw that the wickedness of man was great in the earth, and that every intention of the thoughts of his heart was only evil continually. **6** And the Lord regretted that he had made man on the earth, and it grieved him to his heart."

- **Section 4: 7** "So the Lord said, 'I will blot out man whom I have created from the face of the land, man and animals and creeping things and birds of the heavens, for I am sorry that I have made them.' **8** But Noah found favor in the eyes of the Lord."

At first glance, the narrative in Genesis 6 can seem a bit disjointed. In verses 1 and 2, nothing appears out of the ordinary—men and women are getting married, part of the natural cycle of life. But then, in verse 3, God suddenly decides to limit man's lifespan. Is this a good thing or a bad thing? It feels somewhat random. Even more puzzling is the mention of the Nephilim, seemingly notable figures, but what are they about?

By verse 5, things take a darker turn. God is deeply displeased by the wickedness of humanity, but the narrative jumps from weddings to widespread wickedness without much explanation. And again, what role do the Nephilim or the "mighty men" play in this? In verse 7, everything spirals out of control as God decides to wipe out mankind. What happened?

These verses have perplexed readers for centuries, and some have even written entire books on them. The mystery deepens in Genesis 6:1-2, where the phrase "sons of God" appears, saying that they took the "daughters of men" as their wives. This cryptic statement has puzzled scholars and theologians for generations, leading to several theories about who the "sons of God" were and why their unions with human women were so problematic that they contributed to the cause of the flood. Here are the three leading interpretations:

The Fallen Angels Theory

Many biblical scholars and theologians throughout history have held the view that the "sons of God" mentioned in Genesis 6:1-4 are fallen angels. They root this interpretation in several key Scriptures and support it with the broader context of biblical teachings on angels and their interaction with humanity. They come to the conclusion that the angels came to Earth when man began to multiply and took women (daughters of Adam and/or his descendants) and had children with them, who were the Nephilim. The Nephilim were mighty warriors who caused chaos on the earth and were giants.

Key Scriptures and Arguments. In these verses, whether you interpret it to mean that their offspring with human women resulted in the birth of the Nephilim or not, it seems logical to believe that it is speaking about angelic beings, based on similar language used in other parts of the Bible.

- **Job 1:6:** "Now there was a day when the **sons of God** came to present themselves before the Lord, and Satan also came among them."

  In this context, "sons of God" clearly refers to angelic beings who have access to God's presence. This supports the idea that the term "sons of God" in Genesis 6 could also refer to angels, specifically fallen ones who defied God's order.

- **Jude 1:6-7:** "And the angels who did not stay within their own position of authority, but left their proper dwelling, he has kept in eternal chains under gloomy darkness until the judgment of the great day—just as Sodom and Gomorrah and the surrounding cities, which likewise indulged in sexual immorality and pursued unnatural desire, serve as an example by undergoing a punishment of eternal fire."

  This passage suggests that certain angels left their designated realm and engaged in actions that were outside of God's design, often interpreted as the sin of intermingling with human women. The connection to "unnatural desire" supports the interpretation that these angels engaged in a grievous act similar to what is described in Genesis 6.

- **2 Peter 2:4-5:** "For if God did not spare angels when they sinned, but cast them into hell and committed them to chains of gloomy darkness to be kept until the judgment; **if he did not spare the ancient world, but preserved Noah,** a herald of righteousness, with seven others, when he brought a flood upon the world of the ungodly..."

  Peter links the sin of the fallen angels to the judgment of the ancient world by the flood, implying that their actions were a significant factor in the corruption that led to the flood.

Theory Criticism

- One significant issue with the fallen angel theory is the question of how spiritual beings could take on physical forms capable of reproduction with humans, let alone produce offspring as extraordinary as giants. While there are biblical examples, such as in Genesis 18:1-8, where angels appear in human form and engage in human activities—like eating a meal with Abraham—there is no direct evidence to suggest that they could engage in sexual reproduction. Additionally, Jesus's words in Matthew 22:30, where He says that angels "neither marry nor are given in marriage," directly challenge the idea that angels were designed for or capable of marital unions with humans. Angels have always been depicted as male in spiritual form and do not reproduce. This raises the question of how a being, not created for reproduction, could somehow engage in biological reproduction. This leaves a significant gap in the fallen angel theory, as it requires accepting that angels could transform into physical beings capable of human reproduction, an idea that lacks clear scriptural support.

- Another major issue is the narrative's focus on human wickedness as the cause of the flood, which seems inconsistent if the central problem was the union between the "sons of God" (angels) and the "daughters of men." **Genesis 6:5** clearly states the cause of the flood: "The Lord saw that the wickedness of man was great in the earth, and that every intention of the thoughts of his heart was only evil continually." This places the blame squarely on humanity, yet the previous verses briefly mention the Nephilim and focus heavily on the actions of the sons of God and their relationships with human women. If fallen angels were truly responsible for corrupting humanity, it raises several questions: Why was man's lifespan limited immediately after these unions were mentioned? And why was the flood punishment directed at mankind and not at the angels themselves? The narrative's emphasis on human wickedness, and the absence of direct judgment on the angels, suggests that the core issue was human moral failure, not angelic interference. While there may have been a known backstory involving angels and Nephilim, the text here emphasizes human responsibility, weakening the argument for the fallen angel theory as the primary cause of the flood.

This shift from the actions of angels to the wickedness of humanity creates a narrative tension. If the union between the sons of God and the daughters of men was the primary reason for divine intervention, it would make sense for the text to emphasize that issue throughout. Instead, it quickly transitions to a condemnation of human hearts and intentions, making it difficult to see the angelic unions as the central cause for the flood. This discrepancy weakens the fallen angel theory as it fails to fully account for why humanity, rather than angels, is punished for the corruption that led to the flood.

The Sethite Theory

This view suggests that the "sons of God" were the descendants of Seth (Adam and Eve's third son), who were considered righteous. The "daughters of men" were from the line of Cain, who had been marked by God for his evil deeds after killing Abel. This theory interprets the marriages as a breakdown in the separation between the godly and ungodly lines of humanity.

Theory Criticism

- One of the central weaknesses of the Sethite theory is that, while the line of Seth is often considered godly due to figures like Enoch and Noah, there is no direct scriptural statement labeling all of Seth's descendants as righteous or all of Cain's as evil. This is important because it weakens the theory's foundation. If the Bible does not clearly distinguish between these groups as inherently good or evil, then the argument that intermarriage between them is the primary cause of divine punishment becomes difficult to sustain. The theory relies heavily on assumptions and lacks direct textual backing.

- The Sethite theory also struggles to explain why unions between the lines of Seth and Cain would provoke God's decision to send the flood. Genesis 6:5 points to widespread human wickedness as the cause, stating that "every intention of the thoughts of his heart was only evil continually." While the theory posits that intermarriage led to moral corruption, the text focuses on humanity's wickedness as a whole rather than a specific union between two family lines. If the spread of sin and wickedness was the primary cause of the flood, the Sethite theory does not clearly demonstrate why these marriages were pivotal in God's decision to wipe out humanity. It leaves a gap in explaining the broader moral and spiritual decay that warranted such a drastic divine response.

The Divine Kingship Theory

In this interpretation, the "sons of God" are not angels or humans from specific lineages but rather powerful rulers or kings who claimed divine status or were viewed as god-like by their subjects. These rulers may have practiced polygamy, taking many wives and oppressing their people. This theory suggests that the phrase "sons of God" refers to their perceived divine authority.

Theory Criticism

- This interpretation emphasizes the sociopolitical aspects of early civilizations, suggesting that powerful rulers or kings claimed divine authority and took wives from among their people. However, this approach seems out of step with the era described in Genesis 6, which portrays a more foundational stage of human development, where the focus is on moral and spiritual corruption rather than the establishment of structured kingdoms or divine kingship. The theory shifts the narrative into a political lens that doesn't align with the biblical text's emphasis on spiritual decay and divine-human interaction.

- The theory downplays or omits the spiritual context implied by the phrase "sons of God." In most other biblical contexts, such as in Job 1:6 and Job 38:7, "sons of God" refers to divine or angelic beings. In the New Testament, the term refers to the divine relationship of mankind with God, as seen in John 1:12, Romans 8:14, and Galatians 3:26. However, in this narrative, the term may suggest a worldly status or elite right rather than a purely spiritual designation. Interpreting the "sons of God" as merely human rulers or kings undermines the broader biblical tradition that associates this term with a higher, spiritual calling, making it inconsistent with the spiritual failure described in the text. The passage in Genesis 6 implies more than just earthly rulers engaging in polygamy—it points to a deeper spiritual failure, where the descendants of Adam chose wives based on lust, disregarding their spiritual responsibilities. This theory fails to fully account for the spiritual aspects implied in the text.

- Forceful unions are unlikely. The suggestion that the phrase "they took as their wives any they chose" implies forceful or non-consensual unions seems to be a stretch. In the biblical text, this phrasing is commonly used to describe marriage arrangements and does not inherently indicate coercion. Instead, it suggests a consensual arrangement or personal choice in the selection process, as seen in other parts of the Bible where similar language is used. This weakens the argument that these unions were forced and driven by oppressive rulers exercising unchecked power.

The Unresolved Mystery: Piecing Together a Plausible Explanation

What I believe all those who have crafted their theories have missed is one crucial piece of information: science. By integrating what we now know about the world during the likely time that Adam and Eve were created, we can bridge the gap between the biblical narrative and historical and scientific evidence, forming a more coherent explanation.

This is similar to how ancient biblical laws surrounding leprosy were initially misunderstood. In Leviticus, we find detailed instructions for identifying leprosy, quarantining the infected, and performing rituals for cleansing. For centuries, these practices were seen purely as religious mandates, difficult to justify. However, with the advent of modern science, we now understand that these laws served a vital public health function—quarantining those with infectious diseases was essential for preventing outbreaks. Ancient wisdom, long misunderstood, becomes clearer when viewed through the lens of scientific understanding.

I fully acknowledge that no one will ever know precisely what transpired during the period from Adam and Eve's creation, which I suggest occurred between 11,500–10,000 BC, to the flood around 6000–5000 BC. This era has sparked countless opinions and debates that may continue indefinitely. However, by piecing together plausible elements, we can begin to form an outline that offers insight into what this time might have looked like and how, in His wisdom, God resolved the challenges humanity faced in the beginning.

Everything changed when Adam and Eve gained the knowledge of good and evil. This awakening to sin led to their expulsion from Eden and into a world filled with harshness and decay. They immediately became aware of their nakedness and sought to cover themselves, marking the beginning of an understanding of morality—particularly sexual morality—and introduced the challenges of navigating relationships outside their former state of innocence, including the issue of incest.

God's response to sin entering the world was swift. Adam and Eve were not given a grace period to adjust to their fallen state, nor would such an extension make sense if it allowed for unchecked sexual immorality. Some might argue that the law forbidding incest was not yet given, but the Bible is clear that the law exposes sin that already exists. In the absence of explicit laws, conscience serves as a guide. As Paul explains in Romans 2:14-15, "when Gentiles, who do not have the law, do by nature things required by the law ... they

show that the requirements of the law are written on their hearts, their con-
sciences also bearing witness." Adam and Eve's immediate recognition of their
nakedness reflects this moral awakening.

In Eden, Adam and Eve lived in a state of innocence where nakedness
was not associated with shame or immorality. Genetic concerns, such as the
risks of close interbreeding, were irrelevant due to their initial genetic perfection. As they began to multiply, concerns about incest would have naturally resolved themselves over a few generations, well before the laws against
incest were established, as seen in Leviticus. Marriages with more distant relatives, such as first cousins (permitted under biblical law), would have contributed to a healthy, diverse population over time.

While Adam and Eve were still commanded to multiply, the complexity of morality—including the implications of incest—emerged fully in the
fallen world. This shift underscores the profound change brought about by
their disobedience and the entrance of sin into creation.

If Adam and Eve were the first and only humans, then their children would
have had to marry each other to fulfill God's command. But now, once they
became aware of good and evil and their nakedness, such a scenario seems
contradictory, given God's later prohibition of incest in Leviticus 18:6-18.
The context for these sexual laws is provided in Leviticus 18:3, which states:
"You shall not do as they do in the land of Egypt, where you lived, and you
shall not do as they do in the land of Canaan, to which I am bringing you.
You shall not walk in their statutes."

Leviticus 18:6 begins a detailed list of prohibitions regarding sexual relations with close family members:

- "None of you shall approach any one of his close relatives to uncover
  nakedness. I am the Lord."

- "You shall not uncover the nakedness of your father, which is the
  nakedness of your mother; she is your mother, you shall not uncover
  her nakedness."

- "You shall not uncover the nakedness of your father's wife; it is your father's nakedness."

- "You shall not uncover the nakedness of your sister, your father's daughter or your mother's daughter, whether brought up in the family or in another home."

In ancient Hebrew, "uncovering nakedness" is a common idiom or euphemism used to describe sexual relations. This phrase conveys the idea of engaging in intimate, sexual acts without directly stating it, reflecting the cultural and linguistic norms of the time for addressing sensitive topics in the biblical text.

These verses clarify that the laws in Leviticus were given to prevent the Israelites from imitating the immoral practices they had witnessed in Egypt or would encounter in Canaan. God was calling them to be different, to uphold a higher standard of holiness.

So how do we reconcile this apparent contradiction if the origins of humanity, starting with Adam and Eve, seem to necessitate the very actions later condemned in Leviticus? If God explicitly prohibits incestuous relationships in Leviticus, why would He allow or even necessitate such relationships at the very beginning of human history when sin entered the world through Adam? This apparent contradiction poses a significant challenge to the traditional interpretation of the Genesis narrative.

A Broader Understanding: What Science Tells Us

Modern archaeological evidence strongly suggests that Homo sapiens evolved over more than 100,000 years, during which time, as I would propose, God fine-tuned the DNA necessary to create Adam and Eve. These early humans were biologically the same as modern man but lacked the spiritual quality that God endowed to His chosen creation. Adam and Eve's unique place in history is that they were the first humans made in God's image, possessing a living soul, as described in Genesis 2:7:

Romanized Hebrew: "Vayyitzer YHWH Elohim et-ha'adam afar min-ha'adamah, vayyipach b'apav nishmat chayyim, vayehi ha'adam lenefesh chayyah"

Word-for-Word English Translation: "And formed YHWH God the man dust from the ground, and breathed into his nostrils breath of life, and became the man a living soul."

When God created Adam and placed him in the Garden of Eden, it becomes clear that His plan likely extended beyond Adam and Eve's immediate descendants. It included the integration of their lineage with the preexisting population of Homo sapiens. Through this intermarriage, Adam and Eve's descendants would pass on the breath of life—existence itself—a soul as an eternal being, and the moral conscience uniquely endowed by God, thus spreading His divine image throughout the earth.

Without this inherent moral law, the world would be forever subjected to a potentially greater population of people with no inner sense of right and wrong, living much as they had for millennia—kill or be killed.

The moral compass inherent in the soul of man would be essential for the establishment of order and civility, as great civilizations cannot thrive without a shared sense of right and wrong. Even though not in direct connection with God, such as His chosen people, mankind would still have this imprinted moral law guiding their decisions and interactions. As Romans 1:19-20 states, "Since what may be known about God is plain to them, because God has made it plain to them ... so that people are without excuse." In this way, God's plan bridged the spiritual gap between His chosen creation and the broader human population.

According to archaeological evidence, by 10,000 BC, the broader world was already populated by Homo sapiens, modern humans. Estimates suggest the global population ranged between one and five million people, with smaller concentrations in regions such as the Near East, where Eden is traditionally located.[49] Even as early as 11,500 BC, a substantial number of Homo sapiens would have already existed.

These humans, though intelligent and capable, played a crucial role in the development of mankind but lacked the direct communication with God and the divine image that Adam and Eve possessed. However, through the intermingling of Adam, Eve, and their descendants with this preexisting population, God facilitated the spread of His divine image and moral law. This plan not only preserved the early human population but also set the stage for salvation through Christ to be made available to all mankind. Furthermore, it prevented the need for incestuous relationships, which are explicitly condemned in Leviticus.

While we can only speculate how all of this might have unfolded if the knowledge of good and evil had not entered the picture, it seems apparent that God had a plan to address the consequences of sin. Rather than allowing Adam and Eve's beginning to be tainted by His abhorrence of sexual immorality, He ensured that their integration with modern humans would allow humanity to continue in full stride, even in a fallen world that came sooner than initially intended.

In this way, God's plan not only preserved the integrity of His moral law but also ensured that humanity could thrive in a world now touched by sin. The blending of genetic material from the pre-Adamites with that of Adam and Eve's descendants fortified the human lineage, making it robust enough to withstand the challenges that would arise as they spread across the earth. Through this process, God's wisdom in preparing for all eventualities becomes evident. Even in the face of sin, His plans are both just and merciful, ensuring the continued flourishing of His creation.

Temperament of Early Mankind (Pre-Adamites)

Adam and Eve came into existence when these early Homo sapiens, still largely dependent on hunting and gathering, exhibited a range of behaviors from cooperation and social bonding within their groups to territoriality and aggression. Archaeological findings, including skeletal remains with signs of trauma and ancient weapons, suggest that interpersonal violence and conflict between groups were not uncommon. While capable of friendly interactions and alliances, these early humans could also be dangerous, living without an inherent moral code and governed instead by the natural law of survival.

Natural Law: The Relationship of Sin and Law

In my decades working in the funeral industry, I've attended thousands of committal services, where the body is placed in its final resting place. One verse that I've heard time and again, and which has always intrigued me for its paradoxical statement, is from 1 Corinthians 15:55-56:

> [55]O death, where is your victory?
> O death, where is your sting?
> [56]The sting of death is sin, and the power of sin is the law.

This verse often comes to mind, especially when reflecting on times I defended you boys for minor infractions of the law, like underage drinking or smoking. While I supported the law, there were moments when I wished for a little leniency—a chance to let a minor offense slide. What this taught me is that sin is intrinsically tied to the presence of the law—the greater the law, the greater the awareness of sin as actions that separate you from civil society. Without law, there is no inherent consequence or "sting" of sin—no separation from civil society, even though the wrongdoing itself may still exist. As Romans 7:8 says, "For apart from the law, sin was dead." The law brings awareness of sin (wrongdoing), but where there is no law defining an action as wrong, the power of sin—its ability to create separation—is diminished.

Just as the laws you broke defined the wrongdoing, so too does the biblical concept of sin depend on the existence of law. Without a law to transgress, the very notion of sin becomes meaningless—everything would be permissible. This is the essence of the biblical teaching: the power of sin lies in the law that defines it. The sting of death (separation) is felt because sin exists, and sin exists because of the laws given to us—or, in the case of being created in God's image, the violation of an inherent sense of right and wrong.

This understanding sheds light on the debate about when death entered the world. Some argue that physical death could not have existed before Adam's sin because sin is what brought death into the world. However, the verse from Corinthians suggests that it was the "sting" of death—the separation from God—that required the existence of law. Before Adam and Eve, there was no divine law for early humans to break, nor did they possess the image of God or a soul imprinted with a sense of right and wrong. They were like Adam and Eve before the fall, created without an understanding of good and evil. Therefore, the concept of the sting of death due to sin, as we understand it, was not applicable to the pre-Adamic world, and they were held to a different standard of acceptance.

Death—the natural cycle of life—was created by God and deemed "good" in the pre-Adamic world as part of His creation. Before the introduction of divine law, there was no sin associated with causing death, as sin cannot be imputed where there is no law. Although this existence was harsh and challenging, it was distinct from the life God intended for those created in His image.

This idea aligns with Romans 5:12-13: "Therefore, just as sin came into the world through one man, and death through sin, and so death spread to all men because all sinned—for sin indeed was in the world before the law was given, but sin is not counted where there is no law." Adam's disobedience introduced the knowledge of sin into the world. While wrongdoing may have existed before Adam, it was not counted as sin because there was no law to define or impute guilt. Only with Adam's awareness of the law did sin bring about its full consequence: separation from God.

Now, before anyone argues that Adam and Eve's early actions, such as incest, could be justified because they were not under the law (later forbidden to their descendants under Mosaic law), let me remind you of another key point from Romans 2:14-15: "For when Gentiles, who do not have the law, by nature do what the law requires, they are a law to themselves, even though they do not have the law. They show that the work of the law is written on their hearts, while their conscience also bears witness, and their conflicting thoughts accuse or even excuse them."

Adam and Eve became immediately aware of their transgressions, including sexual immorality, when they covered themselves after sinning. Their conscience, previously innocent, became a witness to their newfound understanding of right and wrong.

The True Death: Spiritual, Not Physical

When the Bible speaks of death entering the world through sin, many interpret this as physical death. However, this interpretation overlooks the deeper spiritual dimension described in Genesis. In Genesis 2:17, God warns Adam, "for in the day that you eat of it you shall surely die." Yet Adam and Eve did not physically die immediately after their disobedience. Instead, what was lost was their spiritual connection with God—a separation often referred to as spiritual death, which lies at the heart of the biblical narrative.

Paul highlights this in Romans 6:23: "For the wages of sin is death, but the free gift of God is eternal life in Christ Jesus our Lord." Here, the focus is on spiritual death—the ultimate consequence of sin, which is separation from God. While physical death became part of humanity's reality, the more profound and devastating consequence was the broken relationship with the Creator.

Ephesians 2:1-2 underscores this idea, describing humanity as spiritually "dead" in trespasses and sins: "As for you, you were dead in your transgressions and sins, in which you used to live when you followed the ways of this world and of the ruler of the kingdom of the air, the spirit who is now at work in those who are disobedient." This passage illustrates that spiritual death is a state of being cut off from God, even while physically alive. After the fall, this spiritual death became humanity's defining condition, leading to the need for reconciliation through Christ. Redemption, then, is not merely about overcoming physical death but about restoring the spiritual life lost in Eden.

Thus, when Scripture refers to death entering the world through sin, the primary focus is on spiritual death—separation from God. Adam and Eve's continued physical existence after their disobedience underscores this point: they were expelled from the Garden, cut off from direct fellowship with their Creator, and left to navigate a world marked by spiritual estrangement. This spiritual death is the most profound consequence of sin and is central to the redemptive narrative of Scripture.

Cain's Fear and the Pre-Adamite World

When God banished Adam and Eve from Eden, He likely did not place them directly in harm's way—Eden was a set-apart, protected region. Genesis 2:5 states, "When no bush of the field was yet in the land and no small plant of the field had yet sprung up ..." This suggests that Eden, before God cultivated it, was not a region that attracted animals, birds, or even other human populations.

However, after God filled Eden with vegetation and the second creation of creatures mentioned in Genesis 2, Adam and Eve, upon being cast out, would have faced challenges not only from the land itself (not including the animals), but also from the surrounding people—some of whom could be both friendly and dangerous. This context provides a plausible explanation for why Cain feared for his life when he was driven out of Eden to wander the earth after killing his brother Abel. Cain's fear likely stemmed from the lawless pre-Adamite population, as he expressed to God in Genesis 4:13-15:

> *Cain said to the Lord, "My punishment is greater than I can bear. Behold, you have driven me today away from the ground [again, a local region], and from your face I shall be hidden. I shall be a fugitive and a wanderer on the earth, and whoever finds me will kill me." Then the Lord said to him, "Not so! If anyone kills Cain, vengeance shall be taken on him sevenfold." And the Lord put a mark on Cain, lest any who found him should attack him.*

It can't go without saying lightheartedly that I personally would not have found much comfort in that. After all, I'd still be dead, and it probably wouldn't have been a pleasant encounter! But such was Cain's circumstance—he'd just have to accept it, take it or leave it.

Now, some might argue that Cain's fear stemmed from the "other sons and daughters" of Adam and Eve, and that Cain and Abel were nearing one hundred years old when these events occurred, so there could have been others. However, Genesis 5:3-5 provides a clear sequence of time: "When Adam had lived 130 years, he fathered a son in his own likeness, after his image, and named him Seth. The days of Adam after he fathered Seth were 800 years; and he had other sons and daughters. Thus all the days that Adam lived were 930 years, and he died."

This passage clearly indicates that when Seth was born, Adam was 130 years old. With Abel gone, the population of humanity created *in God's image* was reduced to four—Adam, Eve, Cain, and Seth. The verse also specifies that Adam had other sons and daughters only *after* Seth's birth, during the subsequent eight hundred years. To interpret it otherwise is to force a narrative that is not supported by the text, trying to justify who or what could have caused Cain's fear, outside of the discovered existence of early modern man.

The Neolithic Revolution: A New Way of Life

As Adam and Eve began life outside of Eden, they were still relatively young in terms of experience and understanding. They began to cultivate the land and raise livestock—activities that would become foundational to what we now recognize as the Neolithic Revolution. Their efforts likely influenced the pre-Adamite populations they encountered—early Homo sapiens who had not yet developed these advanced agricultural practices.

Moments in history like this should amaze us. Yet, many in the Christian community abandon such events when trying to relate them to the Bible, even though they clearly echo the biblical account of Adam and Eve. God gave Adam and Eve all the seeds they needed to start this revolution in Genesis 1:29: "And God said, 'Behold, I have given you every plant yielding seed that is on the face of all the earth, and every tree with seed in its fruit. You shall have them for food.'"

Christians throw this bit of history down on the ground like a sword of truth and skeptics or those seeking to destroy the Bible's authorship will pick it up and wield it against shaky believers, cutting them down by the thousands. This same intellectual disengagement happens when people try to place Adam and Eve's creation 50,000 to 100,000 years ago, in an attempt to account for Mitochondrial Eve's DNA being present in all human beings today. But to do so, one must grapple with the inconsistency: why would Adam and Eve, who lived less than one thousand years according to the text, delay initiating the agricultural advancements God equipped them to start? Such a timeline creates more questions than it resolves.

It just doesn't make sense when the obvious is staring us in the face: the biblical timeline and historical events like the Neolithic Revolution complement each other. Instead of discarding science, we should embrace it as a tool that enriches our understanding of the Bible's unfolding narrative.

It would have been during this time that Cain and Abel were born. Cain, following his father Adam's example, became a farmer, while Abel became a keeper of livestock. This division of labor reflects the early stages of the changing way of life, not just for them, but for humanity during this new period of significant transition. The tools, social structures, and agricultural practices that Adam and Eve initiated would eventually lead to the rise of civilizations.

Around 10,000 BC, in regions like the Fertile Crescent, people began to domesticate plants such as wheat and barley, and animals such as sheep, goats, and dogs. This led to the development of farming and the establishment of permanent settlements. The agricultural advancements and social structures developed by Adam and passed on to their descendants played a crucial role in this transformative period.

The Bible tells us that Cain eventually found a wife, a question that has puzzled many readers, theologians, and scholars for centuries. The most logical explanation is that, as time went by and Adam and his sons explored the region, they began to encounter an existing civilization—one that God likely informed them about. Although this civilization could be dangerous, historical records suggest that not all were hostile. Cain's wife most likely came from the pre-Adamite population, as did the descendants of Adam's other children, until enough generations had passed that incestuous relationships were no longer an issue. While Adam's descendants had the responsibility to multiply and likely intermarry with this preexisting civilization, they would have also had the opportunity to marry within their now distant relatives. This may have been what Noah and his sons did, especially Seth, to maintain a lineage that would transcend to the coming of Christ.

This theory aligns with both the biblical narrative and the scientific understanding of human origins, avoiding the problematic notion of incest that contradicts God's later laws.

The Corruption of Adam's Lineage: The Path to the Flood

As the story of Adam and Eve unfolds, it becomes clear that God's original plan for humanity centered on a direct, intimate relationship with Him. God chose a specific land within the created world as a sacred place, and in it, He established the Garden of Eden—a sanctuary where heaven and earth intersected. This sacred space was much like the holy places seen throughout the Bible, such as the tabernacle during the Israelites' wandering in the wilderness and the Temple of Solomon in Jerusalem. Adam and Eve, created in His image, walked and spoke with God in this divine setting, enjoying unparalleled communion with their Creator.

Adam, as the first patriarchal figure, was the beginning of a lineage that God would work with closely throughout much of the Old Testament. Adam and Eve were tasked with filling the earth, reflecting His glory, and maintaining their divine relationship. However, after the fall, sin entered the world, and this relationship began to unravel, replaced by the harsh realities of nature and the consequences of human choices.

The timeline from Adam's creation to the flood spans thousands of years.

During this time, Adam's descendants multiplied and began to intermarry with the pre-Adamite population, which archaeological discoveries confirm had existed for centuries. These pre-Adamites, or modern humans (Homo sapiens), though biologically similar to Adam's lineage, lacked the spiritual knowledge and divine image imparted by God. This intermarriage was not merely a biological blending of peoples; it played a pivotal role in spreading God's image and spiritual knowledge throughout the world. However, this integration happened sooner rather than later in human history, leading to a profound spiritual compromise as the divine legacy carried by Adam's lineage encountered the pre-Adamite population.

The pre-Adamites, without the moral law or knowledge of God, were meant to be positively influenced by Adam's descendants. However, it was the descendants of Adam who gradually adopted the customs and ways of earlier mankind, drifting further from the divine path. Evidence of this cultural and spiritual blending can be seen in archaeological sites that reveal early civilizations engaging in religious practices reflecting worship of other gods, animals, or nature.

For example, sites such as Göbekli Tepe in Turkey, on the outskirts of the region of Eden, one of the earliest known religious structures, depict animal worship and show no clear connection to monotheistic practices.[50] Similarly, Çatalhöyük, another ancient site, reflects early religious expression but involves symbolism around animal deities and fertility goddesses, suggesting a shift away from a divine moral law. These findings support the notion that early humans, though developing religious thought, were veering from the spiritual legacy that Adam and Eve were meant to pass on.

Over time, this intermingling caused Adam's descendants to lose their spiritual distinctiveness. As they spread further and mixed with pre-Adamite cultures, their spiritual heritage became increasingly diluted. Rather than intermarrying and populating the land with a new generation born in the image of God—and teaching these populations about Him—they assimilated into the pre-Adamite way of life, which was rooted in survival instincts and primitive spirituality rather than divine law. As a result, the knowledge of God faded, and the distinction between those created in God's image and those who did not know Him became increasingly blurred.

Despite more of humanity being born with the image of God through intermarriage with Adam's lineage, the gradual erosion of faith led to increasing wickedness. Over generations, as time passed and society expanded, God's presence became more of a distant memory. The moral law, intended to be preserved and passed down through Adam's descendants, was corrupted. Humanity, having received the divine image but failing to uphold its spiritual responsibility, fell deeper into sin. This culminated in the wickedness described in Genesis 6:5: "The Lord saw that the wickedness of man was great in the earth, and that every intention of the thoughts of his heart was only evil continually."

A Second Look at Genesis 6:1-8

Now, with this narrative in mind, let's walk back through the account in Genesis 6:1-8 to explore what these Scriptures are actually saying.

Section 1

> When **man** began to multiply on the face of the land and daughters were born to them, **the sons of God** saw that the **daughters of man** were attractive. And they took as their wives any they chose. (Genesis 6:1-2)

The term "man" here seems to encompass all of humanity, both the descendants of Adam and the pre-Adamic population. The phrase "daughters of man" likely refers predominantly to the daughters of these pre-Adamite populations, whose numbers by this point in history would have far exceeded those of Adam's direct descendants. The mention of their attractiveness suggests the motive behind these relationships. Adam's descendants "chose" as they desired, basing these marriages on lust for beautiful women rather than seeking women of good character.

The real point of debate in these verses centers around the identity of the "sons of God," a phrase that has sparked much argument. However, when we consider the broader narrative, the most logical interpretation is that the "sons of God" refers to Adam's lineage—the righteous descendants entrusted with upholding God's will. They were placed within the land of Eden, a sacred sanctuary within the broader untamed world. The Bible's primary focus is on the history of humanity, not angels. While angels are present in Scripture, their role is more peripheral; they are rarely, if ever, the driving force behind major historical events involving mankind.

To interpret "sons of God" here as angels would elevate them to the primary agents behind one of the most catastrophic events in human history. This interpretation would shift the narrative to the origins of the Nephilim, placing the responsibility for mankind's corruption on angelic beings. Such a reading moves the focus away from humanity's own moral failings and is inconsistent with the Bible's overarching theme, which centers on mankind's moral and spiritual struggles rather than external, supernatural forces being the root cause of corruption.

The phrase "sons of God" appears in the Bible multiple times, both in the Old and New Testaments. The exact number of occurrences depends on the translation, but here are the key instances:

Old Testament. The phrase is usually translated from the Hebrew "bᵊnê hāʾĕlōhîm," meaning "sons of God" or "sons of the gods." It occurs primarily in the following passages:

- **Genesis 6:2, 4**—The "sons of God" take the "daughters of men" as wives, which appears to have been a consensual arrangement. This likely refers to the righteous men (descendants of Adam) marrying women from the broader population (pre-Adamites), potentially leading to a spiritual and moral decline.

- **Job 1:6**—The "sons of God" present themselves before the Lord, and

Satan is among them. This scene can be understood as a meeting on earth, not in heaven. It likely involved the descendants of Seth, the religious leadership of God's chosen people at that time. Since this occurs around 2000 BC, before the establishment of the Israelite nation, God still maintained a hands-on approach with humanity. Both God and Satan are depicted as working on earth—God is interacting with mankind, and Satan is described as "going to and fro on the earth, and walking up and down on it." This suggests that this divine assembly took place on earth, where Job, the leadership of mankind, and Satan were present, rather than in a heavenly realm.

- **Job 2:1**—A similar scene as in Job 1:6, where the "sons of God" gather again before the Lord, and Satan appears once more. This is the second meeting during Job's trials, and again, the context suggests that it occurred on earth. Satan, after wandering the earth, returns to continue his attack on Job. Neither of these passages suggests a heavenly setting, but rather a continuation of God's hands-on interaction with humanity on earth during this time.

- **Job 38:7**—Refers to the "sons of God" shouting for joy when God laid the foundations of the earth. Here, the "sons of God" are clearly angels, as God speaks to Job from the whirlwind, recalling the creation when the angels celebrated His work. But again, this is a conversation here on earth, where God is actively working with mankind, as He speaks to Job directly about creation and His interactions with both the physical and spiritual realms.

- **Deuteronomy 32:8** (in some translations and manuscripts like the Dead Sea Scrolls)—Refers to God dividing the nations according to the number of the "sons of God" (though some translations use "sons of Israel"). This passage likely refers to righteous men, descendants of Noah, who were assigned to lead the divided nations, by name, as outlined in Genesis 10. This is a division of mankind into seventy nations, with a descendant of Seth assigned to each one. It is unlikely that there would have been an additional seventy angels assigned to the leadership of mankind. Throughout the Bible, angels are depicted as messengers, not leaders. The reference to "sons of God" here fits within the broader biblical narrative of God's interaction with human leadership, consistent with His hands-on approach during this time in history.

New Testament. In the New Testament, the phrase "sons of God" is usually translated from the Greek *huioi theou* and is often used to refer to humans who are followers of God or believers in Christ. Key examples include:

- **Matthew 5:9**—*"Blessed are the peacemakers, for they shall be called sons of God."* This suggests that the "sons of God" are those who promote peace and righteousness, aligning themselves with God's will and purpose for human relationships and societal harmony.

- **Luke 20:36**—*"For they cannot die anymore, because they are equal to angels and are sons of God, being sons of the resurrection."* This verse refers to those who, having been found worthy of resurrection, are granted eternal life and are called "sons of God." It highlights the future state of the righteous in the resurrection, sharing in divine favor and immortality.

- **Romans 8:14**—*"For all who are led by the Spirit of God are sons of God."* This emphasizes that anyone who lives by the guidance of the Holy Spirit is considered a "son of God," reflecting a relationship with God based on spiritual direction and faithfulness.

- **Romans 8:19**—*"For the creation waits with eager longing for the revealing of the sons of God."* This speaks to the idea that creation itself anticipates the ultimate revelation and glorification of those who are the true followers of God—those who live as His sons and daughters. It emphasizes the purpose of creation being fulfilled: God placing souls on earth in human form, and those who, by choice, follow God and His ways, reflecting His image as a son or child of God. Through the redemption and transformation of the faithful, creation's purpose is ultimately realized, as God's image is made manifest in those who choose to walk in His light.

- **Galatians 3:26**— *"For in Christ Jesus you are all sons of God, through faith."* This indicates that through faith in Jesus Christ, believers are adopted into God's family as His children. This verse underlines the idea that faith in Christ, rather than ethnic or legal adherence, is what defines someone as a "son of God."

Sons of God as Righteous Men—Humanity's Greatest Failure. The phrase "sons of God" in Genesis 6 refers not to angels, but to men who were called to be righteous—individuals created in God's image and entrusted with moral stewardship over the earth. These men were not merely ordinary humans; they were a special creation, living souls distinct from the moral condition of early man before them. Their role was to bear righteousness, acting as spiritual leaders set apart to guide and transform humanity in alignment with God's will, serving as beacons of moral integrity in a world teetering on the edge of spiritual darkness.

However, they utterly failed. The text says, "They took as their wives any they chose." This phrase marks a significant breakdown in discernment and judgment—decisions they willingly made based on lust, resulting in a departure from their divine purpose. By choosing partners with this shallow foundation, these righteous men aligned themselves with worldly desires and disregarded their divine responsibility. Instead of forming relationships that could have fulfilled their goal—potentially with members of the pre-Adamite population who may have been more adaptable to their spiritual mission—they allowed themselves to be led astray by the desires of the flesh, choosing women who introduced spiritual corruption. Their failure was not just personal but systemic—by abandoning their duty to uphold righteousness, they enabled the moral decay of all mankind.

Throughout the Bible, God holds all of humanity to a high standard, especially leaders, the "sons of God." Adam and the generations up to Noah were elevated to positions of moral responsibility, tasked with guiding their generation, which included all mankind, toward righteousness. Their lives were marked by direct interaction with God, and with that privilege came the burden of greater accountability. This is clearly expressed in Psalm 82:1-4:

> *God has taken his place in the divine council; in the midst of the gods he holds judgment: "How long will you judge unjustly and show partiality to the wicked? Selah. Give justice to the weak and the fatherless; maintain the right of the afflicted and the destitute. Rescue the weak and the needy; deliver them from the hand of the wicked."*

In this passage, God rebukes the rulers (called "gods" here in the sense of earthly authorities) for their failure to protect the weak, the needy, and the fatherless. He calls them to correct their ways and to administer justice to those who cannot defend themselves. This expectation of leadership and righteousness would have been the same from creation to the flood.

Many scholars, though not all, believe this "divine council," also translated as "the congregation of the mighty" (KJV) or "the great assembly" (NIV), refers to a heavenly court, where God presides over spiritual beings. However, when we turn to John 10:34-36, where Jesus is accused of blasphemy, we see Him refer to this very Scripture, making it clear that "gods" in this context refers to human rulers. Jesus responds to the accusations of blasphemy by quoting Psalm 82, saying, "Is it not written in your Law, 'I said, you are gods'?" He continues, "If he called them gods to whom the word of God came—and Scripture cannot be broken—do you say of him whom the Father consecrated and sent into the world, 'You are blaspheming,' because I said, 'I am the Son of God'?"

Here, Jesus is clearly using Psalm 82 to refer to human leaders—those who were entrusted with authority and responsibility under God's rule. These "gods" are not angelic beings or part of a heavenly court; they are mortal men given divine responsibility to lead justly. When Jesus says, "to whom the word of God came," He is referring to the human leaders in Psalm 82 who received God's law and authority. Jesus then makes a connection to His own role as the Word of God, sent to these same human leaders. In other words, He's saying that if those leaders, who were mere mortals, were called "gods" because they received God's word, then it's not blasphemy for Him—God's living Word—to call Himself the Son of God. Jesus is emphasizing that these men, though referred to as "gods" because of their role as representatives of divine justice, are still human and accountable to God, just as He is divinely sent to fulfill the law they were given.

This supports the interpretation that in Psalm 82, the "divine council" refers to an earthly assembly of human leaders who were judged for failing to fulfill their God-given duties. Jesus's use of this passage in John confirms that the "gods" referred to here are men, illustrating God's direct involvement with humanity, placing men in positions of authority and holding them accountable when they failed to uphold His standards.

Just one more thing to note: God is standing in the midst of the "gods" in Psalm 82. Let's include the Hebrew text so we don't have to contend with interpretive opinion:

Psalm 82:1

Elohim (**God**) nitzav (**stands**) ba'adat-El (**in the assembly of God**);
bekerev elohim (**in the midst of the gods**) yishpot (**He judges**).

First, the verse clearly says that God is **in the midst** or present among the "gods" and strongly implies that God is physically or spiritually present among them, actively holding them accountable for their actions. This contrasts with the image of God reigning from a distant heavenly throne, emphasizing instead His direct engagement with these rulers of humanity.

Standing in the midst of the gods implies that God is not removed from their presence but is intervening directly, indicating judgment and involvement in earthly matters. The setting of this "divine council" or "assembly of gods" takes place where the rulers (or "gods") are, further reinforcing the idea that this is likely an earthly assembly where God has come to judge their failure to administer justice.

In addition, in Scripture, when God is depicted in heaven, He is most commonly described as sitting on His throne. This imagery emphasizes God's sovereignty, authority, and kingship. However, there are a few instances where God is depicted as standing, but these tend to be connected to moments of judgment, action, or intercession.

God Sitting on His Throne (Common Depiction)

- **Isaiah 6:1**—Vision of God's Glory

  "In the year that King Uzziah died I saw the Lord **sitting** upon a throne, high and lifted up; and the train of his robe filled the temple."

- **Revelation 4:2**—John's Vision of Heaven

  "At once I was in the Spirit, and behold, a throne stood in heaven, with one **seated** on the throne."

- **Psalm 47:8**—God's Sovereign Rule

  "God reigns over the nations; God **sits** on his holy throne."

These passages emphasize God's reign, power, and the idea that **He is seated in His heavenly court**, ruling with authority.

God Standing (Often Related to Action or Judgment on Earth)

- **Psalm 82:1** (CSB)—Judgment

  *"God **stands** in the divine assembly; he pronounces judgment among the gods."*

Here, "**God stands**" in judgment over the "gods" or rulers, indicating His active role in bringing justice when speaking with those in authority over mankind on earth.

- **Amos 9:1**—Judgment Against Israel

  *"I saw the Lord **standing** beside the altar, and he said: 'Strike the capitals until the thresholds shake, and shatter them on the heads of all the people.'"*

  In this passage, God is **standing** beside the altar as a sign of impending judgment on Israel. In this vision, He is here on earth.

The sons of God in Genesis 6 were similarly chosen. They had the divine responsibility to stand as moral pillars, but when they failed, it wasn't just a personal shortcoming—it was the failure of the very ones who were meant to uphold God's will on earth. The consequences of their failure were far-reaching. Their compromise led to a greater spiritual collapse, causing the darkness of sin to envelop all of humanity in the land.

The gravity of their failure explains why the full weight of God's wrath fell upon mankind. This was not about angels; it was wholly about the failure of human leadership. These sons of God, created in God's image, endowed with His spirit, were meant to be the stewards of humanity. They were supposed to guide the world out of darkness and into the light of God's righteousness. Instead, they betrayed their calling, and the moral corruption spread unchecked.

Section 2

Then the Lord said, "My Spirit shall not abide in man forever, for he is flesh: his days shall be 120 years." The Nephilim were on the earth in those days, and also afterward, when the sons of God came in to the daughters of man and they bore children to them. These were the mighty men who were of old, the men of renown. (Genesis 6:3-4)

Immediately following the root cause of the corruption leading to the flood, God's decision to limit man's lifespan to 120 years in Genesis 6:3 reflects His recognition that humanity, now deeply corrupted, could no longer sustain itself spiritually. "My Spirit" refers to God's breath of life, the very soul imparted to humanity. By declaring that His Spirit would not abide in man forever, God acknowledged the finiteness of human life, recognizing that extended lifespans had become periods of prolonged wickedness rather than opportunities for spiritual growth. Despite His great patience—allowing thousands of years for humanity to course-correct—the moral decline continued, driven by Adam's descendants lusting after beauty in pre-Adamite women and forgetting their divine origins. God's drastic intervention was not impulsive; it came after an extended period of waiting. Yet, with only one man, Noah, remaining faithful, God acted before a complete moral collapse could occur, preserving humanity's spiritual destiny and His ultimate plan for redemption.

This brings us to one of the Bible's greatest mysteries—the Nephilim. Growing up, I seldom heard much about them, and even today, many people are unfamiliar with this subject. It's one of those areas in the Bible that is often avoided due to its complexity, yet it likely played a role in the decay of moral values and may have contributed to the cause of the flood. Therefore, I will offer some insight—not only because it's important but also because it's intriguing.

What does the passage actually say about the Nephilim? The text states that the Nephilim were on the earth "in those days" and also afterward. This has often been interpreted to mean both before and after the flood. The passage also mentions the sons of God taking daughters of men as wives and having children with them. This has led many to believe that the Nephilim were the offspring of these marriages, becoming "mighty men" and "men of renown."[51]

However, after closely examining what Genesis 6:1-2 says, it becomes clear that the passage isn't suggesting that the Nephilim were the offspring of anyone. It simply mentions that the Nephilim were on the earth in those days, known for their strength, valor, or perhaps their notorious deeds—coinciding with the time "when the sons of God (mankind) came in to the daughters of man (womankind), and they bore children to them (humankind)."

The idea that the Nephilim were the offspring of angels and humans is a later interpretation, primarily derived from non-canonical sources like the Book of Enoch. Enoch 6-7 describes how certain angels (called Watchers) descended to earth, took human wives, and produced giant offspring. This is where the notion of angelic-human hybrid Nephilim originated. However, the Book of Enoch is not part of the canonical Bible, and this theory is not directly supported by the biblical text. Genesis 6 only briefly mentions the Nephilim, with another brief reference in Numbers 13:33, as part of the fearsome giants in Canaan, but their origins are not elaborated upon there either. One could suggest that the ancient audience was already familiar with the backstory, which may explain why it was not further detailed in the biblical text.

Although there is no clear fossil record proving the existence of giants, the Bible does offer an account of giants, such as Goliath, whom David famously defeated. According to 1 Samuel 17:4, Goliath's height was "six cubits and a span," which translates to roughly nine feet, nine inches tall. While this height is impressive, it is not the outlandish twenty to one hundred feet that some legends suggest. Such exaggerated claims belong to the realm of myth, not fact.

Throughout history, there have been occasional reports of fossilized remains of giants or extremely large humanoid skeletons, but these have either been debunked as hoaxes or identified as misidentified remains of large animals, such as mammoths. The scientific community has yet to find credible, peer-reviewed evidence supporting the existence of such giants.

That being said, I believe giants did exist in biblical times. The Bible indicates that the extinction of giants, often referred to as the Nephilim or Anakim, occurred primarily during the conquest of Canaan by the Israelites. Various passages mention giants in the land and their eventual defeat. By the time of David's reign, the giants had mostly been eradicated, with only a few isolated individuals or families remaining.

It seems plausible that the Nephilim played a role in the moral decay that led to the flood. If they were fierce warriors without any moral law, they would have contributed significantly to the problem of unchecked violence and corruption.

Section 3

The Lord saw that the wickedness of man was great in the earth, and that every intention of the thoughts of his heart was only evil continually. And the Lord regretted that he had made man on the earth, and it grieved him to his heart. (Genesis 6:5)

Genesis 6:5 makes it clear that humanity—not angels—bore the blame for the escalating wickedness. The failure of the sons of God to maintain their righteous leadership led to the complete moral degradation of the human race.

God's disappointment and judgment were not arbitrary. He wasn't punishing humanity for failing to meet impossible standards; He was holding them accountable for squandering the gift of moral leadership He had entrusted to them. It was a betrayal that harmed and disadvantaged all of humanity for the sake of personal indulgence. The sons of God were meant to be protectors of righteousness, but by turning away from their calling, they allowed spiritual corruption to engulf the earth.

God had always taken a hands-on approach with mankind. He didn't abandon humanity after placing them on earth; rather, He walked with Adam in the garden, made promises to Noah, and established covenants with Abraham. Throughout, God actively guided and instructed His people. But the failure of the sons of God in Genesis 6 represented a catastrophic breach in this relationship. Those who were supposed to be God's hands and feet on earth—the ones tasked with ensuring that humanity stayed aligned with His will—utterly failed.

This narrative offers a powerful explanation for centuries of confusion regarding why God's verdict fell so heavily on mankind in Genesis 6. It wasn't about angels leading humanity astray—it was the failure of human beings to live up to the divine image in which they were created. The flood was not just an act of punishment; it was a necessary reset—a cleansing of a world that had lost its moral compass due to the failure of those who were meant to reflect God's image and lead humanity in righteousness.

Beyond a Coloring Book Page in Sunday School

The story of the flood is more than just a pivotal moment in human history—it's a sobering reflection on the human spirit and its connection to the divine. When God, in His righteous judgment, decided to cleanse the earth and begin anew, it was not a story of destruction but one of resilience, renewal, and His unwavering commitment to humanity's purpose.

This narrative resonates deeply with us because it reflects the divine spirit within humanity—the refusal to give up, the determination to strive when the stakes are highest, and the belief that some causes are too important to abandon. God's judgment during the flood underscores His holiness, but His preservation of Noah reveals His steadfast faith in His creation. Just as God would not forsake His purpose for humanity, we see within ourselves that same spark of divine tenacity—a determination to persevere for righteousness against all odds.

Throughout history, this spirit of resilience has driven humanity to overcome even the most overwhelming challenges. It's what compels us to reach beyond what seems possible, fueled by a divine hope within us. Consider the soldiers who stormed the beaches of Normandy, charging into a literal hell and unimaginable adversity for the sake of freedom and the future. Their courage wasn't just an act of human will; it was a reflection of God's spirit in us—the light that refuses to yield when the cause is righteous.

As St. Francis of Assisi said, "All the darkness in the world cannot extinguish the light of a single candle."[52] Noah, though just one man surrounded by a world of corruption, was that candle. His faith illuminated a path forward for humanity, proving that even in the darkest times, a single spark of trust in

God can ignite a new beginning. Noah's obedience to God's call ensured that hope and renewal were not extinguished but preserved for future generations.

Today, the ripple effects of Noah's faithfulness continue to shape the world. In God's wisdom, the flood was not the end but a necessary reset to purify creation and pave the way for the ultimate redemption through Christ. Over twenty-five percent of the world today follows Christ, and countless others are influenced by biblical principles.[53] This legacy of faithfulness and renewal transcends time, reminding us that God's purposes endure.

We are children of God, created in His image with His spirit within us. This divine essence fuels our deepest convictions, our courage to face adversity, and our hope for a better future. Whether in monumental acts of bravery or quiet moments of trust, God's spirit shines in us, lighting the way forward, just as Noah's faith did thousands of years ago.

The story of the flood is not merely a biblical tale; it's a mirror that reveals the enduring strength of the human heart when aligned with God's purpose. It shows us that no matter how dark the world may seem, the light of faith can pierce through, ensuring that the cause is never lost, and the future is always worth saving.

CHAPTER 6

Intelligent Design

From the beginning of human inquiry, we've sought to understand the world around us. Science, as a tool of discovery, has revealed astonishing details about the universe—its physical laws, biological processes, and, with the help of the Hubble telescope, has even allowed us to look back to the very moment when time began. Through this process, we've learned how things work, from the mechanics of planets to the microscopic intricacies of cells—DNA, in particular, stands out as a stunning testament to complexity beyond brilliance.[54] Yet, as we peer deeper into the intricate details of this design, we are confronted with a thought-provoking question: *Are these natural laws and complexities the product of chance, or do they point to evidence of purposeful design?*

Naturalism suggests that everything in the universe, including life itself, arose purely from natural causes—undirected processes that brought all time, space, and matter into existence in a single split second, followed by the gradual development of biological life.[55] According to this view, the universe's existence and the emergence of complex life-forms are accidents, the result of blind forces acting over vast stretches of time. Those who hold this belief have argued their case effectively, and no doubt have shaken the foundations of faith in a creator. Evolution is a household term and permeates schools across the globe—the leaders in this theory are capable and well-regarded thinkers.

Unfortunately, they were the first to embrace non-biblical understandings, which threatened century-long biblical teachings, but they did so with a better grasp of emerging knowledge. For example, the Big Bang theory has arguably been one of the most challenging concepts for traditional interpretations of the Bible. It has become a deep line in the sand, argued adamantly from both sides. Ironically, I've always thought that it made the most sense, even though it was outside traditional teaching. *How else would you create a universe?* That question always ran through my mind. It seemed like the perfect way to do it. Now we know, it's likely the only way to do it. Everything that will ever exist in the universe is already in the universe, and that won't ever change.[56] This is based on the law of conservation of mass—the first law of thermodynamics.

The universe is made up of space, time, and matter. Einstein's theory of relativity demonstrated why a Big Bang was necessary.[57] The theory essentially states that space, time, and matter are interdependent—they cannot exist without one another. They must come into existence simultaneously. If you don't have space, where would you put matter? If you don't have matter, what would fill the space? And if you don't have time, when would it exist? All of these components had to emerge at the same instant—within a tiny fraction of a second—which aligns with the concept of the Big Bang. And if the universe required a Big Bang, who caused it?

With only a Bible in hand, one may feel ill-equipped to counter such arguments, as the Bible is not a science textbook. Often, the best strategy is to engage them on their own terms, using science to respond to their scientific claims. Quoting Scripture to those who do not accept it as authoritative is unlikely to sway them; they base their argument on science, and science is your strongest defense.

To challenge the plausibility of nature as an unguided force, it's only fitting to examine nature itself. The more we learn about the universe, the more we find evidence that challenges the perspective of pure chance. An alternative explanation emerges: certain aspects of the universe are so finely tuned and intricately complex that they point toward design rather than random, undirected processes.

This is the foundation of intelligent design. At its core, intelligent design argues that the precise conditions required for life and the complexity found in biological systems point to a purposeful Creator, rather than random events. This chapter will explore these ideas further, beginning with the concept of "fine-tuning"—the observation that the universe's physical constants are calibrated with astonishing precision, suggesting an underlying intelligence guiding these processes.

Throughout history, some of the greatest scientific minds, from Isaac Newton to Albert Einstein, have acknowledged the possibility of a grand design behind the workings of the universe. Newton marveled at the order and precision of the cosmos, seeing in its laws the hand of a Creator. Einstein, though not religious in a traditional sense, once remarked, "The most incomprehensible thing about the universe is that it is comprehensible," implying that the universe operates on rational, predictable laws that suggest a deeper reason behind its existence.

Compounding Improbabilities: The Odds of Design

One of the most compelling aspects of the argument for intelligent design is the increasing improbability of multiple complex systems evolving purely by chance. Each individual system—whether it's the bacterial flagellum, the human eye, or DNA replication—can be subject to scrutiny and counterarguments by evolutionary biologists. However, when we consider the odds of all these systems arising independently and successfully through undirected processes, the improbability compounds exponentially.

Imagine trying to draw the ace of spades from a deck of 52 cards. The chances of success are 1 in 52. Now, imagine drawing the ace of diamonds immediately afterward; the odds of doing this are 1 in 52 multiplied by 1 in

51, which is 1 in 2,652. Each subsequent card drawn in perfect sequence continues to compound the odds—1 in 50 multiplied by 1 in 2,652, which is 1 in 132,600, then 1 in 49, and so on—until the odds of drawing all 52 cards in the correct order becomes astronomically improbable.

In fact, the odds of drawing all 52 cards in the correct order from a shuffled deck are 1 in 80,658,175,170,943,878,571,660,636,856,403,766,975, 289,505,440,883,277,824,000,000,000. This mind-boggling number (over eighty unvigintillion) demonstrates just how unlikely such an event would be.

Now, imagine that there are only fifty-two complex biological systems that must exist and work together for life to function—each one akin to drawing a card from the deck. The odds of these systems all evolving by random chance would be as improbable as drawing all fifty-two cards in perfect sequence. The improbability doesn't remain static; it compounds with each new system, making the odds of them all evolving together by chance astronomically small.[58] This leads us to a crucial question: Is it more reasonable to believe that all of these systems evolved through undirected processes, or does the sheer improbability point to the existence of a designer who intentionally set them in place?

In the following sections, we will explore the compelling evidence that supports the idea of a universe designed with purpose. From the fine-tuning of cosmic constants to the intricate complexity of biological systems, the evidence suggests more than mere chance. It points to intelligence.

The Fine-Tuning of the Universe

The universe is an extraordinary place, filled with countless wonders that stretch beyond the limits of human comprehension. However, what stands out most in the cosmic story is not just the grandeur of the stars or the intricacy of galaxies, but the precision with which the universe itself operates. This precision, often referred to as "fine-tuning," points to something more than random chance. It suggests that the universe was set up in such a way that even slight deviations in its physical laws would have rendered life—and even the universe itself—impossible.

Scientists have identified several physical constants that govern the structure and behavior of the cosmos.[59] Among these are the force of gravity, the electromagnetic force, the strong and weak nuclear forces, and the cosmological constant that governs the rate at which the universe is expanding. If any one of these constants were even slightly different, life as we know it could not exist. The odds of these constants aligning perfectly by chance are staggeringly low, leading many to argue that the universe is not a cosmic accident, but the product of an intelligent designer.

Take, for example, the precision of gravitational pull. Gravity not only keeps objects on Earth from floating away into space but also plays a crucial role in maintaining the balance of gases in our atmosphere. One of the most essential gases we need for life is oxygen, while ammonia, which can be harmful in large amounts, does not accumulate in the air we breathe. Although ammonia is lighter than oxygen, it is broken down through natural processes, while oxygen remains abundant, thanks to the precise balance that gravity helps maintain. Gravity's fine-tuning is so extraordinary that even a tiny deviation—measured to 1 part in 10^{40}—could disrupt the balance of life-sustaining conditions on Earth.[60] This precision ensures that our planet retains the critical gases needed for life, allowing the complex systems of our atmosphere to function harmoniously.

Grains of Sand on Earth

Imagine every grain of sand on every beach and desert across the entire planet. Estimates suggest there are about 7.5×10^{18} grains of sand on Earth. Now, that's already a mind-boggling amount. But to grasp the level of precision required for life to exist, consider this: if the force of gravity were altered by even 1 part in 10^{40}, life as we know it would be impossible. To put that into perspective, if you multiplied the number of grains of sand on Earth by itself multiple times, you would still fall short of approaching 10^{40}. The odds of such fine-tuning occurring by chance are so incredibly small that it's hard to imagine a universe without intelligent design behind its creation.

Gravity, as described by Einstein's theory of general relativity, is the result of the bending or warping of the fabric of space and time (spacetime) by matter. This can be visualized like a trampoline. If you place a bowling ball in the center of the trampoline, the weight of the ball bends the fabric, creating a dip. Now, if you place a marble on the edge of the trampoline, it will naturally roll toward the center due to the curvature created by the bowling ball. This is how gravity works: matter bends spacetime, and other objects follow the curves in that fabric, creating what we perceive as gravitational attraction.

On the atomic level, things work a bit differently, revealing the complexity of forces that hold matter together. While gravity operates on a large scale to hold the atom on Earth, the electromagnetic force is the dominant force within atoms. In an atom, the nucleus is made up of protons and neutrons. The protons within the nucleus carry a positive charge, which attracts negatively charged electrons that orbit the nucleus much like a tiny solar system.

Here's where it gets fascinating: the electrons move around the nucleus in specific quantum orbits, or energy levels. The balance between the electromagnetic attraction of the nucleus and the momentum of the electrons keeps them in stable orbits. If the electron had too little energy, it would spiral into the nucleus, collapsing the atom. If it had too much energy, it would escape, and the atom would break apart. The balance is so precise that the electron remains in a stable orbit, neither collapsing into the nucleus nor flying away. It's like giving the marble just enough force to roll around the edge of the trampoline without falling toward the bowling ball, but not so much force that it flies off the trampoline.

This compound relationship between gravity and the electromagnetic force highlights the complexity and fine-tuning that underpins all matter. While gravity governs the marble made up of atoms, the electromagnetic force governs the atoms that make up the marble, all working together so that you have a marble to play with. Together, these forces create a harmonious system that sustains life and maintains the delicate balance required for a stable universe.

The Wisdom of the Heavens: Ancient Insight and Modern Discovery

There are times when the wisdom of the Bible speaks to the genius of the universe, and also to the mystery of how people who wrote it thousands of years ago could have known truths that modern science is only now beginning to understand. Jeremiah 10:12 says, "It is he who made the earth by his power, who established the world by his wisdom, and by his understanding stretched out the heavens." The phrase "stretched out the heavens" is seen by some as an ancient reference to the expanding universe—a concept confirmed by modern astrophysics. The universe has been expanding for 13.8 billion years, since the Big Bang, at an astounding rate of 43,500 miles per second. The importance of this expansion lies in how it allows for the formation of galaxies, stars, and planets, creating the necessary conditions for life and shaping the very structure of the cosmos.

The precision of the Big Bang is a wonder. In one moment of rapid expansion—an event some describe as explosive—all matter and energy came into existence, and the rate of this expansion had to be incredibly fine-tuned. If the expansion had been even slightly greater, the universe would have expanded too quickly, causing gases to spread out and preventing the formation of stars, planets, and galaxies. On the other hand, if the expansion had been just a little slower, gravity would have pulled everything back together, causing the universe to lose its momentum and collapse in on itself. This delicate balance allowed the universe to expand at exactly the right rate, creating the conditions necessary for the cosmos as we know it to form. Such extraordinary precision points to a deeper order or design behind the universe's creation.

We Are Truly Alone in the Universe

The more we explore the cosmos, the more we realize just how special and rare Earth's location is. Even within 10 million light-years of observation, no planet has been found that replicates the precise conditions required for life as Earth does. The combination of factors that make Earth habitable is extraordinarily unique—our perfect distance from the sun, our stable star, our protective magnetic field, and our abundance of liquid water. Together, these factors create a delicate balance that sustains life. When we consider just how vast the universe is and how remote we are from other potentially habitable worlds, it becomes clear that Earth may truly be one of a kind.

From this perspective, the idea that we are alone in the universe becomes more plausible. Even if intelligent life exists elsewhere, it would have to be incredibly far away. The distances in space are mind-boggling—even within the ten million light-years we can observe clearly, no planet has shown signs of being suitable for life. Earth's position in the Goldilocks Zone, where conditions are just right, is so rare that it sets us apart from anything else we've observed in the universe.

Now, consider the possibility of alien life visiting Earth. If intelligent beings existed beyond this ten million light-year range, and they somehow had the technology to travel at the speed of light (the fastest speed possible), it would still take them ten million years just to reach us. By that time, Earth—and possibly even humanity—would have changed beyond recognition. The idea that an alien civilization could visit us is not only unlikely but almost impossible given the distances involved.

Even for planets much closer, the challenges of interstellar travel are immense. The energy required to cross such vast distances would be incomprehensible. The universe is expanding, and the farther out we look, the more remote and unreachable other galaxies become. The sheer remoteness of our solar system, nestled in the Milky Way, makes Earth feel like a tiny, isolated island in a vast cosmic ocean.

Given what we know today, the odds of alien life reaching Earth are astronomically low. While science fiction often entertains the idea of extraterrestrial visitors, the reality of our location in the universe suggests otherwise. Earth's uniqueness and isolation, combined with the immense distances separating us from even the nearest galaxies, reinforce the notion that we may be truly alone, at least in the sense of any direct contact with other life-forms.

Recently, UFO sightings have become more prevalent, and with almost everyone carrying cellphones equipped with video cameras, unexplained objects moving through the sky have been recorded more frequently. While over ninety percent of these sightings have been explained as natural phenomena or man-made objects, a small number continue to elude clear explanation. There have even been reports of unidentified objects hitting the ground, leaving evidence of impact but no trace of what caused it. However, this still doesn't lead me to believe that a life-form from another part of the galaxy has discovered Earth. Instead, it reminds me of something a funeral director I worked with often said when closing a casket for the last time: "Never to be seen again ... by *human* eyes, that is." Then he would give you a sneaky smile out the corner of his eye. Take that for what you will when considering the unexplained in the sky.

All in all, in the grand expanse of space, Earth stands out as a remarkably rare and isolated gem, and the idea of space aliens visiting our remote corner of the universe remains not just improbable, but an incredible long shot against the backdrop of cosmic distances.

The Case for Intelligent Design

These examples—and many others—reveal a universe that appears to be perfectly suited for life. The precise calibration of physical constants raises an important question: is this the result of blind chance, or is it evidence of an intelligent designer who fine-tuned the universe for a purpose?

The fine-tuning argument doesn't claim to have all the answers about how the universe works, but it challenges the notion that such an ideal arrangement could have arisen by chance from nothing. It brings to light two very different beliefs: Do you believe that something (all of creation) came from nothing with no Creator (nothing)—naturalism? Or did something come from nothing, but from something greater—a designer or Creator? Those are the two choices. For me, the sheer improbability of everything aligning so perfectly—whether in the forces that govern matter, the expansion of the universe, or the conditions that make life on Earth possible—suggests that more is at work than random, undirected processes. Behind the elegance and precision of the universe lies the compelling possibility of a mind—a designer—who set these conditions in place with purpose and intentionality, allowing for the wonder and complexity of life to unfold.

Irreducible Complexity: A Case for Design

Biological systems are marvels of intricate design, displaying a level of complexity that is both astonishing and difficult to explain through purely natural processes. One concept that has emerged in discussions about design in biology is irreducible complexity, which suggests that certain biological structures are so interdependent that they could not have arisen through gradual, step-by-step evolutionary processes. Instead, these systems seem to require all of their parts to be present and function simultaneously, much like a well-engineered machine. This section will explore examples of irreducible complexity and how they point to the possibility of intelligent design.

The idea of irreducible complexity was popularized by biochemist Michael Behe, who argues that certain biological systems could not function if any one of their parts were removed. A classic example of this is the bacterial flagellum, a whip-like structure that enables bacteria to swim. The flagellum is composed of multiple proteins that work together to create a rotary motor, which propels the bacterium through its environment.[61] If any part of this motor is missing or non-functional, the entire system would fail. This raises a significant question: how could such a complex system evolve piece by piece if its parts are only useful when they all work together?

In a traditional Darwinian view, evolution occurs gradually, with small mutations providing slight advantages that accumulate over time. However, in the case of irreducibly complex systems like the bacterial flagellum, the gradual accumulation of parts seems unlikely. The flagellum is an all-or-nothing system—without the complete set of components, the bacterium would not benefit from any partial structure. This points to the possibility that such systems were designed, fully formed, rather than slowly evolving through random mutations.

The Human Eye: A Window into Design

Another frequently cited example of complexity in biology is the human eye. The eye is an incredibly sophisticated organ, capable of capturing light, focusing it, and converting it into electrical signals that the brain can interpret. The process involves multiple finely tuned parts, including the cornea, lens, retina, optic nerve, and various photoreceptor cells (rods and cones). Each of these parts must work together seamlessly for vision to occur.

Critics of Darwinian evolution argue that the development of the eye poses significant challenges to the theory of gradual evolution. How could such a complex organ evolve through small, successive changes if any intermediate form of the eye would be non-functional and provide no survival advantage? While Darwin himself speculated that eyes might have evolved from simpler light-sensitive patches of skin, the rapid development and intricate coordination required for fully formed vision suggest that the eye may be a product of design rather than random mutation.

The Human Blood-Clotting Cascade

The blood-clotting process, or coagulation, is another intricate biological system that involves a series of reactions where one protein activates another, leading to the formation of a clot. This cascade is an example of irreducible complexity because if one factor is missing, the entire system fails, either causing uncontrolled bleeding or dangerous clotting. The delicate balance of this system showcases how multiple parts must work together simultaneously to achieve a life-sustaining function.

The existence of different blood types is indeed fascinating, and while the exact reason for this variation isn't fully understood, there are a few potential benefits that could point to why a Creator might design different blood types.

1. **Adaptation to Disease:** Different blood types have been shown to offer varying levels of resistance to certain diseases. For example, individuals with type O blood have been found to be more resistant

to severe malaria, while those with type A blood are more prone to infections like smallpox. This variation could be seen as a protective measure, ensuring that no single disease could wipe out an entire population, as genetic diversity provides resilience to a variety of health threats.

2. **Immune System Diversity:** The antigens present on red blood cells (which define blood types) play a role in how the immune system identifies and reacts to foreign substances. Different blood types can offer a diversity of immune responses, helping populations withstand different pathogens and diseases. This diversity may allow humanity to thrive in varied environments with different health challenges.

3. **Evolutionary Resilience:** From an intelligent design perspective, the existence of multiple blood types could be seen as a way to ensure genetic variation and resilience within the human population. By having this diversity, populations are less likely to be vulnerable to the same environmental or medical challenges, thus preserving the species.

4. **Potential Role in Reproduction:** There's some speculation that blood type might play a subtle role in reproductive success. Certain blood type combinations between parents may influence factors like fertility, gestation, and even the health of offspring. This could suggest that variation in blood types helps in ensuring healthier, more adaptable future generations.

While it's difficult to say definitively what the exact purpose of different blood types is, the benefits related to disease resistance and immune system diversity suggest that they could serve as a protective mechanism in a well-thought-out design, ensuring the survival and flourishing of humanity in a wide variety of conditions.

The Human Immune System

The immune system is incredibly complex, involving multiple layers of defense. The adaptive immune system, in particular, uses T-cells and B-cells to recognize and target specific pathogens. The immune system can "remember" previous infections and respond more effectively in the future, an ability that points to a highly sophisticated and finely tuned mechanism for protecting the body from disease. The coordination of these cells in recognizing and eliminating threats is another example of a system that seems too complex to have arisen through random mutations alone.

DNA Replication: The Blueprint for Life

At the molecular level, the complexity of DNA replication provides another compelling argument for design. DNA, the molecule that carries genetic information, must be copied accurately every time a cell divides.[62] This process involves a host of enzymes and proteins that work in concert to unzip the double helix, synthesize new strands, and proofread the new DNA to ensure that errors are minimized. The precision and efficiency of this process are staggering—any mistakes in copying can lead to mutations, which might be harmful to the organism.

The sheer complexity of DNA replication, with its multitude of interdependent steps and specialized enzymes, raises the question of how such an intricate system could have evolved through random mutations alone. It seems far more likely that DNA, with its information-rich structure and self-replicating capabilities, was designed with a purpose in mind. The fact that life depends on the flawless functioning of this system further underscores the idea of a purposeful designer behind its creation.

Each of these examples—whether the bacterial flagellum, the human eye, the blood-clotting cascade, the immune system, or DNA replication—demonstrates a level of intricacy that is difficult to explain through gradual, unguided processes. The more we explore these systems, the clearer it becomes that they function as finely tuned mechanisms, where every part must be in place for the whole to work. This level of complexity, where systems depend on multiple interlocking components, challenges the notion that random mutations alone could have produced such precision.

Rather, the evidence points to a purposeful designer, one who has carefully crafted these systems with intention and intelligence. The intricate design present in biological systems is not just a testament to the complexity of life, but also a reflection of the creative mind behind it. When we consider the incredible odds against these systems arising by chance, it becomes clear that intelligent design offers the most plausible explanation for the origin and function of life.

The Genius of Autonomous Design

It's often said, "Give a man a fish, and you feed him for a day; teach him how to fish, and you feed him for a lifetime." The higher thinking lies in the creation of systems that sustain themselves throughout time, without the need for constant oversight. This is exactly what God has done with the universe: a self-sustaining, perfectly balanced system that requires no further intervention. This concept of autonomous creation—systems that harmonize to sustain life—echoes through every fiber of the natural world.

Many of us may believe that God is constantly at the wheel, steering the ship of the universe as it expands through space. But perhaps that idea comes from our own limitations—the fact that we, as humans, have never been able to replicate such a system; therefore, the concept is hard to grasp. What has mankind ever created that sustains itself for millennia? If anything, our contributions often disrupt the systems God has put in place. From harmful chemicals like PFOA, used by DuPont in the production of Teflon, to disasters like the BP oil spill, man's attempts frequently result in adverse effects on the world's ecosystems. In the case of PFOA, even though it was phased out in 2015, traces of it still remain in our environment and, alarmingly, in human bloodstreams, highlighting the persistent impact of our actions. Conversely, nature's resilience was evident in the aftermath of the 2010 BP oil spill. While the damage was extensive, natural processes, such as oil-degrading bacteria in the Gulf, played a significant role in breaking down some of the spilled oil, leading to a recovery beyond initial expectations. Nevertheless, these events remind us of how delicate these systems are and how human interventions can create long-lasting consequences.

God's systems are timeless, designed to sustain life in perfect harmony. This doesn't speak to the absence of God, but rather to the genius of God—who created systems so perfect that they work without constant intervention. This brilliance surpasses anything mankind has ever accomplished, and it is reflected in everything we see in nature. It's the ultimate demonstration of a higher power: a creation that continues to thrive long after its initial spark.

Autonomous Systems That Sustain Life

The universe and Earth are full of autonomous systems that operate without continuous oversight, ensuring the flow of energy and life. Some of the key systems include:

- **The Water Cycle (Hydrological Cycle):** This system moves water through the processes of evaporation, condensation, and precipitation, transporting it through the atmosphere, ground, and oceans.[63] It ensures a steady supply of fresh water for all living organisms and ecosystems, as well as human use.

- **The Carbon Cycle:** This cycle moves carbon between the atmosphere, oceans, and living organisms, regulating the planet's climate and supporting life through photosynthesis.

- **The Nitrogen Cycle:** This process converts atmospheric nitrogen into forms that plants and animals can use to build proteins and DNA, crucial for sustaining ecosystems.

- **The Genetic Code:** The DNA blueprint allows organisms to grow, repair, and reproduce autonomously, passing down genetic information from generation to generation.

- **Plate Tectonics:** The movement of Earth's plates recycles materials, shapes the landscape, and helps regulate the planet's temperature by cycling carbon between the atmosphere and the deep Earth.

- **The Seasons:** Earth's axial tilt and orbit around the sun create the cycle of seasons—spring, summer, fall, and winter. These seasonal changes regulate temperature, precipitation, and daylight, creating diverse habitats and supporting the growth cycles of plants and animals. Seasons also drive agricultural cycles, ensuring food production.

- **The Ocean Currents:** Ocean currents, driven by wind, Earth's rotation, and temperature differences, regulate global climate by distributing heat from the equator to the poles. This moderates temperatures and supports marine ecosystems, making Earth more hospitable.

- **The Day-Night Cycle:** The rotation of Earth on its axis creates the day-night cycle, which helps regulate the biological rhythms of living organisms. Circadian rhythms control sleep, metabolism, and behavior, ensuring that life operates in sync with the planet's natural cycles.

- **Earth's Atmospheric Layers:** The various layers of Earth's atmosphere, including the troposphere, stratosphere, and mesosphere, each serve critical functions. The stratosphere, for instance, contains the ozone layer that protects life from harmful UV radiation, while the troposphere is where weather patterns develop, distributing water and nutrients.

Protective Systems of the Universe

- **The Ozone Layer:** The ozone layer in Earth's stratosphere absorbs the majority of the sun's harmful ultraviolet (UV) radiation, protecting living organisms from genetic damage and reducing the risk of skin cancer, cataracts, and other harmful effects.

- **Earth's Magnetic Field:** Generated by the movement of molten iron in Earth's core, this magnetic field shields our planet from harmful solar wind and cosmic radiation, preventing the atmosphere from being stripped away and protecting life on the surface.

- **Jupiter's Role as a Shield:** Jupiter, the largest planet in our solar system, plays a crucial protective role by deflecting comets and space debris with its strong gravitational field.[64] Without Jupiter, Earth would face more frequent impacts from asteroids and comets, potentially causing catastrophic events.

- **Planetary Alignment:** The arrangement of planets in the solar system, particularly the gas giants, helps to stabilize the inner solar system by reducing the likelihood of destabilizing gravitational interactions. This allows Earth's orbit to remain relatively stable over long periods, fostering the development of life.

- **The Moon's Gravitational Influence:** The moon stabilizes Earth's axial tilt, which is responsible for the planet's relatively stable climate and regular seasons. Without the moon, Earth's tilt would fluctuate, leading to chaotic climate changes that would make life more difficult to sustain.

The Remarkable Design of the Human Body

The human body is one of the most astounding creations, a masterpiece of intelligent design that operates with precision and complexity. From our ability to think and adapt to our body's capacity to heal itself, every system works in harmony to sustain life. The body is not just a vessel; it is a dynamic, self-regulating system, constantly adjusting to changes in our environment, fighting off illness, and allowing us to thrive. Its incredible resilience and functionality are a testament to the design that enables us to live, adapt, and grow.

- **The Skin:** The body's largest organ, the skin acts as a protective barrier, shielding us from harmful pathogens, regulating temperature, and preventing fluid loss. It also has the resilient ability to heal itself, closing wounds and regenerating tissue. Additionally, the skin plays a critical role in synthesizing vitamin D when exposed to sunlight, supporting bone health and immune function.

- **The Reproductive System:** This is where the true miracle of life happens. The reproductive system is finely tuned to support the creation of new life, from the intricate hormonal balance that regulates fertility to the process of pregnancy and childbirth. The human reproductive system ensures that life continues through future generations, a testament to the design of life itself.

- **The Brain:** Often called the most complex organ in the universe, the brain controls all bodily functions, processes emotions, stores memories, and allows for reasoning, creativity, and abstract thinking. It constantly adapts through a process called neuroplasticity, rewiring itself based on experiences and learning.

- **The Immune System:** The body's defense system is constantly on alert, identifying and eliminating harmful pathogens like viruses and bacteria. It can recognize and remember previous infections, providing immunity and protection over time. The immune system's adaptive nature is what enables vaccines to work.

- **The Cardiovascular System:** This system circulates blood throughout the body, delivering oxygen and nutrients to cells while removing waste products. The heart, a remarkably efficient pump, works continuously to keep blood flowing, even under strenuous conditions.

- **The Respiratory System:** The lungs allow for the exchange of oxygen and carbon dioxide, a process essential for life. The body's ability to increase its oxygen intake during physical activity or at high altitudes showcases its adaptability to different environments.

- **The Digestive System:** This system breaks down food into essential nutrients that the body can absorb and use for energy, growth, and repair. The complexity of digestion, nutrient absorption, and waste elimination underscores the body's ability to extract energy from the environment.

- **The Musculoskeletal System:** Our muscles, bones, and joints give the body structure and mobility. The strength and flexibility of the musculoskeletal system allow for a wide range of movements, from fine motor skills to feats of physical endurance.

- **The Healing Power of the Body:** The human body has the life-sustaining ability to heal itself. Whether it's closing a wound, regenerating tissue, or fighting off an infection, the body activates a series of processes to repair damage and restore balance.

- **The Body's Adaptability:** Humans have the unique ability to adapt to a wide range of environments, from extreme heat to freezing cold. The body regulates its temperature through sweating, shivering, and blood vessel dilation, allowing humans to survive in diverse climates.

- **The Nervous System:** The body's internal communication network, the nervous system, allows for rapid responses to stimuli. It controls both voluntary actions, like moving your hand, and involuntary actions, such as reflexes and the regulation of heart rate.

Feeding the World: The Complex Food Systems of Nature

The food systems in nature are remarkably well thought out, designed to not only provide the essential sustenance required for life but also to do so in a way that allows for a rich diversity of tastes and meal styles. These sustainable systems span across the animal kingdom, plant life, and marine ecosystems, offering an endless menu of flavors and nourishment. The variety and abundance of food sources reflect the intelligent design behind them, ensuring that life thrives while catering to diverse needs and preferences worldwide. Here's an overview of the main components:

Animal Kingdom (Terrestrial Animals)

There are numerous species of animals that humans have traditionally consumed as part of their diet. These include:

- **Mammals:** Common examples include cattle, pigs, sheep, goats, and deer. There are around 60-80 edible mammal species that are commonly farmed or hunted globally.

- **Poultry & Birds:** Chickens, turkeys, ducks, geese, and quails are widespread in human diets. In total, there are around 20-30 edible bird species commonly consumed.

- **Game & Exotic Animals:** Some cultures eat a variety of wild game or exotic animals such as kangaroos, ostriches, or guinea pigs. Overall, around 1,500 species of terrestrial animals are consumed by humans.

Marine Life (Fish and Seafood)

Marine ecosystems provide an enormous range of food sources:

- **Fish:** There are about 32,000 species of fish, with 1,000-2,000 considered regularly edible and harvested worldwide, including salmon, tuna, cod, and mackerel.

- **Crustaceans & Mollusks:** This includes crabs, lobsters, shrimp, oysters, clams, and mussels. There are approximately 300-400 edible species of crustaceans and mollusks.

- **Seaweed:** Seaweed is also part of marine ecosystems and is consumed in many coastal cultures. There are around 20-30 species of seaweed that are commonly edible.

Edible Plants

Plants provide the majority of the world's food and are a key component of food ecosystems:

- **Grains:** Wheat, rice, corn, barley, and oats are among the primary grains that feed the world. There are approximately 40-50 major grain crops grown worldwide.

- **Fruits & Vegetables:** Over 20,000 species of edible plants exist, though humans consume less than 200 species regularly. Common examples include apples, bananas, spinach, carrots, and tomatoes.

- **Nuts & Seeds:** Edible nuts (like almonds, walnuts, and cashews) and seeds (like sunflower, chia, and flax seeds) are derived from around 50-100 species.

Fungi & Edible Insects

- **Mushrooms & Fungi:** There are around 100-200 species of edible fungi, with mushrooms being the most widely consumed.

- **Edible Insects:** Insects like crickets, grasshoppers, and beetles are consumed in many cultures. Around 1,900 insect species are known to be edible.

Other Food Sources

- **Honey:** Bees produce honey, a sweet food source consumed globally, and are part of a broader pollination ecosystem.

- **Algae:** Algae, including spirulina, is consumed in supplements or as food in some parts of the world.

These systems work together, each supporting the other, to create and sustain life in its many forms. From the water cycle that nurtures plants, to Earth's magnetic field that shields us from cosmic radiation, every system plays a crucial role in maintaining balance and harmony. Whether it's the genetic code that orchestrates the growth of organisms, the seasons that regulate ecosystems, or the intricate food webs that nourish life, the planet operates as an intricately woven network of autonomous processes. Even the human body, with its wondrous capacity for healing, adaptation, and reproduction, is a testament to this intelligent design. Together, these systems form a resilient, self-sustaining creation, operating in ways both seen and unseen, ensuring that life continues to thrive in the most intricate and beautiful ways.

The Origin of Information

Imagine walking along and stumbling upon a watch lying on the ground. For years, people have used this analogy to argue that the watch, with all its intricate parts—gears, hands, glass face, springs, and even ruby to make the jewel bearing—could not have formed by accident. The idea that wind and dust, blowing for millions of years, could somehow come together to form the necessary components of the watch, shaping the glass, tempering the spring, and assembling the metals into perfect alignment, is already a stretch of the imagination. Yet, those who argue for purely natural processes might claim that, given enough time, these elements could indeed come together.

They suggest that the raw materials—sand, metal, and minerals—could form the glass, plastics, and metals needed for the case and hands. With enough heat, pressure, and chance, the spring might even be tempered perfectly to power the watch. As time went on, the wind could blow in just the right way to shape the intricate parts with incredible precision, eventually assembling them into a functioning watch.

And it doesn't stop there. Given even more time, this watch would wind itself and begin to tick. The hands would move in perfect synchronization, marking the seconds, minutes, and hours. Somehow, by pure chance, it would perfectly match the rotation of Earth—tracking the rising and setting of the sun with such precision that at the exact moment of high noon and midnight, the hands would align in perfect harmony, all pointing straight up to 12.

That alone would be astonishing—but here's where it becomes even more incredible. Lying next to the watch is something far more astonishing: a set of instructions. These aren't random scribbles; they are detailed blueprints explaining how every component was made, the precise specifications for each part, and step-by-step directions on how to assemble them into a functioning watch.

And that's where the real question lies—not just in how the watch could have come together by chance, but where did the instructions come from? How did this set of blueprints, containing detailed knowledge and foresight, appear alongside the watch? The watchmaker's existence becomes undeniable—not because of the watch itself, but because of the intricate, purposeful information that lies beside it.

The DNA Blueprint: Information in Biology

In the biological world, DNA functions as that very set of instructions, the blueprint for life itself. DNA carries the detailed information needed to build and maintain every living organism, from the smallest bacterium to the most complex human being.[65] It's not just a collection of molecules randomly assembled—DNA contains a **code**, a sequence of nucleotides that spells out specific instructions for the development and functioning of each organism.

Just as a library filled with books doesn't write itself, DNA contains a vast amount of information, carefully arranged to ensure that life can exist and reproduce. The nucleotide sequences in DNA are akin to letters in an alphabet, spelling out specific instructions for how cells should function, what proteins to make, and how organisms should grow. This is not random data; it is ordered and purposeful.

If we know from experience that information always comes from an intelligent source—whether it's a book written by an author or software coded by a programmer—then the question arises: Where did the information in DNA come from? Random processes like natural selection and mutation may account for certain variations within species, but the origin of the information that defines life points to something more—a purposeful designer.

A Nod to the Bible: The Ultimate Instruction Manual

This concept of life's blueprint brings us back to the Bible, which can be viewed as the instruction book for the world we live in and the life we lead within it. Throughout history, the Bible has demonstrated how life works, offering wisdom and guidance on how to navigate the complexities of existence. Remarkably, the Bible's teachings have shown a deep understanding of how the natural world functions—long before science could confirm these truths.

Take, for example, the creation account in the book of Genesis. Thousands of years ago, before the writer of Genesis could possibly have known how the cosmos was formed, the Bible presented a guide for how creation unfolded. In an age without telescopes, satellites, or scientific inquiry, Genesis describes the creation of light, the separation of waters, the appearance of land, and the formation of life in an order that aligns strikingly well with what modern science now understands about the formation of Earth and the development of life.

This is not a coincidence; it's a testament to the idea that these ancient texts contain truths that transcend human knowledge. Just as DNA contains the blueprint for life, the Bible serves as a blueprint for the world and life itself, providing instructions for how to live, thrive, and understand the universe we inhabit.

Beyond Imagination

Just as the blueprint of DNA points toward design, so does the larger complexity of the universe itself, bringing us to a broader question: How do we reconcile this intricacy with the notion of creation?

When I think about those who argue against intelligent design, I often come to the conclusion that they just don't fully grasp what they're talking about. It's not that they lack intelligence or curiosity, but the sheer magnitude of the universe's complexity is something so far beyond comprehension. Similarly, when I hear arguments from within the religious community that the world was created in six literal days, I understand where they're coming from. On the surface, Genesis seems to tell the story in that way. But, as I've discussed in earlier chapters, the Bible's depth goes far beyond the simple narrative. It's a text perfectly inspired to convey our origins, in a way that humanity could understand for centuries, without overwhelming us with the intricacies that we're only now beginning to grasp.

Being a bit facetious, I sometimes imagine God sitting back and watching us with a knowing smile or perhaps a shake of the head, thinking, "You really have no idea how intricate all of this is, do you." Maybe He's even pondering the irony of us insisting that He created the entire universe in less than seventy-two hours. I can almost hear Him musing, "Why would they assume *yom* meant a literal day when I took seven days just to bring down the walls of Jericho? If something as straightforward as that took time, how much more so the creation of the entire universe?" This masterpiece, after all, took billions of years to unfold.

The intricate information stored within DNA is like a detailed blueprint, just as a watch comes with precise instructions for its assembly. It's difficult to explain how such a system, packed with precise and purposeful information, could have arisen by accident—or equally, how all of it could have come together in just seventy-two hours, as though it were a design so simple. The reality is, no matter which side of the argument you're on, the complexity of life and the universe is far beyond what we often give it credit for. When we take a step back and reflect, it becomes clear that life, in all its complexity, points toward something far greater than chance—toward the presence of a designer.

The Signature of Intelligence

Jerry Clower, an American stand-up comedian from the 1970s, often told funny stories about his Southern upbringing and the adventures of *Jerry and*

Marcel Ledbetter, especially their coon-hunting escapades. We listened to him whenever we had the chance on the radio, and one story stuck with me about a famous scientist and his chauffeur.

This scientist was frequently called upon to give his signature lecture across the country. His chauffeur, who drove him to these engagements, would always sit in the back of the room and listen to the speech.

One day, while driving to yet another lecture, the chauffeur started to vent. "It's just not fair," he said. The scientist, curious, asked, "What's not fair?"

"Well, I've driven you to these events all over the place, and every time you give the same speech! I've heard it so many times that I think I could give it better than you can. Yet you're the one who gets paid handsomely, while I just drive."

The scientist thought for a moment and then proposed an idea. "Alright, why don't we switch roles today? Nobody at this event knows who I am. You'll give the lecture, and I'll sit in the back as your chauffeur."

They pulled over and swapped their clothes.

When they arrived at the venue, the chauffeur, now dressed as the scientist, confidently took the stage. Meanwhile, the real scientist, disguised as the chauffeur, sat quietly in the back. Amazingly, the chauffeur delivered the speech flawlessly and even finished a bit early.

Impressed, the moderator said, "Since you've finished a little early, would you mind taking a few questions from the audience?"

Before the chauffeur could decline, someone stood up and asked an incredibly complex, technical question: "Sir, if you were drilling in the Alaskan Maltese Basin, and after drilling 675 feet into the Jurassic stratum of sedimentary limestone, you pulled up the line and examined the bit, what would the pH acidity of the shale on the drill bit be?"

The chauffeur stood there, stunned for a moment, then said, "Sir, that is by far the simplest question I've ever been asked in all my years of lecturing! In fact, it's so simple that I'm going to let my chauffeur sitting in the back answer it for you!"

If only life were so simple—perhaps anyone, or even no one, could have created the universe. But it's nowhere near that simple.

Brilliant Complexity of Design

Throughout this chapter, we've explored the fine-tuning of the universe, the intricate complexity of biological systems, and the perplexing origin of information within DNA. Each of these elements, when examined closely, presents overwhelming evidence pointing toward a purposeful and intelligent designer.

The fine-tuning of the physical constants that govern the universe—so precise that even the smallest deviation would render life impossible—demonstrates that the universe is no random accident. The complexity of biological systems, from the irreducibly complex structures like the bacterial flagellum to the highly sophisticated process of DNA replication, reveals a level of design that could not have arisen through gradual, step-by-step natural processes alone. And the vast amounts of information encoded within DNA, functioning like a detailed instruction manual for life, offer further proof of intentionality and design.

As we reflect on the complexity around us, we are reminded that behind the awe-inspiring beauty of the universe is a mind that designed it—a Creator whose fingerprints are found in every system we observe. The logical conclusion from this evidence is clear: a universe so finely tuned, systems so intricately interwoven, and information so purposeful cannot be the product of mere chance. Just as the existence of a watch points undeniably to the watchmaker, the evidence all around us points to an intelligent designer—a Creator with purpose, intention, and brilliance beyond our full comprehension. The design we see compels us to acknowledge that we are part of a much grander plan, one authored by a mind far greater than our own.

CHAPTER 7

The Wonders of Personality

When we look at the diversity of life on Earth, it's clear that variety is not always random difference, but it is intricately designed and essential for survival. Just as different blood types help protect humanity against disease and genetic vulnerability, so too does the diversity of human personalities contribute to our ability to thrive as a species.[66] Every personality type brings something unique to the table, ensuring that, together, we can face life's challenges and complexities processing the world around us much like 3D imagery, which provides a multifaceted balance of thought and robust solutions.

It can't go without saying that in the professional arena of psychology, the classification of individuals into personality types remains controversial.[67] Medical analysis, particularly in treating mental disorders, tends to focus on personality traits, which can be measured more consistently and exist on a spectrum, making them easier to quantify. Personality types, on the other hand, attempt to categorize people into distinct groups, which can sometimes oversimplify human behavior.

Science often struggles with the complexity of God's creation because it seeks concrete, measurable data, yet many aspects of human personality and existence transcend simple equations. God's design includes nuances, subjective experiences, and variability that can't always be easily reduced to formulas or clear patterns. While scientific analysis is invaluable, it often faces limitations in areas where the intricacies of human nature are involved—especially in understanding human behavior, spirituality, or relationships, where not everything fits neatly into binary or measurable constructs.

It's much like raising four children in the same home with the same parents, attending the same school, and eating the same meals—yet, for some reason, they turn out completely different.

So while medical science focuses on what it can measure, that doesn't mean other perspectives—like those offered by personality types—aren't valuable. This chapter offers a practical, life-centered approach, understanding personalities as tools for better insight into ourselves and others, without needing to fit neatly into scientific frameworks.

One helpful tool for understanding personality is the Myers-Briggs Type Indicator (MBTI), which categorizes people into one of sixteen personality types based on how they perceive the world and make decisions.[68] The MBTI groups these types into four major categories: Guardians, Artisans, Idealists, and Rationals. Each of these types reflects a specific way of engaging with the world, helping us understand our tendencies and preferences in communication, relationships, and even work. While the MBTI may not be a divine revelation, it provides valuable insight into human nature, reinforcing the idea that our differences are purposeful and essential.

Knowing your personality type not only helps you find fulfillment but also enables you to understand and appreciate the people around you better. Most importantly, if you can identify your strengths and weaknesses, you can work in ways that bring out the best in yourself and others. Relationships can become smoother, teams can function more effectively, and families can better support each other when we understand the inherent traits that make each person unique.

For much of my life, before I understood my personality, I often felt like I didn't fit in. I thought differently than most people around me, and I had a tendency to be very strict about matters. I had a small circle of friends and found large social events draining. Whether it was family gatherings, social occasions, or work events, I could feel my energy disappear within minutes. It wasn't until I was about fifty that the company I worked for had us take the MBTI evaluation, and that's when everything started to make sense. Since then, it's been an invaluable tool in understanding myself and others.

Here's what the evaluation revealed about me. You don't have to dive into it in detail, but it will give you an idea of what such an evaluation can tell about you.

MIKE A. BILLS

Temperament: Architect Rational (INTP), borderline Mastermind Rational (INTJ)

Your temperament is the **Rational** (NT). Rationals are rare, making up no more than five to ten percent of the population. But because of their drive to unlock the secrets of nature and develop new technologies,[69] Rationals have done much to shape the world. Your particular personality type, the **Architect** (INTP), is even scarcer. Individuals of your type make up little more than one to two percent of the total population.

About Your Rational Temperament

There are four types of Rationals (NTs): **Field Marshals, Masterminds, Inventors,** and **Architects.** These four personality types share several core characteristics. Firstly, Rationals are pragmatic people who tend to excel in problem-solving and analytical thinking.

Rationals are ingenious, independent people who can be both strong-willed and skeptical. Typically focused on the world of ideas, Rationals spend much of their time and energy understanding how things work. Known for being strategic leaders and skilled thinkers, Rationals are generally even-tempered, goal-oriented individuals who yearn for achievement and accomplishment. Indeed they can be the kinds of mentors that can help people gain confidence and independence. Valuing logic and pragmatism above almost all else, Rationals can sometimes seem cold and distant to others. It's not that they don't care about the people around them; it's simply that they're more oriented toward ingenuity and results than toward interpersonal exploration.

Architects are master designers of all kinds of theoretical systems, including school/training curricula, corporate strategies, and new technologies. The world is primarily something to be analyzed, understood, explained, and redesigned.

Generally, what is important for Architects like you is to grasp fundamental principles and natural laws. In fact, you'll often use external reality as a kind of raw material that you organize into structural models, be they literal or imagined. Of all sixteen personality types, yours shows the greatest precision of thought and speech. As a result, when it comes to identifying particular distinctions between things or noticing inconsistencies, you are unmatched in detection and resolution. Also, when you put your considerable design and organizational skills to use—even when you're just cleaning out the garage—the results are often elegant, efficient, and coherent.

Being an Architect, you can be a ruthless pragmatist when it comes to ideas. You're also insatiably curious compared to most other people. Because you're one who is often driven to find the most efficient means to any ends, you maintain a lifelong focus on learning. This constant influx of new ideas allows you to always employ the best methods. Architects prize intelligence and may sometimes show impatience with others who have less ability or are less driven. But for the most part you're no snob when it comes to seeking out new knowledge. As a result, you'll gladly listen to amateurs if their ideas prove useful; you'll also ignore experts if theirs do not. Authority derived from office, credential, or celebrity doesn't typically impress you. You're much more compelled by what makes sense. So no matter who speaks the words, only consistent, coherent statements carry real weight with you. It can be difficult for an Architect like you to listen to nonsense without pointing out a speaker's error, even in a casual conversation. As for serious discussions or debates, your skill in framing arguments can be overwhelming to opponents. This gives you a particular advantage in all kinds of professional and personal situations. The discussions you prefer to engage in are most often about a search for understanding. As a result, you may feel it's your mission to eliminate any inconsistencies put forth by others.

As individuals, Architects like you often seem difficult to get to know. Ordinarily you'll be quite shy, except with close friends, and this reserve can be difficult to penetrate. In work situations, you may also prefer to work quietly and alone, rather than spending much time with others gathered around the office water cooler. Your strong ability to concentrate usually keeps you on task. In fact, depending on the assignment, Architects like you may even shut others out. There are times when you may become obsessed with analysis or get caught up in your thought processes to the exclusion of the outside world. Your type is known for this innate ability to close off and persevere until you've comprehended an issue in all its complexity.

Because you can be curious and imaginative, you're usually happy when your work allows you the opportunity to explore the universe of ideas. You're very willing in an organization to offer the leader the benefit of your strategic insights and contingency planning skills. But when those in charge show confusion or demonstrate incompetence, you feel compelled to take charge and get things back on track.

In your ideal work environment, your superiors would create a structure, provide you with resources, set some general expectations, and let you loose. Like other "creatives" (scientists, computer engineers, and even writers and designers), you're apt to do your best work in situations where you can work autonomously and deliver finished products, rather than having to constantly check in or collaborate with others.

Like other Rationals, you are wired to acquire competence and intelligence. As a result, you tend to thrive in intellectually stimulating, innovative work environments where you can be recognized for your expertise.

Famous Rational Personalities

Walt Disney, Mark Twain, **Abraham Lincoln**, Dwight D. Eisenhower, Ulysses S. Grant, **John Adams**, Douglas MacArthur, William Tecumseh Sherman, Napoleon Bonaparte, **Thomas Jefferson**, Albert Einstein, Isaac Newton, **Aristotle**, **Stephen Hawking**, **Charles Darwin**, Benjamin Franklin, **Jack Welch**, Bill Gates, **Steve Jobs**, and Steve Wozniak.

Looking at these names, everything started to make sense to me. There was an inherent reason why I was the way I was, though it didn't always work in my favor. Especially in work environments, where most people were Guardian personalities—serious about getting in line and staying there—I began to see why I sometimes felt like the odd one out. My tendency to question authority when I thought they were wrong, or change the test answers in college when the spreadsheet didn't make sense, started to click into place. It also explained why I sometimes came across as annoying or insensitive around the business table, even when my intentions were logical.

I highlighted a few names from that list, not to suggest that I'm on the same level as these individuals, but because it shed light on some of the things I was drawn to growing up. As I mentioned earlier in the book, I hated missing *The Wonderful World of Disney* on Sunday evenings when I had to attend church. The world Walt Disney created was awe-inspiring to me as a child, and I've spent much of my adult life studying Disney's approach to business. Abraham Lincoln has always been one of my favorite presidents—a gifted writer with timeless philosophy. I've watched the *John Adams* mini-series more times than I can count, and I've quoted Thomas Jefferson elsewhere in this book.

One of the most perplexing yet striking statements that stays with me is from Aristotle: "The law is reason without passion." It underpins another statement I often reflect on: "For justice delivered without dispassion is always in danger of not being justice." It stands in contrast to the concept of mercy, which I also believe in deeply—that mercy can only be extended to someone who doesn't deserve it. I've read books by Jack Welch and Steve Jobs, and while I would likely find myself in a heated debate with Stephen Hawking and Charles Darwin, I can understand what drove them and how their rational minds shaped their contributions.

Now that I have this insight, I can truly appreciate how different personality types are essential for the world to function smoothly. Guardians provide structure, Artisans bring creativity and entertainment, Idealists inspire change, and Rationals strategize solutions. It's this balance that enables us to overcome challenges and collectively build a better world. Most importantly, each type offers its contribution in a way that is uniquely their own.

As you've likely noticed, my personality has a strong influence on how this book is written. With a Rational (Architect) personality, I naturally delve deeply into questions, value science, and scrutinize scholarly interpretations of the Bible, often focusing on nuances and details. Someone with a different personality might have taken a more emotional or expressive approach—something I've tried to be mindful of, though it's not my style. Writing this book has been a balancing act, engaging a broader audience while staying true to my analytical nature. Nonetheless, it's been a rewarding journey, and I hope this illustrates how personality affects how we interact with the world.

In the following sections, we'll explore each of the four primary personality types—Guardians, Artisans, Idealists, and Rationals—and how each reflects a unique aspect of God's intricate design for humanity. Understanding how these types complement one another can help you navigate your own life with greater wisdom, fostering harmony in your relationships and appreciating the diversity that makes each of us an essential part of the human experience.

Guardians: The Pillars of Society

Guardians are often seen as the bedrock of society, responsible for maintaining the order and structure that allows communities to thrive. Making up around forty to forty-five percent of the population, Guardians naturally gravitate toward roles that involve leadership, organization, and care for others. They are the individuals who ensure that things run smoothly, that traditions are upheld, and that the fabric of society remains intact.

The Four Types of Guardians in Society:

Supervisors (ESTJ)

- **Traits:** Decisive, organized, natural leaders.
- **Description:** Supervisors thrive in leadership roles and are excellent at managing people and resources. They respect tradition and expect others to follow established rules and procedures.

Inspectors (ISTJ)

- **Traits:** Meticulous, dependable, detail-oriented.
- **Description:** Inspectors are thorough and methodical in their work, valuing accuracy and reliability. They are rule-followers who prefer consistency and practicality in all areas of life.

Protectors (ESFJ)

- **Traits:** Caring, sociable, nurturing.

- **Description:** Protectors are warm, compassionate, and highly attuned to the needs of others. They excel in caregiving roles and work to maintain harmony in social settings.

Providers (ISFJ)

- **Traits:** Supportive, practical, considerate.

- **Description:** Providers are deeply committed to helping others, often putting the needs of friends, family, and community first. They are loyal and hardworking, ensuring that things run smoothly behind the scenes.

The Role of Guardians in Society

Guardians play a vital role as stabilizers in both personal and professional settings.[70] They are practical, loyal, and deeply committed to the systems that have proven effective over time. Whether in families, businesses, or government, Guardians value established rules and protocols, believing that order and consistency provide the foundation for long-term success.

One of the defining traits of Guardians is their sense of responsibility. They take their duties seriously and often put the needs of others ahead of their own. Guardians thrive in structured environments, where expectations are clear, and their efforts to maintain stability and reliability are highly valued. Whether they are organizing teams, managing households, or leading in their communities, Guardians ensure that the systems in place are sustained and run efficiently.

Their loyalty extends not only to their work but also to their relationships. Guardians are dependable and steadfast, often forming the backbone of families and organizations. They are the ones people turn to when they need support, knowing that a Guardian's word is their bond. This deep sense of duty and practicality allows them to contribute to societal stability in ways that few others can.

Guardians' Impact on Humanity

While their reliance on established traditions and rules may sometimes come across as resistance to change, Guardians play an essential role in ensuring that society doesn't lose its way amidst rapid shifts and innovations. They remind us that while change is necessary, it must be grounded in principles that ensure long-term security and stability.

Guardians maintain the structures that hold societies together, and their unwavering dedication to preserving the things that work gives society the continuity it needs to thrive. Their methodical approach ensures that transitions are made smoothly, and their commitment to duty and order prevents chaos in times of uncertainty.

Famous Guardian Personalities

Many notable figures throughout history have embodied the traits of Guardians. These individuals demonstrate the strength, dedication, and leadership that Guardians contribute to society.

- **George Washington**—First US president, known for his duty and commitment to preserving the nation's stability
- **Queen Elizabeth II**—Symbol of stability during her reign, known for steadfast dedication to duty
- **Dwight D. Eisenhower**—US general and president, recognized for his organizational and leadership skills
- **J.R.R. Tolkien**—Author of *The Lord of the Rings*, known for his methodical approach to creating a detailed fictional world

These figures demonstrate the Guardian's potential to lead, serve, and maintain order in a variety of ways, offering a model for those who share similar traits to see their own potential.

In the following section, we'll explore how Artisans bring their creativity and energy into the mix, offering a balance to the structure that Guardians provide.

Artisans: The Creators and Entertainers

Artisans are the spontaneous creators and performers of society.[71] They live in the moment, thriving on new experiences and pushing the boundaries of convention. Often described as adaptable, energetic, and hands-on, Artisans bring excitement, creativity, and innovation to the world. They tend to think outside the box, offering unconventional solutions to problems and making life more dynamic and vibrant.

While Guardians focus on maintaining order and structure, Artisans ensure that life doesn't become stagnant. Their ability to think quickly on their feet, adapt to change, and improvise solutions is crucial for human progress. Whether in the arts, entertainment, or even fields like business and entrepreneurship, Artisans excel in creating new and thrilling experiences.

The Four Types of Artisans in Society:

Promoters (ESTP)

- **Traits:** Energetic, persuasive, risk-takers.
- **Description:** Promoters are bold and action-oriented. They enjoy taking risks, are highly persuasive, and excel in dynamic environments where they can take charge and make things happen.

Crafters (ISTP)

- **Traits:** Independent, hands-on, analytical.
- **Description:** Crafters are skilled at working with tools and technology. They are problem-solvers who enjoy figuring out how things work and often prefer to work independently.

Performers (ESFP)

- **Traits:** Outgoing, playful, charismatic.

- **Description:** Performers thrive in social situations, using their charm and energy to entertain others. They are spontaneous and fun-loving, making them the life of the party and natural entertainers.

Composers (ISFP)

- **Traits:** Sensitive, artistic, introspective.

- **Description:** Composers are deeply in tune with their emotions and the world around them. They express their creativity through art, music, and personal expression, often valuing beauty and authenticity in life.

The Role of Artisans in Society

Artisans are driven by their desire to experience life to the fullest. They are often the ones who bring excitement, color, and spontaneity to otherwise structured environments. In moments of crisis or challenge, Artisans have a unique ability to adapt and find innovative ways to solve problems. Their flexibility and willingness to take risks make them invaluable in fields that require quick thinking and creative problem-solving.

Artisans also play a key role in helping society break free from rigid patterns, introducing new perspectives and inspiring change. They thrive on freedom and are often the ones pushing the envelope in creative industries, whether it's through art, music, fashion, or entertainment. Their contributions remind us that life is not just about maintaining order but also about experiencing joy, expression, and innovation.

Famous Artisan Personalities

Artisans often leave their mark in the world through their artistic talents, entrepreneurial spirit, and ability to entertain and captivate audiences. Some well-known Artisans include:

- **Elvis Presley**—Legendary musician and performer

- **Pablo Picasso**—Revolutionary artist who redefined modern art

- **Marilyn Monroe**—Known for her creativity, charm, and ability to captivate audiences

- **Quentin Tarantino**—Innovative film director known for his unconventional storytelling

- **Bruce Lee**—Martial artist and actor who pushed boundaries in both film and physical disciplines

- **David Bowie**—Visionary musician and artist

- **Marie Antoinette**—A historical figure known for her flair and controversial style

- **Richard Branson**—Entrepreneur with a flair for risk-taking and business creativity

Artisans' Impact on Humanity

Artisans make life more vibrant and exciting. Their role as creators and innovators cannot be underestimated, as they help keep society fresh and evolving. By embracing spontaneity and expressing their creativity in various fields, Artisans bring balance to a world that often relies on structure and predictability. Their unique approach to life ensures that humanity continues to explore new frontiers, discover new possibilities, and find joy in the process.

In the next section, we'll explore how Idealists, with their vision for change and deep sense of purpose, bring inspiration and meaning to balance the creativity and spontaneity that Artisans contribute.

Idealists: The Visionaries and Dreamers

Idealists are the empathetic visionaries who see the world not just as it is, but as it could be.[72] They are driven by a deep sense of purpose and a desire to make a positive impact on the lives of others. Idealists are often described as compassionate, creative, and inspiring, with an unwavering belief in the potential for growth and change. They are the dreamers who inspire movements, push for progress, and advocate for the well-being of humanity.

Where Guardians provide stability and Artisans bring creativity, Idealists fuel change by envisioning a better future. They are motivated by their values, often seeking to improve the world around them through leadership, mentorship, or advocacy. Their passion for personal development and meaningful relationships makes them natural connectors in both their personal and professional lives.

The Four Types of Idealists in Society:

Teachers (ENFJ)

- **Traits:** Charismatic, organized, inspiring.

- **Description:** Teachers are natural leaders who motivate others to reach their full potential. They excel at communication and are driven by a desire to help others grow and succeed.

Counselors (INFJ)

- **Traits:** Insightful, compassionate, reserved.

- **Description:** Counselors are introspective and empathetic, often acting as the moral compass of their communities. They have a deep understanding of people and are driven by a desire to help others achieve personal fulfillment.

Champions (ENFP)

- **Traits:** Enthusiastic, creative, people-oriented.

- **Description:** Champions are highly energetic and spontaneous, constantly exploring new ideas and possibilities. They are driven by a sense of purpose and are often at the forefront of social and creative movements.

Healers (INFP)

- **Traits:** Idealistic, reflective, gentle.

- **Description:** Healers are deeply empathetic and introspective individuals who are guided by their values and beliefs. They are passionate about helping others and often seek careers where they can make a meaningful difference.

The Role of Idealists in Society

Idealists are often drawn to roles that allow them to help others grow and thrive. Whether as counselors, teachers, leaders, or activists, Idealists strive to uplift those around them. Their strong sense of empathy and moral conviction often leads them to champion causes related to social justice, education, and human rights.

Idealists believe that change is possible, and they are willing to challenge the status quo to bring about a more compassionate and inclusive society. Their optimism and unwavering belief in the potential for good make them powerful forces for transformation. They are the ones who inspire others to look beyond their immediate circumstances and strive for something greater, both personally and collectively.

Famous Idealist Personalities

Many well-known figures throughout history and popular culture embody the traits of Idealists. These individuals are often remembered for their vision, passion, and commitment to making the world a better place.

- **Martin Luther King Jr.**—Civil rights leader and visionary

- **Mahatma Gandhi**—Leader of India's nonviolent independence movement

- **Nelson Mandela**—Anti-apartheid revolutionary and former South African president

- **Mother Teresa**—Humanitarian and founder of the Missionaries of Charity

- **John Lennon**—Musician and peace activist

- **Princess Diana**—Advocate for humanitarian causes and public service

- **J.K. Rowling**—Author of the *Harry Potter* series, known for inspiring readers to believe in magic and hope

Idealists' Impact on Humanity

Idealists play a crucial role in inspiring change and growth, both on a societal and individual level. Their ability to envision a better future, coupled with their passion for helping others, often leads to groundbreaking social and cultural transformations. They remind us that the world is not static—that progress is possible when driven by empathy, compassion, and commitment to justice.

By championing the causes of the marginalized and advocating for human dignity, Idealists leave a lasting impact on humanity. Their vision, paired with their drive to create a better world, helps us move forward toward a future filled with hope and possibility.

In the next section, we will explore how Rationals bring a different form of insight, using logic and strategy to develop solutions that help humanity navigate the complex challenges we face.

Rationals: Architects of Innovation

Rationals are the problem-solvers and innovators of society. They are driven by a deep curiosity about how the world works and are constantly seeking to understand, analyze, and improve systems. Rationals are often described as logical, independent, and strategic thinkers who value knowledge and efficiency above all else. They are the architects of new ideas, technologies, and processes that help humanity advance and solve complex challenges.

While Guardians provide stability, Artisans bring creativity, and Idealists inspire change, Rationals focus on figuring out how things work and finding ways to make them better. Their pursuit of knowledge and logical solutions often leads them to careers in science, engineering, technology, and strategic leadership. They are the people who ask "Why?" and "How?" and will not stop until they uncover the answers.

The Four Types of Rationals in Society:

Field Marshals (ENTJ)

- **Traits:** Commanding, organized, goal-oriented.

- **Description:** Field marshals are born leaders who excel at organizing people and resources to achieve long-term goals. They are strategic thinkers who focus on efficiency and results.

Masterminds (INTJ)

- **Traits:** Strategic, independent, visionary.

- **Description:** Masterminds are future-oriented planners who are constantly thinking about how to improve and optimize systems. They are highly independent and prefer to work on their own terms.

Inventors (ENTP)

- **Traits:** Inventive, energetic, intellectually curious.

- **Description:** Inventors are enthusiastic problem-solvers who love coming up with creative solutions to complex problems. They are quick thinkers and excel at brainstorming new ideas and possibilities.

Architects (INTP)

- **Traits:** Logical, innovative, reflective.

- **Description:** Architects are analytical and introspective individuals who focus on understanding how systems work. They enjoy theoretical thinking and often come up with new ideas to explain the world around them.

The Role of Rationals in Society

Rationals thrive in environments where they can think critically, solve problems, and explore new ideas. They are the ones who build frameworks that allow society to function more efficiently. Whether in fields like engineering, research, or strategic planning, Rationals are always looking for ways to streamline processes and innovate.

Rationals also excel in leadership roles, particularly when it comes to strategy and long-term planning. They are known for their ability to see the bigger picture and devise solutions that can be implemented on a large scale. Rationals often challenge established systems, not because they are inherently rebellious, but because they believe there is always a better way to do things.

Famous Rational Personalities

Many of the greatest minds in history have been Rationals, leaving an indelible mark on society through their innovations, leadership, and problem-solving abilities. Some notable Rationals include:

- **Nicola Tesla**—Inventor and electrical engineer known for his groundbreaking work on alternating current

- **Marie Curie**—Pioneering scientist in the field of radioactivity

- **Elon Musk**—Entrepreneur and innovator behind Tesla, SpaceX, and other ventures

- **Galileo Galilei**—Astronomer, physicist, and engineer who made significant contributions to the scientific revolution

- **Thomas Edison**—Prolific inventor responsible for the electric light bulb, phonograph, and many other innovations

Rationals' Impact on Humanity

Rationals play a vital role in driving technological and intellectual progress. Their ability to break down complex problems and find innovative solutions is crucial in a world that is constantly evolving. Whether through scientific breakthroughs, technological advancements, or strategic leadership, Rationals push humanity forward by challenging the status quo and seeking more efficient ways of doing things.

Their impact on humanity extends far beyond immediate practicalities. Rationals are often the architects of systems that revolutionize how we live, from the technologies that power our daily lives to the strategic solutions that guide entire nations. Their relentless pursuit of knowledge and understanding has led to some of the most important discoveries and innovations in human history.

In conclusion, Rationals bring a level of insight and strategic thinking that complements the strengths of Guardians, Artisans, and Idealists. Together, these personality types create a balanced and dynamic society where each plays a critical role in ensuring humanity's survival and advancement.

Understanding and Interacting with Different Personalities

Recognizing and understanding personality differences is essential for improving relationships, parenting, and teamwork. While we may share environments, each of us approaches life through our own unique lens, shaped by our individual personalities. This explains why children raised in the same household can grow up to be so different from one another. Their personalities determine how they process and react to information, often leading to distinct perspectives, behaviors, and approaches to life's challenges.

The Role of Personality in Parenting and Family Dynamics

As a parent, it's essential to recognize that each child is wired differently. Four different children may process a single message four different ways, based on their personality type. For instance, a Guardian child may respond well to clear rules and structure, while an Artisan child might resist rigidity and thrive in more spontaneous environments. An Idealist child may need emotional connection and encouragement, whereas a Rational child prefers logic and autonomy. Understanding these differences can help parents tailor their communication and expectations to each child's unique strengths and needs.

Gender can also influence how personality traits manifest. While personality is not determined by gender, certain traits may be more pronounced in boys or girls due to social expectations or biological factors. Recognizing this can help in fostering balanced environments where both genders can express their personalities authentically. Regardless, understanding the role of personality differences—whether through science or personal belief—can enhance your ability to navigate relationships.

Your Children Entering the Structured World of Education

A child's personality expresses itself not only at home but also in school, a structured environment that often challenges their individual needs. Traditional schooling can sometimes be at odds with a child's unique personality traits, and this tension may manifest in various ways. A famous example is Thomas Edison, who struggled in the traditional school system. His teachers described him as "addled" and difficult to teach because he didn't conform to classroom expectations.

When someone is described as "addled," it suggests that their thinking is disorganized or unclear. In the context of Thomas Edison, his teachers used the term to imply that he had difficulty understanding or following along in class, though in reality, it was more likely that his unique way of thinking didn't fit into the traditional educational mold. His mother, recognizing his curiosity and unique way of thinking, chose to homeschool him. Edison's difficulties in school didn't stop him from becoming one of the greatest inventors of all time—a testament to how certain personalities, especially those that lean toward innovation and creative thinking, may not thrive in rigid academic environments.

This example highlights the importance of understanding how your child's personality interacts with their environment, especially in school, which may not always accommodate their natural tendencies. Here's how different personality types may express themselves in the classroom:

Guardians (ESTJ, ISTJ, ESFJ, ISFJ)

- **Role in School:** The "rule-followers" and "responsible students."

- **How They Express Themselves:** Guardians tend to thrive in structured environments with clear expectations and rules. They are often seen as the tattletales because they are naturally inclined to enforce rules and report when others aren't following them. They appreciate order and may be the ones who organize their desks, turn in assignments early, or volunteer to help the teacher. Guardians are dependable and enjoy fulfilling their responsibilities, making them excellent class monitors or team leaders in group projects.

- **Challenges:** Guardians might struggle when the classroom lacks clear guidelines or when classmates disrupt order. They may get frustrated with more spontaneous students (like Artisans) who don't seem to take things as seriously.

Artisans (ESTP, ISTP, ESFP, ISFP)

- **Role in School:** The "creative thinkers" and "class clowns."

- **How They Express Themselves:** Artisans are more spontaneous and hands-on learners who thrive when they can use their creativity. They're the students who may doodle in the margins or come up with creative solutions during class projects. Some might take on the role of class clown, using humor or lightheartedness to entertain their peers. They're also risk-takers, which could make them prone to acting out if they feel restricted by the structure of the classroom.

- **Challenges:** Artisans can get bored quickly in traditional learning environments that require sitting still for long periods. They may struggle to follow strict rules or detailed instructions, preferring to figure things out as they go.

Idealists (ENFJ, INFJ, ENFP, INFP)

- **Role in School:** The "peacemakers" and "dreamers."

- **How They Express Themselves:** Idealists tend to be empathetic and sensitive students who care deeply about their peers. They often try to mediate conflicts, encourage others, and are drawn to creative or expressive subjects like literature, art, or drama. In group settings, they're often the ones who want to ensure everyone feels included and that harmony is maintained. They are imaginative and can daydream or get lost in their thoughts during class.

- **Challenges:** Idealists may struggle with criticism or harsh feedback, as they are highly sensitive to emotional tones. They might have difficulty focusing on tasks that don't align with their personal values or interests and can be distracted by their imaginative inner world.

Rationals (ENTJ, INTJ, ENTP, INTP)

- **Role in School:** The "strategists" and "analytical thinkers."

- **How They Express Themselves:** Rationals are often the students who excel in subjects that require critical thinking, logic, and problem-solving. They love complex subjects like math, science, or debate. These students are likely to challenge teachers, not out of disrespect, but because they genuinely want to understand the reasoning behind instructions or rules. Rationals are more likely to think independently and may not care much for peer approval.

- **Challenges:** Rationals may come across as aloof or detached because they tend to prioritize logic over emotions. They can also become impatient with repetitive tasks or lessons they find unchallenging, and they might struggle in subjects that require less analytical thinking and more emotional engagement.

How These Personalities Might Interact in School

- **Tattletales:** Guardians are likely to take on this role because of their strong sense of responsibility and duty to follow rules. They may feel it's their job to enforce classroom order.

- **Class Clowns:** Artisans, especially ESFPs or ESTPs, might seek attention through humor and spontaneity, providing entertainment to their peers.

- **Peacemakers:** Idealists, particularly ENFJs or INFPs, are more likely to intervene when classmates are fighting or feeling left out, striving for harmony.

- **Challengers:** Rationals, especially INTJs or INTPs, might challenge teachers on logic or strategy, asking "why" more than simply accepting things at face value.

By understanding these personality tendencies, teachers can create environments that accommodate each type's strengths, encouraging creativity, harmony, and intellectual growth in the classroom.

The Politics of Personality: How Society Finds Balance

In the world God created, personalities play a vital role in maintaining societal balance. Just as different blood types protect humanity from vulnerability to disease, the variety of personality types prevents society from swinging too far in one direction or the other. The distribution of personality types—Guardians, Artisans, Idealists, and Rationals—forms the foundation of how we interact with the world and, ultimately, how we engage in politics and society at large.[73]

We often see this dynamic reflected in political polarization, which is mirrored in society's poll numbers during elections and major political movements. Many people find themselves bewildered by the unwavering positions others hold on the opposite side of an issue. This confusion can be traced back to the differences in personality types and how each group processes and responds to the world. For example, Guardians, who make up roughly forty to forty-five percent of the population, are naturally inclined to resist change and uphold tradition and structure. This makes them the bedrock of political stability on both sides of the spectrum, contributing to the rigidity of base voters. Artisans, who are present-focused and pragmatic, also tend to align with Guardians to maintain the structure of the status quo, accounting for up to seventy-five percent of the population.

This results in two halves of society that are relatively immovable—thirty-five percent in one political camp and thirty-five percent in the other. These groups form a foundation that is unlikely to shift drastically in any direction. The Guardians and Artisans in each camp often look at the other with bewilderment, unable to understand how the other side can see the world so differently, yet they provide the critical balance that prevents society from veering too far in one direction.

The most fluid shifts in political sentiment come from Idealists and Rationals, who are driven by better ideas and long-term strategies. Idealists, comprising fifteen to twenty percent of the population, are moved by visions of a better future, while Rationals, making up ten to fifteen percent, are motivated by what they believe is the most logical or strategic path forward. These two groups play the key role in moving society, albeit slowly, in one direction or the other. Only when leaders present new ideas that appeal to Idealists and new strategies that resonate with Rationals does society see political movement.

This dynamic creates a balancing effect. Guardians and Artisans act as the bedrock, slow to change and resistant to drastic shifts, while Idealists and

Rationals provide the fluidity necessary to prevent stagnation. Even when Idealists and Rationals shift, the process is slow and methodical, like lava gradually flowing, because they must first convince the foundation—Guardians and Artisans—to join them.

In essence, this balance of personalities—rooted in God's grand design—ensures that humanity doesn't run off the edge of a cliff when swayed by a single idea or leader. It stabilizes society by creating a natural check on extreme change, allowing us to evolve while maintaining the structures that keep us grounded. This system of balance is essential for long-term societal survival and progress, much like how each personality type contributes to the overall harmony of human life.

This natural balance of personalities is why the American system of government, as crafted by the Founding Fathers, was designed to maintain stability by ensuring the free flow of ideas, beliefs, and values from the people. They understood that when society's natural push and pull between different perspectives is allowed to flourish, it stabilizes the nation. However, when governments become rigid and restrict this flow, rebellion and major conflict often arise.

Governments rooted in socialism or communism tend to suppress the natural flow of societal ideas, beliefs, and values that emerge from the grassroots. These systems often allow a small fraction of leaders to control the majority of society, imposing their narrow worldview and desires. This stifling of diversity in thought and personality leads to devastating consequences for humanity, as power and fear become the tools used to maintain control. Historical examples, such as the Holocaust under Nazi rule, demonstrate how governments that do not allow the free exchange of ideas and that impose rigid control over society can lead to horrific outcomes.

In contrast, a government rooted in freedom allows personalities to flow freely and maintain balance without the need for oppressive tactics. The American system, with its checks and balances, safeguards this flow, ensuring that the natural differences in personality types lead to thoughtful and deliberate progress rather than chaos. It is this system, designed to mirror the diversity of human nature, that helps society remain stable and prevents any one group from seizing unchecked power.

The Dynamics of Personality in the Business World

Just as the framework of society depends on a balance of personalities, so too does the success of businesses—whether under corporate guidance or proprietorship. To a certain degree, the broader oversight of regulations and market forces protects society, but the core dynamics that drive success or failure often mirror the same principles we see in human interactions and personality diversity.

Most businesses begin at a grassroots level, and the personalities involved play a crucial role in determining the outcome. It's no secret that many small businesses fail, and statistics show that around twenty percent of small businesses fail within the first year, while half fail by the fifth year. One of the leading causes of this failure is the lack of diverse personalities contributing to the foundation of the business. In many cases, small businesses, especially sole proprietorships, rely on a single personality type—the owner.[74] This is a critical weakness because it lacks the balance that Guardians, Artisans, Idealists, and Rationals bring to the table.

For example, a sole proprietor may have a visionary idea but lack the organizational skills of a Guardian or the creative flexibility of an Artisan. Without the input of diverse perspectives, the business can struggle to establish the systems and structure necessary for long-term success. The founder may excel in one area but lack the comprehensive insight needed to adapt and grow the business as it expands.

This is why many small businesses that succeed often do so by recognizing the need for balance early on. They bring in employees, partners, or consultants who provide the missing pieces, whether that's the practical approach of a Guardian to maintain order, the innovative thinking of an Artisan, or the strategic long-term vision of a Rational. Successful businesses often start with a great idea but grow into larger, more organized companies by incorporating a diverse set of personalities that create a structural system of checks and balances. This framework allows the company to adapt, scale, and thrive over time.

However, just as the absence of personality diversity can doom small businesses, even large corporations can fail if they allow their leadership to become too homogenous. As businesses grow, there's a tendency for leaders to surround themselves with like-minded individuals—"birds of a feather flock together." This is especially true in the corporate world, where hiring practices often favor those who fit the established culture. Guardians and Artisans, who value order and stability, may dominate the leadership ranks, while Idealists and Rationals, who challenge the status quo and focus on long-term strategy, may be sidelined or discouraged from contributing.

This polarization can create a situation where new ideas and strategies—often spearheaded by Idealists and Rationals—are stifled in favor of maintaining the status quo. In boardrooms, innovative ideas can be taken to dark alleys and beaten to death because they introduce discomfort or require change. Without this balance of personalities, a company can lose its ability to innovate, adapt, and stay competitive.

A recent and glaring example of this dynamic reveals itself in the downfall of Anheuser-Busch. This company, once a giant in the brewing industry, made strategic missteps that many attribute to a leadership team that became polarized in their thinking. As their leadership became more focused on a "woke" agenda, they alienated large segments of their customer base, causing a sharp decline in sales and public trust. This shift in focus may have been driven by leaders who lacked the diverse input of voices that might have warned against this course of action—voices from Guardians concerned with tradition, or Rationals pointing out the long-term risks to the company's core brand.

In business, just as in society, balance is key. Companies that thrive do so because they incorporate a diversity of thought and personality, recognizing that each brings value to the table. Whether it's the stability and order provided by Guardians, the creativity and excitement of Artisans, the vision of

Idealists, or the strategic thinking of Rationals, a successful business ensures that all perspectives are heard and valued. When this balance is lost, companies risk making decisions that are out of touch with their market, their employees, and their long-term viability.

Understanding the dynamics of personality in business is crucial for long-term success. When businesses fail to recognize this, they risk becoming too rigid or too polarized, which can lead to poor decision-making and, ultimately, failure. Whether you're a small business owner or a corporate leader, embracing the diversity of personalities within your organization can ensure stability, creativity, and long-term growth.

Incorporating gender-based or ethnic-based hiring systems in leadership positions, while often rooted in noble intentions, can fail to achieve long-term success if it overlooks the importance of personality diversity. Businesses thrive when they harness the unique strengths of varied personality types, not when hiring decisions are driven primarily by demographic factors. While it's critical to offer equal opportunities for all individuals—regardless of nationality, gender, or physical challenges—true success comes when the right personalities are in place to complement and balance the team.

As the Declaration of Independence famously states, "We hold these truths to be self-evident, that all men are created equal." This principle serves as a cornerstone of American values, ensuring that all individuals are granted equal rights and opportunities. It's essential that American businesses embrace this by hiring individuals from all walks of life. However, while diversity of background and experience is valuable, hiring practices that focus solely on these characteristics without considering personality dynamics can miss the mark.

The question ultimately becomes: Can the person do the job and bring the necessary personality difference that is crucial to the overall success of the business? By focusing on personality, businesses can create environments where individuals thrive, contribute meaningfully, and balance the team's collective strengths. Ethnic and gender diversity should absolutely be part of an inclusive hiring process, but the priority must remain on assembling a team whose personality traits will enhance the company's ability to function effectively, adapt, and innovate.

In the end, successful companies build teams where the diverse personalities—whether they are Guardians, Artisans, Idealists, or Rationals—work in harmony. The balance between structure, creativity, strategy, and vision is what drives long-term growth and stability. When this diversity of thought and temperament is prioritized, businesses are better equipped to navigate the complex challenges of today's world.

What Each Personality Can Bring to the Business Table

Guardians

Strengths:

- **Stability and Order:** Guardians excel at creating and maintaining structure. They ensure that processes run smoothly and that the company operates within established guidelines and systems.

- **Loyalty and Reliability:** Their dedication to their work makes them highly dependable employees who value tradition and consistency.

- **Attention to Detail:** Guardians are meticulous and excel at following through on tasks. They focus on ensuring that all necessary steps are taken to achieve a goal, preventing errors and oversights.

Weaknesses:

- **Resistance to Change:** Guardians may be hesitant to embrace new ideas or methods, preferring to stick with established practices.

- **Overreliance on Structure:** While structure is important, they may struggle when the business requires adaptability or creative problem-solving.

Artisans

Strengths:

- **Creativity and Innovation:** Artisans thrive on thinking outside the box and bringing fresh ideas to the table. They are often the ones who can generate exciting new solutions to problems.

- **Adaptability:** They are flexible and quick on their feet, able to pivot and adjust plans based on new information or sudden changes.

- **Energy and Enthusiasm:** Artisans bring a lively energy to their work, helping to keep morale high and pushing the team forward with their excitement for new challenges.

Weaknesses:

- **Lack of Long-term Focus:** Artisans may struggle with long-term planning or consistency, sometimes preferring to focus on the moment rather than considering future consequences.

- **Impulsivity:** Their enthusiasm can lead to taking risks that haven't been fully thought out, which can sometimes cause issues if not balanced by more cautious team members.

Idealists

Strengths:

- **Vision and Inspiration:** Idealists are dreamers, always thinking about what could be and how things can improve. They are often the ones pushing for change and progress.

- **Empathy and Emotional Intelligence:** Their strong sense of compassion and understanding makes them excellent at managing relationships and fostering collaboration within a team.

- **Strong Ethics:** Idealists are motivated by a desire to make the world a better place, which can lead to them advocating for causes that align with the company's values.

Weaknesses:

- **Over-idealism:** Their lofty visions can sometimes be impractical, and they may become frustrated when reality doesn't align with their idealistic goals.

- **Conflict Avoidance:** Idealists tend to shy away from confrontation, which can lead to unresolved issues festering within a team or company.

Rationals

Strengths:

- **Strategic Thinking:** Rationals excel at analyzing complex problems and developing logical, long-term solutions. They often take a big-picture view, making them ideal for leadership roles that require vision and strategy.

- **Problem-solving:** Rationals are skilled at cutting through emotions and distractions to identify the core issue and solve it efficiently.

- **Innovation and Efficiency:** They are constantly looking for ways to improve systems and processes, making the business more stream-lined and effective.

Weaknesses:

- **Lack of Patience for Emotional Issues:** Rationals may struggle to connect emotionally with team members and may come across as cold or unapproachable.

- **Over-analysis:** They can get bogged down in details, overthinking issues to the point of inaction or missing the opportunity for a quick win.

By understanding the strengths and weaknesses each personality type brings to the business table, companies can harness these qualities to build a well-rounded, efficient, and innovative team. This balance ensures that no critical aspect of business is overlooked and that all bases are covered when it comes to creativity, strategy, structure, and human connection.

The Importance of Personality Fit in Your Career

I didn't fully understand the impact of personality on career satisfaction until later in life. As a Rational personality, I thrived on strategic thinking, innovation, and solving complex problems. Yet, I found myself in the funeral industry, an environment deeply rooted in tradition, emotional interactions, and a strong social component. While I succeeded in this field and raised my family in a comfortable middle-class environment in Keller, Texas, much of my time was marked by frustration.

Fortunately, I worked for a corporation in Fort Worth, Texas, a company that in the beginning was highly innovative and became a dominant force in the funeral industry. The company handled over thirty-five percent of the market in Fort Worth, managing more than 2,500 cases annually from just two iconic locations and overseeing two beautifully maintained cemeteries with over 2,000 interments per year. This success was largely due to the for-ward-thinking leadership that valued growth and excellence, but as the early leaders of innovation retired and weren't replaced, I often found myself at odds with the emotional and traditional nature of the industry.

Had I understood my own personality earlier in life, I might have made different career choices. I was constantly trying to introduce strategic changes to an industry that was resistant to anything that deviated from tradition. This left me feeling like I wasn't fully utilizing my strengths as a Rational personal-ity—strengths that focus on long-term strategies, innovation, and efficiency.

Each personality type is wired differently by God, and finding the right career that matches your inherent design can lead to a much more fulfilling work life. While I found success in the funeral industry, I also recognized the tension between my natural personality and the demands of the job. Understanding who you are, how you process information, and what environment allows you to thrive can help you avoid frustration and find a career path that brings joy and purpose.

In the next section, we'll explore how different personality types align with various career paths, helping you identify where you might find the most satisfaction in your own professional journey.

Guardians: Structured and Reliable Careers

- **Best Careers:** Accounting, law enforcement, healthcare administration, education, human resources

- **Why They Thrive:** Guardians excel in careers that require organization, stability, and adherence to rules. They are natural caretakers and managers, and they find satisfaction in upholding traditions and ensuring that systems run smoothly.

Artisans: Creative and Dynamic Careers

- **Best Careers:** Graphic design, marketing, event planning, performing arts, skilled trades

- **Why They Thrive:** Artisans thrive in hands-on, creative, and fast-paced environments. They bring a fresh perspective and are at their best when they can innovate, create, and entertain others.

Idealists: Inspiring and People-Oriented Careers

- **Best Careers:** Counseling, teaching, social work, ministry, creative writing

- **Why They Thrive:** Idealists are driven by their passion for helping others and their desire to inspire positive change. They excel in environments where they can make a difference in people's lives and help them achieve their potential.

Rationals: Strategic and Analytical Careers

- **Best Careers:** Engineering, research, information technology, strategic consulting, entrepreneurship

- **Why They Thrive:** Rationals are problem solvers who love to strategize and innovate. They flourish in careers that challenge them intellectually and allow them to implement logical, long-term solutions.

Finding the right career is more than just chasing a paycheck or following a path of convenience. When you take the time to understand your God-given personality, you can find work that brings fulfillment and a sense of purpose. This understanding can transform a job into a calling, leading to a life where you feel aligned with who you were created to be.

The Power of Two Personalities: *Synergy*

Marriage is one of the most significant partnerships a person can enter into, and like every other area of life, it is deeply affected by the personalities of those involved. The idea of two people coming together to create something greater than they could alone is a beautiful example of *synergy*—where the whole becomes greater than the sum of its parts. The Bible echoes this wisdom in Ecclesiastes 4:9-10: "Two are better than one, because they have a good return for their labor: If either of them falls down, one can help the other up." This concept of mutual support is central to a successful marriage.

The natural result of marriage, the greatest example of this synergy, is offspring. Children are not just the product of love and commitment but also a reflection of the union's power to create life. Together, husband and wife create something greater—a legacy that neither could accomplish alone. This legacy manifests in their children, who carry forward a combination of both personalities and traits, creating a lasting impact on the world.

However, just like in careers, personalities play a massive role in the success or failure of marriage. Many relationships begin with passion—a force so strong that it can overshadow deeper issues. But passion alone cannot sustain a marriage. Over time, life tests the relationship, and it's often the clash of personalities that becomes the final conflict. While passion may be the initial spark, true compatibility lies at a deeper level. The stress of daily life, decision-making, and long-term goals can bring out aspects of our personalities that are often hidden at the start. As the saying goes, "What's down in the well will come up in the bucket." If two people are misaligned in their core personalities, it's only a matter of time before this surfaces and creates tension.

This misalignment is one reason why many marriages fail. Statistics show that nearly half of marriages end in divorce, often due to unmet expectations, poor communication, and a lack of understanding between partners. Personality conflicts are a significant part of this dynamic. People often enter relationships driven by passion and chemistry, without considering whether their deeper personalities—how they handle conflict, make decisions, and view the world—are truly compatible.

Fine-Tuning Your Personality for Wholeness

Understanding your personality plays a significant role in becoming a whole person because it helps you recognize your natural strengths, weaknesses, and tendencies. Being a whole person is a basic building block of all relationships, but more so in marriage. When you are aware of your personality type, you gain insight into why you think, feel, and behave the way you do. This knowledge enables you to navigate life's challenges more effectively and grow into a more fulfilled person. Being whole means you are self-sufficient—you are able to stand on your own without needing someone else to fill in the gaps or sustain you. You are not dependent on another person for your emotional well-being, your sense of identity, or your ability to function in life. This foundation of self-reliance allows you to enter into relationships from a place of strength rather than need.

Understanding your personality can lead to becoming a more whole and fulfilled person.

1. **Self-Acceptance:** Knowing your personality helps you accept yourself for who you are. Instead of constantly trying to fit into someone else's expectations, you learn to embrace your natural tendencies. This self-acceptance allows you to stop fighting against your nature and start appreciating your unique qualities.

2. **Improved Decision-Making:** Understanding your personality helps you make better decisions—whether in relationships, career choices, or personal goals. By aligning your decisions with your core strengths and preferences, you create a life that suits you rather than feeling out of place or unfulfilled.

3. **Emotional Awareness:** When you understand your personality, you become more aware of how you process emotions and respond to stress. This awareness helps you manage your emotional reactions better and promotes emotional growth, which is vital to becoming whole.

4. **Personal Growth:** Recognizing your personality traits provides a roadmap for personal development. You can focus on enhancing your strengths while addressing areas that need improvement. For example, a Rational may need to work on emotional connection with others, while an Idealist may need to practice logical problem-solving.

5. **Better Relationships:** Knowing your personality type helps you understand how you interact with others and why certain relationships work better for you. This knowledge allows you to form deeper connections and maintain healthier relationships.

6. **Clarity in Career:** Understanding your personality can guide you toward a career that aligns with your natural abilities, leading to greater job satisfaction and fulfillment. A career that matches your personality allows you to use your strengths to their fullest.

7. **Self-Confidence**: As you gain a deeper understanding of your personality, you build confidence in your abilities. When you know what makes you unique, it becomes easier to trust yourself and your decisions.

The Misconception of "Completing" Each Other in Marriage

A common misconception in relationships is that two people who are not fully whole can "complete" each other. This romanticized idea suggests that someone with emotional gaps or insecurities can find a partner to fill those voids. However, in practice, this rarely works. Instead of complementing each other, such relationships often result in emotional exhaustion, as each person tries to take from the other what they lack.

True synergy in marriage occurs when two whole people—fully developed, self-aware, and emotionally healthy—come together. When both people are secure in who they are, the partnership becomes about giving rather than taking. When two people who are 100% whole come together, they create a relationship filled with love, support, and purpose. Their union becomes greater than just 200%, as they work together to build a life that is stronger than what either could achieve alone.

On the other hand, if two people enter a relationship expecting it to fill their emotional gaps and make them whole, they often find themselves struggling. Instead of bringing their full, independent selves to the partnership, they come together with unmet needs that leave the relationship incomplete—like having two TVs but only one remote that works. This imbalance creates frustration and resentment, as each person looks to the other to provide what they lack. Over time, the relationship can shift from being about love, partnership, and growth to a constant tug-of-war, where both try to compensate for their own deficiencies by taking from the other.

This dynamic is easily seen in various relationship issues. For example, one partner might seek out marriage as a way to avoid responsibility—perhaps they don't want to work, assuming that their partner's strong work ethic will cover for them. Over time, this imbalance breeds resentment, as the hard-working spouse feels overburdened while the other enjoys the benefits without contributing. Another example could be a spouse who is unconcerned with maintaining a clean and organized home. Their lack of attention to detail may leave the other partner frustrated, constantly cleaning up after them. Or, one person might be naturally insensitive, frequently making social blunders that their spouse has to fix. In each of these cases, the incomplete partner places an unfair burden on the other, expecting them to fill in the gaps they haven't worked on themselves, leading to tension and emotional exhaustion.

The key to a strong, healthy marriage is for both partners to bring their wholeness to the relationship. By working on themselves first, they can offer their best to each other and grow together. This is the true essence of synergy—two people, fully formed and committed, creating something greater than the sum of their parts.

Understanding your personality and that of your spouse is crucial for building a lasting marriage. It allows both partners to appreciate their differences, communicate effectively, and work toward common goals. In the end, it's not about finding someone to "complete" you. Completing *you* is up to *you*. It's about first completing yourself, becoming whole and finding someone who complements you and enhances the life you're already living.

Ultimately, this is the journey of life—finding oneself in the world God intentionally created for you with purpose. From the ingenious planet designed for life, to the intentional diversity of people who work together to manage it and thrive, to the succinct fit of a lifetime helpmate, everything reflects a creation with you in mind. You are uniquely you. That may be hard to grasp with billions of people in the world, but it's true. There has never been, nor will there ever be, another you. Yet, in the midst of life's demands, we can often forget why we matter. When exhaustion sets in and the weight of responsibility presses down, much of the time it's about understanding what makes us tick. And so, we take a step forward to examine what drives the cycle of your life—energy.

CHAPTER 8

The Energy Cycle and Our Personal Lives

From the intricate systems in nature that sustain life—water, food, shelter—to the complex interdependence of our personalities and relationships, God has masterfully designed creation to function in balance.

According to *Merriam-Webster's Dictionary*, one definition of "life" is "the quality that distinguishes a vital and functional being from a dead body." But life is meant to be more than just existing.

One of my favorite movies, *City Slickers*[75], captures this struggle. It follows three middle-aged friends—Mitch Robbins, Ed Furillo, and Phil Berquist—who feel trapped in routines that no longer bring fulfillment. Mitch sells advertising, Phil endures a loveless marriage while managing his father-in-law's grocery store, and Ed, though successful in business, wrestles with commitment. For Mitch's thirty-ninth birthday, Ed and Phil gift him a two-week cattle drive adventure.

During the trip, the three men share their "best day" and "worst day." Mitch recalls his first baseball game with his father. Phil surprises everyone by choosing his wedding day—because, for once, he saw his father look at him with pride. Then, when asked about his worst day, Phil pauses and dryly responds, "Every day since has been a tie."

It's a humorous but revealing line. Many of us reach points where we feel like we're simply going through the motions—functional, but not fully alive. As responsibilities grow, the carefree days of childhood fade, and life often unfolds differently than we imagined.

Yet, I believe life is meant to be a blessing despite its difficulties. When God breathed life into creation, it wasn't for mankind to merely exist but to thrive. Jesus said, "I came that they may have life and have it abundantly" (John 10:10). While He was referring to eternal life, I believe this also applies to our time on Earth—life filled with purpose, joy, and meaning.

If life were meant to be devoid of goodness, why would we long for an abundance of it? God's design includes experiences that bring joy: the abundance of flavorful food—our source of energy—deep relationships, lifelong marriage, the love of children, and an even greater love for grandchildren. These blessings reflect God's intention for us to experience more than mere survival.

But life gets complicated. Joys fade—food becomes scarce, relationships fracture, marriages dissolve, children grow distant, and grandchildren get caught up in the relentless pace of life. When we lose sight of God's design, uncertainty can overshadow the blessings meant to enrich us.

Yet, what if difficulty isn't a sign that something is wrong, but a reflection of how life is structured? Understanding the flow of energy—how it is gained, spent, and replenished—can provide insight into why life feels exhausting. Hardship is not always a sign of failure; it is part of the natural rhythm of existence. By recognizing these cycles, we can learn to manage energy wisely, reduce unnecessary burdens, and regain balance.

Powering Life on Earth

Deep beneath the surface of Texas, just outside San Antonio, lies Natural Bridge Caverns—one of the largest cave systems in the U.S. Over tens of thousands of years, nature has sculpted breathtaking formations of stalactites and stalagmites, each growing at a rate of about one inch per century. One of the most awe-inspiring formations is *The Watch Tower*, a towering spire stretching fifty feet from the cavern floor—a silent witness to the slow, unrelenting passage of time.

During a guided tour, there's a moment that leaves a lasting impression. At the deepest part of the cave, the guide flips a switch, plunging the space into absolute darkness. The blackness is so complete it feels tangible. You raise your hand inches from your face, but it vanishes into the void. Even the silence is heavy, as though sound itself has been swallowed by the earth.

This experience starkly reminds us of how much we rely on energy to shape our world. Without it, there is no movement, no warmth, no life. Energy is so integrated into our daily existence that we rarely think about it—until, like in the cave, it's suddenly gone.

The same realization hits when we go without food—our primary source of energy. Hunger, fatigue, irritability—these aren't just physical discomforts; they are signals that our energy reserves are depleting. Much like the darkness in the caverns, these sensations make us acutely aware of how essential energy is to sustain every part of life.

What Is Energy?

From the moment we are born, our bodies are connected to a constant flow of energy. A baby cries every few hours, demanding nourishment to sustain life. Energy fuels everything—from the steady beat of our heart to the simplest task of lifting a hand. Even in sleep, our bodies continue to draw from it, regulating breathing and repairing cells. Our dependence on this flow is both constant and unavoidable—a built-in reminder of our connection to the cycle of life.

I remember, in grade school, seeing a picture of Benjamin Franklin's famous kite experiment. The image showed Franklin standing in a storm, flying a kite with a key attached, lightning striking, illuminating the discovery of electricity. But while dramatic, that bolt was simply releasing energy—not creating it. The source of energy had always been there; Franklin simply found a way to harness it.

This is true for all of life. A thriving world—and a thriving life—doesn't just fall into place. It takes work. It takes energy. Life is a constant flow and exchange of energy—a delicate balance between order and disorder, growth and decay. Just as our personalities shape how we interact with the world, the fundamental laws of energy and matter shape everything around us.

For this discussion, we can categorize energy on Earth into two basic types: biological energy (which sustains living organisms) and non-biological energy (which powers technology and infrastructure). But both forms ultimately trace back to the same source—the sun.

The sun is the great provider of life's energy, fueling everything from the smallest plant to the largest ecosystem. Its light powers photosynthesis, sustaining the food chain, and its warmth drives weather patterns, ocean currents, and even the cycles that shape our environment. It's no coincidence that the first thing God addresses in creation is *light*: *"Let there be light"* (Genesis 1:3). Before anything else could take shape, there had to be *energy*. This underscores the necessity of the sun's presence from the beginning, ensuring that Earth's life-supporting systems were set in motion.

Energy in Living Systems

Biological energy is the foundation of life. It begins with photosynthesis, where plants and microorganisms capture sunlight and convert it into chemical energy stored as glucose. This stored energy then flows through the food chain: herbivores consume plants, carnivores eat herbivores, and humans consume both. Plants serve as the vital link between the sun and all living things, making solar energy accessible to every organism.

Even during photosynthesis, plants produce the oxygen we breathe, creating a continuous cycle in which we harness the sun's energy to sustain life. Without this process, life as we know it would not exist.

Energy Beyond Living Systems

Non-biological energy doesn't directly fuel living organisms but is still essential for human activity. While solar power is the most direct form, other energy sources—like wind, water, and fossil fuels—are also connected to the sun.

- Wind energy results from the sun heating Earth's surface unevenly. Warm air rises, and cooler air moves in to replace it, creating wind currents that can be harnessed for energy.

- Hydropower originates from the sun's heat driving the water cycle. Solar energy evaporates water, which then falls as precipitation, often at higher elevations. As the water flows downhill due to gravity, its energy is captured and converted into mechanical and electrical power.

- Fossil fuels, such as coal and oil, are essentially ancient sunlight. Millions of years ago, plants and microorganisms trapped solar energy through photosynthesis. When they died and were buried under sediment, that energy became stored in fossil fuels. When we burn these fuels, we're tapping into energy that originated from the sun long ago.

In both biological and non-biological systems, 99.9% of the energy we use on Earth can be traced back to the sun. Yet, despite its abundance, energy is not limitless—it must be harvested, stored, and replenished. And when that balance is disrupted, we feel it.

The Unstoppable Flow of Time and Energy

I grew up in an era where country music captured the heartbeat of American life. One song, *Okie from Muskogee* by Merle Haggard[76], became an anthem for tradition, celebrating a world that seemed stable and unchanging. It painted a picture of small-town life where things stood firm against the chaos of cultural upheaval.

But the truth is, life isn't static. Change is not just inevitable—it's fundamental to how the universe operates. No matter how much we long for stability, energy is always in motion, and with motion comes transformation.

Oklahoma is well known for its violent thunderstorms—particularly tornadoes. When we moved to the countryside, where the sky stretched endlessly above us, lightning storms became mesmerizing displays of raw, untamed energy. The bolts would streak unpredictably across the sky, illuminating the heavens in chaotic brilliance.

That's the nature of energy—it doesn't sit still. It moves, flows, and disperses, always traveling in one direction.

This directional flow of energy is closely tied to something even more fundamental—time itself. Physicist Arthur Eddington coined the term, *The Arrow of Time,* to describe the fact that time has a natural, irreversible direction. We see this in everyday life—things don't unburn, unmix, or unbreak. Stir cinnamon into a bowl of oatmeal, and no matter how much you stir in the opposite direction, it won't separate back into a neat pile. Instead, it disperses even further. This is because energy, once spent, spreads outward—just like time moves forward, never reversing.

This principle applies to everything in life. All things change—every second, every day, every year—until the end of time. The natural tendency of the universe is to move toward disorder, and it requires energy to maintain order.

A Great Start to a Bad Day

How many times have you heard someone groan in frustration, *"What are the odds of that happening?"* Just when you think nothing else can go wrong—it does.

Imagine this: It's been raining all night, and the pigpen is a muddy mess. You're out there in the morning, trying to feed the hogs, but they're jostling and bumping into you. Suddenly, you lose your footing and fall face-first into the mud. Before you can get up, the pigs start crowding around, nearly trampling you. In a panic, you grab the first thing you can—a board about the size of a baseball bat. You swing it to fend them off, but in the process, you accidentally strike the one pig you had planned to show at the upcoming fair—right in the head. And, as if on cue, the pig drops dead on the spot.

Now, that might sound too absurd to be true, but it actually happened to a friend of mine in high school. He had invested a lot of money in that pig, and of all the pigs to hit, that was the *last* one he would have chosen. The odds of such an unlucky coincidence were staggering.

This exact scenario might not have happened to you, but we've all had moments that make us shake our heads in disbelief. You drop your toast, and it lands butter-side down. You send an email before finishing it. Your cell phone slips from your hand—straight into the toilet.

Welcome to Murphy's Law. *Murphy's Law* states: "Anything that can go wrong will go wrong." It's a humorous but painfully accurate way to describe life's inevitable misfortunes. But is it really just "bad luck"? Or is there something deeper at play?

The truth is, Murphy's Law isn't just a saying—it reflects a real, observable pattern in how the universe operates. And that pattern is disorder. Left on its own, life tends to fall apart—not come together. We experience this every day:

- Your house doesn't stay clean unless you actively maintain it.
- Your body doesn't stay in shape without effort.
- Relationships don't strengthen without intentional care.

This isn't just a metaphor—it's a fundamental law of the universe. The reason Murphy's Law holds true is the same reason your coffee gets cold, metal rusts, and plans unravel. It all comes down to The Second Law of Thermodynamics—one of the most powerful principles in science. This law states that in any energy exchange, some energy is always lost to disorder, also known as entropy. In other words, things naturally break down over time unless energy is applied to keep them in order.

If you don't put effort into maintaining something, it deteriorates. Entropy is why life requires work. This means that when things go wrong, it's not just bad luck—it's how the world works. Understanding this can help us stop feeling like life is conspiring against us and instead start working with these natural principles to bring balance.

And that's where energy comes in. Everything—our work, our relationships, our well-being—depends on how well we manage, replenish, and direct our energy to counteract disorder.

Managing the Flow of Life's Energy

The *First Law of Thermodynamics* states that energy cannot be created or destroyed; it can only change form. The word thermodynamics itself helps explain this: "thermo" refers to heat energy (primarily from the sun), and "dynamics" refers to how that energy moves and works. This means that life operates within a constant exchange of energy that must be sustained.

In a closed system, the energy we expend must be replenished by the energy we consume—primarily through food. The key term here is closed system—meaning we don't receive additional outside help. There's no external source supplementing our energy needs, no one covering our costs.

The *Second Law of Thermodynamics* tells us that in every energy exchange, some energy is lost as waste heat, making systems inefficient. This is why perpetual motion machines—devices that could run indefinitely without additional energy—are impossible. They violate this fundamental rule.

The same is true for us. We require constant energy input to function, live, and survive. The sun provides more than enough energy every second of daylight, freely available and abundant. However, harvesting and utilizing that energy takes effort—whether through photosynthesis, human labor, or technological systems.

Even our modern conveniences require energy input. When we flip a light switch, we're tapping into an energy system that someone had to build and maintain. Energy isn't free—whether it's physical effort, money, or resources, it must be replenished. Similarly, in life:

- The more complex or demanding our responsibilities, the more energy we require.

- If we don't replenish that energy, we experience exhaustion—physically, emotionally, or spiritually.

- Since we can't create energy from nothing, life becomes a continuous cycle of consumption, transformation, and replenishment.

This reality applies to every aspect of life. If you don't intentionally balance energy input and output, you'll burn out. Everything in life, from the smallest cell to the grandest civilization, follows the same fundamental pattern—energy must flow to sustain life. This means that thriving isn't about resisting energy loss—it's about mastering its flow.

- If we accept that disorder is inevitable, we stop being surprised when things go wrong.

- If we recognize that energy must be replenished, we learn to manage it wisely.

- If we embrace the need for effort, we stop longing for effortless stability and start working *with* the natural rhythms of life.

So, where's the missing link? How does energy truly flow through us, and how can we harness it for a thriving life? That's what we'll explore next.

The Current of Money

Throughout history, survival was directly tied to physical effort. If you wanted food, you had to hunt, fish, or farm. If you needed shelter, you had to gather materials and build it yourself. The energy you spent had an immediate return: work equaled survival.

But as societies advanced, this direct exchange of energy changed. Instead of every person laboring to secure their own resources, civilizations developed systems where some people worked the land while others specialized in different skills—blacksmithing, trading, and carpentry. This shift allowed for progress, but it also introduced a new form of energy exchange: money.

Money IS Stored Energy

At its core, money represents stored human effort. Rather than directly harvesting food or materials, people now work specialized jobs, earning money in exchange for their labor. That money can then be spent on accessing goods and services—essentially transferring one person's stored energy to another. Consider a loaf of bread:

- In the past, you'd plant wheat, harvest it, grind it into flour, and bake the bread yourself.

- Today, you spend money to buy it at a store. But what is that money? It represents the energy you expended at your job, now converted into a currency that allows you to acquire the bread without growing it yourself.

This same principle applies to everything we buy—housing, electricity, fuel. Every dollar spent is a transfer of energy, reflecting the work someone had to do to produce or provide a resource.

Energy Exchange and the Hidden Costs of Modern Life

In a world where money is the dominant form of energy exchange, inefficiencies multiply. Unlike the direct system of working the land and eating what you grow, today's economy introduces middlemen, industries, and infrastructures that each take a portion of the energy before it reaches you.

Buying a hamburger feels effortless—just order, pay, and enjoy. But behind that quick transaction is a vast chain of energy and effort:

- The wheat for the bun and the lettuce, tomatoes, and onions were grown using sunlight, water, fertilizers, and farm equipment. The beef came from cattle raised on feed, water, and land, all requiring energy.

- The grain was milled into flour, the vegetables harvested, the beef processed into patties, and everything transported—each step relying on fuel, machinery, and refrigeration.

- The grill, fryer, and storage all use electricity and gas. The restaurant itself requires lighting, heating/cooling, and water—all powered by energy.

- The wrapper, napkins, and bag were manufactured, printed, and delivered. The restaurant's marketing—from digital ads to billboards—requires design, production, and electricity.

- Employees take your order, prepare the meal, and keep the restaurant running. Their wages come from the cost of the meal, which is ultimately an exchange of energy—your past work (money) for their current work (service).

A simple hamburger represents a massive, interconnected system of energy and labor. Every convenience has a cost—whether in fuel, work, or money—all tracing back to the fundamental principle—nothing happens without energy.

Understanding the Loop: Energy → Money → Energy

Money, then, is not just paper or digital numbers—it is the currency of energy exchange. Every time we earn, spend, or save, we are managing our personal energy reserves. The modern cycle looks like this:

1. *We work, expending physical and mental energy.*

2. *We earn money, which represents that expended energy in a storable form.*

3. *We spend money on food, shelter, and utilities, converting it back into usable energy to continue working.*

The challenge? Inefficiencies in this cycle deplete us more than we realize. Wasteful spending, unnecessary labor, and hidden energy drains make modern life feel more exhausting than it should be.

Recognizing money as stored energy changes how we approach it. It shifts our perspective from spending mindlessly to managing energy efficiently, ensuring that the effort we exert is not lost to unnecessary drains.

This principle will become even more important as we explore where energy is lost, how it can be conserved, and what it means to truly regain balance in our lives.

The Unseen Loss of Energy

As children, we rarely notice energy waste. Our parents absorb the inefficiencies—providing food, keeping the lights on, and handling life's hidden costs. But as we grow older and begin managing our own resources, energy leaks become unavoidable and a problem we have to deal with.

Every task we undertake, whether physical or mental, is subject to inefficiency. From basic activities like cooking and cleaning to the mental strain of work and relationships, there is always a loss of energy along the way. And once we have children of our own, that loss compounds—because now, we're also covering their inefficiencies.

The Daily Energy Drain

Think about the start of a typical workday. You wake up, make coffee, get dressed, and commute to work—each step consuming energy. But much of this energy is lost in inefficiencies:

- Washing clothes, preparing outfits, and getting ready each morning take time, effort, and resources (water, electricity, and mental energy), yet none of it directly contributes to your work.

- Sitting in traffic burns fuel, time, and patience. You're paying for gas, wear on your car, and lost time—all uncompensated.

- The pressure of deadlines, difficult negotiations, and social interactions with coworkers and customers drain mental energy—often more than the actual tasks at hand.

- Decision fatigue—constant small choices from what to wear to how to phrase an email, add up, reducing your ability to focus on more substantive work.

None of these efforts are directly rewarded, yet they all contribute to energy loss—financially, physically, and mentally. Recognizing these drains is the first step toward managing energy more effectively.

The Cycle of Energy Loss at Home

You leave for work, but your home doesn't pause its demands just because you're gone. Energy inefficiency continues in the background, unnoticed but constant.

The dishes you washed last night? They're already piling up again, requiring more water, soap, and effort—over and over, day after day. The house you cleaned yesterday? Your kids (or pets) have undone it within hours, meaning the time and energy you spent restoring order were temporary at best. And the air conditioning that runs all day while you're away? It's quietly consuming energy and money without providing immediate comfort or benefit.

Even outsourcing these tasks doesn't eliminate the energy loss—it simply shifts it. Take, for example, hiring a house cleaner. On the surface, it seems like an efficient use of money—you get a clean house without spending your own time and effort. But if we break it down, the total energy exchange looks like this:

- The cleaner's physical energy investment, which is now externalized but still required.

- Their travel time, fuel, and vehicle expenses, meaning additional energy is burned just to get the job done.

- Their cleaning supplies and equipment, which must be purchased and replenished—an effort that requires its own time and energy investment.

- Taxes and business overhead, which further add to the unseen costs.

- The time for scheduling and coordination, which you still have to manage.

- Gratuities and other fees, additional expenses that don't directly contribute to the cleaning itself.

No matter how we approach it, there's no such thing as a truly effortless system—energy is always being used, whether it's your own or someone else's, which compounds the energy usage. The very act of outsourcing means additional layers of energy expenditure—more transportation, more resources consumed, more inefficiencies introduced into the process. Life is a constant balancing act of managing and redistributing energy, but entropy ensures that maintaining order always requires more effort than letting things fall apart.

Looking at the big picture, the total energy loss is often greater than if you had done the work yourself. This doesn't mean outsourcing is always wrong—sometimes it's necessary. But when energy efficiency is the goal, we must consider whether we are truly saving energy or simply shifting the burden elsewhere.

The same happens when we substitute material gifts for emotional energy in relationships. The gift itself becomes a form of inefficiency—a costly delay of the inevitable confrontation or honest conversation. It represents an attempt to invest physical energy where emotional energy is needed, creating an inefficient mismatch. Investing time and genuine attention directly into relationships yields better results and prevents wasted energy overall.

Emotional energy can feel draining and uncomfortable, which is why people often avoid it. But taking a direct approach is often the most effective and efficient way to reach a true solution. I've always believed that "a sharp knife cuts the quickest and hurts the least" in managing relationships, whether personal or professional. This approach isn't about being unkind; it's about offering direct honesty, a practice that takes courage and is rooted in compassion. Jesus highlights the value of honesty in communication in Matthew 5:37, saying, "Let what you say be simply 'Yes' or 'No'; anything more than this comes from evil." Here, Jesus encourages us to speak with sincerity and straightforwardness, without misleading or watered down and confusing information. This advice aligns with the idea that people know how to adapt to honesty. Direct communication not only respects others but also saves us from the inefficiencies that arise when we avoid the truth.

This principle applies to energy management as well. Avoiding direct solutions—whether in relationships or daily tasks—leads to wasted effort. The more efficiently we deal with problems at their root, the less energy we lose to unnecessary complexity.

Even something as small as leaving lights on has hidden costs. It's easy to dismiss with, *"I'll just pay the bill,"* but that bill reflects:

- The power plants generating electricity.
- The workers maintaining the grid.
- The infrastructure supporting the entire system.

Each use comes at a fractional cost, seemingly insignificant in the moment, but it accumulates throughout the month. A hidden loss of energy—both financial and physical—that could have been entirely avoided by simply turning off the light when it wasn't needed.

In the end, we often throw money and energy at problems, thinking it will simplify life, not realizing that money is a form of our stored energy. But whether it's outsourcing tasks, indulging in material comforts, or neglecting relationships, these choices often create hidden inefficiencies that drain our energy and resources. The key is recognizing and addressing these underlying inefficiencies to live more intentionally and conserve our energy for what truly matters.

In the Bible, Solomon offers wisdom on this: "Better is a handful of quietness than two hands full of toil and a striving after wind." (Ecclesiastes 4:6).

Reducing the Waste of Our Energy

There's an episode of *All in the Family* where Archie Bunker's wife, Edith, tries to conserve energy by quickly opening and closing the refrigerator door. To keep the cool air in and reduce energy waste, she flings the door open, blindly grabs whatever she can in two seconds, and then slams the door shut. The result? Nine times out of ten, she grabs the wrong item! Archie's classic look of disbelief— *"You've got to be the dumbest person on the planet!"*—made it hilarious, but the scene illustrates a real-life point about wasting energy, whether it's from unnecessary actions or inefficiency.

In all seriousness, simplifying life in practical ways can reduce unnecessary work and wasted energy. Think about something as simple as taking off your clothes. You can remove your shirt right-side out just as easily as inside-out, but if you take it off inside-out, you'll need to use extra energy later to turn it right-side out before doing laundry. The goal is to eliminate the need for that extra step. Similarly, dropping clothes directly into the hamper instead of leaving them scattered around saves the energy of having to gather them from every corner later.

This principle of eliminating inefficiencies applies not just to our personal lives but also to business. In the world of business, a well-known concept called *Kaizen* focuses on continuous improvement and reducing wasted effort. One of the best demonstrations of this principle can be seen in a YouTube video called, *Toast Kaizen.*

In the video, making toast—a seemingly simple task—illustrates how inefficient processes can accumulate over time. The bread is far from the toaster, the butter is stored cold and hard in the refrigerator, and utensils are kept across the room. Each time the person makes toast, extra energy and time are wasted moving back and forth. When it's time to spread the butter, the cold butter tears the bread, adding another layer of inefficiency and frustration.

The solution in the video demonstrates how small adjustments—like keeping butter at room temperature near the toaster and storing utensils within easy reach—can drastically reduce the effort and energy needed. This is the essence of Kaizen; making small, incremental changes to improve efficiency.

Kaizen doesn't just advocate speeding up inefficient processes—it seeks to eliminate unnecessary steps altogether. By storing bread and butter closer to the toaster and keeping everything needed for the task within arm's reach, the energy required to make toast is minimized. Even layering tasks—like loading dishes into the dishwasher while waiting for the bread to toast—enhances overall efficiency.

This is the heart of what we're discussing—not just working harder or faster within inefficient systems but removing the need for extra energy in the first place. Whether in your personal life—like turning off lights when you leave a room—or in business, where processes are streamlined to eliminate wasted effort, the goal is to reduce energy drain by focusing on working smarter, not faster or harder.

The Value of Your Energy in Work and Leadership

Most people—about ninety percent—work for someone else. Businesses function as systems that extract energy from employees in exchange for wages. This labor is then converted into products or services that generate profit. Ideally, this exchange is mutually beneficial, where employees receive fair compensation for their energy, and businesses thrive through their contributions.

However, not all companies value energy equally. Some offer fair wages, benefits, and work-life balance, ensuring employees feel valued and compensated appropriately. Others extract far more energy than they return, leading to burnout, dissatisfaction, and diminished well-being.

The most extreme historical example of energy exploitation was slavery, where human labor was forcibly taken without compensation or concern for well-being. While slavery has been abolished, the issue of fair compensation remains relevant today. Many workplaces still undervalue employees, offering low wages, excessive hours, or high-stress conditions that drain energy without adequate return.

Even high-paying jobs aren't immune to energy costs. Long commutes, high-pressure environments, and relentless schedules consume more than just time—they take a toll on mental bandwidth, relationships, and personal growth. True career sustainability isn't just about financial compensation; it's about ensuring that your energy is respected, rewarded, and balanced.

Where you invest your energy is one of the most important decisions you'll make. The best opportunities provide not just financial stability but also the freedom to build stronger relationships, pursue personal goals, and maintain well-being. Work should provide a return that allows you to thrive, not just survive.

The Work Economy: Energy for Money Exchange

At its core, work is an exchange of energy for stored energy—money—which we then use to obtain food, shelter, and other necessities. However, while the cost of food energy (our input) is relatively equal for most people, the return on energy spent (our output) can vary greatly.

Some may earn $15 per hour, while others earn $40 per hour or more—even though both are exerting similar effort. The difference isn't simply how hard they work but how effectively their energy is applied. Maximizing this return comes down to three key factors:

1. **Quality Fit**—*Aligning work with your natural strengths to reduce wasted energy.*

2. **Relevance**—*Matching skills with high-value industries to ensure a greater return.*

3. **Investment in Yourself**—*Continually improving your abilities to remain valuable in a changing economy.*

Quality Fit: Aligning Work with Your Strengths

The quality of your work determines its value. Everyone has unique strengths, and when your job aligns with those strengths, your effort becomes more efficient, more rewarding, and ultimately more valuable. Instead of simply working harder, the key is to work smarter—ensuring that every bit of energy you invest leads to a greater return. Since energy, once spent, can't be reclaimed, maximizing its impact means finding work that not only sustains you financially but also enriches your personal and professional life.

A key factor in this is understanding your personality. Your personality influences how you process information, interact with others, and solve problems. Aligning your work with your natural tendencies reduces energy waste and increases efficiency. For example:

- A naturally analytical person may struggle in a high-energy sales environment but thrive in data analysis or strategic planning.

- A highly creative person may feel stifled in repetitive administrative work but excel in marketing, design, or content creation.

- A hands-on problem solver may find office work draining but flourish in a trade or technical field.

- A rational thinker who thrives on innovation may feel stifled in an industry that values tradition, such as funeral services or long-standing family businesses. These environments are often dominated by Guardian personalities, who prioritize stability and resist change. When a forward-thinking individual works in such a setting, their natural drive for innovation may be at odds with the prevailing culture, creating a persistent energy drain due to misalignment.

The better your job aligns with your innate abilities, the more efficiently you can invest your energy—leading to higher returns and greater career satisfaction.

Relevance: Matching Skills with Demand

Even the most well-developed skills won't yield a high return if they aren't in demand. Some professions—such as healthcare, technology, and skilled trades—command higher compensation because they solve critical needs.

However, success isn't about picking a single career path—it's about understanding where your skills fit into the economy and refining them to maximize their worth.

Many assume that skill alone determines value, but in reality, how a skill is applied makes all the difference. Two people can have the same ability, yet one earns significantly more because they understand how to position their skills within high-value industries. For example:

- A talented writer who creates marketing copy for businesses may earn significantly more than one who writes personal essays with no commercial demand.

- A mechanic specializing in electric vehicle repair will have greater job security than one focused solely on outdated car models.

By investing in yourself, developing in-demand skills, and strategically applying them where they are most valued, you can maximize the return on your energy investment and build a sustainable, fulfilling career.

Consider this: You spend $20 a day on food to fuel your body for work. The next day, you exchange that energy for wages over an 8-hour shift. There's a massive difference between earning $15 per hour ($120 total) and $40 per hour ($320 total).

The energy your body consumes has the same intrinsic value for everyone, but how effectively you exchange it in the marketplace determines your return. In this example, working for $15 per hour results in a $200 loss of potential earnings because the market supports a much higher return for the same physical energy output. The key is to minimize energy loss by aligning your work with its highest market value.

Investment in Yourself: Stay Valuable in a Changing Economy

Even if you've found the right career fit and positioned your skills in high-demand industries, your value in the workforce isn't static—it evolves with the economy. The most successful people continually invest in themselves, adapting to modern technologies, trends, and market shifts to stay competitive.

Long-term career sustainability depends on lifelong learning and skill development. No matter the field, those who refine their abilities and expand their knowledge increase their earning potential and job security. Consider these approaches to investing in yourself:

- Expanding your knowledge is one of the smartest investments you can make, especially if your company is willing to cover the cost. Even if a training session or course seems tedious, take full advantage of it—you never know when that knowledge will become valuable. Read books on business, motivation, and human behavior to gain insights that most people overlook. The more you understand how industries, markets, and people operate, the more leverage you will have in your career.

- Be open to learning from those who are smarter than you. Never take offense at constructive criticism from someone more experienced—it's often the most valuable feedback you'll ever receive. Highly intelligent people can be brutally honest, but that's because they focus on results, not feelings. Instead of reacting emotionally, extract the lesson from their critique and use it to improve.

- Be the smartest person in the room by seeking knowledge beyond what is required. The most successful people don't just learn what's necessary for their job; they explore how their role fits into the bigger picture. Developing a well-rounded understanding of finance, leadership, negotiation, and problem-solving will set you apart, even in specialized fields. The more you know, the more control you have over your career trajectory.

- Don't be afraid to embrace change—even if someone younger figured it out first. Change is the reason you have a cell phone in your hand instead of a rotary dial. Those who see better, faster, or smarter ways of doing things get to sit in the front seat of progress and become part of the solution, not the problem. The moment you reject innovation simply because it comes from a younger generation, you risk becoming obsolete.

Just like in the natural world, stagnation leads to decline. A worker who stops growing in their field eventually sees diminishing returns on their energy investment. But those who proactively sharpen their skills and seek new knowledge increase their resilience, expand their options, and maximize their long-term return on energy spent.

Church Leadership: The Stewardship of Your Energy

Throughout history, church leadership has held tremendous power over its followers, extending its influence beyond spiritual guidance to include the management of vast resources. Managing these resources—whether in the form of financial contributions or the emotional and spiritual energy of a congregation—comes with great responsibility. The Catholic Church in the Middle Ages is a prime example of how mismanagement can lead to a system of control and inequality that profoundly affects the people.

During this period, the Church exercised significant authority over European society, regulating not only spiritual matters but also much of daily life, often using fear and control as its primary tools. The sale of indulgences—a practice in which the church sold forgiveness for sins—essentially placed the fate of one's soul in the hands of the clergy. In my opinion, much of this leadership will have a lot of explaining to do to God one day. Nonetheless, people were convinced that their salvation could only be secured through monetary contributions—the people's energy—leading to widespread corruption. This abuse of power starkly contrasted with how God Himself had managed forgiveness and worship in the earliest history of humanity.

In those early days, from Adam and Eve through to figures like Abraham and Moses, God led humanity directly, and forgiveness of sin was established through a sacrificial system. People engaged with God personally, and sacrifices served as a means of atonement. This practice was later formalized in the Mosaic Law, prescribing specific rituals and sacrifices to cleanse sin, with priests acting as intermediaries for purification and forgiveness. However, as time went on, Israel began to desire a king like other nations, rather than continuing to rely solely on God's direct leadership. God allowed this shift, beginning with King Saul, and while kings ruled the people, priests retained a critical role in the religious and ceremonial aspects of life. Yet, as power consolidated under kingship, both the monarchy and the priesthood became vulnerable to corruption, with leadership often straying from God's intentions and exploiting their positions of power.

Finally, with the coming of Jesus in the New Testament, a transformative change occurred. Jesus came not to abolish the law, but to fulfill it (Matthew 5:17), offering a way for people to connect with God directly. Through His life, teachings, and ultimate sacrifice—giving His own life on the cross—He provided a means of forgiveness that surpassed the need for continual animal sacrifices or priestly mediation. His message emphasized a personal, faith-based relationship with God, accessible to all, regardless of background or status, shifting the focus to individual accountability and the gift of personal salvation.

In contrast to Jesus's model of selfless service, the wealth amassed by the Church in later centuries stood in stark opposition to the needs of the common people. Rather than leading and uplifting followers, the Church often exploited them, creating a system where the few benefited at the expense of the many. This was quite different from the direct, personal connection to God that had been intended, which through His son, Jesus, culminated through the ages to focus on individual faith and devotion rather than institutionalized control.

Psalm 82 offers insight into God's expectations of just leadership. Here, God stands in an assembly of rulers and chastises them for failing to care for the people properly: "How long will you judge unjustly and show partiality to the wicked? Give justice to the weak and the fatherless; maintain the right of the afflicted and the destitute" (Psalm 82:2-3). This divine reprimand clarifies that true leadership must prioritize justice, care, and responsibility for the well-being of all people, especially those of lesser status. This call for compassionate leadership reflects the behavior of many modern business and government leaders, who form inner circles of entitlement, often ignoring the struggles of those less fortunate.

Jesus rebuked the religious leaders of His day for similar failures. In Mark 12:38-40, He warned: "Beware of the scribes, who like to walk around in long robes and like greetings in the marketplaces and have the best seats in the synagogues and the places of honor at feasts, who devour widows' houses and for a pretense make long prayers. They will receive the greater condemnation." Jesus sharply criticized these leaders for their focus on appearances, status, and personal gain, rather than truly serving their people. They enjoyed the privileges that came with leadership but failed to responsibly manage the spiritual and material resources entrusted to them, exploiting the vulnerable instead of supporting them as they had been called to do.

Following this rebuke is the well-known story of the widow's mite, found in Mark 12:41-44. As Jesus watched people making their offerings at the temple, a poor widow put in two small copper coins, worth only a penny. Jesus pointed her out to His disciples, saying, "Truly, I tell you, this poor widow has put in more than all those who are contributing to the offering box. For they all contributed out of their abundance, but she out of her poverty has put in everything she had, all she had to live on."

While this story highlights the widow's incredible faith, it also sheds light on the neglect of religious leaders who would willingly accept her last coins without concern for her well-being. In the context of Jesus's earlier rebuke, it becomes clear that her sacrifice, though noble, exposes the failure of those in power to care for the vulnerable. The leaders were more concerned with the energy they could extract from society and ignorant of the genuine cost, failing to ensure that the poor, like the widow, were protected and provided for.

Fast-forward to today, and I see similar patterns of energy mismanagement in certain church leaders. Owners of sprawling estates, private airstrips and aircraft are unquestionably excessive in their management of the church. This wealth, funded by the contributions of their congregations, represents a massive extraction of energy from people who are often led to believe that their financial offerings will secure blessings or favor from God. This lifestyle of some church leaders raises critical questions about whether they are truly stewarding the resources entrusted to them for the good of all, or simply indulging in personal luxury.

I also think leaders who advocate for the "prosperity gospel," a philosophy that equates financial success and material wealth with God's blessing seems misleading. This messaging can distort the true meaning of stewardship, often encouraging followers to pursue wealth rather than deepening their faith. This approach can alienate many, as not everyone experiences financial prosperity, and linking riches to righteous living is misleading. It creates a potentially delusional connection between money and salvation, subtly suggesting that prosperity is necessary to belong or to receive God's favor. In reality, of all things in life, only God's grace is truly free. The prosperity gospel blurs the line between spiritual growth and material success, leading many to believe that wealth is the ultimate measure of divine approval.

As we've discussed with business leaders, the same principle applies to church leaders—stewardship is about using resources wisely, not for personal enrichment. Leadership in the church, more than anywhere else, should reflect God's call for justice, humility, and care for the people. Leaders should be trusted to use the energy—whether in the form of contributions, time, or spiritual devotion—entrusted to them for the benefit of the entire congregation and community outreach, whether local or broad. When they fail to do this, the people suffer, and the true mission of the church is lost.

This leads to disillusionment among believers, particularly younger generations, who may see the church as just another institution that extracts more than it gives. It's no wonder that mistrust grows, and many turn away from organized religion, feeling that the spiritual energy they pour into it is not being fairly managed.

So, always be mindful of how you invest your energy, even within the church. This is not to suggest that organized religion is inherently flawed—on the contrary, the New Testament encourages believers with the words, "Do not neglect to meet together, as is the habit of some, but encouraging one another" (Hebrews 10:25). I believe that the church Christ established is meant to be a supportive, organized body that strengthens and encourages us in life—but it is still an organization of people. And, as history has shown, not every group of people identifying as a church may fully reflect God's original intent. There is a valuable place for your energy within the church—one that, when grounded in the teachings of the New Testament, brings care and assistance to society. Yet it is also a place where, at times, some may misuse the resources and trust placed in them.

Keeping Life Simple

There is a memorable scene in the popular mini-series *Lonesome Dove*, when Gus McCrae, played by Robert Duvall, is talking to Lorie (Lorena), the young woman he has a soft spot for. She's crying, heartbroken and dreaming of going to San Francisco, imagining the excitement and opportunities awaiting her there. Gus, who understands the hardships and fleeting nature of big dreams, gently tries to ground her, advising her to appreciate the simpler pleasures in life. Gus says to her, *"Lorie darlin', life in San Francisco is still just life. If you want only one thing too much, it's likely to turn out to be a disappointment. Now, the only healthy way to live, as I see it, is to learn to like all the little everyday things. Like a sip of good whiskey in the evening, or a soft bed, or a glass of buttermilk, or say, a feisty gentleman like myself."*[77]

In his simple, endearing way, Gus is encouraging Lorie to find contentment in life's small pleasures rather than placing all her happiness in a distant dream. It's a wonderfully wise moment that captures Gus's character and the deeper theme of *Lonesome Dove* about finding beauty in the everyday, especially in the rugged life they lead.

It's such a well-written scene because it encapsulates Gus's wisdom and warmth. He's trying to tell her, in his own way, that happiness can be found in simple contentment, rather than constantly yearning for more. This message has resonated with so many, and it's one of the reasons Gus is such a beloved character: he reminds us that life doesn't have to be complicated to be fulfilling.

If ever there was a consistent theme in the Bible, it is the call to keep life simple. I believe God fully understood the flow of energy in life and how endless pursuits can drain us, leading to disenchantment, weariness, and emptiness. Solomon, one of the wealthiest and wisest kings, experienced this firsthand. Reflecting on the emptiness he found in riches and luxury, he observed, "Then I considered all that my hands had done and the toil I had expended in doing it, and behold, all was vanity and a striving after wind, and there was nothing to be gained under the sun" (Ecclesiastes 2:11). In the end, Solomon concluded that all worldly pursuits are ultimately "vanity" or futility, advising that the most important thing in life is to "Fear God and keep his commandments, for this is the whole duty of man" (Ecclesiastes 12:13).

Like Gus's advice to Lorie, which echoes in the timeless wisdom of Solomon, we can all find peace in seeking balance and appreciating the beauty of everyday blessings. Life, when centered around meaningful relationships, simple pleasures, and faith, holds a special fulfillment that endless pursuits cannot provide. Here are some small yet profound ways to keep life simple and draw happiness from the essentials.

Social Circles and True Friends

Social media can consume an incredible amount of time and energy, often without people realizing it. Platforms like Facebook, Twitter, and Instagram create the illusion of connection, but investing too much energy in these virtual networks can detract from important relationships, especially with family members who deserve more attention and effort. It's easy to fall into the trap of prioritizing online personas and engagements over real-life connections, leading to inefficient use of emotional energy.

Just as physical inefficiencies drain our energy, so do emotional and social ones. Spreading ourselves thin over numerous shallow connections—whether through social media, casual acquaintances, or surface-level interactions—can leave us exhausted and unfulfilled. In contrast, building deeper, more genuine relationships allows us to channel our emotional energy more effectively, fostering true connection and reducing the fatigue that comes with maintaining too many superficial ties.

The wisdom of the Bible speaks directly to this. Proverbs 18:24 says, "A man of many companions may come to ruin, but there is a friend who sticks closer than a brother." This verse reminds us that having one or two close friendships outside of the family can be more valuable than trying to maintain numerous shallow connections. Focusing our energy on fewer but deeper relationships results in a stronger sense of satisfaction and saves us from the emotional drain of trying to be everything to everyone.

In my life, I've had a number of friendships that have come and gone, but one true friendship has endured for a lifetime—that of my friend, Steve Reichert. When I look back, outside of family, my greatest happiness has come from the adventures and memories we've shared. From childhood explorations of dry creek beds to the challenges of wheat harvest, to the numerous adventures in the Wichita Mountains and skiing trips in the western mountain ranges, no other friendship compares. Sometimes we'd see each other daily for years, while at other times, a year or more might pass between visits. Yet, no matter the time apart, our friendship has always picked up right where it left off.

Our friendship hasn't been without its challenges. Steve can be maddeningly stubborn—to the point you'd feel like shooting him, and in a strange way, that's exactly what happened! When we were kids, he was once at a friend's house after school when things escalated between them, and his friend grabbed a shotgun. As Steve tried to run out of the house, he was shot near the back door. He survived, but probably still carries some birdshot in him to this day. True to his forgiving nature, Steve forgave this friend and remained in contact with him over the years.

Even I've had my moments. Once, when we were kids exploring a creek in the country, we disagreed about which direction to go. Steve, as usual, stubbornly marched off his way, so when he got a little distance down the creek bed, I impulsively shot him in the back of the leg with my pellet gun! I know, crazy! But such were the antics of our youth. Through all the arguments, mishaps, and misadventures, our friendship has remained unshakeable.

A true friend like Steve is more than just someone to share good times with; he's someone who endures every challenge, every laugh, and every setback. Life's happiness isn't in numbers but in quality, and one true friend can mean more than a thousand acquaintances. They're a rare treasure, and their support, loyalty, and shared history make life richer, simpler, and more fulfilling.

Energy and Your Body

Not all the energy we take into our bodies is high-quality energy. The food we consume significantly impacts our energy efficiency, with some foods creating more inefficiencies than others. Highly processed foods or those rich in unhealthy fats and sugars often provide poor-quality energy—they take longer to metabolize, offer minimal nutrients, and are more likely to be stored as fat rather than used immediately. This contributes to sluggishness, metabolic inefficiency, and weight gain.

Eating out, while a nice getaway and an opportunity to experience new foods, adds even more inefficiencies to the process. Beyond the energy used in meal preparation, there's the energy spent getting ready, traveling, and the cost of the restaurant itself—staff, facilities, and service—all of which compound the overall energy expenditure. The convenience comes at a price, not just financially but in terms of energy efficiency.

By contrast, choosing simple, whole, nutrient-dense foods—those rich in essential vitamins, minerals, and proteins—allows our bodies to function more efficiently. Preparing meals at home with fresh, high-quality ingredients eliminates much of the waste associated with dining out and ensures that the energy we consume is working for us, not against us. Occasionally skipping a traditional heavy meal in favor of something lighter and more efficiently processed, such as a well-balanced meal replacement shake, can also help. These shakes provide nearly 100% of the essential nutrients, proteins, vitamins, and minerals the body needs while being easily digestible and metabolized, resulting in sustained energy without the slow, inefficient burn of heavier meals.

Energy Extraction and Efficiency

The human body operates under the principles of energy balance, much like a closed system in thermodynamics. The energy extracted from food must equal the energy expended over time, or an imbalance occurs. However, the body is not 100% efficient in extracting energy from food, as the digestive process itself consumes energy (thermogenesis). Each macronutrient requires different amounts of energy to metabolize:

- Protein: ~20-30% of its energy is lost as heat.
- Carbohydrates: ~5-10% is lost.
- Fats: ~0-3% is lost.

This means that for every calorie consumed, only a fraction is actually available for biological work, movement, and cellular function. The more efficiently a food can be metabolized, the better energy return the body receives.

Energy Storage and Imbalance

If energy intake exceeds immediate energy needs, the surplus is stored primarily in two forms:

1. **Glycogen**—*Short-term storage in muscles and the liver, readily available but with limited capacity.*

2. **Fat**—*Long-term storage, highly energy-dense but not as readily accessible for quick energy needs.*

The problem is that fat stores are inefficiently converted back into usable energy. Once stored, fat requires a controlled metabolic state (such as fasting or extended activity) to break down. Even then, not all of it is directly converted into ATP (the body's energy currency) for immediate use. This is why it's easier to gain weight than to lose it and why maintaining a steady energy balance is key to sustained physical and mental performance.

Energy Input vs. Output: Why Balance Matters

Unlike an efficient battery that can store and instantly release energy, the human body prioritizes survival over convenience—meaning that stored fat is not as easily or efficiently converted back into usable energy compared to immediately available carbohydrates.

A person consuming more energy than needed for daily biological functions and activity will accumulate stored fat. This is why an overabundance of energy intake does not directly translate into greater energy output. Instead, excess energy is stored rather than immediately available for movement, thinking, or work.

When the body needs energy beyond its immediate intake, it first draws from glycogen stores, which are quickly accessible. Only when those are depleted does the body begin breaking down stored fat—but this process is slower and less efficient than directly using food-based energy sources.

Practical Takeaways: How to Balance Your Energy
1. Prioritize High-Quality Energy Sources

- Choose whole, nutrient-dense foods over processed, low-nutrient alternatives. Examples: fresh vegetables, fruits, lean meats, eggs, nuts, and whole grains instead of sugary snacks, white bread, or processed meals.

- Opt for lean proteins, complex carbohydrates, and healthy fats to ensure efficient energy metabolism. Examples: chicken, fish, quinoa, sweet potatoes, brown rice, avocados, olive oil, and almonds.

2. Avoid Unnecessary Energy Storage

- Be mindful of overeating, especially processed foods that are easily stored as fat. Examples: chips, soda, fast food, pastries, and refined sugars contribute to excess energy storage with little nutritional benefit.

- Implement intermittent fasting or portion control to encourage the body to use stored energy rather than constantly storing excess. Eating smaller, balanced meals can help regulate energy use.

3. Match Energy Intake with Output

- Ensure that the energy consumed through food aligns with daily physical and mental exertion. If you're sedentary, overeating high-calorie foods leads to excess storage, whereas an active lifestyle requires nutrient-dense energy sources.

- Regular physical activity helps maintain the body's natural balance between input and output. Strength training, cardio, and even simple movements like walking or stretching prevent excess energy from turning into fat.

4. Understand How Your Body Uses Energy

- Carbohydrates provide quick energy but burn fast. Examples: bananas, oats, whole wheat bread, brown rice, and beans.

- Protein supports muscle maintenance and metabolic activity but is less efficient for immediate energy use. Examples: chicken, fish, eggs, Greek yogurt, tofu, and lentils.

- Fats provide long-term energy storage, but accessing it requires more effort from the body. Examples: avocados, nuts, seeds, olive oil, and fatty fish like salmon.

- Overeating any of these macronutrients results in energy being stored rather than used, leading to inefficiency and potential weight gain.

The laws of thermodynamics apply to the human body just as they do in physics. The body's energy system functions best when energy input equals energy output. When energy is extracted efficiently, stored wisely, and utilized properly, the body thrives. But when energy is mismanaged, stored inefficiently, or consumed in excess, it leads to metabolic inefficiency, weight gain, and sluggish performance.

By understanding these principles, we can make more informed choices about how we eat, move, and sustain our energy levels. Simplifying our approach—choosing whole, nutrient-dense foods, reducing unnecessary energy waste, and being mindful of how we fuel our bodies—allows us to maintain steady energy without unnecessary complexity.

The Energy Drain of Debt

Debt is one of the biggest reasons to keep life simple. It is a major drain on personal energy—both mentally and financially. The problem with debt is that it doesn't just drain what we've already earned; it also demands that we earn even more in the future to pay it off, often with interest. By simplifying our lifestyle and reducing unnecessary spending, we can preserve more of our energy, ensuring that our work benefits us rather than being siphoned away by financial obligations. Keeping life simple isn't just about minimalism—it's about maximizing the return on our time and effort while avoiding the energy drain of financial strain.

The Compounding Burden of Interest

Interest on debt magnifies this issue. Every payment on interest alone is a transfer of our hard-earned money without receiving anything tangible in return. Interest payments represent one of the most inefficient uses of energy, as they siphon away our financial strength—energy that could be directed toward better pursuits, investments, or even rest. Instead, we become locked in a cycle of working harder just to pay for energy that never truly existed in the first place.

If money is a representation of stored energy, then interest artificially inflates the system without an actual energy input, creating an imbalance much like a perpetual motion machine—something that cannot exist according to the laws of physics. Eventually, the system collapses because real energy (labor, resources, production) cannot keep up with the compounded burden of debt.

Biblical Wisdom on Debt and Interest

The Bible provides surprising insight into debt—insight that aligns with modern economics and energy balance principles. Much like the order of creation described in Genesis aligns with scientific understanding, biblical guidance on lending and borrowing suggests a higher intelligence and keen foresight into financial sustainability.

Old Testament Prohibitions Against Interest (Usury)

> **Exodus 22:25:** "If you lend money to any of my people with you who is poor, you shall not be like a moneylender to him, and you shall not exact interest from him."

This verse makes it clear that Israelites were not to charge interest on loans to the poor among them.

> **Leviticus 25:35-37:** "If your brother becomes poor and cannot maintain himself with you, you shall support him as though he were a stranger and a sojourner, and he shall live with you. Take no interest from him or profit, but fear your God, that your brother

may live beside you. You shall not lend him your money at interest, nor give him your food for profit."

Again, the focus is on helping those in need rather than profiting from them.

> **Deuteronomy 23:19-20:** "You shall not charge interest on loans to your brother, interest on money, interest on food, interest on anything that is lent for interest. You may charge a foreigner interest, but you may not charge your brother interest, that the Lord your God may bless you in all that you undertake in the land that you are entering to take possession of it."

This passage distinguishes between Israelites and foreigners, emphasizing fair treatment among one's own community.

New Testament Perspective

> **Luke 6:34-35:** "And if you lend to those from whom you expect to receive, what credit is that to you? Even sinners lend to sinners, to get back the same amount. But love your enemies, and do good, and lend, expecting nothing in return, and your reward will be great, and you will be sons of the Most High, for he is kind to the ungrateful and the evil."

Jesus expands the principle beyond Israel, advocating for selfless giving rather than lending for profit.

A Violation of Energy Balance

What is easily read as good stewardship in the Bible takes on a deeper significance when we understand money as stored energy. Just as the laws of thermodynamics dictate that energy must be balanced—it cannot be created from nothing—interest violates this natural order by fabricating money (energy) out of thin air. Instead of reflecting the true value of labor and resources, interest inflates the cost of borrowing, creating an artificial demand for more energy than was originally expended.

This imbalance forces individuals to work harder and expend more energy just to repay what was borrowed, often at a loss. The result is a cycle of inefficiency, where debt demands a constant input of effort to sustain something that never truly existed in the first place.

It's no coincidence that the biblical warnings against usury focused on the poor—those already struggling to draw enough energy from their food and balance it with what they received in return. God designed the universe to function on principles of sustainability, and Jesus, fully aware of the natural laws governing energy balance, understood that these same principles applied to finance as well. This is likely why God forbade charging interest among the Israelites:

- A loan is an exchange of stored energy—the lender gives the borrower money, and the borrower returns it over time, creating a balanced trade.

- Interest, however, disrupts this balance. The borrower must generate additional energy (through labor and effort) beyond what was received, yet the lender has done nothing additional to create this extra energy.

- The energy required to repay interest has no corresponding input from the lender. It is an artificial demand on the borrower, forcing them to work harder for energy that never truly existed in the first place.

This imbalance is likely why the Bible speaks against interest so strongly. The biblical authors, inspired by God, seemed to understand that a borrower would be forced to produce energy in excess of what they received, creating an unsustainable system where the poor would struggle unfairly to escape the debt.

A Different Way of Doing Things: The Strength of Community

A story I told in Chapter 1, *My Genesis*, illustrates how a system without interest created a fair, balanced exchange of energy and strengthened our small community.

When I was a small boy, my brother Tim and I would often go to Taft Grocery, a small store where we would pick up essentials—bologna, cheese, bread, and mayonnaise—without exchanging money. Instead of requiring immediate payment, the store owner would write it down in a ledger, and from time to time, my father would stop in and pay the bill when he could.

My father was self-employed, and his income was inconsistent. This system of trust and fair trade allowed him to provide food for our family even during slow weeks without the added pressure of interest. Had interest been tacked onto these balances, my father would have had to work even harder—beyond his already full workload—to not only repay the debt but also generate extra energy to cover the fabricated cost of interest.

What made our community special was this mutual understanding and support. No one was looking to exploit their neighbor. Instead, fair trade, trust, and cooperation made life easier for everyone. If our small-town system had operated like modern banking, where every delay in payment came with added interest, life would have been much harder. Families like mine would have been trapped in a cycle of working just to repay energy that was never truly exchanged.

Why National Debt is a Threat to Energy Stability

The same principles apply on a global scale. Nations accumulate debt with interest, essentially fabricating future energy from nothing. But since real energy—labor, resources, and production—must be generated to repay that debt, there comes a point where it is no longer possible. The system collapses when the demand for repayment exceeds the citizens' capacity to extract enough energy to pay it back.

A government does not generate wealth—it only manages the wealth of its citizens. When a government borrows money, it is not shouldering the burden itself; it is committing current and future generations to produce more than what they need to meet basic needs, just to repay a debt they never individually agreed to. Over time, this imbalance forces greater taxation, inflation, or economic hardship, as citizens struggle to pay back not only the initial amount borrowed but also the artificially imposed demand for energy that was never truly created in the first place.

The Fall of Rome: A Lesson in Energy and Economic Collapse

History repeatedly shows that when a civilization's debt surpasses its ability to generate real wealth, collapse follows. One of the clearest examples is the fall of the Roman Empire, which suffered from economic mismanagement, excessive debt, and a failure to balance energy production with its financial system.

At its height, Rome controlled vast resources, but as the empire expanded, it relied heavily on borrowed wealth—much like modern nations today. Instead of maintaining a balanced system where wealth was backed by real energy (agriculture, labor, and trade), Rome turned to debt, taxation, and inflation to sustain its growing military and bureaucracy. With conquest slowing and resources dwindling, the empire could no longer generate enough real energy to sustain itself. Instead of cutting spending, Rome debased its currency—reducing the silver content in coins while keeping the same face value—mirroring the modern practice of printing excess fiat currency. This led to massive inflation, making everyday goods unaffordable for common citizens. Heavy taxation further drained productivity, forcing farmers and laborers into debt and eventually leading to economic collapse.

Much like Rome, modern nations rely on debt-backed economies, borrowing against future energy that does not yet exist. Governments print money without real productivity backing it, leading to inflation, debt bubbles, and economic instability. Rome's mistake was believing it could fabricate wealth without real energy input. The lesson is clear: when debt exceeds the ability to produce real value, collapse is inevitable—whether for an empire, a nation, or an individual.

The Illusion of Wealth: Why Gold Alone Holds No True Value

Some may argue that gold and other natural resources can back up a nation's debt, providing a safety net in times of crisis. At first glance, this seems reasonable—gold has long been considered a store of value. However, when examined through the lens of energy balance, it becomes clear that even gold is only valuable if there is enough extracted and stored energy to sustain its worth. Without energy—whether in the form of labor, industry, or resources—gold is just an inert metal, unable to generate wealth on its own.

Gold's value exists only when energy is applied to extract, refine, and utilize it. If gold is buried deep in the ground and no one has the energy, technology, or labor to mine it, it has no more practical worth than a rock. The same applies to other resources like oil, coal, or rare minerals—they must be actively harnessed to be of any use. Simply possessing these resources does not create wealth; they must be converted into usable energy to maintain their value.

Even if a country has vast gold reserves, that gold only retains purchasing power if the economy remains productive. If a nation spends gold on goods but fails to replace that value with new energy—through labor, innovation, or resource extraction—the gold itself becomes worthless. This is why economies built solely on natural resource wealth often collapse when those resources run out or lose market value.

A striking example of this is Spain's 16th-century economic collapse. After discovering vast amounts of gold and silver in the Americas, Spain became the richest nation in Europe. But instead of using this wealth to develop sustainable industries, Spain relied on imported gold to fund its economy. Inflation skyrocketed, making local industries uncompetitive, and when the flow of gold slowed, Spain found itself bankrupt despite possessing more gold than any other nation.

Wealth Comes from Energy, Not Stockpiled Resources

The true value of any resource, even gold, is tied to the energy required to extract, trade, and sustain it. If there is no extracted and stored energy to replace it, then its worth vanishes. Gold, like money, is merely a representation of value—but that value is meaningless if the real economy producing goods and services collapses. A straightforward way to understand this is through the Island Test.

Imagine two islands: One has mountains of gold but no food, no labor force, and no energy production. The other has no gold, but fertile land, skilled workers, and a strong energy system. Which island is wealthier?

The answer is obvious: The island with real energy production will thrive, while the island with gold alone will starve.

This proves that real wealth comes from energy production, not stockpiled material assets. Gold is only valuable in a system where it can be exchanged for goods produced by human energy. Without production, it's just shiny metal.

The Hidden Cost of Borrowing

Of course, there are times when debt is a practical necessity—such as taking on a mortgage for a home, which provides long-term stability and equity, as long as interest remains reasonable, and the property increases in value. In such cases, the debt serves a productive purpose, aligning energy expenditure with future financial security.

However, debt taken on for non-essential purchases—like financing a new car when an older model would suffice or charging vacations and entertainment to a credit card—quickly becomes an energy trap. Instead of working for you, this type of debt erodes financial and personal energy, creating long-term inefficiencies:

- Financing a vehicle not only accrues interest but also depreciates the car's value, meaning the borrower loses both financial energy (money) and physical energy (the declining worth of the car).

- Credit card purchases for meals out, gadgets, and entertainment might seem minor, but if balances aren't paid within the grace period, high-interest debt quickly erodes wealth. Financing larger non-essential purchases like televisions, travel, and luxury items compounds the problem. Unlike a home, which can appreciate in value, these purchases immediately lose their worth, still requiring energy (money) to pay them off. This simply turns convenience into a financial burden.

To maintain control over financial energy, we must be mindful of how debt impacts both our present and future. Borrowing may offer short-term convenience, but it often results in long-term inefficiencies, requiring far more energy to repay than was initially gained. Reducing financial obligations allows us to preserve our energy for lasting investments rather than wasting it on unnecessary interest and debt cycles. The most reliable way to avoid the entrapment of debt is to minimize borrowing whenever possible and commit to living simply within our means.

Resisting the Pull of Chaos

As we've explored, the flow of energy in life is constant and unavoidable. From the biological energy that sustains our bodies to the non-biological energy that powers our homes and technologies, we operate within the limits of how much energy we can consume, transfer, and sustain efficiently. Yet, energy alone is not enough—without structure, discipline, and intention, disorder takes over.

Life does not naturally maintain balance. Left unchecked, entropy pulls everything toward chaos—from personal health and relationships to societies and civilizations. The answer is not simply to work harder or generate more energy, but to use energy wisely, reducing inefficiencies and directing effort toward what truly matters.

Fighting against this drift toward disorder isn't just about physical maintenance—it extends to our emotional resilience, moral foundations, and societal stability. Without intentionality, things fall apart. But with purposeful action and sustained effort, we can resist the pull of chaos and create a life of order, meaning, and lasting impact.

The Unexpected Benefit: Innovation Through Struggle

Paradoxically, the same force that threatens to unravel our lives—entropy— also drives adaptation and refinement. The struggle against decay is not merely a hardship; it is an essential mechanism woven into the fabric of existence, pushing life to evolve, civilizations to advance, and individuals to sharpen their abilities.

Rather than seeing entropy as an obstacle, it can be understood as an engine of progress. The natural world constantly resists disorder: trees develop deeper roots to withstand storms, ecosystems stabilize through interdependence, and even the human body repairs itself in response to injury. Likewise, human civilization innovates not simply because struggle exists, but because the laws of nature compel us to counteract entropy.

From the earliest days of civilization, the need to resist disorder led to the development of tools, agriculture, and engineering. Advances in medicine, infrastructure, and technology are not merely conveniences but necessary responses to the natural tendency of systems to break down. Washing machines and dishwashers, for example, do not exist simply for comfort— they optimize energy use and reclaim time from repetitive tasks. Justice systems and moral structures prevent societal collapse, reinforcing order where entropy would otherwise bring instability.

This is the irony of entropy: while it is often seen as a destructive force, it is also the reason life is dynamic and ever-improving. The very fabric of existence ensures that we do not remain stagnant but are continually refining, adapting, and pushing forward.

Moral Decay and Its Devastating Effects

While entropy and disorder can wreak havoc in physical and societal structures, the effects of moral decay are even more profound. When individuals and communities stray from a moral framework, the consequences can be devastating, not only in personal lives but on a much larger scale.

In the Bible, Jesus was asked to identify the greatest commandment, and His response serves as a guide for moral stability. Jesus said the greatest commandment is to love God with all your heart, soul, and mind (Matthew 22:37-38). He then added that the second commandment, intricately linked to the first, is to love your neighbor as yourself (Matthew 22:39). These two commandments, Jesus said, are the foundation upon which all the law and the prophets rest. They provide the moral compass necessary for human interaction and the maintenance of order. When humanity follows these principles, society thrives. When these are ignored, moral decay ensues.

One of the most poignant examples of moral decay on a societal level is the story of Anne Frank, a Jewish girl who, along with millions of others, became a victim of Adolf Hitler's regime. Anne Frank's family fled Germany to escape the Nazi persecution of Jews, but they were eventually captured after hiding in Amsterdam for two years. Her diary, written during that time, provides a vivid and heartbreaking account of her life in hiding and the fear that hung over her family. Anne Frank died at the Bergen-Belsen concentration camp in 1945, just months before it was liberated.[78] She was one of over 100,000 innocent Jews in the Netherlands, and millions more across Europe, caught in the crosshairs of Nazi brutality.

The Holocaust, in which six million Jews were murdered, was the direct result of moral decay on a national scale.[79] Hitler's regime spread hatred and justified genocide through propaganda and fear, creating a system that led to unimaginable chaos, disorder, and destruction. This moral decay was not limited to Germany's leadership; it permeated much of the population, who either actively participated or turned a blind eye. It took enormous amounts of energy—through resistance movements, military intervention, and global effort—to put an end to Hitler's reign of terror.

Anne Frank's story reminds us that moral decay can lead to the suffering of the innocent. As societies allow hatred, bigotry, and fear to take root, the consequences are devastating. The example of the Holocaust illustrates that moral decay doesn't just impact individuals but can unravel entire nations, plunging them into chaos.

The fight against such decay can never be neglected; it must be an ongoing, vigilant endeavor to prevent the devastating effects of moral entropy. What may have started in the mind of one individual—like Hitler—quickly infected an entire society, creating a challenge of monstrous proportions that took immense energy and sacrifice to bring under control.

The key is prevention. Moral leadership, societal vigilance, and collective action are not only needed to restore order after things have gone awry but, more importantly, to prevent decay from ever taking hold. This proactive approach is the most effective way to keep chaos and destruction from spreading, ensuring that society remains grounded in justice and compassion.

The Tug on Life

In July 2018, I took a trip to visit my father in Oklahoma. He had finally succumbed to Merkel cell carcinoma, an aggressive form of skin cancer, and was now confined to a bed in the front room of my parents' home. By this time, he couldn't speak, but we could still talk to him, and you could tell he knew we were there—his eyes would meet yours, and he could hold your gaze. Often, I would see him reaching out into the air, as if grasping something only he could see, carefully placing it elsewhere. Even then, he was arranging things, putting everything in its place—just like he always had. That was my dad. Everything had its place, and everything was kept in order. Not that there weren't some pretty big piles of stuff here and there, but even those were neatly stacked wherever they were.

Little did I know that this visit would be the last. He had been sleeping for most of the day, and just before I decided to head back to Fort Worth, I sat down next to his bed and put my hand on his chest. His breathing had become shallow. As I sat there for a moment, he opened his eyes, and I could tell something was different. He could barely move, but he looked right at me, then glanced over to where my brother Tim was standing. They were all talking on the other side of the room, and I'm sure my dad could hear them. He looked back at me, then again at Tim, as if to say, *"Get him."* I called Tim over, and when he rushed to my dad's side, I saw how completely focused my dad was on him. It was a testament to their bond—Tim had been a constant companion to our father throughout his life. With Tim's hands on his shoulder, my hand on his chest, and my sister across from me, my dad quietly slipped away. My dad was a great man.

Watching my father's last moments brought into sharp focus the inevitability of entropy, the universal force which pulls all things, from our bodies to our societies, toward disorder unless actively countered. The meticulous order my dad maintained throughout his life, and even in his final moments, was giving way to the forces of decay, a reminder of the constant battle against disorder we all face.

Such is the cycle of life—man was created from the dust of the ground, and we still are today. When God created Adam, He skipped a few steps because He can, but He gave us the system of reproduction in His place, allowing for the same miracle of life. Mothers gain the necessary raw materials from plants (which absorb nutrients from the ground), or from animals that feed on these plants. Regardless, we originate from the earth and come to life through the energy provided by the sun. When our bodies can no longer harness the energy needed to sustain life, we return to the ground.

In many ways, life is a constant battle against the pull toward disorder. This ongoing struggle is a fundamental part of existence, reflecting the delicate balance between chaos and structure in a world where disorder is the default state. It is deeply connected to our awareness of life. The moment we withdraw the energy needed to maintain balance in our relationships, homes, and responsibilities, disorder starts to seep in. Friction surfaces in our relationships, clutter accumulates in the home, and the lawn needs to be mowed again. This slow drift into chaos reminds us that life requires continuous effort and care to keep things functioning as they should.

By contrast, when we achieve order and harmony in our lives, we function more efficiently, both mentally and physically. Humans seem to be wired for structure—an organized environment promotes peace of mind, reduces stress, and allows us to focus on growth rather than survival. In an ordered environment, we can think more clearly, make better decisions, and feel a sense of control over our surroundings. When our homes, relationships, and tasks are aligned, we conserve energy that would otherwise be spent managing chaos.

Order and routine create predictability, which the brain naturally craves. With fewer distractions and sources of stress, we're able to channel our energy toward productive and fulfilling activities. In this way, achieving order allows us to thrive, rather than merely exist in a state of reaction to the chaos around us. This suggests that order may indeed be the innate, default condition of human existence—a state where we are at peace, creative, and capable of fulfilling our higher potential.

Consider luxury hotels and resorts as an example. People often save for months and pay a premium to escape the chaos of everyday life and immerse themselves in meticulously controlled environments. From Dubai to California, luxury hotels like the Ritz-Carlton succeed by going to great lengths to counter entropy. Pristine linens, meticulously combed beaches, and seamless interactions all contribute to the inner sense of peace and order people crave. The more these spaces minimize disorder, the more valuable and desirable they become, temporarily offering guests the comfort of perfect organization.

Maintaining order requires a careful balance of time and energy because our supply is limited. This is especially evident with children, who spend most of their energy playing and eating, leaving little for tasks like cleaning up after themselves. The dinner table and their rooms can quickly shift from organized spaces to chaotic messes. Until they learn to put their clothes in the hamper or clean up their own messes, it falls on parents to pick up the pieces—turning clothes right-side out, gathering items scattered across the house, and restoring order. As life becomes busier, the continual expenditure of your own energy to manage these tasks can become overwhelming.

This is where the words of Benjamin Franklin come into play: *"Tell me and I forget, teach me and I remember, involve me and I learn."*[80] In the same way, teaching little Johnny to take responsibility for his own messes—whether it's cleaning up after dinner or putting his clothes in the hamper—helps him manage his own time and energy. Establishing a routine, such as setting times for dinner, play, and homework, provides structure that allows him to blossom. A simple change, like adding a decorative hamper to his room, can help contain the mess of clothes scattered everywhere, creating a more organized space. By teaching these habits early on, you reduce your own energy expenditure, enabling you to manage the increasing demands of a busy life.

Societal Structures and the Fight Against Decay

The struggle against entropy extends beyond individual lives—it affects entire societies. Local governments, law enforcement, and political systems must continually invest energy to prevent decay. When infrastructure, safety, or governance is neglected, urban deterioration, social disorder, and political corruption follow. Just as we must maintain our homes and relationships, societies must combat disorder through reforms, accountability, and innovation to sustain stability.

At the local level, cities must invest in infrastructure to prevent urban decay. Roads need repair, water systems require maintenance, and public spaces must be kept clean. Without attention, potholes become hazards, water systems corrode, and parks turn into neglected spaces, decreasing quality of life, increasing safety risks, and lowering property values.

Law enforcement and public safety also require ongoing energy. Without proper staffing, training, and updated equipment, the ability to enforce laws and maintain order weakens, leading to increased crime and civil unrest. Agencies must constantly adapt and improve community relations to sustain stability.

At the broader societal level, political systems experience entropy through corruption, inefficiency, and inequality. If a government fails to maintain transparency, checks and balances, and reforms, it risks becoming bloated and dysfunctional. History has repeatedly shown that civilizations collapse when governance becomes complacent or corrupt, allowing entropy to erode societal structure.

On a national scale, governments must manage resources, balance budgets, and maintain infrastructure and services. Neglecting these responsibilities leads to deteriorating roads, failing institutions, and economic instability. Public health systems must be upheld to prevent disease outbreaks, education must evolve to meet new challenges, and national security must adapt to modern threats.

From local communities to entire nations, systems need constant energy, effort, and innovation to prevent decay. When left unchecked, entropy accelerates decline—but with deliberate investment and vigilance, societies can sustain stability and progress. The same principles that govern personal life and purpose apply at every level of civilization: what we fail to maintain, we eventually lose.

Intentional Living: Defying Entropy with Purpose

Life is an ongoing exchange of energy. From the moment we take our first breath, we enter into a system where energy must be continuously received, transformed, and given back. We extract energy from the land through food, convert it into work and action, and store it in various forms—whether in money, relationships, or the legacy we build over time. Yet, this flow is not automatic; it requires intention, wisdom, and balance.

At every stage of life, we are either managing energy well—investing it in purposeful work, relationships, and growth—or wasting it on distractions, inefficiencies, and fleeting pursuits. The challenges we face—personal struggles, societal injustices, economic hardships—are often the result of an imbalance in this exchange. Too often, systems extract more energy than they return, leaving people drained, disillusioned, and searching for meaning.

Entropy will always work against us. It erodes our physical health, our sense of purpose, and even the moral fabric of society. When my father died, I saw this firsthand. The moment life left his body, the fight against entropy ended. His body, once strong, began its journey back to dust. No matter how hard we fight it, everything eventually gives way to entropy.

And yet, even as I faced this reality, I realized something remarkable. What he had done with his energy throughout his life was not lost. The physical energy that sustained his body was gone, but the energy of his love, wisdom, and influence remained. It was etched in my memories, in the values he instilled in me, in the lessons that shaped who I am. His impact did not fade with his body—it carried forward in a different form.

This isn't just a personal experience—it is a universal truth. History itself is a testament to the power of life's energy defying entropy's decay. Anne Frank, though surrounded by chaos, poured her energy into words that outlived her physical existence. She could not stop the entropy of war, but she overcame the entropy of being forgotten. Her thoughts, recorded in the dim light of a hidden attic, still resonate today—because energy, when applied with purpose, leaves a mark that does not simply vanish.

This is the essence of our existence. It's not about chasing comfort or wealth, nor is it about avoiding hardship. It is about using the energy we have to make a difference that echoes beyond our time. The Bible states in Psalm 112:6, "For the righteous will never be moved; he will be remembered forever." Being remembered is not about personal glory; it is about the good we leave behind—an example for future generations to follow.

So, the real question is: Where and how do we invest our energy? Do we squander it on pursuits that drain us without return, or do we use it to build something lasting? Jesus spoke of an abundant life (John 10:10)—not a life of ease, but a life of purpose, where energy is invested in things that truly matter.

The world will always demand more of our energy than we can sustain. It will tempt us to chase after things that consume rather than fulfill. But God, in contrast, freely provides—giving us the energy of the sun, the richness of the land, and the breath in our lungs. When we align ourselves with His design—living in a way that conserves, restores, and shares the energy we've been given—we find peace, balance, and purpose.

At the end of our days, what will matter most is not how much energy we consumed, but how well we used it—not what we stored up on earth, but what we gave to others, which is stored as treasures in heaven (Matthew 6:19-20). The Bible tells us that our deeds will follow us beyond this life (Revelation 14:13), meaning that what we do here isn't lost—it echoes into eternity. Did we exhaust ourselves on things that faded, or did we use our energy to love God, serve others, and leave the world better than we found it? The call given to Adam and Eve—to steward and sustain the earth—remains part of our responsibility today, ensuring that the generations who come after us have a foundation to build on.

So, the challenge is this: Will we passively let entropy take its course, or will we be active stewards of the energy we've been given?

The flow of energy through our lives is not just a scientific reality—it is a spiritual calling. And how we direct it determines the kind of life we build and the legacy we leave.

CHAPTER 9

Where Is God?

n 1993, a haunting photograph taken during the famine in Sudan brought the world face-to-face with unimaginable suffering.[81] Captured by Kevin Carter, a Pulitzer Prize-winning photojournalist, the image showed a little boy, originally thought to be a girl, no older than five or six, crouched in the dust, his frail body weakened from starvation. He was making his way to a United Nations food distribution center alone, yet the short distance seemed insurmountable for his starving body as he lay physically exhausted on the ground.

The child, alone and vulnerable, appeared barely able to take another step. Behind him, a vulture lurked ominously, waiting. This image became a symbol of human suffering, evoking outrage and compassion worldwide.

Carter explained that journalists were advised not to touch famine victims to avoid spreading disease, a guideline that posed a deep ethical challenge in moments like this. He reported that the child managed to move on after the photo was taken. However, the emotional weight of the image and the global backlash deeply affected Carter. Though he won the Pulitzer Prize in 1994 for this photo, he struggled with guilt and depression. Tragically, just a few months after receiving the award, Carter died by suicide.

Carter's photograph transcended the facts; it provoked deep questions about suffering, compassion, and divine intervention. How could such immense suffering exist in a world filled with sunlight, fertile soil, and water? Where is God in moments like these?

This is one of the most difficult questions people grapple with. It may be one of the primary reasons people give up on religion, second only to the Bible being cast as myth and out of sync with science. Whether rich or poor, minister or skeptic, the question of why God allows such harshness confuses many.

As recounted in Walter Isaacson's biography of Steve Jobs, a pivotal moment in Jobs's early life led him to question his faith in God.[82] At thirteen, Jobs came across a magazine cover depicting the suffering of starving children in Biafra, Nigeria. Troubled, he approached his Lutheran pastor with a series of questions. First, he asked if God knew everything, even down to which finger Jobs would raise before he did it. The pastor affirmed this. Jobs then showed the magazine cover to the pastor and asked, "Does God know about this and what's going to happen to those children?" The pastor struggled to provide an answer that satisfied Jobs. This marked a turning point for the young Jobs, who began to distance himself from organized religion.

One might expect ministers to have a deeper understanding of suffering, yet many struggle to reconcile harsh realities with the concept of a loving, omnipotent God. When faced with questions about suffering, responses are often unsatisfying, boiling down to a call for *"faith"* without deeper exploration. This can lead many to question their beliefs or abandon them altogether.

When I consider everything discussed in this book, I believe the answer to Steve Jobs's question is simple—yes, God is aware of what happens on Earth. But I also believe the world must function within the systems He designed, without requiring His constant intervention. 2 Peter 1:3 offers a perspective: "His divine power has given us everything we need for a godly life through our knowledge of him who called us by his own glory and goodness." In other words, God has not left us defenseless but equipped us with the knowledge and resources to both survive and thrive in a world that requires resilience and wisdom.

Take Earth as an example. Its abundance of resources—water, minerals, fertile soil—along with the energy supplied daily by the sun forms a self-sustaining system that fuels the cycle of life. God has created a world rich in food and other essentials for life to thrive. The natural systems that sustain the universe showcase the intricate balance established at creation—a balance that does not require His micromanagement.

Our bodies, too, are marvels of design, equipped to adapt, heal, and overcome challenges. Our immune systems fight infections, bones and muscles regenerate after injury, and our minds develop solutions to complex problems. Humanity possesses the innate ability to work within these systems to enhance and sustain life.

I don't believe it was ever part of God's plan to continually intervene and "fix" the world. Instead, He placed us in this well-ordered creation with the responsibility to manage it, to learn from it, and to thrive within its boundaries. Human beings, endowed with intelligence and creativity, were tasked with stewarding the earth's resources and each other.

Underlying Causes of Pain and Suffering Today

If we look closely at the reality of suffering today, we see that much of it is influenced by human lifestyle choices, health decisions, and natural processes. The primary causes of death in the United States include heart disease, cancer, unintentional injuries (such as accidents), chronic respiratory diseases (like COPD), stroke, Alzheimer's, diabetes, liver disease, kidney disease, and complications from influenza and pneumonia.

These causes illustrate how a combination of genetic predispositions, lifestyle behaviors, and preventable conditions shape the extent of human suffering. While personal choices are linked to factors such as heart disease and cancer, environmental or genetic influences contribute to others, such as accidents and respiratory illnesses.

As a funeral director, I can attest to this firsthand. The mass of services we conducted, upwards of forty percent of the Fort Worth, Texas, market, consistently resulted from the natural cycle of life and inadvertent failures of humanity—whether through preventable illnesses, accidents, or lack of timely medical care.

The Human Cause of Suffering: The Myth of Divine Neglect

Many people struggle with the idea that suffering and death result from God's neglect. However, a closer look at tragic events often reveals that they are caused by human decisions and societal structures rather than divine inaction.

The famine in Sudan, captured by Kevin Carter's photograph, was not due to God withholding food. It was the result of civil war, corruption, and governance failure. Similarly, the 2004 Indian Ocean earthquake and tsunami, which claimed over 230,000 lives, underscores human fragility. While natural disasters are beyond human control, the decision to build homes near coastlines reflects humanity's pursuit of beauty and resources while often underestimating potential risks.

History also illustrates the danger of attributing suffering to divine neglect. Atrocities justified by religious authority, such as during the reign of Henry VIII, were born of human ambition, not divine will. Similarly, the Holocaust resulted from moral decay and the failure of political systems to resist evil, not God's neglect.

Human-made suffering is evident in the prevalence of accidental deaths. Drunk driving, for instance, stems from recklessness, not divine design. These risks are created by human hands, not by God.

To attribute the chaos and suffering in the world to divine neglect overlooks humanity's role in shaping its destiny. The moral decay that leads to suffering is not God's doing; it is the result of human failure to create just and compassionate societies.

Pain and Suffering: A Catalyst for Progress

While suffering is undeniably tragic, it also serves as a force that propels humanity forward. In God's wisdom, painful experiences foster innovation, resilience, and growth. The struggle to overcome adversity often becomes a catalyst for unimaginable progress.

Humanity has responded to crises with ingenuity. War and infections in the early twentieth century led to the development of penicillin. Automobile fatalities spurred innovations like seat belts and crash-resistant plastics. Advancements in cancer treatments, vaccines, and surgical techniques emerged as direct responses to human suffering.

Beyond medicine, crises like the *Titanic* prompted safer maritime regulations, while environmental disasters led to innovations in cleaner energy and more effective protections.

The Genius of the Human Mind: Innovation Through Adversity and Struggle

The human mind is phenomenal, capable of creativity, problem-solving, and innovation. God's design allows humanity not only to endure but to overcome hardship. Some of the greatest innovations—anesthesia, vaccines, radiation therapy—emerged from times of war, famine, and natural disasters.

While suffering is painful, it can drive progress. God's plan enables humanity to face challenges and improve life through innovation and compassion. Struggles compel us to create solutions that prevent future suffering, turning hardship into a catalyst for bettering life for future generations.

As President John F. Kennedy famously said during the quest for the moon, *"We go to the moon not because it is easy, but because it is hard."*[83] At the time, mankind was far from achieving this monumental leap into space. Yet, in a short period, the human spirit triumphed, landing a man on the moon. This shows how embracing challenges leads to greatness.

This speaks to the essence of human progress: through persistence, innovation, and determination, we can overcome even the most daunting obstacles. Just as mankind reached for the stars and touched the moon, we can rise above today's difficulties, knowing that the journey itself often leads to greatness.

The Harmony of Creation

God's creation is a masterpiece of balance and precision. From the fine-tuning of the cosmos to the interdependent ecosystems on Earth, everything is designed to function in harmony. The natural cycles—such as the water cycle, plant growth through photosynthesis, and the changing of seasons—are evidence of divine order.

When humans align their actions with these natural systems, creation thrives. Sustainable agricultural practices, advances in energy production, and conservation efforts help ecosystems recover from damage by allowing natural processes to restore balance.

The Breakdown of Divine Order Through Mismanagement

While God's design is inherently balanced, when humanity fails to respect divine order, suffering often follows. Human greed, neglect, and shortsighted decisions disrupt the natural balance, leading to consequences that are felt for generations.

The Dust Bowl of the 1930s serves as a stark reminder of how mismanagement of the land leads to catastrophe.[84] Similarly, overfishing, deforestation, and pollution are modern examples of how ignoring natural limits leads to scarcity and suffering. When natural systems are pushed to their breaking points, the results are clear: depleted fisheries, eroded topsoil, and polluted water sources. These issues disproportionately affect the poorest and most vulnerable populations, leading to food shortages, health crises, and loss of livelihoods.

Human-caused suffering often arises when we disrupt natural harmony through carelessness or exploitation. Marine ecosystems, for example, are particularly vulnerable. Overfishing threatens not just individual species but destabilizes entire ecosystems. One of the most well-known examples is the collapse of the Newfoundland cod fishery in the 1990s.[85] Overfishing decimated the population, leading to economic devastation and the collapse of an entire industry.

Another stark example is the destruction of coral reefs. Coral reefs provide habitat for approximately twenty-five percent of marine species and play a critical role in coastal protection. However, unsustainable fishing practices, pollution, and climate change have caused widespread coral bleaching and destruction. The Great Barrier Reef has lost nearly half of its coral cover in recent decades.[86]

This echoes my personal experience deep-sea fishing off the coast of Port Aransas, Texas. We would venture up to sixty miles offshore to fish the abundant Red Snapper beds. However, with modern technology, other boats would track our position, and once we left, they would strip the Red Snapper beds of fish. This pressure, without regard for sustainability, highlights how the immediate reward of a full catch often blinds us to long-term consequences, reflecting the broader issue of overfishing and environmental mismanagement.

Human Suffering as a Consequence of Disruption

When divine order is disrupted by human negligence or willful ignorance, it is not God who causes suffering, but humanity itself. Famine, for instance, is often less about insufficient food production and more about political instability, economic injustice, and poor distribution systems. Kevin Carter's photograph of a starving child in Sudan was not the result of divine neglect but rather human failure to provide necessary resources.

Natural disasters like earthquakes and tsunamis are beyond human control, but the suffering that follows is often worsened by poor preparation, inadequate infrastructure, and unsafe living conditions. God's creation includes the forces of nature, but human negligence increases the toll on life.

Restoring Divine Order Through Responsibility

It is humanity's responsibility to restore order by managing the world's resources wisely. This includes making choices that align with sustainability and fostering equitable systems that prevent harm to vulnerable populations. Organizations working toward environmental conservation, sustainable farming, and social justice play critical roles in realigning human activity with God's divine order.

Scripture reminds us that humans are not owners but caretakers of creation. As Psalm 24:1 states, "The earth is the Lord's, and everything in it." Understanding this divine ownership calls for humility and care in how we treat the environment and one another.

While global issues may seem distant, the truth is that they touch all of us. Our daily choices impact the quality of life for ourselves, others, and future generations. Small actions, such as reducing waste, conserving energy, and supporting sustainable products, have ripple effects. These choices help reduce pollution, conserve resources, and preserve biodiversity.

The harsh realities we face—environmental degradation, water shortages, and food scarcity—are often the result of collective mismanagement. But just as these problems are caused by human actions, they can be mitigated by individual efforts. By conserving water, using renewable energy, or reducing our carbon footprint, we help ease the burden on the planet and improve the quality of life for ourselves and others.

Our mindful decisions alleviate suffering, create a legacy of hope, and foster a sustainable future. The energy we save, the resources we preserve, and the compassion we show today will shape the world that future generations inherit. Life's challenges are undeniable, but by taking responsibility for our choices, we can reduce unnecessary suffering and build a more compassionate world.

Continuing the Journey toward Solutions

While history provides examples of innovation born from adversity, progress continues today. In the face of challenges like global hunger, access to clean water, and advancing healthcare, modern technology, medical breakthroughs, and environmental stewardship are paving the way for solutions that improve life worldwide.

In agriculture, innovations like genetically modified crops, vertical farming, and precision agriculture are helping to combat food insecurity, ensuring sustainable food sources even as farmland becomes scarce. Advances in diagnostics and personalized medicine are transforming healthcare, enabling earlier detection of diseases like cancer and improving outcomes.

The need for clean water has driven advancements in portable filtration systems, desalination plants, and atmospheric water generators, providing drinkable water in drought-stricken regions. These breakthroughs offer hope to millions who suffer from water scarcity, improving health and contributing to economic stability.

In addition, renewable energy innovations—such as solar, wind, and hydroelectric power—are reshaping how we power the world. These options help protect the environment and reduce costs, benefiting both households and industries.

While renewable energy technologies are sometimes met with skepticism, there are innovations I personally embrace. For example, battery-operated tools and lawn equipment offer a safer alternative to gas-powered versions. One major benefit is eliminating the need for flammable gasoline in the home, a constant concern with children around. Using battery-powered tools reduces reliance on fossil fuels and creates a safer environment for our families.

Small innovations like these remind us that solutions don't always have to be monumental. They often start with the decisions we make daily.

A Collective Human Response: From Local to Global

Beyond technological innovation, modern efforts to tackle social and environmental issues show an increasing global responsibility. The World Food Programme (WFP), as the largest humanitarian organization addressing hunger, works globally with significant US support.[87] WFP's vital interventions help combat hunger caused by conflict, natural disasters, and climate change, ensuring food distribution in crisis zones while supporting long-term development.

Businesses are also making an impact through the "buy one, give one" philosophy, exemplified by companies like TOMS and Warby Parker. These social enterprises link corporate responsibility with charitable giving, ensuring that for every product sold, a corresponding product or service reaches those in need. While effective, some critics suggest they address symptoms rather than systemic issues in regions of aid.

Meanwhile, the rise of plant-based and lab-grown meat introduces forward-thinking solutions to the environmental and ethical concerns surrounding traditional livestock farming. These alternatives offer a sustainable approach to feeding a growing global population but can provoke debate among traditional farmers or communities whose livelihoods depend on meat production.

Together, these initiatives reflect humanity's collective drive to innovate and address global challenges, merging corporate responsibility, sustainable practices, and humanitarian efforts to build a better world.

Innovation as an Ongoing Journey

The same spirit of human ingenuity that gave us penicillin, seat belts, and safety regulations continues to drive progress today. God's gift of creativity and problem-solving remains key to overcoming adversity. Solutions to today's challenges are actively being developed on a global scale.

Humanity's ability to thrive in the face of hardship reflects our divine design and purpose: to solve problems, care for one another, and steward the world we've been given. Modern innovations remind us that progress is an ongoing journey. Like past generations, we continue to push the boundaries of what is possible, taking up our role in God's design as stewards and innovators, driven by the belief that a better world is always within reach. This ongoing innovation is a testament to human resilience and the divine gift of creativity within each of us.

Are Miracles Still Part of His Plan?

In the Bible, miracles serve as divine displays of God's power. From the opening sentence that began it all, "God created the heavens and the earth," God's power and glory are on full display. His direct intervention in the lives of humankind extends throughout the entire history of the Old Testament.

These events are more than just supernatural occurrences; they are deeply purposeful, designed to reveal God's nature, guide His people, and demonstrate His sovereignty. Here are some of the greatest miracles in the Old Testament, each highlighting different aspects of God's character and His relationship with humanity.

- **Parting of the Red Sea** (Exodus 14). God parted the Red Sea, allowing the Israelites to escape Egyptian slavery. This miracle symbolizes **His power to deliver** His people from impossible situations.

- **The Ten Plagues of Egypt** (Exodus 7-12). God sent ten plagues to free Israel, demonstrating **His supremacy** over Egypt's gods and nature itself, showing His determination to liberate His people.

- **Manna in the Wilderness** (Exodus 16). For forty years, God provided manna and quail for the Israelites, teaching them **He is reliable** for daily needs.

- **The Fall of Jericho** (Joshua 6). God miraculously brought down Jericho's walls through obedience, demonstrating **His power** and the importance of faith.

- **The Sun Standing Still** (Joshua 10). During a battle, God stopped the sun and moon in the sky, giving Israel time to secure victory, showing **His control over time and nature.**

- **Elijah and the Fire from Heaven** (1 Kings 18). God sent fire from heaven in response to Elijah's prayer, proving His **sovereignty over false gods** and leading Israel back to worship Him.

- **The Fiery Furnace** (Daniel 3). God protected Shadrach, Meshach, and Abednego from the fiery furnace, demonstrating His **ability to protect** His faithful servants even from death.

- **Jonah and the Great Fish** (Jonah 1-2). God sent a great fish to save

Jonah after he fled from His command, illustrating His **control over creation** and willingness to give second chances.

These miracles were not merely acts of divine power; they underscored different aspects of God's nature—His sovereignty, justice, mercy, and faithfulness—and His desire to reveal Himself to humanity. In the Old Testament, miracles were often signs that pointed to God's covenant with His people, His promises, and His plan for their future. They remind us that while God's ways may be beyond our understanding, His interventions are always aimed at guiding humanity toward a deeper relationship with Him.

God's Miraculous Intervention through Jesus: A New Level of Divine Involvement

In the New Testament, God's intervention in the lives of His creatures took a different form. This time, God walked on the earth once again, just as He had with Adam and Eve in the cool of the evening in the Garden of Eden. However, this time He came in the person of His Son, Jesus Christ. Jesus became God's miraculous intervention on earth, not only to affirm His divine nature but also to reveal God's character, mercy, and love in a tangible way. His presence among humanity was once again a hands-on approach, a direct interaction with His creation. Through His words and actions, Jesus walked and talked with people, meeting them in their daily lives, much like the early days in Eden.

Jesus's miracles served as a testament to His identity as the Messiah and provided a foretaste of the Kingdom of God. They were designed to bring people to faith, to demonstrate God's power, and to embody God's compassion for humanity. Through Christ, God engaged directly with mankind, offering healing, teaching, and the hope of eternal life.

The Greatest Miracles of Jesus

- **Turning Water into Wine** (John 2:1-11). Jesus's first recorded miracle took place at a wedding in Cana.

- **Feeding the Five Thousand** (Matthew 14:13-21). In one of the most well-known miracles, Jesus fed a crowd of over five thousand people with just five loaves of bread and two fish.

- **Walking on Water** (Matthew 14:22-33). During the night, a storm arose, and the disciples were terrified as they struggled against the waves. Jesus then came toward them, walking on the water.

- **Healing the Blind Man** (John 9:1-12). Jesus spat on the ground, made mud with the saliva, and applied it to a man's eyes. He instructed the man to wash in the Pool of Siloam, and upon doing so, the man regained his sight.

- **Raising Lazarus from the Dead** (John 11:1-44). Lazarus, a dear friend of Jesus, fell ill and died. Jesus approached the tomb and called out, "Lazarus, come out!" Lazarus emerged from the grave, alive and still wrapped in his burial clothes.

- **Calming the Storm** (Mark 4:35-41). A violent storm suddenly arose, threatening to capsize the boat. Jesus rose and rebuked the wind. The wind died down, and there was a great calm.

- **Casting Out Demons** (Mark 5:1-20). Jesus encountered a man possessed by a legion of demons. Recognizing Jesus's authority, the demons entered pigs, which then rushed into the sea and drowned.

- **Healing the Paralytic** (Mark 2:1-12). Four men lowered a paralyzed man to Jesus. Seeing their faith, He healed him physically, instructing him to pick up his mat and walk.

- **The Resurrection** (Matthew 28:1-10). The most extraordinary miracle of Jesus's ministry was His own resurrection after crucifixion. Jesus was buried in a tomb, and on the third day, He rose from the dead.

Why Jesus Performed Miracles

Jesus's miracles were not just acts of compassion; they were deliberate signs meant to reveal His divine identity and the nature of God's Kingdom. They served several key purposes:

1. **Affirming His Divine Authority:** Miracles authenticated Jesus's claims to be the Son of God. They demonstrated that He had authority over nature, sickness, death, and the spiritual realm. This authority was essential to His mission and message, confirming that He was the promised Messiah.

2. **Revealing God's Character:** Through His miracles, Jesus revealed God's love, mercy, and compassion. He healed the sick, fed the hungry, and raised the dead, showing that God's heart is for the broken and the suffering. These acts provided a glimpse of God's Kingdom, where suffering, pain, and death are no more.

3. **Inviting Faith:** Miracles were a call to faith. Jesus often performed miracles in response to faith or to inspire faith in others. They were meant to lead people to recognize who He was and to trust in Him for salvation. In many cases, Jesus's miracles transformed not just bodies but hearts, drawing people into a deeper relationship with God.

4. **Demonstrating the Kingdom of God:** Jesus's miracles were signs of the in-breaking Kingdom of God. They pointed to a future reality where God's rule would be fully realized, characterized by healing, restoration, and peace. Each miracle was a foretaste of this coming Kingdom, offering hope and renewal in a world marred by sin.

From Miracles to the Power of Love

As the apostolic age came to a close, a noticeable shift occurred in how God's miraculous power was displayed on earth. During Jesus's ministry and the early years of the church, miracles served as divine signs of God's power and validation of the gospel message. These miraculous events were never meant to be ongoing practices for all generations but rather served a specific purpose at a specific time: to establish the foundation of the early church and confirm the divinity of Christ.

Miracles like raising the dead, healing the sick, and speaking in tongues authenticated the message of Christ and the authority of His apostles. Hebrews 2:3-4 explicitly states that God testified to the message of salvation "by signs, wonders, and various miracles, and by gifts of the Holy Spirit distributed according to his will." This passage suggests that miraculous acts were not a permanent feature of Christian life but were tools God used to confirm the truth during a period when His word was being solidified and spread.

Similarly, in 1 Corinthians 13:8-10, Paul explains that prophecies will cease, tongues will be stilled, and knowledge will pass away—pointing to a time when miraculous gifts will no longer be necessary. Instead, something more enduring will take their place: love. As Paul emphasizes, "Now these three remain: faith, hope, and love. But the greatest of these is love" (1 Corinthians 13:13). The miraculous signs were temporary, but love is eternal. Paul uses the analogy of a child maturing into adulthood to illustrate that just as a child outgrows certain behaviors, the church would eventually move beyond the need for miraculous signs.

Miracles through the apostles were signs of their authority, as Paul states in 2 Corinthians 12:12, where he refers to miracles as "the marks of a true apostle." Once the apostles had laid the foundation of the church, their role—and the need for ongoing miraculous signs—came to an end. Acts 19:11-12 recounts "extraordinary miracles" performed by Paul, emphasizing that even during the apostolic age, these were unique events tied directly to apostolic ministry.

As the New Testament continued to be written and the church matured, the miraculous gifts became less frequent. By the time Paul wrote to Timothy, he advised him to use wine for his stomach ailments (1 Timothy 5:23), suggesting a shift from miraculous healing to practical, natural solutions. This reflects a transition in how God's involvement in the world would manifest—through the abilities, intellect, and compassion He endowed humanity with, rather than through direct, miraculous intervention.

The Transition to Love and Human Ability

What we see in the New Testament is not the removal of God's involvement in the world, but a shift toward His ultimate plan: the empowerment of humanity to carry out His work through love. Jesus, in His teachings, emphasized that the greatest commandments were to love God and to love your neighbor as yourself (Matthew 22:37-40). This new law of love replaced the old law, transforming how we relate to God and each other.

In fact, Jesus's entire ministry was about love—He performed miracles not just to display power, but to show compassion, heal the sick, and uplift the marginalized. Yet, His ultimate mission was to transform hearts, not just bodies. His message in 1 Corinthians 13 is that while miracles may fade, love is eternal. Love is the enduring miracle that each of us can carry forward into the world. The lasting legacy of Christ's ministry is not just in the miraculous events, but in the way He changed human hearts to love deeply and sacrificially.

Empowering Us to "Be the Miracle"

As the apostles' era came to a close, the church entered a new phase, one in which God's power was manifested through human action, love, and innovation. This is what Paul means when he speaks of growing up and putting away childish things (1 Corinthians 13:11). The miraculous gifts of the apostles were like training wheels for the early church, guiding them toward maturity. Now that the church is established, God works through the gifts He has placed within humanity—our ability to love, to create, to heal, and to build.

This shift can be likened to learning how to ride a bicycle. As children, many of us learned to ride with our father's guiding hand. At first, he held onto the bike, steadying us as we wobbled and nearly fell. Each time, he was there to catch us before we hit the ground. Again and again, he would push us forward, let go, and run alongside, ready to intervene if we lost our balance.

But there came a moment when, after much practice and encouragement, he pushed us, let go, and watched as we finally took off on our own. We were set free from his direct intervention, not because he stopped caring, but because he had equipped us with the skills to ride on our own.

We see this in modern medicine, in acts of compassion, in the pursuit of justice, and in the development of technologies that improve life for countless people. These are not miraculous in the traditional sense, but they are no less a reflection of God's power working through the genius of His creation— the children of God. Just as Jesus empowered His disciples to continue His work after He ascended, God now empowers us to "be the miracle" for those around us. Through love, we can heal, restore, and bring hope to the world.

Love Is the Greatest Commandment

In the end, love becomes the miracle. It is what remains when everything else fades away. Love transforms lives, rebuilds communities, and reflects God's eternal presence in the world. While the miraculous signs and wonders of the early church have passed, the power of love remains—and it is through love that we fulfill Christ's call to be His hands and feet in the world today.

As we move forward in faith, we remember that the true legacy of Christ and the apostles is not just the miracles they performed, but the love they demonstrated. It is this love that we carry with us, and through it, we have the power to change the world.

The Miraculous Power of Humanity

On the afternoon of November 23, 2023, Kendra, my daughter-in-law, was driving home with my granddaughter Karsyn, thirteen, and grandson Tommy, five. They had spent Thanksgiving at Kendra's mother and stepfather's home in the small town of Paradise, Texas. As evening approached, they packed up the car and set out for Keller, a mere twenty miles away. It was an unfamiliar route, one of those narrow, two-lane asphalt roads that can be deceptively straightforward during the day but turn treacherous as the shadows lengthen.

Kendra drove cautiously but confidently, traveling around sixty miles per hour. The road stretched out before them, a ribbon of asphalt winding through the rolling Texas countryside. Karsyn sat quietly in the front seat looking out the window, lost in her thoughts, while Tommy babbled away in the back, his voice blending with the hum of the engine. For a moment, everything was normal, just an ordinary drive home after a family holiday.

Then, in the distance, Kendra noticed what looked like a dip in the road. It was approaching fast—too fast. Instinctively, she began to brake, the car slowing slightly as they braced for the dip, but within seconds, everything around them exploded into chaos.

The car was wrenched violently to the side, crashing into the oncoming embankment with a force that seemed to crush the air out of the world itself. The airbags detonated with explosive force, filling the cabin with a choking cloud of white. Glass shattered, spraying like lethal confetti in every direction. The deafening noise of tearing metal, screaming brakes, and shattering glass merged into a single cacophony of terror. The acrid stench of burning rubber and gasoline invaded their lungs, mingled with the dry, earthy smell of disturbed dirt and dust.

Kendra's mind was a whirl of fear and confusion. In the haze of smoke and disorientation, she heard Tommy's high-pitched screams from the back seat, a desperate, piercing wail that cut through the din like a knife. People appeared as if out of nowhere, running toward the car, shouting in panicked voices. Across the road, another vehicle lay mangled beneath the massive bulk of a semi-trailer, a grim testament to the violence of the crash.

And amidst this maelstrom, there was an unsettling silence. Kendra turned, her heart in her throat, and looked at Karsyn. Karsyn sat motionless, her body slumped against the seat, her eyes closed, her small frame eerily still. The world seemed to stop. In that fleeting, endless moment, a sense of dread washed over Kendra. Life, in a single heartbeat, had been frozen in time.

What Kendra hadn't realized, being unfamiliar with the road, was that what she thought was a dip was, in fact, an intersection where the road she was on met another highway. They were barreling toward it with no warning. The stop sign that should have alerted her to slow down and stop had been knocked down earlier that morning at around seven o'clock, left ignored and unreplaced by the Texas Department of Transportation. What should have been a routine drive turned into a nightmare in the blink of an eye.

I've often thought of a line from the movie *Forrest Gump* when reflecting on this time in our lives.[88] In the film, young Jenny prays with her childhood friend, Forrest, after running to the cornfields to hide from her abusive father. As they knelt together, Jenny's prayer was simple and heartbreaking: *"Dear God, make me a bird so I can fly far, far away."* Jenny was living in an abusive home; her father was an alcoholic who would often come after her when he was drunk. Forrest narrates this moment with childlike honesty, saying, *"God works in mysterious ways. He didn't turn Jenny into a bird that day. Instead, he had the police come, and they took her away to live with her grandma."*

Such is how our lives work today. We have free will to make our own decisions, and these choices can have devastating consequences on the world around us. Jenny's father chose to drink, and in doing so, he cast a shadow of fear and pain on those closest to him. This is the nature of true free will; its consequences are permitted by God, for without the possibility of both good and bad outcomes, free will would not truly exist. In Karsyn's case, it wasn't a miracle that she survived the accident—it was a narrow escape from the devastating effects of entropy, the ever-present decay in life that constantly requires energy to keep it at bay.

Earlier that morning, chaos had been set in motion when the stop sign was knocked down. This disruption required someone to expend energy to restore order by putting the sign back up. However, in their free will, they neglected to do so. God wasn't to blame for the wreck; the fault lay squarely with human action—or inaction. Yet, even amid this chaos, God ultimately provided the miracle of life. Not by preventing the accident or turning Karsyn into a perfectly healthy person instantly, but through the miraculous potential of humanity itself.

Within minutes, if not seconds, the innovations of man began to work the miracles of God's creation. A cellphone call to 9-1-1 set off a chain of responses that showcased human ingenuity. The sheriff's department was notified, and paramedics were dispatched instantly. Within minutes, a helicopter—a marvel of modern technology—took to the sky, flying over twenty miles from downtown Fort Worth to reach the scene. The emergency responders on the ground worked quickly to stabilize Karsyn's body, their hands and minds applying the skills and knowledge developed through years of medical advancement. Moments later, she was rushed to the emergency room of one of the finest children's hospitals in the United States.

There, in the hands of gifted surgeons and medical staff, the real work of healing began. They meticulously repaired the internal damage she had sustained, using techniques and tools that would have been unimaginable a few generations ago. Days later, they would miraculously fuse her cracked vertebrae, allowing the incredible design of her body to begin the process of self-repair. Her broken elbow, too, would heal, thanks to the delicate balance of medical intervention and the body's natural ability to mend itself.

This is the miracle of God today—not through direct intervention, but through the divine creation of us to be His instruments of miracles to mankind. In the midst of chaos and suffering, the miraculous power of humanity, endowed by God, becomes the channel through which healing and hope flow.

Today, Karsyn has essentially made a full recovery, at least outwardly. To the casual observer, she is just like any other young teenager, living her life and moving forward. Yet, her journey through this trauma has left its marks—both physically and emotionally. She carries three visible scars as reminders of that day: one on her back from the fusion of her vertebrae, another on her stomach from the internal repairs, and a third on her elbow. They are silent witnesses to the fragility of human life and the extraordinary efforts made to preserve it.

In the grander scheme, experiences like this one are not just isolated moments of crisis; they become catalysts for growth and learning. They propel humanity forward, compelling us to improve, adapt, and become more resilient. The ordeal that Karsyn and our family went through is a testament to the intricate balance between the vulnerability of life and the capacity for recovery that God has placed within us. It was a painful reminder of how quickly life can change, but also of how the systems and capabilities we've developed as a society can spring into action when needed most.

Such events push us to examine and refine our responses. Emergency responders analyze their performance to improve for future incidents, medical professionals learn new lessons that influence their practices, and engineers study accidents to enhance safety features in cars and infrastructure. Even the Texas Department of Transportation, through the structure of our court system, must confront the negligence that left the stop sign down, learning from this tragedy to prevent similar occurrences in the future. In this way, our frailties and failures become the driving forces behind societal advancements. Each crisis, every brush with entropy and chaos, serves as a lesson that shapes a more prepared, more thoughtful future.

Karsyn's recovery is not just a story of medical success; it's a story of the miraculous power of humanity in the face of life's uncertainties. We are reminded of our collective journey—how each scar, each lesson learned, contributes to the broader narrative of human progress. Her scars, though symbols of a terrifying day, are also symbols of resilience, a testament to the strength of the human spirit and the marvel of the human body's design. They remind us that while life is frail, we are equipped with an incredible capacity for healing, growth, and adaptation.

In the end, events like this one teach us that God's miracles today often come through the collective efforts of humanity. They come through the hands of surgeons, the advancements of medical science, the rapid response of emergency teams, and the compassion of communities. In each crisis, in each recovery, we see a glimpse of the divine at work—not in the absence of suffering, but in the way humanity rises to meet it. And as Karsyn moves forward in life, those scars will be both a reminder of what was overcome and an inspiration for what can be achieved through the miraculous power of God's design within us.

The Miraculous Power of Prayer

I hope you can see by now that things have changed. The Bible does recount many miracles, but they were not random acts; they served specific purposes in revealing God's power and affirming Jesus's divine mission. Today, the expectation of physical miracles as a normative response to prayer can lead to disappointment and a crisis of faith when these miracles do not occur. This misunderstanding can result in spiritual isolation and doubt, with individuals questioning God's presence and love when they do not receive the miraculous answers they expected.

Much of this misunderstanding is perpetuated by certain religious teachings that present the power of prayer as a direct portal to divine intervention, expected to counteract the effects of free will and the natural laws of decay and disorder. While prayer is indeed powerful, many groups suggest it should lead to an immediate overturning of life's harsh realities, which can be counterproductive to understanding how God's creation truly works. The world is not the Garden of Eden; while it is designed for life to thrive, it is also a place where hardships exist. This dual nature of the world is part of God's design, balancing life-sustaining systems with the harsh realities of existence.

God never promised that life would be easy, and in the Bible, He often provides practical guidance to help His people navigate the challenges of a fallen world. For instance, in the Old Testament, God gave the Israelites detailed instructions on how to live, including specific laws about cleanliness and health. These laws, such as those found in Leviticus, were not merely spiritual commands; they were also practical measures to prevent the spread of disease and protect the community. Instructions on washing after touching something unclean, isolating those with infectious diseases, and properly handling food and waste were divine wisdom given in a time when the understanding of germs and hygiene was nonexistent. God provided these guidelines not to make life more difficult but to teach His people how to live within the realities of a world where disease and decay are present.

This demonstrates that while God is always present, He also expects humanity to take an active role in navigating the complexities of life. He has embedded within His creation principles and systems that require human engagement, wisdom, and responsibility. However, this message is often confused within the church itself, where the understanding of miracles and divine intervention can sometimes be misconstrued.

Much of the confusion stems from various Scriptures in the Bible that are often cited in support of miraculous expectations. However, it's essential to understand what these references are actually saying in their full context.

Matthew 7:7-8—"Ask, Seek, Knock"

Ask, and it will be given to you; seek, and you will find; knock, and it will be opened to you. For everyone who asks receives, and the one who seeks finds, and to the one who knocks it will be opened.

In this passage, part of Jesus's Sermon on the Mount, Jesus teaches the principles of the Kingdom of God and righteous living. He encourages persistence in prayer, but the focus is not necessarily on miraculous interventions. Instead, it is about seeking a deeper relationship with God, aligning one's will with His, and trusting Him for guidance and provision. When Jesus speaks of asking, seeking, and knocking, He is inviting us to pursue God earnestly. The "giving" mentioned here often refers to spiritual insights, wisdom, and the presence of God rather than physical miracles. The heart of this teaching is about nurturing a relationship with God and finding fulfillment in His presence rather than in specific outcomes.

Philippians 4:6—"Do Not Be Anxious"

Do not be anxious about anything, but in everything by prayer and supplication with thanksgiving let your requests be made known to God.

Paul wrote this letter to encourage believers to find peace in God despite their circumstances. He urges them to present their requests to God through prayer with a thankful heart. The emphasis here is on God's peace as a response to prayer, indicating an internal transformation rather than a promise of miraculous change in circumstances. When believers bring their anxieties to God, the result is not necessarily the removal of their problems but the peace of God that "surpasses all understanding" (Philippians 4:7). This peace serves as a guard over the heart and mind, offering calm reassurance even amid life's storms.

John 14:13-14—"Ask in My Name"

Whatever you ask in my name, this I will do, that the Father may be glorified in the Son. If you ask me anything in my name, I will do it.

Jesus speaks these words to His disciples, preparing them for His departure. He encourages them to continue His mission, assuring them of God's support in their efforts. To ask "in Jesus's name" means to pray in alignment with His character, mission, and will. It's not a blank check for miracles but a call to seek God's will and purposes. The focus here is on the heart's alignment with God's will rather than an expectation of miraculous intervention. When prayers are offered in Jesus's name, they are meant to reflect His heart, His love for others, and His desire for God's Kingdom to be realized on earth.

James 1:5—"Ask for Wisdom"

If any of you lacks wisdom, let him ask God, who gives generously to all without reproach, and it will be given him.

James addresses believers facing trials and in need of guidance, encouraging them to ask God for wisdom. This promise is not about the removal of trials but about the inner transformation that comes from gaining wisdom to navigate life's difficulties. God's response is to equip the believer internally to handle external challenges. The focus is on developing discernment and strength to endure hardships rather than expecting an immediate miraculous solution. Through this wisdom, believers can see their trials from a divine perspective and make decisions that reflect their faith and maturity.

James 4:2-3—"You Do Not Have because You Do Not Ask"

You desire and do not have, so you murder. You covet and cannot obtain, so you fight and quarrel. You do not have because you do not ask. You ask and do not receive, because you ask wrongly, to spend it on your passions.

James confronts the selfish desires and wrongful motives that can taint our prayers. He clarifies that God does not respond to self-centered prayers but to those that align with His will. This passage suggests that the effectiveness of prayer is tied to the heart's intentions. When prayers are selfless and in line with God's purposes, they become more about internal alignment with God's will than about external changes. The message here is that prayer is not a means to fulfill personal desires but a way to cultivate a heart that seeks God's desires.

Mark 11:24—"Believe That You Have Received"

Therefore I tell you, whatever you ask in prayer, believe that you have received it, and it will be yours.

Jesus teaches about faith and the power of prayer, but the broader context of Scripture shows that this faith is about trusting in God's will and timing rather than expecting an immediate miraculous outcome. True faith in prayer is about trusting God's nature and His overarching plan. It involves a heart posture that seeks God's Kingdom first, accepting His response—whether it is a change in circumstances, a change in the heart, or a deeper understanding of His will. The essence of this teaching is that faith looks beyond the immediate and trusts in God's ultimate good.

1 John 5:14-15—"According to His Will"

And this is the confidence that we have toward him, that if we ask anything according to his will he hears us. And if we know that he hears us in whatever we ask, we know that we have the requests that we have asked of him.

John emphasizes the confidence believers have when their prayers align with God's will. This verse directly ties the effectiveness of prayer to God's will, suggesting that prayer is less about changing God's mind and more about aligning our hearts with His purposes. The assurance here is that God listens and responds to prayers that come from a heart seeking His will. The focus is on cultivating a relationship where the believer's desires are shaped by their understanding of God's nature and His plans for the world.

God Listens and Responds to the Heart

These passages, when understood in their full biblical context, emphasize that prayer is fundamentally relational. It's about bringing our desires, fears, and needs before God and trusting Him to respond in ways that align with His will and foster our spiritual growth. While miraculous interventions do occur in Scripture, these verses often highlight inner transformation, peace, wisdom, and alignment with God's purposes as the primary responses to prayer. God's response to prayer is often about changing our hearts, providing us with strength and peace, and guiding us through life's complexities rather than intervening in miraculous ways that defy the natural order.

The context of all these verses must necessarily be defined by Jesus's purpose on earth, which essentially defines His works. Did Jesus come to perform miracles as His primary mission, or was His main goal to seek and save the lost, teaching the gospel's message of salvation? Fortunately, Jesus provides clear insights into His works and purpose throughout the New Testament. While miracles were an important aspect of His ministry, they served mainly to authenticate His identity and message. Jesus's primary work was to reveal God's truth, call people to repentance, and offer salvation. Here are some key passages where Jesus defines His works and purpose:

In Luke 19:10, Jesus states, "For the Son of Man came to seek and to save the lost." This declaration, made after His encounter with Zacchaeus, succinctly describes His mission. Jesus's ultimate purpose was to bring salvation to humanity. His works involved actively seeking out those who were spiritually lost and offering them redemption and a restored relationship with God.

In John 4:34, Jesus emphasizes, "My food is to do the will of him who sent me and to accomplish his work." Here, Jesus underscores that His work was to fulfill the will of God the Father. His mission was not self-driven but directed by the Father's plan. This "work" involved proclaiming the Kingdom of God, teaching about God's nature and will, and ultimately sacrificing Himself for the salvation of humanity.

John 17:4 records Jesus's words: "I glorified you on earth, having accomplished the work that you gave me to do." In His prayer before the crucifixion, Jesus declares that He has completed the work given to Him by the Father. This work included His teachings, His life of perfect obedience, and His actions that revealed God's character and plan for salvation. Through this, Jesus brought glory to God, which was central to His purpose.

In John 10:10, Jesus reveals His intention: "I came that they may have life and have it abundantly." His purpose was to provide not just physical life but also abundant spiritual life. His works included teaching the truths of God's Kingdom, demonstrating God's love and grace, and offering a pathway to eternal life through faith in Him.

In John 18:37, during His dialogue with Pilate, Jesus declares, "For this purpose I was born and for this purpose I have come into the world—to bear witness to the truth. Everyone who is of the truth listens to my voice." Jesus defines His purpose as testifying to the truth—truth about God, humanity's need for salvation, and the way to eternal life. His teachings, actions, and ultimately His sacrifice were all aimed at revealing this truth to the world.

Finally, Matthew 20:28 reiterates the theme of service and sacrifice: "Even as the Son of Man came not to be served but to serve, and to give his life as a ransom for many." Jesus emphasized that His work was about serving humanity. He did not come to be served but to serve, and His greatest work was giving His life for the redemption of many.

Jesus's works were primarily about revealing God's nature, fulfilling God's redemptive plan, and teaching the principles of the Kingdom of God. While miracles were an essential part of His ministry, they were secondary to His central mission: to bring salvation, to teach truth, and to offer Himself as a sacrifice for sin. Through His teachings, actions, and sacrifice, Jesus accomplished the work that the Father sent Him to do. Thus, the "greater works" that His followers would do involve spreading this message of salvation and continuing the mission of making disciples, impacting the world with the truth of God's love and grace.

Understanding "Greater Works" in John 14:12

The interpretation of John 14:12 has been debated, and the phrase "greater works" can be understood in different ways. Here's a breakdown of both viewpoints:

Greater Miracles

Some interpret "greater works" to mean that believers will perform miracles greater in number or scale than those Jesus performed. However, this interpretation raises some challenges:

- **Nature of Jesus's Miracles:** Jesus's miracles—raising the dead, walking on water, feeding thousands—were unparalleled. While the apostles performed miracles after Jesus's ascension, these were done to affirm the gospel's message and the power of God, not to surpass Jesus's works.

- **Authority and Purpose:** Jesus performed miracles to reveal His divine nature and the Kingdom of God. If "greater works" were to mean more spectacular miracles, it could imply a misunderstanding of the purpose behind Jesus's miracles, which were to point to His identity as the Son of God and the coming of His Kingdom.

Greater in Impact

A more likely interpretation is that "greater works" refers to the spread and impact of the gospel message rather than the miraculous deeds themselves:

- **Wider Reach:** Jesus's ministry was primarily confined to a specific region (Israel). After His ascension, His followers carried the message to the ends of the earth. This expansion of the gospel's reach can be seen as "greater" in scope and influence.

- **Transformation through the Gospel:** The "greater works" could also refer to the spiritual transformation of lives through the preaching of the gospel. While Jesus performed miracles that transformed physical conditions, His followers would go on to transform hearts and lives through the message of salvation.

- **Empowerment by the Holy Spirit:** Jesus's departure and the sending of the Holy Spirit empowered believers to carry out the mission of spreading the gospel, leading to the birth and growth of the Church. This movement's lasting impact on the world can be seen as a "greater work" in the sense that it fulfills Jesus's mission on a global scale.

While Jesus performed extraordinary miracles, His statement about "greater works" likely points to the mission of spreading the gospel and the transformative power of faith in the lives of countless people across the world. It emphasizes the broader impact believers would have, not necessarily in terms of more spectacular miracles, but in their ability to reach the world with the message of Christ.

Misunderstandings of Prayer and Miracles

A significant source of disillusionment with God and the church often arises from a misunderstanding of how God interacts with humanity today through prayer. Many struggle with the idea of selective intervention—wondering why their prayers for a miracle go unanswered while others seem to receive divine intervention. Questions like "Why is my child not healed?" or "Why did this happen to me?" become difficult to resolve when God seems silent and does not respond with miraculous intervention.

This misunderstanding is compounded by the tendency to label events as "miracles" when they may simply be the result of natural circumstances. We often use the term "miracle" as a catch-all for situations that science can explain, such as surviving an accident due to a seat belt or the body's ability to heal after medical treatment. While these moments are certainly unexplainable and can be seen as God's providence working through natural means, they are not miracles in the biblical sense. This overuse of the term can make religion seem out of touch with reality for many, further contributing to feelings of disillusionment.

Believing that God still intervenes selectively and miraculously through prayer in some lives but not others can lead to feelings of isolation and questions of fairness. Why would one person's child be healed while another's is not? Such perceived selectivity can create feelings of unworthiness or anger toward God, fostering a damaging narrative of "selective worth." This notion suggests that only those who receive miracles are favored by God, leaving others to feel marginalized and abandoned. Understanding that God's plan today is not about performing miracles on demand, but rather about guiding humanity through wisdom, resilience, and inner transformation, helps to realign our expectations and fosters a deeper, more authentic faith.

I remember my mother-in-law, Elaine, struggling with her health toward the end of her life. There was a time when everyone thought her time had come as she lay in the hospital, unresponsive for days. Suddenly, she made a turn for the better, enough so that she was able to come home and live for another year or so. Many called it a miracle. But here was the problem I had with the thought that God had miraculously intervened to bring her back to some measure of health: if it was truly a divine intervention, why was it only partial? She still needed in-home care and relied on a wheelchair to move around.

In all the miracles recorded in the Bible, miraculous intervention was always whole and complete. God never left someone partially healed. When Jesus restored sight to the blind man, it wasn't partial—he was fully restored, likely with perfect vision. When Jesus raised Lazarus from the dead, Lazarus didn't return to life with lingering illnesses; he was completely revived. Miraculous healings in the Bible were total and transformative, not half-measures.

If we believe that God still performs miracles in the same way today, then we face a troubling question: why would He intervene to give someone a few more difficult months or years, but not heal the countless children just a few miles away at Cook Children's, many of whom may not live out the year? These children and their families pray fervently for a miracle, yet many do not receive the outcome they hope for. This inconsistency becomes hard to reconcile unless we shift our understanding of how God works in our lives today.

These questions reveal the problems that arise when we misunderstand the purpose of prayer in the present day. Many see prayer as a means to invoke miracles, and when the miraculous outcomes they pray for do not materialize, it can lead to confusion, disillusionment, and feelings of abandonment. However, the true purpose of prayer becomes clearer when we understand that, in many ways, God has chosen to work through humanity. We are not God, but we are His hands and feet in the world. This is not a pedestal to stand on; it is a call to action and a tremendous responsibility.

Being the hands of God means that we are tasked with the work of intervening, healing, and supporting one another. God has equipped each of us with the ability to make a difference in the lives of others through compassion, innovation, and the unique gifts He has given us. Through advancements in medicine, the comfort of community, and the resilience of the human spirit, we become His instruments of love and care in a world that is still filled with pain and suffering.

This is not to say that life will always be perfect or that every prayer will result in a desired outcome. The world remains a place of adversity and struggle, which is a part of God's design for us to grow and thrive. Through hardships, we learn, adapt, and develop a society that can provide care, support, and hope. Prayer, in this context, is not about suspending the natural order or receiving every wish granted.

Rather, prayer is about seeking wisdom, strength, and peace. It is through prayer that we find the courage to confront challenges, the clarity to heal and innovate, and the love to reflect God's presence in the world. Prayer connects us to God's guidance and helps us align our hearts with His purposes. It transforms us, empowering us to be His hands in the world, and reminding us that we have a role to play in bringing about His will on earth.

A Shift in Salvation: From Collective Leadership to Individual Relationship

In the Old Testament, the pattern of salvation was mediated through religious leaders. People brought sacrifices to the priests to atone for their sins, with the high priest serving as an intermediary between God and humanity. The system required collective worship and adherence to the law, with temple rituals and sacrifices symbolizing the people's need for God's forgiveness and favor.

However, in the New Testament, there is a profound shift. Christ became the ultimate sacrifice, offering atonement once and for all. This act of self-giving love set humanity free from the need for ongoing sacrifices and the mediation of religious leadership for forgiveness. Jesus opened the way for each individual to have a direct, personal relationship with God. Through prayer, each person can now approach God one-on-one, without the need for an earthly intermediary. This transition emphasizes the personal nature of salvation and significant accessibility of God's grace to all who seek it.

This change foreshadows how God's intervention works today. Just as He has given us full control over our salvation, He has also placed in humanity's hands the responsibility for its own destiny. God has once again moved His creation forward, entrusting us to take an active role in the world. This concept is encapsulated in the following poem:

GOD SAID NO

I asked God to take away my habit.

God said, No.

It is not for me to take away, but for you to give up.

I asked God to make my handicapped child whole.

God said, No.

Her spirit is whole, her body is only temporary.

I asked God to grant me patience.

God said, No.

Patience is a byproduct of tribulations; it isn't granted, it is earned.

I asked God to give me happiness.

God said, No.

I give you blessings; happiness is up to you.

I asked God to spare me pain.

God said, No.

Suffering draws you apart from worldly cares and brings you closer to me.

I asked God to make my spirit grow.

God said, No.

You must grow on your own, but I will prune you to make you fruitful.

I asked God for all things that I might enjoy life.

God said, No.

I will give you life so that you may enjoy all things.

I asked God to help me love others, as much as He loves me.

God said…

Ahhhh, finally you have the idea.

God has given us the power to be the miracle today. Prayer is not a means to summon divine intervention to change our circumstances but a way to find God and receive His guidance. Through prayer, we align ourselves with His will, find the strength to face our challenges, and become the instruments of His love and purpose in the world.

The Power of Prayer Today: Seeking Peace, Comfort, and Understanding

Jesus's teaching on prayer, particularly in the Lord's Prayer (Matthew 6:9-13), centers on seeking God's will, daily sustenance, forgiveness, and spiritual deliverance. The prayer goes:

> *Our Father in heaven, hallowed be your name.*
> *Your kingdom come, your will be done, on earth as it is in heaven.*
> *Give us this day our daily bread,*
> *and forgive us our debts, as we also have forgiven our debtors.*
> *And lead us not into temptation, but deliver us from evil.*
> (Matthew 6:9-13)

The emphasis is not on asking for miraculous intervention but on aligning oneself with God's plan. The Lord's Prayer serves as a guide for this alignment, touching on various aspects of our spiritual and physical needs.

> *"Your kingdom come, your will be done,*
> *on earth as it is in heaven."*

This is a request for God's reign and will to be realized in our lives and the world around us. It's a call for us to seek His purposes above our own, inviting God to shape our desires and actions to reflect His love, justice, and mercy. God helps us in this area by transforming our hearts and minds, enabling us to live out His principles of love, humility, and service in our daily lives.

> *"Give us this day our daily bread."*

Here, we ask for our basic needs—physical sustenance and provision. It's a reminder that God is the source of all that we need and that we rely on His provision daily. God meets these needs often through the natural processes of the world He created, through the work we do, and through the generosity of others. It's an invitation to trust in His care and to be content with what He provides.

When considering what this request truly means, we can better understand the division of responsibilities between what God has entrusted to humanity and what He Himself continues to sustain. In Genesis 1:28, God gives humanity specific responsibilities over creation: "And God blessed them. And God said to them, 'Be fruitful and multiply and fill the earth and subdue it, and have dominion over the fish of the sea and over the birds of the heavens and over every living thing that moves on the earth'" (Genesis 1:28).

This dominion is not a license for exploitation but a call to stewardship. God entrusted mankind with the care of animals, plants, and the resources of the earth. This means that while God provides the systems that support life—the sun, the water cycle, the atmosphere—He has given us the responsibility to manage the more immediate aspects of our world. We are to cultivate the land, care for the creatures, and look after each other, using these resources wisely to meet our needs and the needs of others.

God's role involves sustaining the broader systems that make life possible. Psalm 104 beautifully describes God's ongoing involvement in creation, where He provides for every living thing and maintains the order of the natural world:

> *You make springs gush forth in the valleys; they flow between the hills; they give drink to every beast of the field; the wild donkeys quench their thirst. Beside them the birds of the heavens dwell; they sing among the branches. From your lofty abode you water the mountains; the earth is satisfied with the fruit of your work.* (Psalm 104:10-13)

This passage illustrates how God oversees the grand systems of creation, providing water, food, and the cycle of life. In this way, God handles the big things—the sun that rises each day, the earth that sustains life, the seasons that change in their appointed times. These are not within our control, nor are they our responsibility.

When considering global issues like climate change due to burning fossil fuels, I find myself questioning if this falls within God's realm of responsibility. While we have a duty to be wise stewards of the earth, it's hard to imagine that we possess the power to fundamentally disrupt or destroy the planet beyond God's ability to sustain it. Jesus spoke of His return when it was time for judgment, and I don't think He will arrive one day to find an empty world and ask, "Where did everyone go?"

> *"And forgive us our debts,*
> *as we also have forgiven our debtors."*

This part of the prayer acknowledges our need for forgiveness and challenges us to extend the same grace to others. It's a spiritual request, asking God to cleanse us of our wrongdoings and help us live in harmony with others. God helps us by offering His boundless grace, teaching us the importance of forgiveness, and empowering us to let go of resentment and bitterness.

> *"And lead us not into temptation, but deliver us from evil."*

This is a plea for God's guidance and protection. We ask God to help us avoid the pitfalls of sin and to steer us away from situations that could lead us astray. God aids us by providing wisdom and discernment, giving us the strength to resist temptations, and delivering us from harmful influences. His guidance often comes through His Word, the prompting of the Holy Spirit, and the counsel of others who walk in faith.

Through these petitions, the Lord's Prayer teaches us that the power of prayer lies not in asking for miraculous changes but in seeking a deeper connection with God. It's about aligning our desires with His will, trusting in His provision, seeking His forgiveness, and relying on His guidance. In these ways, God helps us grow spiritually, find peace, and navigate life's complexities with a heart tuned to His purposes.

Addressing Jesus's Prayer in Gethsemane: Was It a Request for a Miracle?

When Jesus prayed in Gethsemane, He did indeed ask for something: "My Father, if it is possible, let this cup pass from me; nevertheless, not as I will, but as you will" (Matthew 26:39). This moment was a deeply human expression of Jesus's anguish. The prospect of Roman crucifixion was a harrowing burden, and His plea to "let this cup pass" was a natural request for deliverance from immense suffering.

However, this request is distinct from seeking a miraculous intervention as we might think of it. Jesus wasn't asking for a supernatural alteration of reality; rather, He was sharing His deepest concerns and laying them before the Father. He knew the path ahead and its necessity for the redemption of humanity, yet He still expressed His human desire to avoid such pain. The core of His prayer was submission: "not as I will, but as you will." This demonstrates the essence of prayer—bringing our desires to God while yielding to His greater plan. Jesus's prayer illustrates that God welcomes our honesty and emotions in prayer.

The Power of Prayer: Moving Beyond the Physical Realm

This perspective on prayer points us toward how God works within humanity today, not through miraculous interventions that defy the natural order but within the spiritual and emotional realms. Prayer becomes a means for God to work in our hearts, providing peace and comfort, and sometimes even mobilizing others around us to offer support.

This ties back to the concept of free will, which God allows to reign supreme in the world. The reality of free will means that people make choices that affect themselves and others, sometimes leading to suffering. However, when we seek God's counsel through prayer, He can influence the hearts and minds of those within our circles, prompting them to act in ways that align with His will. God's intervention often comes through the compassion, wisdom, and actions of people around us rather than through direct supernatural acts.

Just a few weeks before your mom passed away, I left the company I had worked for over three decades. For a short time, I went to work for a smaller funeral home in Granbury, Texas, about forty miles away, where I didn't know anyone, and no one knew me. One day, I conducted a graveside service at the Texas State Cemetery, near the state capitol in Austin. After the service ended, the wife of the deceased sent her granddaughter to give me a tip—some money.

This was something I would never accept, so I told the granddaughter, "Thank you, but I can't accept this." She walked back to her grandmother, and a moment later, she returned, saying, "My grandmother really wants you to have it. It would be easier if you just accepted it because that's just her way." So, I reluctantly accepted the bill and put it in my pocket.

After everyone had left, I took the bill out to put it in my wallet, and that's when I experienced a moment I will never forget. This family did not know me. They had no idea that your mom had recently passed away. But written on the outside of that $20 bill, in blue ink, was your mom's name—Laura.

Seeing her name brought a wave of comfort to me, though I'm not sure I can fully explain it. It was a quiet reminder of her, a small but meaningful sign. While I can't explain how or why this happened, I believe this is one of the ways God works. He often influences the thoughts and actions of those around us to bring comfort and help to those in need. Jesus touches on this idea in John 14:10, saying, "Do you not believe that I am in the Father and the Father is in me? The words that I say to you I do not speak on my own authority, but the Father who dwells in me does his works." While we are not Jesus, this passage reminds us that God can work through us. I don't know who wrote "Laura" on that $20 bill or how it ended up in my hands, but I believe it found its way to me through the workings of God and the actions of others.

This is where God works today through prayer—within the people in our circles, our communities, and many times across the globe through world charities and missions. The prayers of those in need are laid on the hearts of those who can help. This can be seen in the Cindy Ramsey Center, part of the Met Church in Keller, Texas, which plays a significant role in addressing food insecurity in the Fort Worth area.[89] Established as its own nonprofit in 2017, it serves as a local mission for the church, offering services like food distribution, crisis counseling, home repairs, and financial literacy to those in need.

The center's food outreach is substantial, providing over 2.2 million pounds of food to families in 2023 alone. With both an indoor market and an outdoor mobile market, they collectively serve more than one thousand families each week. This demonstrates how the center actively works to answer the prayers of many through love, compassion, and direct community involvement, aligning with the idea that prayer often inspires real-world actions that reflect God's love.

This reinforces the theme that God's response to prayers frequently comes through acts of love and service by others, showing that miracles happen in everyday acts of kindness and generosity.

In the end, the power of prayer lies not in its ability to summon divine miracles at our command but in its capacity to transform our hearts, align us with God's will, and mobilize us to act as His hands in action in a broken world. Today, we are the miracles—vessels of God's love and grace, equipped to bring healing, comfort, and hope. When we pray, we connect to this divine purpose, finding peace and strength to face life's challenges, knowing that God is with us, not just in supernatural interventions but in every act of kindness, every moment of grace, and every quiet assurance of His presence.

CHAPTER 10

The Mosaic of God's Design

As I come to the end of this journey we've taken together, I find myself reflecting on all the conversations, questions, and discoveries that have shaped the pages of this book. My desire has been to guide you through the complexities of faith and science, of tradition and discovery, so that you might find clarity where so many today are left with confusion.

It seems like the deeper science delves into the mysteries of the universe, the further it takes us from traditional understandings of the Bible. Every new discovery, whether in astronomy, biology, or anthropology, seems to stretch the gap between what we have believed and what we are learning. And for many, this is a breaking point—an obstacle too great to overcome. It is not uncommon to find those who, unable to reconcile the two, simply give up on faith, feeling as though the Bible no longer speaks to the world they see unfolding before them.

This, I believe, is a tragedy, because each scientific discovery brings us closer to marveling at God's handiwork, reminding us that the divine narrative of the Bible remains relevant and awe-inspiring. The atmosphere we live in now, where science and faith often seem at odds, is leaving many without the tools to harmonize the truths found in both. But I am convinced that the Bible, when viewed through a lens that understands both its divine inspiration and its cultural context, is not in opposition to the discoveries we are making today. In fact, I believe that the more we learn, the more we discover the fingerprints of God in the very fabric of the universe.

Looking Back to the Intelligent Design for Life

Science has revealed that our universe is billions of years old. It doesn't matter whether you hold to a Young Earth (YEC) or Old Earth (OEC) perspective, as this understanding is not directly tied to salvation. However, it deepens our appreciation of God's creation and demonstrates the Bible's relevance in the modern world. Discoveries show that space, time, and matter began in an instant with the universe's expansion from a singularity—an event science calls the Big Bang. Their very existence points to a cause beyond space, time, and matter—a cause the Bible unmistakably identifies as God. Furthermore, we have uncovered the processes behind the formation of galaxies, stars, planets, and the extraordinary complexity of life—all pointing to a universe finely tuned for our existence.

When we interpret the Bible's account of creation not as a rigid, twenty four-hour timeline but as expansive phases of development—where *"evening and morning"* mark the completion of each creative period—we see alignment with scientific revelation. The ancient writers, inspired by God, conveyed truths that resonate with modern insights. The universe unfolded over immense stretches of time, and with each stage, God prepared for humanity's arrival and His ultimate plan for redemption.

As Isaiah 45:18 reveals, God "did not create [the earth] to be empty, but formed it to be inhabited." Creation was never aimless; it was purposeful from the beginning.

Earth, with its intricate design and abundant resources, stands as a testament to its purpose of sustaining life. Since its formation, its environment was finely tuned to support a wide array of living organisms. The atmosphere, rich in oxygen and nitrogen, not only forms breathable air essential for count-less species but also acts as a protective shield, filtering harmful solar radia-tion and moderating temperatures. The presence of water in its liquid form provides the essential foundation for life, while the diversity of climates and ecosystems, ranging from lush rainforests to arid deserts, ensures that every form of life has a habitat in which to thrive.

Earth's vast food sources, from the bounty of the seas to the fertile soils pro-ducing endless varieties of plants, demonstrate the planet's capacity to nourish life. Beyond food, Earth's resources, such as timber for shelter and tools and fossil fuels for energy, have enabled humanity to grow, adapt, and advance. Even the minerals beneath the surface and renewable resources like sunlight and wind testify to a world designed not only for survival but for flourishing.

Earth was designed to sustain life and serve as the setting for God's grand plan. Positioned in a "Goldilocks" location—not too close to the sun to scorch its surface, nor too far to freeze—Earth's placement underscores its unique-ness in the cosmos. But what exactly was this divine plan?

Creation and Purpose: A World Prepared for Humanity

Before the beginning of time, before the first star was born or the first molecule came together, God had already planned your creation—a begin-ning with the end in mind. His purpose was that one day, you would have the opportunity to live in eternity in His presence as a son or daughter of God. You were created with intentionality and purpose. This divine plan was set in motion with the promise of eternal life at its core. As Titus 1:2 affirms, "in hope of eternal life, which God, who never lies, promised before the ages began."

The human fossil record reveals that God uniquely designed our bodies as vessels—physical forms, each capable of becoming a dwelling place for an individual soul. This distinction between body and soul sheds light on the existence of life before Adam and Eve. Scientific evidence shows that intelli-gent beings inhabited Earth long before the biblical timeframe associated with Adam and Eve. These beings, while possessing survival instincts and notable intelligence, lacked the divine spark of a soul. They lived by natural laws and instincts, much like animals in the natural order. Though capable and intelligent, they were without moral consciousness or the unique spiritual purpose the Bible attributes to humanity. Only after Earth was fully prepared and the human form perfected as a vessel did God introduce souls into humanity, beginning with Adam and Eve—the first Homo sapiens to embody the soul of man. This marks a shift in Genesis 2, which picks up where Genesis 1 leaves off in verse 25, signaling a pivotal turning point.

Genesis 1:26 presents a unique moment in the creation narrative. In the previous creation periods, the phrase "And God said" (*Vayomer Elohim*) appears only once per act of creation. However, in the sixth period, it appears twice—first in verse 24, when God commands the earth to bring forth living creatures, and again in verse 26, when He declares, "Let us make man in our image." This deliberate repetition signals a significant shift. Up to this point, Earth was alive with animals and intelligent beings capable of survival and adaptation. Yet none were like this new creation: beings made in His image, endowed with a soul capable of knowing Him.

This shift in Genesis is not just the continuation of the sixth day but a pivotal event. The phrase "Let us make man in our image" introduces a spiritual dimension that did not exist before, even in other human-like species. While all living things reflect aspects of God's creativity, only this new creation—a new humanity—would bear His image in a distinct way. It was no longer merely about survival or adaptation. Here was a creation that could engage in relationship with God, possessing moral and spiritual capacity: the soul of humankind.

In verse 26, the narrative shifts from the creation of the earth as a whole, which had unfolded over hundreds of thousands of years, to the land of Eden, where God establishes a new relationship with humanity—Adam and Eve—and begins to nurture this unique, soul-bearing creation.

Toward the end of the sixth day, or period of creation, God chooses the region of Eden to begin a second creation. This has long perplexed theologians, and many skeptics view this retelling of creation as a contradiction because the order of events differs from Genesis 1. However, this difference is intentional—God now creates in reverse order, mirroring the original creation account in Genesis 1.

As discussed in earlier chapters, the sequence unfolds in a structured pattern: from the heavens and the earth to the land and sky, then to Adam, the garden, the animals, the birds, and finally, Eve. God plants a garden and places Adam within it to initiate His redemptive plan for humanity. In this act, He bestows a soul within Adam and Eve, setting humanity's true purpose into motion.

Interestingly, the evidence of this story can even be traced to the genetic heritage of every person alive today. We all carry DNA markers from a common maternal ancestor, known as Mitochondrial Eve, who lived between 100,000 and 150,000 years ago—around the middle of the sixth period of creation. Her DNA links all humanity, reflecting God's careful handiwork through the ages.

This also explains why genetic studies do not reveal a genetic bottleneck associated with the time of Adam and Eve. If Adam and Eve were the first Homo sapiens created in the image of God, their genetic lineage would have naturally blended with existing human populations through intermarriage as society developed. Rather than a drastic population reduction, their lineage became part of the broader human story, allowing their divinely crafted DNA to spread throughout humanity.

It is also reasonable to believe that God, in His wisdom, crafted their DNA with the resilience it would have developed from the beginning of humankind. Our physical bodies, refined through the ages and formed from the earth's dust, were designed as earthly homes for our souls. From the earth, they came, and to the earth, they will return; yet our souls will return to God, their Creator.

Scripture emphasizes this separation between body and soul, underscoring the eternal nature of the soul. Here are a few passages that clarify this distinction:

- **Matthew 10:28:** "And do not fear those who kill the body but cannot kill the soul. Rather fear him who can destroy both soul and body in hell."

- **Ecclesiastes 12:7:** "And the dust returns to the ground it came from, and the spirit returns to God who gave it."

- **Luke 23:46:** "Then Jesus, calling out with a loud voice, said, 'Father, into your hands I commit my spirit!' And having said this, he breathed his last."

These verses remind us that while our bodies are mortal and part of Earth's cycle, our souls belong to God and are destined for eternity. God's careful preparation of the world over billions of years reflects His intentionality, ensuring that when humanity was created in His image, we could inhabit a world rich with resources, structure, and purpose. The distinction between body and soul, and the perfection of each over time, reveals a God who, since the earliest days, crafted a world ready to receive beings created to know and love Him.

Seeing the Garden of Eden and Beyond through Science

In understanding creation, science often provides insight where the Bible allows room for discovery. Take, for example, humanity's evolving understanding of the universe's structure. Ancient civilizations believed that the sun revolved around Earth—a perspective that made perfect sense based on what they could observe from their limited vantage point. The Bible reflects this in Ecclesiastes 1:5, which says, "The sun rises, and the sun goes down, and hastens to the place where it rises." This verse poetically captures the movement of the sun across the sky, as seen from Earth, suggesting a daily journey where the sun seems to vanish in the west, only to reappear in the east by some unseen path.

Only through scientific advances did we come to understand that this view was not a literal heliocentric model but rather an expression of human perspective—a poetic rendering rather than a scientific claim. Science, in this way, allows us to see such verses as observational descriptions written in language accessible to the people of that time, rather than as obstacles to a more accurate model of the universe.

This same kind of insight makes the timing of Adam and Eve clearer. Archaeology shows that around 10,000 BC, humanity transitioned from a hunter-gatherer lifestyle to farming, tending livestock, and settling in permanent communities. This period, known as the Neolithic Revolution, marked a shift in human civilization—introducing agriculture, animal domestication, and the development of permanent settlements. These advancements laid the foundation for organized societies, technological progress, and structured communities.

The Bible, which serves as an ancient record of human history, describes Adam and Eve as being given 'the seeds of all things good to eat.' It also records Abel raising livestock and Cain farming the land, further reinforcing this connection to early agricultural society. Based on this, Adam and Eve likely came into existence around 11,500 to 10,000 BC—aligning perfectly with both science and biblical history.

In Chapter 5, we explored the hidden generations within biblical genealogies, revealing how the Bible accounts for longer time spans, which we also see reflected in scientific discoveries today. When genealogies are expanded, they encompass much longer periods than simply adding up each individual's age. This insight also resolves what initially seems puzzling—how the major patriarchs, from Adam to Lamech, all lived during a certain period with long overlapping lifespans, creating the impression that they were alive at the same time.

However, the absence of other descendants of Adam within these genealogies suggests a different picture—one where these patriarchs likely lived consecutively rather than simultaneously, with each succeeding the other over time, much like the prophets of the Old Testament. This perspective aligns with a broader historical framework and clarifies how biblical records emphasize spiritual succession rather than strict chronological overlap.

This expanded timeline also helps resolve another major question: how the population grew large enough to build the Tower of Babel. Traditional biblical chronologies, when taken at face value, suggest that only about 100 years passed between the flood and the Tower of Babel. However, this short timeframe presents a challenge, as constructing such a monumental structure would have required both a vast population and advanced technology. It also raises the question of how humanity could so quickly unite in rebellion against God so soon after experiencing a catastrophic event like the flood.

By recognizing longer time spans within genealogies, we can see that the post-flood world had significantly more time to repopulate and develop complex societies. This perspective not only aligns with scientific discoveries of early civilizations but also with the natural progression of human expansion and technological advancement.

This also parallels the broader biblical theme of God establishing sacred spaces. Just as the Jews, after reaching the Promised Land, built a Temple where God would dwell with His people, Eden was the first sacred dwelling place of God on Earth. Like the temples throughout the Old Testament, the Garden of Eden was rich in gold and precious minerals, symbolizing its significance as a divine space. It was a place of unparalleled beauty, peace, and spiritual intimacy—distinct from the outside world, where God's presence shaped humanity's destiny.

Adam and Eve were a divine presence, bearing the image of God and carrying within them the moral and spiritual nature that would be spread throughout the world. They were the beginning of conscious living and moral discernment—qualities that science cannot fully explain.

Adam and Eve's purpose extended beyond mere dominion; they were tasked with populating the earth with soul-bearing beings entrusted with a divine moral compass. As stated in Genesis 1:28, "And God blessed them. And God said to them, 'Be fruitful and multiply and fill the earth and subdue it.'"

Here, God's intent was for humanity to rise above the pre-Adamic, soulless state—a condition that science has shown existed for hundreds of thousands of years—fully reflecting their creation in His image as children of God, accountable to Him and endowed with divine purpose.

The Flood and Humanity's Renewal through Noah

Again, the science of archaeology can offer insights into what life was like for Adam and Eve and the challenges they faced. Homo sapiens, having existed for millennia, likely lived alongside Adam and Eve. This historical context helps explain where Cain found his wife—not through an incestuous union with a sibling, but by intermingling with pre-Adamic humans. This resolves two long-standing biblical puzzles.

First, it clarifies where Cain's wife came from after he was banished from Eden for killing Abel. Genesis 4:17 states, "Cain knew his wife, and she conceived and bore Enoch." This suggests that Cain found his wife shortly after settling in the land of Nod, east of Eden, rather than already being married before his exile. This aligns with the idea that he intermarried pre-Adamic humans, rather than condemning a sibling to banishment for his actions in addition to committing incest.

Second, it dispels the disturbing notion that humanity's beginnings required incest, something that God later forbade in Mosaic Law. Even though incest was not yet explicitly written into the law in Cain's time, sin did not originate with the law; the law merely exposed it. Incest was always a sinful nature.

Archaeological discoveries also offer clues about the pre-Adamic population. Sites like Göbekli Tepe reveal social groups engaged in religious rituals, yet these early belief systems were deeply tied to the natural world, focusing on animals rather than moral or spiritual enlightenment. These practices suggest an untamed, instinct-driven humanity, lacking the moral discernment that Adam's descendants carried.

As Adam's descendants intermingled with pre-Adamic humans, the influence of soulless existence threatened to draw the entire world into chaos. When humanity was on the brink of complete moral collapse, God chose to intervene, resetting the land with the flood while preserving Noah and his family.

The Local Flood: A Just and Targeted Judgment

Noah was unique—a man who had been tested by living amid moral decay yet remained steadfast. His faithfulness set him apart in a world that had become increasingly corrupt. The flood was not a reckless destruction of the entire world but a precise judgment on the region where the corruption had overtaken God's intended moral order.

This supports the local flood perspective—a cleansing of Eden, the sacred space that God had established on Earth, much like how later temples in Israel were consecrated and purified when defiled. The original Hebrew text also supports this, emphasizing that the flood reset the creation of Genesis 2, purging the land where Adam's lineage had spread. A local flood model also makes more sense logistically—it explains why:

- The ark's size could accommodate the animals. If the flood were global, Noah would have needed to house animals from all over the planet, including species that were nowhere near Eden.

- Noah was able to step off the ark into a world that was still functional. A global flood would have destroyed all ecosystems and wiped out all plant life, making immediate survival impossible.

- The flood's purpose was moral renewal. If God's goal was to cleanse human corruption, it makes sense that His judgment would focus where that corruption existed rather than eradicating all life indiscriminately.

Clearing a Major Contradiction in a Global Flood View

This local flood interpretation also resolves a major contradiction that arises if the flood were global. Psalm 104:6-9 clearly refers to the events of Day 3 of creation, when God separated the waters from the land and established permanent boundaries for the seas. While some attempt to argue that this passage refers to the flood of Noah, the broader context of Psalm 104 makes it clear that it is describing the formation of the earth itself, not a later catastrophic event. These verses explicitly state that once God set the boundaries of the waters, they would never again cover the entire earth:

> *You covered it with the deep as with a garment; the waters stood above the mountains. But at Your rebuke the waters fled, at the sound of Your thunder they took to flight... You set a boundary they cannot cross; never again will they cover the earth. (Psalm 104:6-9)*

This passage affirms that God's decree during creation established a lasting order. If the flood in Noah's time had been global, it would have directly contradicted this creation account, where God explicitly decreed that the waters would never again cover the entire earth. The local flood perspective aligns perfectly with this declaration, as it describes a regional judgment rather than a reversal of God's creation decree.

These eight individuals—Noah, his wife, his sons, and their wives—stood at the dawn of a new era for humanity. As the sole survivors of the flood in this region, they represented a fresh start, entrusted with the task of rebuilding and fulfilling God's divine mission with renewed purpose and resilience.

Like Adam and Eve before them, Noah and his family were re-tasked with replenishing the earth and fostering a moral foundation within humanity. Shem's descendants carried the direct line of moral accountability, later preserved in the chosen people—the Israelites. Meanwhile, Ham and Japheth's descendants dispersed across the earth, likely intermingling with pre-Adamic populations, helping to spread the divine spark throughout humanity, and would eventually become the Gentile nations.

This also helps clarify where human diversity came from. Scientific research shows that genetic variation within humanity has developed over hundreds of thousands of years through migration, adaptation, and population bottlenecks. Studies indicate that anatomically modern humans originated in Africa and began dispersing across the world at least 130,000 years ago, carrying with them the foundations of the diversity we see today. As Noah's descendants intermingled with these existing populations, their lineage naturally merged into the expanding human civilization, explaining the genetic variation observed across different peoples and cultures. Rather than all diversity stemming from a small, post-flood population, it had already been well-established, aligning with both science and biblical history.

As civilization expanded, pre-Adamic populations became fully integrated into soul-bearing humanity. This process fulfilled God's plan, leading to the fullness of time when all people—Jew and Gentile alike—were ready to receive the gospel.

When Jesus came, His mission reflected what Adam and Noah had started. Once a moral consciousness had been instilled in all of humanity, Christ issued a new commission—not to spread moral awareness, but to proclaim the gospel within humanity's moral understanding. Through Jesus, God's promise was realized: salvation was made available to all of humanity, uniting Jew and Gentile under one divine purpose.

This was the culmination of a plan carefully orchestrated long before it unfolded in time. Prophecies throughout Scripture foretold the coming of the Messiah—from the suffering servant in Isaiah 53 to the prediction of His birthplace in Micah 5:2. These ancient promises found their fulfillment in Jesus Christ, whose life, mission, death, and resurrection completed the story God had been writing from the beginning.

What began with Adam finds its fulfillment in Christ. As 1 Corinthians 15:45 declares, "The first man Adam became a living being; the last Adam became a life-giving spirit." Through Adam, souls entered the world; through Christ, they are given the way back to God. This fulfillment is echoed in the Great Commission (Matthew 28:18-20), where Jesus commands His followers to carry the gospel to all nations. From Eden to eternity, God's plan has remained constant: to create mankind with intention and extend an open invitation into His presence.

The Forgiveness of Sin

When Adam and Eve sinned, humanity's separation from God began, and with it, a divine plan to reconcile mankind to Himself. Central to this plan was the concept of sacrifice—an acknowledgment of God's sovereignty over life and creation. Sacrifice, at its core, was more than an act of obedience—it was a visceral and deeply emotional experience meant to underscore the gravity of sin and its consequences. The death of an innocent creature was a jarring reminder, making the cost of sin unmistakably clear.

The first recorded mention of sacrifice occurs in Genesis 4:3-5, where Cain and Abel brought offerings to God. Abel offered the firstborn of his flock, involving the shedding of blood, while Cain brought fruit from the ground. God accepted Abel's offering but rejected Cain's. This was not favoritism; rather, it was the nature of the sacrifices that made the difference. Abel's offering acknowledged the sanctity of life and the seriousness of sin through the shedding of blood, while Cain's lacked this recognition.

Cain's anger at God's rejection revealed something far deeper than simple jealousy—it exposed a rebellious heart that utterly disrespected God's plan and authority. The Bible states that jealousy was Cain's motive, but his actions suggest a much darker and twisted response. In what can be seen as defiance, Cain likely rationalized his rebellion with mockery.

One can imagine the storm of jealousy swirling in Cain's mind: *"If blood is what you want, if a cherished creature's blood pleases you, then here is the most cherished blood of all—Abel's blood."* Rather than humbling himself before God and offering the proper sacrifice, Cain's jealousy led him to take what was sacred and twist it into an act of contempt. Abel, who had done nothing wrong, became the target of Cain's rebellion. He slaughtered his brother, spilling innocent blood in a perverse imitation of the sacrifice God desired.

This was no ordinary murder. Cain's act mocked God's provision for atonement and spit on the grace He had extended through the sacrificial system. In this heinous act, Cain's jealousy boiled over into outright defiance. The blood of Abel, innocent and unblemished, cried out to God from the ground. Genesis 4:10 poignantly records God's words to Cain: "The voice of your brother's blood is crying to me from the ground." The ground, already cursed after Adam's sin, now bore witness to an even graver act of defiance—the shedding of innocent blood, an affront to the sanctity of life that God Himself had breathed into humanity.

This was more than disobedience; it was a complete rejection of God's mercy—a plan built on humility, faith, and dependence on Him. It was the ultimate act of rebellion, and it would not go unnoticed.

God's response to Cain was both just and merciful. Though He pronounced judgment, banishing Cain and marking him as a wanderer, He also placed a protective mark on him, preventing others from taking vengeance. Even in the face of such defiance, God extended grace, showing that His mercy and justice are intertwined.

Cain's act demonstrated a complete disregard for the destructive nature of sin. He ignored it with his initial offering to God and was oblivious to its weight when he killed his brother Abel. Sin was not just an offense—it carried the potential to unravel creation itself, corrupting not only the body but the soul of mankind. It was the ultimate separator from God. This reality would be fully realized in the time of Noah, when mankind in the region thought only of evil.

Ultimately, sin and God could not coexist. God created mankind to be eternal, yet in their fallen state, they were in danger of eternal separation from Him. But in His mercy, God provided a way for humanity to atone for this condition. He instituted sacrifices as a means for people to acknowledge their sin and approach Him in faith.

Throughout the Old Testament, sacrifices were central to humanity's relationship with God. It was a system He required, yet it was also an act of mercy. The system wasn't arbitrary but deeply significant—a reminder of mankind's corruption of life, which was in the blood, and a return of the body, which God had given. The animal symbolized these realities, allowing for temporary atonement, as mankind was incapable of presenting himself blameless before God. Leviticus 17:11 explains:

> For the life of the flesh is in the blood, and I have given it for you on the altar to make atonement for your souls, for it is the blood that makes atonement by the life.

This system of atonement was always meant to be temporary. No one could enter the world as a man, reach the age of accountability, face the full weight of temptation, and remain sinless, presenting themselves holy before God. Sin triumphed over the human condition.

In His mercy, God accepted the life of a pure animal—its sinless blood (life) and innocent (pure) body returned to Him—as a temporary substitute for mankind's fallen state. But true redemption required more. It required one from humanity itself to be this sacrifice and finally atone (that is, to take responsibility and make restitution) for the corruption mankind had brought into God's creation. Until that day came, there was no path to full restoration.

That day finally came through Jesus Christ. As the Lamb of God (John 1:29), Jesus fulfilled every requirement of the sacrificial system. He was unblemished—not only free from physical defect but also sinless in His moral and spiritual nature. As 1 Peter 1:18-19 declares, "You were redeemed . . . with the precious blood of Christ, a lamb without blemish or defect."

The story of Cain and Abel foreshadows Christ, revealing the contrast between justice and redemption. Abel's blood cried out from the ground, bearing witness to sin's consequences, while Christ's blood would atone for sin, offering reconciliation with God.

The Bible does not specify what Abel's blood was saying, but throughout Scripture, innocent blood calls for justice:

- **A cry for justice:** Abel's death was a moral offense, and in biblical language, innocent blood demands accountability before God (Psalm 9:12, Numbers 35:33).

- **A cry for divine judgment on Cain:** Bloodshed pollutes the land, and God Himself ensures judgment on the guilty.

- **A cry for righteousness to prevail:** This theme is echoed in Revelation 6:9-10, where the martyrs cry out, "How long, O Lord, holy and true, until You judge and avenge our blood?"

Abel's blood called for judgment, but Christ's blood speaks a better word—mercy and redemption. Unlike Abel's blood, which demanded justice, Christ's blood speaks of mercy and forgiveness. Hebrews 12:24 declares, "Jesus, the mediator of a new covenant, and to the sprinkled blood that speaks a better word than the blood of Abel." His sacrifice did not call for punishment but instead provided atonement.

By becoming human, Jesus fulfilled the role that no other sacrifice could achieve. The blood of animals, while significant, could not truly atone for sin because it lacked the spiritual capacity to represent humanity fully. Only a man could stand in place of mankind, yet no one was without blemish—until Christ. In Him, the purity God required was fully realized, and His perfect sacrifice bridged the separation between God and humanity.

It is in Jesus that redemption is found. He explained, "I am the vine; you are the branches. If you remain in me and I in you, you will bear much fruit; apart from me you can do nothing." (John 15:5). Through Christ, humanity could finally be united with God.

This was a new covenant—a new agreement with God. As Jesus declared at the Last Supper:

> This cup that is poured out for you is the new covenant in my blood (Luke 22:20).

Unlike the Old Testament sacrifices, which were repeated endlessly, Christ's sacrifice was final and complete. Hebrews 10:10-12 explains:

> And by that will, we have been made holy through the sacrifice of the body of Jesus Christ once for all. Day after day every priest stands and performs his religious duties; again and again he offers the same sacrifices, which can never take away sins. But when this priest had offered for all time one sacrifice for sins, he sat down at the right hand of God.

Understanding this is much like one of the world's favorite pastimes—football, particularly the Super Bowl champions. The tradition for the winning team is to receive Super Bowl rings. While we often picture only the players receiving the rings, the team typically presents rings to a wide range of individuals, including players (active roster, inactive roster, or injured reserve), coaches, trainers, executives, personnel, and general club staff. They are all champions by association with the success of the team. If you're not part of the team in some way, then you don't get a ring. The reward is based entirely on association.

In the same way, salvation is based on being associated with Christ. He is the winning team who secured the ultimate victory over sin and death, and through our union with Him, we share in His triumph.

I've often thought of this new covenant like when I was growing up and we would go to the drive-in theater. Every so often, admission wasn't per person but per vehicle. Only the driver had to pay, and everyone in the car was given a free pass as long as they were in the car. If you misbehaved that day, you might not get to go, but if you were in the car, your admission was covered.

This is the way of salvation. So long as you are part of the church that Jesus established, one of many branches of the vine, the cost of this salvation is freely given—a gift of grace offered to all who accept it. In a sense, you just need to get in the car and behave.

To ensure that His followers would never forget the magnitude of His sacrifice, Christ instituted the Lord's Supper. This act, shared with His disciples on the night He was betrayed, serves as a lasting reminder of His fulfillment of the old sacrificial system. The bread represents His body, given for humanity—a perfect and unblemished offering. The fruit of the vine signifies the new covenant in His blood, the unity believers have with Him, and the eternal life He gives.

The Lord's Supper is not just a ritual—it is a declaration of Christ's sufficiency and a reminder that His body and blood accomplished what no other sacrifice could.

Baptism: A New Beginning through Water

Baptism, introduced as an essential practice for believers, carries rich symbolic meaning that reaches back to one of the earliest stories of renewal in the Bible—the flood. The apostle Peter draws this connection in 1 Peter 3:20-21:

> *Because they formerly did not obey, when God's patience waited in the days of Noah, while the ark was being prepared, in which a few, that is, eight persons, were brought safely through water. Baptism, which corresponds to this, now saves you, not as a removal of dirt from the body but as an appeal to God for a good conscience, through the resurrection of Jesus Christ.*

The flood was a pivotal moment in history when God cleansed the earth of its corruption, preserving Noah and his family as the foundation for a renewed humanity. Through the waters of the flood, the earth was both judged and given a fresh start. Similarly, baptism symbolizes a cleansing—a washing away of the old life—and a new beginning in Christ. Just as Noah and his family emerged from the ark into a renewed world, believers emerge from the waters of baptism into the newness of life with God.

Baptism also reflects the believer's personal identification with Christ's death, burial, and resurrection. As Paul writes in Romans 6:4, "We were buried therefore with him by baptism into death, in order that, just as Christ was raised from the dead by the glory of the Father, we too might walk in newness of life." This act of immersion into water represents the believer's old life being buried, while rising from the water signifies the resurrection to a new life in Christ.

This connection between the flood and baptism reminds us that both events signify not only judgment but salvation. Baptism is not merely a ritual but an outward declaration of faith, trust, and surrender to God's redemptive work.

Jesus Himself affirmed the importance of baptism, not only through His command to His disciples in the Great Commission but also through His own baptism by John the Baptist. He instructed His followers, "Go therefore and make disciples of all nations, baptizing them in the name of the Father and of the Son and of the Holy Spirit" (Matthew 28:19), establishing baptism as a central act of faith.

Though sinless, Jesus chose to be baptized "to fulfill all righteousness" (Matthew 3:15), modeling the humility and obedience He calls His followers to emulate. In baptism, we align ourselves with His example, demonstrating our commitment to God and acknowledging our place in His redemptive plan.

As the flood marked a new beginning for the earth, baptism marks a new beginning for the believer. It is a public acknowledgment of the freedom and renewal found in Christ—a freedom that allows us to walk with God in a relationship as intimate as the one He shared with Adam and Eve in Eden.

From Dependence to Freedom: God's Fostering of Humanity

From the dawn of creation in Eden, God's relationship with humanity was deeply personal. In Eden, He walked with Adam and Eve in a direct and intimate connection, sharing a relationship unmediated by anything or anyone else. Humanity, in its earliest days, depended entirely on God, living in simplicity and trust.

As history progressed, this closeness transformed. Though God remained present, humanity's relationship with Him became less direct. Over time, intermediaries arose—prophets, priests, and leaders who served as bridges between humanity and God. Through these chosen individuals, God guided His people, offering instruction, wisdom, and opportunities to seek Him.

As their independence grew, He allowed them to pull away, granting them the freedom to govern themselves. This shift became evident when the Israelites demanded a king to rule over them, desiring to be like the surrounding nations. The prophet Samuel, troubled by this request, sought God's guidance. Though God warned that a human king would bring burdens and hardships, He granted their desire, saying, "It is not you they have rejected, but they have rejected me as their king" (1 Samuel 8:7).

Thus, Saul became Israel's first king, followed by David, the man after God's own heart. David's reign marked a pivotal moment in biblical history, as God established a covenant with him, promising that his lineage would lead to the Messiah. This era reflected a maturing relationship, as humanity took on greater responsibility while still being called to seek and follow God.

Centuries later, that promise found its fulfillment. With the coming of Jesus Christ, the relationship between God and humanity entered a new chapter. Jesus, both fully God and fully man, walked among us, teaching, healing, and living as an example of what a personal connection with God could look like. His life demonstrated that God desired not just to guide humanity but to dwell with us, individually and intimately.

One of the most powerful moments symbolizing this shift came at the death of Jesus, when the temple veil was torn from top to bottom. As Matthew 27:51 records:

> *And behold, the curtain of the temple was torn in two, from top to bottom.*

This was no ordinary curtain. The veil, which had long separated the Holy of Holies—the place where God's presence was believed to dwell—from the rest of the temple, was massive in both size and significance.

According to Jewish tradition, this veil in Herod's Temple stood approximately 60 feet high and 30 feet wide and was about 4 inches thick—woven so tightly that it was said even horses tied to each side could not pull it apart.[90]

For centuries, it had symbolized the separation between God and humanity. Only the high priest could enter once a year on the Day of Atonement (Yom Kippur), and only after extensive purification rituals. Its tearing was a divine act, not something any human could accomplish—especially not from top to bottom.

This was God's declaration: the barrier between Him and mankind was gone. His presence was now open to all, no longer confined to a specific place or mediated through a specific priesthood. Jesus had become the ultimate High Priest, providing direct access to God through His sacrifice. As Hebrews 10:19-20 affirms:

Therefore, brothers and sisters, since we have confidence to enter the Most Holy Place by the blood of Jesus, by a new and living way opened for us through the curtain, that is, His body...

The tearing of the veil was a visible sign of the New Covenant—the fulfillment of God's redemptive plan, in which humanity no longer needed a priest to stand between them and God. The way had been opened, once and for all.

This act reflects a great truth: God's desire was always for humanity to come to Him freely, not out of obligation but through love and trust. Jesus not only removed the barriers but actively encouraged a deeply personal relationship with God. In the Sermon on the Mount, He taught, "But when you pray, go into your room and shut the door and pray to your Father who is in secret. And your Father who sees in secret will reward you." (Matthew 6:6). While Jesus was addressing the genuineness of prayer, He was also urging us to develop a one-on-one relationship with God, a connection that is now made possible in His name.

Today, this relationship is available to all who seek it. We no longer depend on priests to intercede for us or rituals to guide us into His presence. Through Jesus, each person can approach God directly, speaking to Him as a child speaks to a loving parent. As Jesus said, "Whatever you ask in my name, this I will do, that the Father may be glorified in the Son" (John 14:13).

This progression mirrors the stages of growth in human life: dependence, independence, and finally, interdependence. In the beginning, humanity depended entirely on God, walking with Him in simplicity. Over time, humanity grew in independence, learning responsibility and the consequences of freedom. Now, through Christ, we are invited into interdependence—a relationship where we freely choose to walk with God, trusting in His guidance while embracing the freedom to love and serve Him fully.

This freedom is deeply personal but also calls for community. While each person has direct access to God, Jesus emphasized the importance of gathering together: "For where two or three are gathered in my name, there am I among them" (Matthew 18:20). The church, as a body of believers, provides encouragement, support, and accountability, but it is no longer the sole mediator of access to God. Each believer is invited to cultivate a personal, vibrant relationship with Him, unmediated by anyone else.

This relationship is rooted in love. As Jesus affirmed, all of God's teachings rest on two principles: to love God with all our heart, soul, and mind, and to love others as ourselves (Matthew 22:37-40). This love transcends rituals and traditions, forming the foundation of a life aligned with His will.

Through Christ, we are free to walk with God as Adam and Eve once did, in a relationship that is both personal and eternal. This freedom is not about independence from God but about choosing interdependence with Him—a life lived in trust, love, and mutual fellowship with the Creator who has always desired to dwell with us.

Equipped for Life, Prepared for Eternity

I often think about my childhood in Oklahoma. I believe most people look back on the time that shaped them—filled with adventure and imagination. We got a few cuts and bruises, maybe even broke an arm, but for the most part, being a child is a grand adventure.

However, as we grow older, there comes the desire for a much grander time. No more homework, no more chores, no more being told what to do all the time. One day, we will have our own car, our own place, and the freedom to do whatever we want to do. It will be glorious—finally, the end of all our problems in life comes and we grow up.

The funny thing is—it's the front end of our problems.

As we step into adulthood, we come to realize a truth that was hidden from us as children: life is tough. And I'm not overlooking some children who start off life with struggles. But no matter who we are, no matter where we come from or when it begins, no one escapes the struggles, complexities, and uncertainties of this world. We carry the weight of responsibility, the burden of choices, the negative impact of others around us and the relentless demands of survival.

Some hardships come from our own mistakes, some from the actions of others, and some from forces far beyond our control. And yet, through all of it—through every failure, heartbreak, and unexpected detour—there remains an undeniable thread running through existence: **purpose.**

Mankind has always searched for purpose. Across every culture, every civilization, and every era of human history—though sometimes misguided—we have asked the same fundamental questions: *Why are we here? What does it all mean?* In *Chapter Two*, we explored how, from the dawn of time, humanity has looked to the heavens, longing to understand our origins, which could be the key to these questions. From the earliest societies to the most advanced civilizations, this search has remained woven into the fabric of our existence. It is part of our very consciousness—a yearning embedded within us, compelling us to seek something greater than ourselves.

These searches have shaped our religions, our philosophies, and our deepest convictions. From far-fetched myths and legends to Buddhism, Hinduism, and Christianity, mankind has consistently clung to the idea of a higher power— an ultimate force responsible for our existence and our purpose in life. No matter what the culture or era, the pattern is the same: we reach beyond ourselves, trying to grasp the truth about where we came from and why we are here.

In this modern age, we stand uniquely apart from those who came before us. We have been afforded a gift that no other generation in history has possessed at such a scale: the *gift of knowledge.* Through science and discovery, we have unlocked mysteries that were once unimaginable. And yet, this very knowledge has also reshaped our understanding of the past, sometimes confirming long-held beliefs, sometimes challenging them, and at times, completely overturning what we once thought was true.

Much of the time, new knowledge helps us. For example, the discovery of different blood types revolutionized medicine.[91] Before this understanding, blood transfusions were often fatal mysteries—some patients thrived, while others died, leaving doctors puzzled. That single piece of knowledge saved countless lives.

Other discoveries, however, have led to consequences we wish mankind had never uncovered—like the ability to build an atomic bomb. This knowledge, while rooted in scientific advancement, carries the weight of catastrophe, threatening the very fabric of society if left unchecked.

Science today continues to have both of these effects—challenging, reshaping, and sometimes affirming what we believe about our existence. While some use scientific discovery to reinforce the idea of a Creator, others wield it as an argument against one. They claim that, despite the universe's natural tendency toward disorder and chaos, somehow, against all odds, it arranged itself into such precise order that life became possible. And yet, when we examine the probabilities, the odds of this happening are so close to zero that they defy logic.

If Christianity were just another myth—one more tale of powerful gods conjured up by human imagination—then it would be no different from the countless legends passed down through time. Yet, Christianity stands apart. Unlike the myths of old, which paint gods in the image of men—full of flaws, selfish ambitions, and distant indifference—Christianity presents something radically different: a direct relationship between Creator and creation even standing apart of other major religions. It is not a story of mankind reaching up to find God, but of God reaching down to reveal Himself to us.

The origins of Christianity are not found in vague oral traditions or fragmented myths, but in ancient writings, meticulously preserved and much of it written by those who lived through the events they describe. What makes these writings remarkable is not just their antiquity, but their continuity—a story told across centuries, by many different authors, all painting the same picture. And what is even more astonishing is how seamlessly this story aligns with what we observe in the natural world.

At its core, the question of our origins and what we believe comes down to reason, logic, and probability. What makes the most sense? What is the most reasonable explanation for our existence and for God?

Reason tells me that in a world prone to chaos, if I find order, something outside of it must have made it that way. This is not blind faith—it is inference drawn from observation. The very laws that govern our universe, from physics to biology, reflect structure, predictability, and precision. If we observe a fossil record that shows hominin species existing for hundreds of thousands of years, denying that evidence outright is not an act of faith—it is an act of willful ignorance. It is the same kind of thinking that fueled the Salem witch trials,[92] the suppression of scientific discovery, and the oppression of new ideas throughout history. Faith and reason were never meant to be at war, but too often, misunderstanding fuels that battle.

What I have never found to be in error in my life is the Bible. Have I found interpretations of it to be flawed? Absolutely. But when examined through the lens of reason, through a sincere search for truth rather than rigid tradition, the core of Scripture has always remained unshaken.

Time and time again, history, science, and experience have affirmed its truth—not because it bends to fit our discoveries, but because it has already accounted for them.

What we see around us is not a contradiction of God's design; it is a confirmation of it. The more we uncover through science, the more we see the intricate order behind existence—an order that the Bible has spoken of all along. Rather than standing in opposition, faith and science seamlessly align, each revealing different aspects of the same truth.

And what is even greater than that? *It makes perfect sense.*

Brushstrokes in Life

Even with a clear expectation, life has a way of circling us back to the same questions. We wrestle with what we thought we knew, only to find ourselves questioning it again. And we usually begin to re-ask these questions when life becomes difficult, when things seem to work against us. Yet none of it can ever make sense if we don't keep in mind why things happen in life.

This world was never meant to be our final destination. Every moment of joy, every struggle, every success, and every heartbreak is a brushstroke in a much larger design. We are not here merely to live, work, and die; we are here to learn, seek truth, and be transformed. The trials we face are not meaningless—they shape us, refine us, and prepare us for something greater than we can imagine.

Life is a journey of growth, and with growth comes challenge. From the moment we take our first steps, we learn through trial, failure, and persistence. In the same way, hardship and testing are not meaningless obstacles but are designed to refine and strengthen us. This process is inseparable from life itself; it is woven into the fabric of human existence by divine intention. Humanity was created with the inherent ability to choose—to freely love and follow God. But that choice gains its deepest meaning through adversity. Love shaped by trials and challenges becomes the purest and truest expression of devotion, forged not out of ease, but perseverance.

Unlike angels, who were not created to experience life with the same vulnerability, limitations, or challenges, we were placed in a world uniquely suited to the development of faith. Our experiences with adversity are not incidental; they are deliberate opportunities to forge a steadfast connection with God. Even when life brings suffering, we discover resilience, purpose, and divine companionship in the process.

This design invites us to embrace each trial as an essential step in our spiritual growth. Just as metals are purified in fire, so too are we refined through life's challenges, emerging with a love and trust in God that is resilient and unwavering. This journey offers something angels cannot experience—a faith forged in the trials of life, enduring not because it is demanded, but because we choose it, freely, day by day.

The Training Ground of Life

In many ways, this refinement through hardship mirrors the training of a United States Marine. Marines endure challenges beyond those of other branches, pushing them to their physical, mental, and emotional limits. This intense testing molds them into the world's most formidable soldiers—unmatched in courage, loyalty, and resilience. The rigorous preparation equips them to endure the challenges of battle, often becoming the difference between survival and defeat.

There is a saying among Marines: *"On the seventh day, God rested; on the eighth day, He created the Marine Corps."*[93] This phrase, though humorous, captures the essence of what it means to be a Marine—elite, disciplined, and prepared for the toughest missions. Their motto, *Semper Fidelis*—"Always Faithful"—reflects not only their bond but also the resilient faith God calls each of us to develop.

Through trials, our faith becomes steadfast, much like a Marine's loyalty to the Corps, enduring through every season of life. Testing transforms us, aligning us more closely with God's purpose and strengthening the relationship He desires with us. This journey of faith is not about avoiding struggle but embracing it as the refining fire that shapes us into who we were meant to be.

Life's Bumpers—A Divine Design

Ultimately, we must ask ourselves: If we do not allow life's adversities to consume us, what power does this world truly have over us? When we trust in God's sovereignty and lean into the eternal hope He provides, the trials we endure lose their grip. This is the power of faith forged in fire—it enables us to walk through life's challenges with assurance, grounded not in the temporary, but in the eternal promises of God's Kingdom.

One of the simplest yet most effective designs in a bowling alley is the use of inflatable bumpers. When inflated, these bumpers fill the gutters, ensuring that even a wildly thrown ball makes its way down the lane, bouncing off the sides until it reaches the pins. Not with as much force or precision as if thrown straight, but nonetheless, it finds its destination. The more erratic the throw, the more the ball relies on the bumpers to correct its path.

God's design in life operates in much the same way. He has built into the world a system of natural consequences that serve as gentle—or sometimes harsh—course corrections to guide us back to the right path.

Touch a hot stove, and you'll quickly learn that some actions bring pain. This isn't cruelty; it's a lesson—a natural consequence built into the design of life to help us avoid harm. In the same way, God allows the systems He created to teach us, even when the lessons are hard. These lessons are not acts of divine punishment; they are part of His design, meant to steer us away from destruction and toward the life we were created to live.

Act Unwisely, and It Will Be Given to You

Sometimes, the struggles we face are not the result of God testing us or refining us but rather the natural consequences of our own choices. Neglecting relationships, indulging in destructive habits, or ignoring wisdom can lead to hardship that feels harsh, yet it is entirely self-inflicted.

When humanity fails to steward the natural world wisely, the results can be devastating—rising seas, failing ecosystems, and natural disasters that remind us of our responsibility to care for creation. These are not arbitrary punishments from God but rather the inevitable consequences of a world governed by order and design. The same principles apply not only to the environment but to every aspect of life, where the laws of nature reflect the wisdom and structure God put in place.

Gravity is a perfect example. Skydiving, mountain climbing, and ladders provide adventure, breathtaking views, and even help us hang Christmas lights—but gravity doesn't take a break for fun. The same force that allows us to explore great heights will also ensure that a fall has consequences. The moral of the story? Whether in nature or in life, when we ignore the order God has established, we suffer the results—not because He is punishing us, but because His creation follows the principles He set in motion.

Build your house on a seashore prone to hurricanes, and the storm will come. It is not divine judgment—it is a reality of nature and choice. Likewise, when we abuse substances, neglect our relationships, or reject the principles of love and forgiveness, the fallout is not what God intended for us, but the unavoidable result of our actions.

The Bible is filled with wisdom and warnings to help us navigate life's challenges and avoid unnecessary pain. Proverbs 14:12 reminds us, "There is a way that seems right to a man, but its end is the way to death." These words are not meant to condemn but to guide—helping us correct our course before we veer too far off track.

God's design is not to shield us entirely from consequences but to allow them to shape and teach us. His natural laws—both physical and spiritual—are meant to guide us toward growth and maturity. When we align ourselves with His wisdom, life's challenges become opportunities to grow stronger. But when we ignore His guidance, the struggle intensifies. And yet, even then, His design provides opportunities for correction and redemption.

Ultimately, God's purpose is not to control us but to guide us. His principles, like the bumpers in a bowling alley, are there to help us find our way back to the center when we stray. The question is not whether consequences will come—they always do. The real question is whether we will heed the lessons embedded in His design or continue throwing ourselves wildly down life's lane, forcing ourselves to learn the hard way what He has already revealed in His Word.

Quiet Lessons of Life

God uses every aspect of life to shape us—even in ways we don't immediately recognize. Some of the most profound lessons come from ordinary experiences, subtle and unassuming, yet deeply transformative. Life, in its temporary nature, holds lessons that are often misunderstood because the greater purpose isn't always visible in the moment.

I've often thought that pets are part of God's thoughtful training for us—small yet significant threads in the tapestry of our lives. They become like family, woven into our daily routines, offering companionship, laughter, and a kind of unconditional love that mirrors the devotion we long for. But beyond the joy they bring, they prepare us for something much deeper.

When my brother Tim and I were young, our first dog was a small, black, white, and brown rat terrier gifted to us by a neighbor. We named him Mittens because of his four white paws—a name that still holds a special place in our memories. Even today, when asked for security questions on websites, if given the option to select a favorite pet, both of us choose "Mittens."

Over the years, other dogs and cats have become cherished parts of our lives and adventures. Johnson, the greatest companion and toughest dog we ever had growing up. Lady, his gentle mother and fierce protector during our hikes. And Tank—who could ever forget him? A massive Staffordshire Terrier who, despite his intimidating appearance, was kind, gentle, and beloved by all.

Each of them is gone now—some tragically—but all left a lasting mark on our hearts. These pets taught us more than just joy and companionship; they taught us about love and loss. When they died, they carried pieces of our childhood with them, and in their absence, we learned how to grieve.

Looking back, I believe God gave us pets as a quiet form of training—a way to experience love in its purest form and to gently prepare us for the reality of loss. It was a silent lesson in carrying grief, equipping us for the inevitable goodbyes of life. When parents, grandparents, and loved ones passed, we bore those losses with greater resilience, because—without realizing it—we had been prepared.

What once seemed like a simple joy turned out to be part of a larger plan—a training ground for learning how to endure loss with grace and trust in God's eternal purposes. This realization has changed the way I view hardship. What we perceive as harsh in life is often misunderstood. God's design allows us to experience temporary things, not to break us, but to teach us—to help us value what is fleeting, to release what we cannot keep, and to deepen our dependence on what is eternal.

These quiet lessons of life are embedded in everything—from the love of a pet to the changing of seasons, and even the fragility of our own lives. The apostle Paul captured this truth in 2 Corinthians 4:17-18:

> *For this light momentary affliction is preparing for us an eternal weight of glory beyond all comparison, as we look not to the things that are*

seen but to the things that are unseen. For the things that are seen are transient, but the things that are unseen are eternal.

Every joy and every loss, every success and every trial, are part of a divine rhythm that draws us closer to God. The fleeting nature of life isn't evidence of its futility but of its purpose. Each moment—whether joyous or sorrowful—is an opportunity to learn, to grow, and to trust more deeply in the eternal promises of God.

Just as our pets taught us to face loss with grace, so God uses the experiences of life to prepare us for greater things. Life's temporary nature is not a curse but a gift, urging us to place our hope not in what fades, but in what endures forever.

These lessons may be quiet and subtle, but they are no less impactful, shaping us in ways we don't always understand—drawing us closer to Him who holds all things in His hands.

A Hard Lesson, A Deeper Love

When Karsyn, my granddaughter and joy of my life, was in elementary school, I would often join her for lunch. One day, I noticed a young boy, perhaps seven or eight years old, with white-blond hair who was blind. He sat at a table designated for students with disabilities, supervised by special education teachers who watched over him and a few other students during their lunch.

What struck me was his routine: he would find his place, unpack his lunch, and, when he was done, his teachers wouldn't step in to help him pack up or clean up. Instead, they firmly encouraged him to do it himself. I watched as he carefully put his containers away, felt around for stray napkins or crumbs that needed to be thrown away, and then made his way to the waste bin— sometimes fumbling as he went. His teachers remained nearby, patiently watching, but they never intervened unless absolutely necessary.

At first, I thought this approach seemed harsh. It would have been so easy for them to step in, to guide him, to save him from the small frustrations and missteps. But over time, as I observed him during these lunches, I realized they were giving him something far more valuable than convenience—they were preparing him for life. Each lunch, they taught him to manage on his own, equipping him with the skills to live independently.

A similar example can be found in the life of Ray Charles, who lost his eyesight at the age of seven.[94] In the movie *Ray*, his mother finds a school willing to accept a blind student, despite the little boy's heartbreaking protests. It was incredibly hard for her to send him out into the world, but she knew that shielding him from struggle would only hurt him in the long run. Watching him suffer tore at her heart, but she understood that true love prepares, not pampers. Had she given in to his tears, had she softened the hardship, he might never have learned to survive in a world that would not always accommodate him. Instead, she helped him develop the independence that allowed him to become one of the greatest musicians in history.

This type of love doesn't coddle—it challenges and strengthens. It is a love that prioritizes growth over comfort, even when the road is hard. While it may seem harsh at first, it reflects a greater care—a love that seeks to equip rather than enable. The same is true of God's love for us.

Just as we lovingly guide our children to become their best, so does God lead us. Discipline is not merely about survival—it is about becoming all we were meant to be. We do not do their homework for them, nor do we take their tests or play their games; we provide guidance, but the work, the effort, and the perseverance must come from them. In the same way, God does not remove obstacles from our path—He allows us to face them, knowing that through struggle, we develop strength, wisdom, and resilience. Hebrews 12:7-10 reminds us of this loving discipline:

> *It is for discipline that you have to endure. God is treating you as sons.*
> *For what son is there whom his father does not discipline? ... Shall we*
> *not much more be subject to the Father of spirits and live?*

The teachers' firmness with the boy, like Ray Charles's mother's persistence, wasn't cruelty—it was preparation. In the same way, life itself is not meant to be heaven, where comfort abounds and challenges are absent. Instead, it is a place where we grow through trials, learn resilience, and develop the endurance that shapes us for the eternal life to come.

Ray Charles's own life demonstrates this truth. Had he not lost his sight, his path might have been entirely different—perhaps ordinary, untouched by the hardships that ultimately forged his greatness. But it was through adversity that his talent, determination, and perseverance were refined. In many ways, this is the story of humanity itself. It is often through struggle that mankind does not merely survive—but thrives.

Training for Something Greater

Life, therefore, is not a party—it is preparation. A necessary step toward something greater. Through the adversities in our relationships, our daily experiences, and even in the simplest joys of life, God is training us. He does not overlook a single moment—each one serves a purpose, preparing us for what is to come.

When we were created in God's image, it wasn't to merely exist—like the dinosaurs or early hominins and Neanderthals, who lived, struggled, and eventually became extinct. Life itself was not the reward—we were made for something far greater. We were made for eternal significance, for a destiny that surpasses the fleeting joys and sorrows of this world.

This is what Jesus brought in the fullness of time—a plan not just for survival, but for eternal life. As He declared in John 10:10:

> *The thief comes only to steal and kill and destroy. I came that they may have life and have it abundantly.*

This abundance of life does not come from a life of ease but from the challenges that shape us, refining us for something beyond this world. Through

Christ, we are given the means to overcome sin, to rise above suffering, and to step into the eternal purpose for which we were created.

Empowered by Design: The Genius of God's Creation

God did not place us in this world helpless. The real neglect by God would have been to cast us into life with no way to navigate it, no ability to grow, no means to survive or adapt. But that is not the case—His genius is empowerment.

We are the only creatures on earth with the ability to reason, innovate, and transform the world around us. The human mind is an extraordinary gift, capable of solving problems, healing the sick, exploring the cosmos, and carrying forward the work God has set before us. It seems clear: God was not afraid to create something remarkable—something great.

Not that we could ever be equal to Him, but He designed us to be incredible. He made us in His image—not just in spirit, but in ability. The genius of His design is not just in the creation of man, but in the creation of a system within man that is sustainable, adaptive, and able to flourish on its own without constant intervention.

This theme is seen throughout Scripture. The Old and New Testaments reveal a steady progression toward the empowerment of mankind. Even in miracles, we see not just God's direct intervention but human participation in His plan. Jesus spoke of greater things to come, and though we may not have the power to create ex nihilo (out of nothing), our ability to carry out the Great Commission through innovation, communication, and mobility is itself miraculous—we were created to be the miracle.

Not in the sense that we replace God or Christ, but that through His design, we were endowed with the capacity to bring about transformation in the world. In the Old Testament, miracles demonstrated God's sovereignty— parting seas, calling down fire, delivering His people with mighty acts. Christ's miracles revealed His identity as the Son of God. Yet, as history unfolds, we see a transition: from dependence on divine intervention to a God-ordained interdependence, where mankind, through wisdom, compassion, and the pursuit of goodness, carries forward His work. The very design of humanity reflects His intent—that we would not merely witness miracles but, by His craftsmanship, become agents of them.

Our advancements in medicine, science, and technology, our ability to heal, to restore, to bring light to dark places—these are not contradictions to faith but confirmations of God's intricate plan. We do not claim credit for these wonders; rather, they testify to the divine blueprint written into our very being. What God created was not just capable of receiving miracles but, in accordance with His design, capable of being a vessel for them. In this, we do as Christ foretold—greater things than even He had done—not by our power, but by the wisdom and order He built into creation itself.

The Story of Job: A Lesson in Perspective

When Job questioned God, struggling to make sense of his suffering, God responded with questions of His own:

> *Where were you when I laid the earth's foundation? Tell me, if you understand. Who marked off its dimensions? Surely you know!* (Job 38:4-5)

> *Can you bring forth the constellations in their seasons or lead out the Bear with its cubs?* (Job 38:32)

Faced with the magnitude of God's wisdom and power, Job realized his limits. He could not explain how the stars were placed in the heavens, how the earth was set in motion, or how the great forces of nature were balanced. He saw, for the first time, how small his perspective was compared to God's eternal plan.

God has equipped us for this life, but we are not God. We have been given wisdom, knowledge, and remarkable ability, yet we must also recognize the limits of human justification and self-defense.

The Final Judgment: The Gift of Christ's Defense

This leads to perhaps the greatest truth of all—we are equipped to thrive in this life, but we are not equipped to stand alone before God.

Abraham Lincoln once said, "He who represents himself has a fool for a client."[95] The wisdom in that statement lies in the reality that none of us can effectively justify ourselves against our own shortcomings.

One day, every person will stand before God to account for their life. And on that day, we will either stand alone—like a fool who tries to defend himself in court—or we will stand with Christ. Jesus warned:

> *Whoever acknowledges me before others, I will also acknowledge before my Father in heaven. But whoever disowns me before others, I will disown before my Father in heaven.* (Matthew 10:32-33)

Without Him, we will have no defense. No lawyer. No justification that will stand before the Almighty. Like Job, we will see our utter inability to argue our case before God.

But for those who are in Christ, we will not stand alone.

Jesus Himself will be our defense, bearing the full weight of our shortcomings. His sacrifice is our justification. And that is perhaps the greatest gift of all—not just that we were designed with the ability to thrive in this world, but that we were not left without hope for the next.

A Final Word to My Children

As I bring this letter to a close, I want you to know how deeply I care about your journey through life. Life is not easy, and God never promised it would be. But He has given us everything we need to help us along the way.

He has given us the wisdom of the Bible to guide us, and He created us with the incredible ability to perceive the world through our senses—hearing, smell, taste, touch, and sight—so that we can learn, adapt, and thrive. He blessed us with intelligence, giving us a mind to think, reason, and understand. He instilled in us internal instincts to navigate challenges and the capacity for relationships— so we can lean on one another for strength, wisdom, and encouragement.

Life's design, though difficult, is intentional. It is meant to shape us, refine us, and prepare us for what lies beyond. When we keep the end goal in mind— a life of eternal joy with Him—it all begins to make sense. My hope for you, as you face life's twists and turns, is that you carry this understanding with you and allow it to bring you peace and clarity.

This journey we've taken together through these pages was my attempt to offer you something lasting. Life is rich with mystery, filled with moments of joy and sorrow, questions and discoveries, doubts and faith. I've wrestled with these questions myself and sought understanding, not only for my own sake but because I want to help you find solid ground in a world that can often feel confusing. Science, faith, and the beauty of the world around us are not in conflict; they form a mosaic that reveals a glimpse of God's heart and intentions.

Remember that life is not without its losses and griefs, but these, too, shape us. They are part of the journey, teaching resilience and compassion. When you walk through life's valleys, hold fast to the lessons of the Bible— listen to the wisdom of nature around you—and trust that both reveal truth. They will be your surest compass.

Seek joy in everyday moments, never give up, and always know that you are deeply loved—not only by me and your mother, but by the God who made you.

My prayer for you is that love, faith, and joy will always be your strongest anchors, holding you in a life rich in meaning and overflowing with peace and happiness. The reason for Creation was your Life, and the reason for your life is your Purpose. Hold this message close and let your purpose guide you forward to the eternal hope that awaits.

With all my love and hope for your future,
Your Dad
Mike A. Bills

WHAT GOD HATH NOT PROMISED
Annie Johnson Flint

God hath not promised skies always blue,
Flower-strewn pathways all our lives through;
God hath not promised sun without rain,
Joy without sorrow, peace without pain.
God hath not promised we shall not know
Toil and temptation, trouble and woe;
He hath not told us we shall not bear
Many a burden, many a care.
God hath not promised smooth roads and wide,
Swift, easy travel, needing no guide;
Never a mountain rocky and steep,
Never a river turbid and deep.
But God hath promised strength for the day,
Rest for the labor, light for the way,
Grace for the trials, help from above,
Unfailing sympathy, undying love.

Re-examining the Flood Narrative through Translation

List of Verses "Earth" vs. "Land"

In the flood account of Genesis 6-9, the Hebrew word often translated as "earth" (*ha'aretz*) appears forty-six times across thirty-five verses. This term can also mean "land," a translation that potentially shifts our understanding of the flood narrative's scope from global to regional. The following list provides each instance of "earth" in its traditional English translation, followed by the Hebrew (Romanized) and a revised version where "earth" is rendered as "land."

Genesis 6:1

- **English:** "When man began to multiply on the face of **the earth**, and daughters were born to them..."

- **Hebrew (Romanized):** "Vay'hi ki hechel ha'adam lerov al pnei **ha'arets** u'vanot yul'du lahem..."

- **English (Revised):** "When man began to multiply on the face of **the land**, and daughters were born to them…"

☑ This is **more sensible** to say "the land" than "the earth." The use of the word **"began"** suggests an initial, localized population growth, which aligns more naturally with the idea of early human settlements being confined to **specific regions.** At that point in history, humanity was not spread across the entire globe but concentrated in particular areas.

Genesis 6:4

- **English:** "The Nephilim were **on the earth** in those days, and also afterward…"

- **Hebrew (Romanized):** "Hanephilim hayu **va'aretz** bayamim hahem ve'gam achar ken…"

- **English (Revised):** "The Nephilim were **in the land** in those days, and also afterward…"

Genesis 6:5

- **English:** "The Lord saw that the wickedness of man was great in the **earth**, and that every intention of the thoughts of his heart was only evil continually."

- **Hebrew (Romanized):** "Vayar YHWH ki rabah ra'at ha'adam **ba'aretz** ve'chol yetzer machsh'vot libo rak ra kol hayom."

- **English (Revised):** "The Lord saw that the wickedness of man was great in the **land**, and that every intention of the thoughts of his heart was only evil continually."

☑ This is more sensible to say "in the land" than "in the earth" as the population at this time in history was most certainly **localized.** This matches the ancient understanding of human settlements being concentrated in specific areas. Using "earth" would imply a more global perspective, which doesn't fit as well with the historical and geographical context of early humanity.

Genesis 6:6

- **English:** "And the Lord regretted that He had made man on the earth, and it grieved Him to His heart."

- **Hebrew (Romanized):** "Vayinachem YHWH ki asah et ha'adam **ba'aretz** vayit'atzev el libo."

- **English (Revised):** "And the Lord regretted that He had made man in the land, and it grieved Him to His heart."

Genesis 6:7

- **English:** "So the Lord said, 'I will blot out man whom I have created from the face of **the land**, man and animals and creeping things and birds of the heavens, for I am sorry that I have made them.'"

- **Hebrew (Romanized):** "Vayomer YHWH em'cheh et ha'adam asher barati mei'al pnei **ha'aretz**, me'adam ad behemah ad remes v'ad of hashamayim ki nicham'ti ki asitim."

- ☑ This verse originally translates to "the land," which is more sensible and supports the idea of localization, as the population at this time in history was most certainly localized.

Genesis 6:11

- **English:** "Now **the earth** was corrupt in God's sight, and **the earth** was filled with violence."

- **Hebrew (Romanized):** "Vatishachet **ha'aretz** lifnei ha'Elohim vatimale **ha'aretz** chamas."

- English (Revised): "Now **the land** was corrupt in God's sight, and **the land** was filled with violence."

- ☑ This is more sensible to say "the land" than "the earth" as the population at this time in history was most certainly **localized**. This matches the ancient understanding of human settlements being concentrated in specific areas. Using "earth" would imply a more global perspective, which doesn't fit as well with the historical and geographical context of early humanity.

Genesis 6:12

- English: "And God saw **the earth**, and behold, it was corrupt, for all flesh had corrupted their way on **the earth**."

- Hebrew (Romanized): "Vayar Elohim et **ha'aretz** v'hinei nishchata ki hish'chit kol basar et darko al **ha'aretz**."

- English (Revised): "And God saw **the land**, and behold, it was corrupt, for all flesh had corrupted their way on **the land**."

Genesis 6:13

- English: "And God said to Noah, 'I have determined to make an end of all flesh, for **the earth** is filled with violence through them. Behold, I will destroy them with **the earth**.'"

- Hebrew (Romanized): "Vayomer Elohim l'Noach ketz kol basar ba lefanai ki mal'ah **ha'aretz** chamas mip'neihem v'hin'ni mash'chitam et **ha'aretz**."

- English (Revised): "And God said to Noah, 'I have determined to make an end of all flesh, for **the land** is filled with violence through them. Behold, I will destroy them with **the land**.'"

Genesis 7:4

- English: "For in seven days I will send rain on **the earth** for forty days and forty nights, and every living thing that I have made I will blot out from the face of **the earth**."

- Hebrew (Romanized): "Ki le-yamim od shiv'ah anochi mamtir al **ha'aretz** arba'im yom v'arba'im laylah ..."

- English (Revised): "For in seven days I will send rain on **the land** for forty days and forty nights, and every living thing that I have made I will blot out from the face of **the land**."

Genesis 7:6

- English: "Noah was six hundred years old when the floodwaters came upon **the earth**."

- Hebrew (Romanized): "V'Noach ben shesh me'ot shanah vayehi hamabul mayim al **ha'aretz**."

- English (Revised): "Noah was six hundred years old when the floodwaters came upon **the land**."

Genesis 7:10

- English: "And after seven days the waters of the flood came upon **the earth**."

- Hebrew (Romanized): "Vayehi l'shiv'at hayamim umey hamabul hayu al **ha'aretz**."

- English (Revised): "And after seven days the waters of the flood came upon **the land**."

Genesis 7:12

- English: "And rain fell upon **the earth** forty days and forty nights."

- **Hebrew (Romanized):** "Vayehi hageshem al **ha'aretz** arba'im yom v'arba'im laylah."

- **English (Revised):** "And rain fell upon **the land** forty days and forty nights."

Genesis 7:14

- **English:** "They and every beast, according to its kind, and all the livestock according to their kinds, and every creeping thing that creeps on **the earth**, according to its kind, and every bird according to its kind, every winged creature."

- **Hebrew (Romanized):** "Hem v'chol hachayah lemiynah v'chol habehemah lemiynah v'chol haremess haremmes al **ha'aretz** v'chol ha'of lemiyno kol tzipor kanaf."

- **English (Revised):** "They and every beast, according to its kind, and all the livestock according to their kinds, and every creeping thing that creeps on **the land**, according to its kind, and every bird according to its kind, every winged creature."

Genesis 7:17

- **English:** "The flood continued forty days on the earth. The waters increased and bore up the ark, and it rose high above **the earth**."

- **Hebrew (Romanized):** "Vayehi hamabul arba'im yom al **ha'aretz** vayarbu hamayim vayi'su et hateivah v'tarum me'al **ha'aretz**."

- **English (Revised):** "The flood continued forty days on the **land**. The waters increased and bore up the ark, and it rose high above **the land**."

Genesis 7:18

- **English:** "The waters prevailed and increased greatly on **the earth**, and the ark floated on the face of the waters."

- **Hebrew (Romanized):** "Vayigberu hamayim vayerbu me'od al ha'aretz v'telech hateivah al p'nei hamayim."

- **English (Revised):** "The waters prevailed and increased greatly on **the land**, and the ark floated on the face of the waters."

Genesis 7:19

- **English:** "And the waters prevailed so mightily on **the earth** that all the high mountains under the whole heaven were covered."

- **Hebrew (Romanized):** "Vayigberu hamayim me'od me'od al ha'aretz v'yikasu kol heharim hagvohim asher tachat kol shamanic."

- **English (Revised):** "And the waters prevailed so mightily on **the land** that all the high mountains under the whole heaven were covered."

Genesis 7:21

- **English:** "And all flesh died that moved on **the earth**, birds, livestock, beasts, all swarming creatures that swarm on **the earth**, and all mankind."

- **Hebrew (Romanized):** "Vayigva kol basar haremmes al **ha'aretz** b'ha'of uvabehemah uvahchayah uv'chol hasheretz hashoretz al **ha'aretz** v'chol ha'adam."

- **English (Revised):** "And all flesh died that moved on **the land**, birds, livestock, beasts, all swarming creatures that swarm on **the land**, and all mankind."

Genesis 7:23

- **English:** "He blotted out every living thing that was **on the face of the earth**, man and animals and creeping things and birds of the heavens. They were blotted out from **the earth**. Only Noah was left, and those who were with him in the ark."

- Hebrew (Romanized): "Vayimach et kol hayekum asher al **p'nei ha'adamah** mei'adam ad behemah ad remes v'ad of hashamayim vayimachu min **ha'aretz** vayisha'er ach Noach va'asher ito bateivah."

- English (Revised): "He blotted out every living thing that was **on the face of the land,** man and animals and creeping things and birds of the heavens. They were blotted out from **the earth.** Only Noah was left, and those who were with him in the ark."

Genesis 8:1

- English: "But God remembered Noah and all the beasts and all the livestock that were with him in the ark. And God made a wind blow over **the earth,** and the waters subsided."

- Hebrew (Romanized): "Vayiz'kor Elohim et Noach v'et kol hachayah v'et kol habehemah asher ito b'teivah vayya'aver Elohim ruach al **ha'aretz**..."

- English Revised: "But God remembered Noah and all the beasts and all the livestock that were with him in the ark. And God made a wind blow over **the land,** and the waters subsided."

Genesis 8:3

- English: "And the waters receded from **the earth** continually."

- Hebrew (Romanized): "Vayashuvu hamayim mei'al **ha'aretz** haloch vashov..."

- English (Revised): "And the waters receded from **the land** continually."

Genesis 8:7

- English: "...and it went to and fro until the waters were dried up from **the earth.**"

- Hebrew (Romanized): "Vayetze yatzo vashov ad yeboshet hamayim mei'al **ha'aretz**."

- English (Revised): "...and it went to and fro until the waters were dried up from **the land**."

Genesis 8:9

- English: "...but the dove found no place to set her foot, and she returned to him to the ark, for the waters were still on the face of the whole **earth**."

- Hebrew (Romanized): "V'lo matza hayonah mano'ach l'chaf raglah vatashav elav el hateivah ki mayim al p'nei kol **ha'aretz**."

- English (Revised): "...but the dove found no place to set her foot, and she returned to him to the ark, for the waters were still on the face of the whole **land**."

Genesis 8:11

- English: "...and behold, in her mouth was a freshly plucked olive leaf. So Noah knew that the waters had subsided from the **earth**."

- Hebrew (Romanized): "V'hinei alei-zayit taraf b'fiyha vayeda Noach ki kalu hamayim mei'al **ha'aretz**."

- English (Revised): "...and behold, in her mouth was a freshly plucked olive leaf. So Noah knew that the waters had subsided from **the land**."

Genesis 8:13

- English: "...Noah removed the covering of the ark and looked, and behold, the face of **the earth** was dry."

- Hebrew (Romanized): "Vayasar Noach et mich'seh titivate v'hinei char'vu p'nei **ha'aretz**."

- **English (Revised):** "…Noah removed the covering of the ark and looked, and behold, the face of **the land** was dry."

Genesis 8:14

- **English:** "In the second month, on the twenty-seventh day of the month, **the earth** had dried out."

- **Hebrew (Romanized):** "U'vachodesh hasheni b'shiv'ah v'esrim yom lachodesh yaveshah **ha'aretz**."

- **English (Revised):** "In the second month, on the twenty-seventh day of the month, **the land** had dried out."

Genesis 8:17

- **English:** "…that they may swarm on **the earth** and be fruitful and multiply on **the earth**."

- **Hebrew (Romanized):** "Vayish'retsu **va'aretz** u'faru v'ravu al **ha'aretz**."

- **English:** "…that they may swarm on **the land** and be fruitful and multiply on **the land**."

Genesis 8:19

- **English:** "Every beast, every creeping thing, and every bird, everything that moves on **the earth**, went out by families from the ark."

- **Hebrew (Romanized):** "Kol hachayah kol haremes v'chol ha'of kol remes al **ha'aretz**…"

- **English:** "Every beast, every creeping thing, and every bird, everything that moves on **the land**, went out by families from the ark."

Genesis 9:1

- **English:** "And God blessed Noah and his sons and said to them, 'Be fruitful and multiply and fill **the earth**.'"

- **Hebrew (Romanized):** "Vay'varech Elohim et Noach v'et banav vayomer lahem pru urvu u'milu et **ha'aretz.**"

- **English:** "And God blessed Noah and his sons and said to them, 'Be fruitful and multiply and fill **the land.**'"

Genesis 9:2

- **English:** "The fear of you and the dread of you shall be upon every beast of **the earth** ..."

- **Hebrew (Romanized):** "U'mora'achem v'chitchem yih'yeh al kol chayat **ha'aretz** ..."

- **English (Revised):** "The fear of you and the dread of you shall be upon every beast of **the land** ..."

Genesis 9:7

- **English:** "And you, be fruitful and multiply, increase greatly on **the earth** and multiply in it."

- **Hebrew (Romanized):** "Ve'atem pru urvu shir'tzu **va'aretz** urvu vah."

- **English (Revised):** "And you, be fruitful and multiply, increase greatly on **the land** and multiply in it."

Genesis 9:11

- **English:** "I establish my covenant with you, that never again shall all flesh be cut off by the waters of the flood, and never again shall there be a flood to destroy **the earth.**"
- **Hebrew (Romanized):** "V'hakimoti et briti itchem v'lo yikareit kol basar od mimei hamabul v'lo yih'yeh od mabul l'shachet et **ha'aretz.**"
- **English (Revised):** "I establish my covenant with you, that never again shall all flesh be cut off by the waters of the flood, and never again shall there be a flood to destroy **the land.**"

Genesis 9:13

- **English:** "I have set my bow in the cloud, and it shall be a sign of the covenant between me and **the earth**."

- **Hebrew (Romanized):** "Et kashti natati b'anan v'hayta l'ot brit beini u'vein **ha'aretz**."

- **English (Revised):** "I have set my bow in the cloud, and it shall be a sign of the covenant between me and **the land**."

Genesis 9:14

- **English:** "When I bring clouds over **the earth** and the bow is seen in the clouds..."

- **Hebrew (Romanized):** "V'haya be'ani anan al **ha'aretz** v'nir'etah hakashet b'anan."

- **English (Revised):** "When I bring clouds over **the land** and the bow is seen in the clouds..."

Genesis 9:16

- **English:** "When the bow is in the clouds, I will see it and remember the everlasting covenant between God and every living creature of all flesh that is on **the earth**."

- **Hebrew (Romanized):** "V'hay'tah hakashet b'anan ur'itiha l'zkor brit olam bein Elohim u'vein kol-nefesh chayah b'chol basar asher al **ha'aretz**."

- **English (Revised):** "When the bow is in the clouds, I will see it and remember the everlasting covenant between God and every living creature of all flesh that is on **the land**."

Genesis 9:17

- **English:** "This is the sign of the covenant that I have established between me and all flesh that is on **the earth**."

- **Hebrew (Romanized):** "Vayomer Elohim el Noach zot ot-habrit asher hakimoti beini u'vein kol basar asher al **ha'aretz.**"

- **English (Revised):** "This is the sign of the covenant that I have established between me and all flesh that is on **the land.**"

Full Narrative of Verses "Earth" vs. "Land"

As promised in the book, the following is a full narrative of Genesis 6-9, where the traditional English translation of the word "earth" is consistently rendered as "land." This alternative translation of *ha'aretz* offers readers a new lens through which to interpret the story of the flood. In these chapters, the revised text maintains the localized scope implied by the term "land," rather than the broader, more global implication often associated with "earth."

By re-examining these passages with "land" as a focal point, readers can gain insight into the potential regional context of the flood and the lives of Noah and his family. This appendix provides an opportunity to consider how translation impacts our understanding of biblical narratives and invites further reflection on the ancient world's historical and geographical landscape.

Genesis 6

1 When man began to multiply on the face of the land and daughters were born to them,

2 the sons of God saw that the daughters of man were attractive. And they took as their wives any they chose.

3 Then the LORD said, "My Spirit shall not abide in man forever, for he is flesh: his days shall be 120 years."

4 The Nephilim were on the land in those days, and also afterward, when the sons of God came in to the daughters of man and they bore children to them. These were the mighty men who were of old, the men of renown.

5 The LORD saw that the wickedness of man was great in the land, and that every intention of the thoughts of his heart was only evil continually.

*6 And the L*ORD *regretted that he had made man on the land, and it grieved him to his heart.*

*7 So the L*ORD *said, "I will blot out man whom I have created from the face of the land, man and animals and creeping things and birds of the heavens, for I am sorry that I have made them."*

*8 But Noah found favor in the eyes of the L*ORD.

9 These are the generations of Noah. Noah was a righteous man, blameless in his generation. Noah walked with God.

10 And Noah had three sons, Shem, Ham, and Japheth.

11 Now the land was corrupt in God's sight, and the land was filled with violence.

12 And God saw the land, and behold, it was corrupt, for all flesh had corrupted their way on the land.

13 And God said to Noah, "I have determined to make an end of all flesh, for the land is filled with violence through them. Behold, I will destroy them with the land.

14 Make yourself an ark of gopher wood. Make rooms in the ark, and cover it inside and out with pitch.

15 This is how you are to make it: the length of the ark 300 cubits, its breadth 50 cubits, and its height 30 cubits.

16 Make a roof for the ark, and finish it to a cubit above, and set the door of the ark in its side. Make it with lower, second, and third decks.

17 For behold, I will bring a flood of waters upon the land to destroy all flesh in which is the breath of life under heaven. Everything that is on the land shall die.

18 But I will establish my covenant with you, and you shall come into the ark, you, your sons, your wife, and your sons' wives with you.

19 And of every living thing of all flesh, you shall bring two of every sort into the ark to keep them alive with you. They shall be male and female.

20 Of the birds according to their kinds, and of the animals according to their kinds, of every creeping thing of the ground, according to its kind, two of every sort shall come in to you to keep them alive.

21 Also take with you every sort of food that is eaten, and store it up. It shall serve as food for you and for them."

22 Noah did this; he did all that God commanded him.

Genesis 7

1 Then the LORD said to Noah, "Go into the ark, you and all your household, for I have seen that you are righteous before me in this generation.

2 Take with you seven pairs of all clean animals, the male and his mate, and a pair of the animals that are not clean, the male and his mate,

3 and seven pairs of the birds of the heavens also, male and female, to keep their offspring alive on the face of all the land.

4 For in seven days I will send rain on the land for forty days and forty nights, and every living thing that I have made I will blot out from the face of the land."

5 And Noah did all that the LORD had commanded him.

6 Noah was six hundred years old when the flood of waters came upon the land.

7 And Noah and his sons and his wife and his sons' wives with him went into the ark to escape the waters of the flood.

8 Of clean animals, and of animals that are not clean, and of birds, and of everything that creeps on the ground,

9 two and two, male and female, went into the ark with Noah, as God had commanded Noah.

10 And after seven days the waters of the flood came upon the land.

11 In the six hundredth year of Noah's life, in the second month, on the seventeenth day of the month, on that day all the fountains of the great deep burst forth, and the windows of the heavens were opened.

12 And rain fell upon the land forty days and forty nights.

13 On the very same day Noah and his sons, Shem and Ham and Japheth, and Noah's wife and the three wives of his sons with them entered the ark,

14 they and every beast, according to its kind, and all the livestock according to their kinds, and every creeping thing that creeps on the land, according to its kind, and every bird according to its kind, every winged creature.

15 They went into the ark with Noah, two and two of all flesh in which there was the breath of life.

16 And those that entered, male and female of all flesh, went in as God had commanded him. And the LORD shut him in.

17 The flood continued forty days on the land. The waters increased and bore up the ark, and it rose high above the land.

18 The waters prevailed and increased greatly on the land, and the ark floated on the face of the waters.

19 And the waters prevailed so mightily on the land that all the high mountains under the whole heaven were covered.

20 The waters prevailed above the mountains, covering them fifteen cubits deep.

21 And all flesh died that moved on the land, birds, livestock, beasts, all swarming creatures that swarm on the land, and all mankind.

22 Everything on the dry land in whose nostrils was the breath of life died.

23 He blotted out every living thing that was on the face of the land, man and animals and creeping things and birds of the heavens. They were blotted out from the land. Only Noah was left, and those who were with him in the ark.

24 And the waters prevailed on the land 150 days.

Genesis 8

1 But God remembered Noah and all the beasts and all the livestock that were with him in the ark. And God made a wind blow over the land, and the waters subsided.

2 The fountains of the deep and the windows of the heavens were closed, the rain from the heavens was restrained,

3 and the waters receded from the land continually. At the end of 150 days the waters had abated,

4 and in the seventh month, on the seventeenth day of the month, the ark came to rest on the mountains of Ararat.

5 And the waters continued to abate until the tenth month; in the tenth month, on the first day of the month, the tops of the mountains were seen.

6 At the end of forty days Noah opened the window of the ark that he had made

7 and sent forth a raven. It went to and fro until the waters were dried up from the land.

8 Then he sent forth a dove from him, to see if the waters had subsided from the face of the ground.

9 But the dove found no place to set her foot, and she returned to him to the ark, for the waters were still on the face of the whole land. So he put out his hand and took her and brought her into the ark with him.

10 He waited another seven days, and again he sent forth the dove out of the ark.

11 And the dove came back to him in the evening, and behold, in her mouth was a freshly plucked olive leaf. So Noah knew that the waters had subsided from the land.

12 Then he waited another seven days and sent forth the dove, and she did not return to him anymore.

13 In the six hundred and first year, in the first month, the first day of the month, the waters were dried from off the land. And Noah removed the covering of the ark and looked, and behold, the face of the ground was dry.

14 In the second month, on the twenty-seventh day of the month, the land had dried out.

15 Then God said to Noah,

16 "Go out from the ark, you and your wife, and your sons and your sons' wives with you.

17 Bring out with you every living thing that is with you of all flesh—birds and animals and every creeping thing that creeps on the land—that they may swarm on the land, and be fruitful and multiply on the land."

18 So Noah went out, and his sons and his wife and his sons' wives with him.

19 Every beast, every creeping thing, and every bird, everything that moves on the land, went out by families from the ark.

20 Then Noah built an altar to the Lord *and took some of every clean animal and some of every clean bird and offered burnt offerings on the altar.*

21 And when the Lord *smelled the pleasing aroma, the* Lord *said in his heart, "I will never again curse the land because of man, for the intention of man's heart is evil from his youth. Neither will I ever again strike down every living creature as I have done.*

22 While the land remains, seedtime and harvest, cold and heat, summer and winter, day and night, shall not cease."

Genesis 9

1 And God blessed Noah and his sons and said to them, "Be fruitful and multiply and fill the land.

2 The fear of you and the dread of you shall be upon every beast of the land and upon every bird of the heavens, upon everything that creeps on the ground and all the fish of the sea. Into your hand they are delivered.

3 Every moving thing that lives shall be food for you. And as I gave you the green plants, I give you everything.

4 But you shall not eat flesh with its life, that is, its blood.

5 And for your lifeblood I will require a reckoning: from every beast I will require it and from man. From his fellow man I will require a reckoning for the life of man.

6 "Whoever sheds the blood of man, by man shall his blood be shed, for God made man in his own image.

7 And you, be fruitful and multiply, increase greatly on the land and multiply in it."

8 Then God said to Noah and to his sons with him,

9 "Behold, I establish my covenant with you and your offspring after you,

10 and with every living creature that is with you, the birds, the livestock, and every beast of the land with you, as many as came out of the ark; it is for every beast of the land.

11 I establish my covenant with you, that never again shall all flesh be cut off by the waters of the flood, and never again shall there be a flood to destroy the land."

12 And God said, "This is the sign of the covenant that I make between me and you and every living creature that is with you, for all future generations:

13 I have set my bow in the cloud, and it shall be a sign of the covenant between me and the land.

14 When I bring clouds over the land and the bow is seen in the clouds,

15 I will remember my covenant that is between me and you and every living creature of all flesh. And the waters shall never again become a flood to destroy all flesh.

16 When the bow is in the clouds, I will see it and remember the everlasting covenant between God and every living creature of all flesh that is on the land."

17 God said to Noah, "This is the sign of the covenant that I have established between me and all flesh that is on the land."

18 The sons of Noah who went forth from the ark were Shem, Ham, and Japheth. (Ham was the father of Canaan.)

19 These three were the sons of Noah, and from these the people of the whole land were dispersed.

20 Noah began to be a man of the soil, and he planted a vineyard.

21 He drank of the wine and became drunk and lay uncovered in his tent.

22 And Ham, the father of Canaan, saw the nakedness of his father and told his two brothers outside.

23 Then Shem and Japheth took a garment, laid it on both their shoulders, and walked backward and covered the nakedness of their father. Their faces were turned backward, and they did not see their father's nakedness.

24 When Noah awoke from his wine and knew what his youngest son had done to him,

25 he said, "Cursed be Canaan; a servant of servants shall he be to his brothers."

26 He also said, "Blessed be the LORD, the God of Shem; and let Canaan be his servant.

27 May God enlarge Japheth, and let him dwell in the tents of Shem, and let Canaan be his servant."

28 After the flood, Noah lived 350 years.

29 All the days of Noah were 950 years, and he died.

Notes

1. Henry Ford, *My Life and Work* (Doubleday, Page & Company, 1922).

2. Ford Motor Company, "Ford Rouge Factory Tour," accessed June 14, 2024.

3. Sidney Fine, *Sit-Down: The General Motors Strike of 1936-1937* (University of Michigan Press, 1969).

4. Richard T. Hughes, *Reviving the Ancient Faith: The Story of Churches of Christ in America* (Eerdmans, 1996).

5. NASA, "Apollo 11 Mission Overview," accessed August 12, 2024.

6. Sears, Roebuck & Co., *Sears Christmas Wish Book*. Various Editions, 1933-1993.

7. U.S. Fish and Wildlife Service, "Wichita Mountains Wildlife Refuge History," accessed August 23, 2024, www.fws.gov.

8. Wilbur Sturtevant Nye, *Carbine and Lance: The Story of Old Fort Sill* (University of Oklahoma Press, 1937).

9. William T. Hagan, *Quanah Parker, Comanche Chief* (University of Oklahoma Press, 1993).

10. Samuel Noah Kramer, *The Sumerians: Their History, Culture, and Character* (University of Chicago Press, 1963), 95.

11. Liliuokalani, *Hawaii's Story by Hawaii's Queen* (Charles E. Tuttle Company, 1964), 41.

12. Mircea Eliade, *The Myth of the Eternal Return* (Princeton University Press, 1974), 45.

13. Wendy Doniger, *Hindu Myths: A Sourcebook Translated from the Sanskrit* (Penguin Books, 1975), 78.

14. The Quran, translated by M. A. S. Abdel Haleem (Oxford University Press, 2005), Surah 7:54-56.

15. Rupert Gethin, *The Foundations of Buddhism* (Oxford University Press, 1998), 118.

16. Stephen Hawking, *A Brief History of Time* (Bantam Books, 1988), 73.

17. Hugh Ross, *The Creator and the Cosmos* (NavPress, 2001), 129.

18. John H. Walton, *The Lost World of Genesis One* (InterVarsity Press, 2009), 56.

19. Bart D. Ehrman, *Did Jesus Exist? The Historical Argument for Jesus of Nazareth* (HarperOne, 2012), 12.

20. Tacitus, *Annals*, Book 15, Chapter 44.

21. Hershel Shanks and Ben Witherington III, *The Brother of Jesus: The Dramatic Story & Meaning of the First Archaeological Link to Jesus and His Family* (HarperOne, 2003), 29.

22. John Calvin, *Institutes of the Christian Religion* (1536), Book 1, Chapter 5, Section 1.

23. Aristotle, *Metaphysics*, Book 12, Section 7; Plato, *Timaeus*, translated by Benjamin Jowett (1892).

24. Neil F. Comins, *What If the Moon Didn't Exist?* (HarperCollins, 1993), Chapter 1.

25. Henry Chadwick, *The Early Church* (Penguin Books, 1967), 202.

26. Albert Pietersma and Benjamin G. Wright (eds.), *A New English Translation of the Septuagint* (Oxford University Press, 2007), Introduction.

27. Urban C. von Wahlde, "Archaeology and John's Gospel," *Biblical Archaeology Review* (July/August 2000).

28. Geza Vermes, *The Complete Dead Sea Scrolls in English* (Penguin Books, 1997), Introduction.

29. Duncan Steel, *Marking Time: The Epic Quest to Invent the Perfect Calendar* (John Wiley & Sons, 2000), Chapter 12.

30. Albert Einstein, *Relativity: The Special and the General Theory*, trans. Robert W. Lawson (Crown Publishing, 1961).

31. Alan H. Guth, *The Inflationary Universe: The Quest for a New Theory of Cosmic Origins* (Perseus Books, 1997).

32. Bradley W. Carroll and Dale A. Ostlie, *An Introduction to Modern Astrophysics* (Pearson, 2017).

33. Donald D. Clayton, *Principles of Stellar Evolution and Nucleosynthesis* (University of Chicago Press, 1983).

34. David Arnett, *Supernovae and Nucleosynthesis: An Investigation of the History of Matter, from the Big Bang to the Present* (Princeton University Press, 1996).

35. NASA, "Hubble Space Telescope Overview," *NASA Science*, 2023, https://www.nasa.gov/mission_pages/hubble.

36. Jacob Neusner, *The Mishnah: A New Translation* (Yale University Press, 1988).

37. Francis Brown et al., *The Brown-Driver-Briggs Hebrew and English Lexicon* (Hendrickson, 1996).

38. Galileo Galilei, *Dialogue Concerning the Two Chief World Systems*, trans. Drake Stillman (University of California Press, 1953).

39. John H. Walton, *The Lost World of Genesis One: Ancient Cosmology and the Origins Debate* (IVP Academic, 2009).

40. Hugh Ross, *A Matter of Days: Resolving a Creation Controversy* (NavPress, 2015).

41. Francis S. Collins, *The Language of God: A Scientist Presents Evidence for Belief* (Free Press, 2006).

42. Nathaniel Jeanson, *Replacing Darwin: The New Origin of Species* (Master Books, 2017).

43. David M. Rohl, *A Test of Time: The Bible—From Myth to History* (Arrow, 1995).

44. Mark Isaak, *The Counter-Creationism Handbook* (University of California Press, 2007).

45. Dennis R. Venema and Scot McKnight, *Adam and the Genome: Reading Scripture After Genetic Science* (Brazos Press, 2017).

46. William Ryan and Walter Pitman, *Noah's Flood: The New Scientific Discoveries About the Event That Changed History* (Simon & Schuster, 1999).

47. Ryan and Pitman, *Noah's Flood*.

48. Brian Verrelli and Sarah Tishkoff, *The Evolution of Modern Humans in Africa: A Comprehensive Analysis* (Annual Review of Genomics, 2004).

49. Richard G. Klein, *The Human Career: Human Biological and Cultural Origins* (University of Chicago Press, 2009).

50. Klaus Schmidt, "Göbekli Tepe: A Prehistoric Stone Temple," *Cambridge Archaeological Journal* (2000).

51. *The Book of Enoch,* trans. by R. H. Charles, 1912. (Non-canonical text).

52. St. Francis of Assisi, *The Admonitions,* trans. by Paschal Robinson, 1926.

53. Pew Research Center, *The Future of World Religions: Population Growth Projections, 2015-2060,* www.pewresearch.org.

54. Michael J. Behe, *Darwin's Black Box: The Biochemical Challenge to Evolution* (Free Press, 1996).

55. Richard Dawkins, *The Blind Watchmaker: Why the Evidence of Evolution Reveals a Universe Without Design* (W. W. Norton & Company, 1986).

56. Stephen Hawking, *A Brief History of Time: From the Big Bang to Black Holes* (Bantam Books, 1988).

57. Albert Einstein, *Relativity: The Special and the General Theory,* transl. by Robert W. Lawson, (Methuen & Co., 1920).

58. William A. Dembski, *The Design Inference: Eliminating Chance Through Small Probabilities* (Cambridge University Press, 1998).

59. Hugh Ross, *The Creator and the Cosmos: How the Greatest Scientific Discoveries of the Century Reveal God* (NavPress, 2018).

60. Roger Penrose, *The Road to Reality: A Complete Guide to the Laws of the Universe* (Vintage, 2007).

61. Behe, *Darwin's Black Box.*

62. James D. Watson and Francis Crick, *Molecular Structure of Nucleic Acids: A Structure for Deoxyribose Nucleic Acid* (Nature Publishing Group, 1953).

63. Peter D. Ward and Donald Brownlee, *Rare Earth: Why Complex Life Is Uncommon in the Universe* (Springer, 2000).

64. Guillermo Gonzalez and Jay Richards, *The Privileged Planet: How Our Place in the Cosmos Is Designed for Discovery* (Regnery Publishing, 2004).

65. Stephen C. Meyer, *Signature in the Cell: DNA and the Evidence for Intelligent Design* (HarperOne, 2009).

66. Daniel Nettle, *Personality: What Makes You the Way You Are* (Oxford University Press, 2007).

67. Robert R. McCrae and Paul T. Costa Jr., *Personality in Adulthood: A Five-Factor Theory Perspective* (Guilford Press, 2003).

68. Isabel Briggs Myers and Peter B. Myers, *Gifts Differing: Understanding Personality Type* (Davies-Black Publishing, 1995).

69. David Keirsey, *Please Understand Me II: Temperament, Character, Intelligence* (Prometheus Nemesis Book Company, 1998).

70. Keirsey, *Please Understand Me II.*

71. Nettle, *Personality.*

72. Keirsey, *Please Understand Me II.*

73. Keirsey, *Please Understand Me II.*

74. Harvard Business Review, "The Business Case for Diversity in the Workplace," Harvard Business Publishing (2018).

75. City Slickers – *City Slickers,* directed by Ron Underwood (Columbia Pictures, 1991).

76. Merle Haggard – Merle Haggard, *Okie from Muskogee* (Capitol Records, 1969).

77. Larry McMurtry, *Lonesome Dove* (Simon & Schuster, 1985).

78. Anne Frank, *The Diary of a Young Girl*, trans. by B. M. Mooyaart (Doubleday, 1952).

79. United States Holocaust Memorial Museum, "Introduction to the Holocaust," www.ushmm.org.

80. Benjamin Franklin, *The Autobiography of Benjamin Franklin*. Various Editions.

81. Greg Marinovich and João Silva, *The Bang-Bang Club: Snapshots from a Hidden War* (Basic Books, 2000).

82. Walter Isaacson, *Steve Jobs* (Simon & Schuster, 2011).

83. John F. Kennedy, "Address at Rice University on the Nation's Space Effort," 12 September 1962. www.jfkli-brary.org.

84. Donald Worster, *Dust Bowl: The Southern Plains in the 1930s* (Oxford University Press, 1979).

85. *Fishing for Truth: A Sociological Analysis of Northern Cod Stock Assessments from 1977 to 1990* (ISER Books, 1994).

86. Terry P. Hughes, et al. "Coral Reefs in the Anthropocene," *Nature*, 546, no. 7656 (2017): 82–90, doi:10.1038/nature22901.

87. World Food Programme, "Annual Report 2023," www.wfp.org.

88. *Forrest Gump*, directed by Robert Zemeckis, Paramount Pictures, 1994.

89. The Met Church, "Cindy Ramsey Center Mission and Outreach," www.metchurch.com.

90. Talmud, Mishnah Yoma 5:1

91. Philip Levine, Nobel Lecture on Blood Groups (Nobel Prize Organization, 1946).

92. Stacy Schiff, The Witches: Salem, 1692 (Little, Brown and Company, 2015).

93. United States Marine Corps historical records.

94. David Ritz, Brother Ray: Ray Charles' Own Story (Da Capo Press, 2003).

95. No verified source; commonly attributed to Lincoln but origin unknown.